The Soul of an

Eagle

The
SouL
of an

EaglE

by
Edmond E. Frank

Copyright 2021

by Edmond E. Frank

All rights reserved. No part of this book may be reproduced by any means or in any form without the express permission of the author.

IngSpk - Paper Back- ISBN 978-1-7348367-5-2

Dedication

This is the true story of my first marriage. I loved that woman but never really saw that it was only about me and how I viewed her. It's all in this book. Did you ever have one of those dreams where everything was so perfect that you absolutely loved it and hated, with all your might, to wake up, even though on some level of mind you knew you were asleep?

My son recently posted the song "Rose-Colored Glasses" to my Facebook page.

Thank you, Son, for the reminder. Sincerely, I still love to remember that dream about your mother. This sequel book tells the account of waking up. All Korean love stories require someone to suffer for love. Hell, I think that's true for most all love stories everywhere. Ours was a true Korean love story.

I dedicate this book to
Shawn Owen Pendleton,
our son.

Acknowledgments

The autobiographical novel *The Courage of a Butterfly* and its sequel were a labor of love, on and off, for over twenty-five years. It could be said they were the schoolground for this writer's ability to write. And there have been numerous teachers scattered throughout the various critique groups over the years. It would be great if I could remember and acknowledge them all by name, but I can't.

I'd like to thank Brian Klemmer of PSI Seminars who first kicked my ass with the truth.

And most of all, Carol Reynolds of Vision Seminars—a visionary, a mentor, and dear friend. It was she who first saw the potential in me and taught me to see it, too, and to use it. It was she who slammed shut every chicken exit that I invented to keep me from writing these books. Carol, I dearly love you—R.I.P.

I wish to thank the Aliante Writers, the Sin City Writers, and the Henderson Writers' Meet-Up Critique Groups. Many in these three groups are published, and all are fellow writers of excellence. They have been of immense support to me. Then there are my beta readers—Betty Hart, Lilly Whelband, Dee Pluta, and Marilyn Crawley.

There is my editor and good friend, Karen Diehl. The excellence of her work makes mine sound intelligent—sometimes. And there is Joyce Mochrie, owner of *One Last Look*, Certified Copy Editor and Proofreader—the best of the best.

There is Joylynn Ross of Pathtopublishing.com, another friend and mentor who is an expert in the publishing industry.

Lastly, there is Bobby Daniels, owner of *Bobby Daniels Graphics*, my cover designer. Probably the most important person in influencing you, the reader, to buy this book, he is a true artist. I highly recommend him to other writers.

Table of Contents

PROLOGUE
Page 1

CHAPTER ONE
9　　Inescapable Sentments

CHAPTER TWO
19　　Masquerading Love

CHAPTER THREE
33　　It's Not the Money, Only the Price

CHAPTER FOUR
45　　The Finger of God

CHAPTER FIVE
55　　Ten Thousand Feet

CHAPTER SIX
69　　Steer on the Kill Floor

CHAPTER SEVEN
81　　Oh, Cheesus!

CHAPTER EIGHT
91　　The Battlefield of Unmet Needs

CHAPTER NINE
101　　Flash Floods of Life

CHAPTER TEN
113   Have Mercy Baby

CHAPTER ELEVEN
123   The Best of Times in the Worst of Times

CHAPTER TWELVE
131   Is Love Such a Hard Thing to Swallow?

CHAPTER THIRTEEN
143   The Saga of Doc

CHAPTER FOURTEEN
151   Doc's Chicken Exit

CHAPTER FIFTEEN
161   Shopping at the Meat Market

CHAPTER SIXTEEN
169   Eagle Quest

CHAPTER SEVENTEEN
181   Single . . . Available . . . Women

CHAPTER EIGHTEEN
191   Hard Hearts Sometimes Break

CHAPTER NINETEEN
203   Protecting That Inner Child

CHAPTER TWENTY
217   Thirty Days Babe . . .

CHAPTER TWENTY-ONE
231   Burying the Past

CHAPTER TWENTY-TWO
241   Of Motorcycle Wheels & Macho Balls

CHAPTER TWENTY-THREE
255   Then Came Ka-Bar

CHAPTER TWENTY-FOUR
265   Life Changes and Remains the Same

CHAPTER TWENTY-FIVE
279   Painting Pink Turds"

CHAPTER TWENTY-SIX
291   Riding a Bad-Ass Machine

CHAPTER TWENTY-SEVEN
305   Lessons, Tests, & Validations

CHAPTER TWENTY-EIGHT
321   Once in the Eclipse of a Blue Moon

CHAPTER TWENTY-NINE
335   The Ghost of Durango Calling

CHAPTER THIRTY
343   Of Moose Milk and Horse Puckies

CHAPTER THIRTY-ONE
351   Loving Mona

CHAPTER THIRTY-TWO
363   The Correction Always Goes >HERE<

CHAPTER THIRTY-THREE
375   Goes Where?

CHAPTER THIRTY-FOUR
387   No Correction Needed

EPILOGUE
395

ABOUT THE AUTHOR
397

SAMPLE CHAPTER FOUR
from *The Courage of a Butterfly*

About This Book

This book is billed as fiction, and some parts are, and while the story itself is based on this author's life—even so, it too must be viewed as fiction. With only a couple of noted exceptions, all of the names have been changed, as have some locations and organizations.

This author tells things as he sees them, and your perception doesn't have to be the same as his. Personal growth is simply having an open mind to where you can change your mind when looking at something differently works better.

This requires other people to share their thinking with you. Can you put your likes and dislikes, and your need to be right, aside long enough to look? Bottom line, that's the definition of an open mind. Just know that change is always uncomfortable.

It seems our society has a problem with the truth. It demands that we wear a façade of pink paint, a color society thinks everyone likes and will accept. Pink is not this author's color.

But like you, it is what he, too, was taught. This author doesn't live according to society's rules—rules whose only purpose is to control our lives. He lives by the laws of truths.

This author's purpose in life is to share a little of that truth with those who want it. For those who don't, his purpose is *not* to fix you. If you're broken, that's *your* job. Looking in the light of truth will show you a viewpoint of life from which you may never have looked before. Is your mind open enough to take in the view? You may even discover the magnificence of what life is all about—your life, not mine.

This book is about those truths that, like gravity, just are. Ignoring gravity works out the same way as ignoring truth. Broken legs or broken lives . . . kinda dysfunctional, don't cha think? Metaphorically so, this book starts with a broken leg.

A personal note from this author to you the reader:

I'm someone who has been to the brink of death and glimpsed into the great beyond. For me, it was a life-changing experience. The main story is my actual life story. But before you start reading it, I would like to offer you a thought

My personal belief is that our lives are run by our soul—and, it is done from a higher, unconscious level. I believe there are therefore, no coincidences—

Everything happens for a reason.

With that thought in mind, as you read through this book, ask yourself this question:

Why did my soul place this book into my hands?

There are a couple of pages in the back marked

"NOTES."

Consider using them.

PROLOGUE

Comb Ridge, Utah—Present Day

Upon regaining consciousness, it takes me a full hour just to get myself free. It's not easy to lift an eight-hundred-pound motorcycle, rocking it an inch or two at a time, and stuffing rocks, dirt—whatever my grasping fingers could reach—up underneath until it forms a sort of lift ramp high enough to clear my broken leg.

But painful now, God, the pain screams a white-hot symphony. The returning circulation is like having my leg cooking in a lobster pot. I don't even want to think about the main issue here. Right now, I'm just grateful that the initial tourniquet action between the bike and a hard spot kept me from bleeding to death while unconscious. The blood has clotted and no longer flows from the wound.

Now free of the bike, I raise up enough to look down into the depths, illuminated fully by the midday sun. *Holy shit! It must be near a thousand feet!* The sheer sandstone drops straight down where I peer over the edge. A soft breeze rises, cooling the sweat of my exertions. Far below, in the jumble of orange boulders, the pinyon and cedars poke forth their crowns, deep green against the rich red of the earth. Had my bike crashed over onto its right side, I would now be down there—a broken, bloodied, mangled corpse.

God, the pain! It would be so easy to just relax and slip over.

"Yes, Jeff. That is the choice you could talk yourself into . . . or maybe, just stay and talk to me."

"Big D?" I look beyond the scratched and dented wreck to the ledge behind, casting about among the stunted trees growing from the meager earth and numerous cracks in the solid rock, looking for him, my dear friend and mentor. He's been my secret companion, recently, on the journey of my life. I met him in an ICU unit at a time when my life appeared to be over, and while I don't like to see him as such, he is also the Angel of Death.

Is that you, come for me at last? I speak to him in our old, familiar way—in my mind.

"Nah . . . not 'at last.'" He chuckles. "I'm only here to keep you company and counsel you, as often I have these last few years." I see him now, a darker smudge, squatting beside the ruins of a Moki Indian dwelling, a scythe cradled by the bones of his left arm. His ivory skull is grinning against the deeper shadows where the rock overhangs the most. "Besides, right now, you could use a friend, don't cha think?"

Fuck! With how my life has turned of late, how do you know I might not end it all now?

"Because when first we met, you asked—in fact, you begged—for this time. No, you will not give it up over a little pain." His laughter rings out freely, not mockingly, rather with a note of kindness. "Besides, haven't you always been afraid of heights?"

"Hmm . . . ur-aaah." My chuckle ends in a groan. *Oh God, Big D, a little pain?* I look down to where the bone protrudes through a rip in the cloth covering my thigh.

"Ah, but you know how to deal with pain. You handled it well these last years in all of its various forms. Yes, you can do it again."

Holding a deep breath, I touch fingers to thumb, then release, letting it out from between teeth no longer clenched. I relax my body, one part at a time, while slowly counting down, centering myself into that place within.

But relaxing each part of my body isn't easy, what with the pain. *Big D, can you distract me somehow?* As always, he hears my every thought. Just as well because to actually speak would break my concentration. Oh, I still feel it screaming but somehow know it is with his influence that I no longer give it any attention.

Now I'm ready. Visualizing the pain, I gather it into a tight ball of monstrous misery, like a big glob of mucus-green snot shot through with the mottled colors of red agony. When it is all gathered, I fling it over the edge and watch it fall into the depths of the canyon, watch it dwindle in size until it is but a faraway thing that can no longer even be seen.

I've not been aware of the time passing—a few minutes or many hours—but I am ready to continue. Now, with only a dull ache, I face the reality of my situation here miles from any traveled path, out of sight on this lonely ledge. Who would even suspect it exists, down here below the edge of this cliff?

What's the point here, Big D? Are you saying that they will find me?

"Oh yes, they will surely find you. It is just a matter of time." There it is, that enigmatic laugh again, the sound of kindness coming from such a gruesome countenance. "With life, it is always a matter of time . . . but then, you know that."

Yes, you've taught me much since first we met.

"And there's much yet for you to learn before we go." He moves over to sit next to me at the edge of the cliff, his leg bones dangling over the edge.

Ah, God . . . I sigh, feeling weaker than I can ever remember. *Look, I'm not really in the mood for lessons just now.*

"Sure you are. It'll help stave off the pain. Talk to me, Jeff."

Talk? About what?

"Just tell me your story."

My story? But you already had me write it all down—a whole damned book full of it, in fact.

"Not that. That was about your life before you met me in that hospital ICU. Begin from the moment when your life, as it then was, ended."

You mean from when you made yourself known to me?

"Close, but you are not searing hamburgers here. Get into the fire with this one. Think, Jeff! When did it all really change for you? I asked you to write about it, and for a while, you even started. Guess that with the completion of your first book you thought it was a request. IT WASN'T!"

I turn to stare, speechless, my jaw sagging with the realization that the apparition facing me is the Reaper, with little to show him as also being my friend Big D.

"I . . . uhh . . . I w-wasn't—" I speak it aloud, stumbling, aware I am beginning to hyperventilate. *Oh, my God, I thought it was a request. Maybe it was of no great concern, but I did write that story. Sure, there was never any good ending, but I thought I finished it in a good place. I—*

"Never mind." He cuts my dry-mouth babble off short, as well as my mindfuck of an excuse. "It will never be done—not in this life. Don't you get that? As to where this consciousness that you are now first began?" He pokes my chest with one boney finger. "You mind-farted completely past that embarrassing part. Start there!"

Taking a deep, shaky breath, I turn to look across the vast gulf of Comb Ridge with the sun low in the west, hot against my face. My mind floats back, remembering another desert and another late afternoon sun, this one viewed from the heights of a hospital room. Yes, it comes to me . . . the smell of the hospital, or rather, the smell of the hospital soap on the wash rag in Meg's hand, and the feel of it sliding down my backside as she bathes me. And then lastly, there is the grunt of her disgust carried over into the words—words that lash forth from her mouth, from my beautiful, loving wife's mouth.

"She-eeet!" Big D's interruption breaks like a gush of ice water against my thoughts. "Don't you mean from your 'bitterly disillusioned, frustratingly unhappy with her life, soon-to-be ex-wife's mouth?' Well . . ."—he pauses as it soaks in—"don't you, Jeff?"

Yeah. "Haaaa-shit!" *That's the way of it. What can I say?*

"The truth, Jeff, only the truth. C'mon. Out with it! There is much about your life that you haven't yet learned, and it's all about facing the truth."

Again, he pauses, and while there is only a red glow coming out of his empty eye sockets, I know he is eyeing me closely. "Now start it out truthfully this time, with Meg's seven little words. Then carry it on through to its present, fucked-over state of affairs. Deal with it. It's there in your saddlebags—several notebooks full. Read it. I'll hear you as you do, then take it all the way forward to right now."

"Oh, God." I groan. *I have slacked off. I can see why you might think I wasn't doing what I was tasked to do.* He ducks his head, eyes now turning a malevolent shade of red. *Oh, sweet Jesus! He does think I've quit on life.*

"That is our bargain—follow your joy with courage and honesty and never quit before your purpose here is complete. And you certainly have quit. Watching you ride that bike sideways down the side of that cliff, I was tempted to let it go on over." The red rage in his eye sockets seems to ease off. "That *is* why we are here, or am I just pissing in the wind to give you this one last chance?"

N-no. A jolt of white-hot agony hits as I move toward my saddlebag. "Aaargh . . . shit!"

Instantly, Big D is back to his old self. "Just hold on. We need to deal with that leg first. You've good reason to quit. Between quitting and dying now, or suffering even more to finish your task"—he nods his head in acknowledgment—"it probably seems like a bitchin'-poor choice." There is certain grim humor in his grin as the glow of his eyes regards the bone sticking out of the gaping wound in my leg. "I think getting that leg stabilized is a priority. Do you want a little time to prepare?"

Oh crap, Big D. I can handle the physical pain . . . shit! Much easier to handle that than the mental shit I've dealt with since meeting you, y'know?

"Yes, Jeff . . . the mental shit? You've done very well there, and you know I couldn't help you, especially not with that pain."

I know.

I pause to look around at this ledge, only about thirty feet below the roadway. This is the only part of it that sticks out far enough to have stopped my motorcycle. Looking up, I note the scratches and gouges left by its downward slide and, for the first time, am aware that next to them are hollows dug out in the side of the sandstone cliff.

A Moki Indian staircase! It climbs the wall where it is not quite so perpendicular to the rest of the cliff. *Of course there would have to be one, what with that Moki dwelling.* The fact that the ancient Indians inhabited and used this ledge for their survival in this desert lends hope for my own. *If they built a shelter here, there must be a spring somewhere, hopefully close by. And the view from here makes a man somehow grateful just to be alive.*

"It is beautiful, Jeff. Has your life since that hospital not also been witness to a like amount of beauty? Has that not been worth the price in pain you paid?"

You know it has, Big D. But right now, I am wondering how I managed to put myself into this sorry-assed situation.

"We'll discuss that, and in time, it will all become clear. For now, you need to dismantle your busted-up bike and take stock in what you have available for your survival. But first, take those front forks apart and set aside that length of rope in your saddlebags. You're going to need them for setting and stabilizing that leg."

He pauses to take note of my reaction to his words, then quickly adds, "Don't sweat it, Jeff. I'll help you with the swelling and in dealing with the physical pain. That I can do. And I've already assisted you with the bleeding. It's the bleeding that sends me so many of my customers—kind of a side effect of giving up on life, y'know?"

He grins his old, familiar grin, and I am again struck with the fact that I can look at his boney skull and know that, like now, there is humor in his grin. "Yes, you've handled your pain with courage, but nothing like you'll need soon. For now, get what you can get done on those forks while there is still some light."

* * *

I wake in a cold sweat, and with a dull, throbbing pain. Looking down in the early morning light, I see my leg is braced by two metal rods that I recognize as the guts of my front forks. Tied tightly between them is my now-straightened broken leg.

"What the fuck!" The words burst forth without conscious thought.

"Relax." The single word seems to carry an unexpected calming effect, the tone coming with that weird intonation that is unmistakably Big D's voice. "I told you I'd help you with the pain. That you don't remember it does not negate the fact that you faced your fear and bore the pain . . . again."

But how?

"Well, see that pinyon pine with the rope tied around it? The other end you tied to your boot. Then it was a matter of just throwing your weight backward . . . well, several times. But hey, you really don't want to remember." He grins again as that realization plays across my mind.

You're right. I shudder. *That's something no one would want to remember. Look, Big D*—I begin to thank him.

"Least I could do." His words come quickly.

Are you concerned that, should I dwell upon it, I'll begin to remember? He doesn't answer directly, but instead, changes the subject.

"Now, there's a notebook at your side. Start from when your life, as it was, ended in that hospital ICU. Your first book needs a sequel, a how-to example from you."

"Aaargh . . . shit!" *Look, Big D. I'm really having trouble getting into writing just now.*

His sigh comes now with a disturbing note. "Look, if you want to make a difference, you need to complete your story. You may not survive this ride." He pauses meaningfully before finishing. "You certainly won't if you quit now." He is eyeing me with intensity.

B-Big D! I have not given up on life. Y-you know that . . . don't you?

"That certainly is the question. Are you even aware that you have stopped following your joy and even been dishonest with yourself on that score? You've made a clean sweep of dishonoring our agreement, and you don't even see it, do you? Ah, Jeff." He shakes his head sadly. "I fear you will not get off this ledge alive."

W-what? How . . . why? My jaw gapes open.

"Now . . ." The cast in his grin now feels of his resolve. "There's a notebook at your side. If you intend to complete this task, start from when your life, as it was, ended in that hospital ICU. Remember those seven little words? Start rewriting Chapter One with them."

A wind comes out of nowhere to fill my eyes and still-opened mouth with sandy grit. I quake at his final words. They shake the very ground around me.

"THIS . . . IS . . . YOUR . . . LAST . . . CHANCE!"

Sometimes the truth of one's life can only be heard in the carnal surety of Death's whisper, a whisper spoken in the darkening of a night that will not again lighten, for Death's visit always brings death. Yet, for a lucky few, it is only the death of a life of lies—and the gift of the truth in life.

Redneck Spirituality—Book One

CHAPTER ONE

Inescapable Sentiments

Tuesday, October 6, 1992—4:45 p.m.

"Why can't you wipe your butt better?" The words ring clear, bell-like in my memory, the death knell of my marriage. Those seven little words formed a pivot point in my life. With them, I released one reality and picked up another, stepped from one pathway onto another, and found myself walking in a direction I'd never gone before.

But back then—what? Twelve, maybe thirteen short years, yet seemingly a lifetime ago, I wasn't aware of it. I shifted onto my side in that hospital bed and gazed in shocked disbelief over my shoulder at my wife, Meg, as she held up the white washcloth. Looking past that cloth, with its pale, telltale, little yellow streak, into her accusing eyes, I noted on her face the twisted grimace of her disgust. Knowing the consequences of any other answer, I simply said, "I'm sorry, dear . . . I will."

But inside, the rage burned. I'd never resented her disdain—not like I did just then. Just then, I didn't want her touching me. In fact, I wished she would leave. For the first time in our marriage, I didn't want her company! Ah, but one should always be careful about what one wishes.

After she left, I lay thinking, going over in my mind the events of recent days. There was no doubt my life had turned serious when I admitted myself to the hospital the previous day. Light-headed and fighting to stay conscious, I'd traversed the hundred yards from the car to the emergency room. That trip was an ordeal of endurance that wouldn't have been possible without Meg's shoulder to lean on during my frequent stops.

* * *

My doctor, Dr. Laring, surmised by his examination that I had some sort of heart problem, but when the test results finally trickled down early this morning, it was found to be a blood clot. An injury to my right calf during a ski-tubing accident at Lake Powell the week before now resulted in a massive clot blocking the blood circulation in my lungs.

When Dr. Laring gave me the news, his manner left little doubt in my mind. It, and the chill in my heart, spoke clearly—*I might not survive*. He'd talked privately to Meg in the hall as she was arriving at lunchtime. During the whole of her visit, her eyes avoided mine. Had he told her something he'd not told me? *Goddamn doctors and their superior, condescending airs!*

"I'm just afraid for you," was all she'd say. I was determined that when next Dr. Laring and I met, I would get some answers.

Him and his officious orders . . . "Stay quietly in bed. Don't so much as lower your legs over the edge." Hell, he didn't even want to let me use the facility, only three steps away. Yeah, I'd do what he said—most of it, anyway. But that last thing . . . I'd ignored that once already. The indignity, the embarrassment, and lack of privacy that went with using a bedpan made some risks seem worthwhile. Besides, it's just so difficult to wipe while using a bedpan.

When Dr. Laring dropped by shortly after Meg left, I was on him like stink on shit. Yeah, he told me all right, even though it was against hospital policy for doctors to give critical patients any gory details. Meg already knew. Hospitals don't give a crap about relatives upsetting patients. I don't know whose shit stunk worse, but he laid his right back onto me with the brutal truth. It ended with, "Frankly, Mr. Williams, I'm surprised you're still alive."

Dr. Laring's truth was the recent reality of my life. Meg's? Hers had been there since our beginning together. Now, alone in my night, I had to deal with both.

God! Why had I flipped out at her remark? During the nearly twenty-five years of our marriage, I'd always known that Meg regarded me as somewhat of a slob. She never made a secret of it, and her remark was not unusual. I always accepted her disdain, even felt it was somewhat justified. Somehow, all that was now changed.

Those seven little words—"Why can't you wipe your butt better?"—were they some kind of wake-up call? Coming, as they did, at the only time in my life when I couldn't lie, those seven words, and the inescapable sentiments they expressed, were . . . just . . . not . . . acceptable.

With them, I began to see my entire marriage, and life, in honesty. Funny how something so painful can bring such a gift. For me, that honesty was all that stood between me and eternity that night when the Angel of Death came for me.

Wednesday, October 7, 1992—1:35 a.m.

Awareness intruded slowly with an incessant buzzing from somewhere far away. Then the voice on the speaker in the darkened hallway snapped my eyes wide.

"Code blue! Code blue, ICU 304!"

There came a rushing of feet and rattling of equipment. Terse mumbles, words I could not quite hear, issued from the room next door. Then one voice barked in command.

"Charging!"

"Clear!" sang out a second.

Ka-thunk! . . . Silence, ominous silence.

"Again! Charging!"

"Clear!"

Ka-thunk! . . . Again, only silence.

"Charging! No, wait." Again, silence stretched several long seconds. "Good work, people, we've got him back."

I released my breath, suddenly aware that I'd been holding it. This was the second code blue I'd witnessed since coming to this ICU. The first had not fared so well. Like a stalk of celery, that one lay silent and pale in his bed across the room, stroked out in a coma now.

Well, that won't be the way of it for me. I grimaced at the gruesome thought. Yeah, I'd goaded Dr. Laring into revealing the facts, all right. Was it his pompous attitude or the way he obviously didn't believe I could handle the truth that made me do it? Now armed with the gruesome details . . . *God! Why did I need to know?*

As if cued by my thoughts, I felt a tightening, like a fist clenching, deep within my chest. The noise that escaped my lips fell pathetically short of a scream.

"Ahhh-hhhh."

Stop it, goddammit! My mind fought for self-control. *You're doing all this to yourself.* "Ahh . . . uhh."

Oh God, no! Like a fist of steel, the clenching suddenly tightened. Even my whispered groans fell silent.

Must stay calm. I gritted my teeth, remembering Dr. Laring's words. They now flashed into my memory, almost as a revengeful goading. ". . . as you begin to suffocate, and your blood pressure drops, your heart will race. Your lungs will pump not so much from lack of oxygen—it's not that noticeable when your blood is not picking up enough—rather, you'll panic. All you badasses do. You'll likely hemorrhage, and your lungs will fill with blood . . ."

No! I will not go out like that, coughing my life away, hurling it, spraying it like red finger paint onto everything in sight. My life has to mean something more. God! Don't let me end as just so much gore some poor, minimum-wage bastard has to clean up.

"No! Oh God, no." In response to my strangled croak, there came a new buzzing and a dark, smothering presence. Turning my head toward the monitor, I saw a flashing red light.

My alarm! Strange, I hadn't heard it when it first went off. *Can't they hear it? Why don't they come?*

The fist within my chest tightened even more and seemed now attached to a presence, an undeniably tactile darkness. My gasp was one of full panic, but somehow the scream refused to come.

"Just relax."

I recoiled at the words, eyes frantic, probing the blanketing darkness for someone—some real person.

The voice continued. "There is nothing to fear. It will all be over way before they can respond."

"But w-why?" I whispered into the deepening blackness. "They . . . n-n-next door. Why . . . d-don't . . . they come?"

"Oh, they will come, and in good time, but it is always so with blood clots like yours. There is nothing they can do now but watch. And they've seen it before. Don't fault them that they stay busy with the one who will live."

My eyes were now held by the red light on the monitor, which had strangely become two. They blinked as if to empathize with his words while the mad squiggle of blue lines across the face of the machine now seemed as a reflection of humor off an ivory jaw gaping from a skull.

"B-b-but . . . it's not m-my . . ."

"Time? Time, now for you, doesn't matter. Your time is now mine!"

"Who . . . huh . . . uhh . . . who are you?"

"Yes, I am who you believe me to be. They call me 'Death,'"—the voice was calm, even matter-of-fact—"and I've come for you."

"Wait! My life . . . n-not finished." My whisper seemed to be accompanied by a strange gurgling. "N-n-not yet!"

"Make it easy on yourself. Simply think what you want to say. I will hear you."

Please, Mr. Death. I am not ready to die yet. I haven't lived! Not really.

"You have had forty-five years." I could hear, more than see, his shrug. "What have you been doing?"

Oh God, Mr. Death, I've thought about it all day and see it so clearly now . . . how I've spent my time doing what others expected of me—my parents, my bosses, my wife. But I've done so little of what I truly wanted. I've wasted my whole life. You can't take me like this—this person I don't want to be!

"Why should I give you more time? What are you willing to do for it?"

Anything!

The twin glows regarded me pensively for a long moment.

"Would you learn the truth about courage? That is . . . about *your* courage?"

What do you mean?

"Do you not secretly regard yourself as a coward?"

My God! How do you—

"Is that not why you are so reluctant to die?" His jaw unhinged into a wide grin. "Cowards always die wishing they'd just once felt like a hero, to just once have known real courage."

Well . . . yes, you could look at it that way, but—

"It matters not how *I* look at it. For you to continue in this life, my first requirement, were I to even consider it, would be that *you* look with honesty at yourself, past and present." His gaze held me transfixed. "Now! Do you have that kind of honesty?"

Yeah, yeah, I do. Sure!

"Not so fast. Such honesty requires a kind of courage that few in this world know." His chuckle held an odd note of challenge. "You are not yet among them."

Look, Mr. Death, I'll do it! Whatever you ask.

"Ha! Good. I will require that you examine your past. You'll write it down, your story, as it comes to you. Remember now, honesty." His ruby stare seemed to flicker in some private merriment as the pressure in my chest melted away. "Oh, and you can call me Big D. We'll be talking from time to time."

Thank you. My sigh comes with a long, easy breath of relief. *It's all settled then?*

"No. Hell, no!" His jeer seems almost to explode. "Don't blow me off so quickly. There is much more!"

More?

"Oh, yes. You see, the funny thing about honesty is that it requires the light of truth."

The light of . . .

"And the funny thing about you"—there was that chuckle again—"is that you have no idea about the truth of life."

Truth of life?

"Huh-ah!" The fist in my chest returned briefly, a quick clutch of agony.

"What are you, some kinda fucking parrot? Listen up!"

Yes! "Huh-ah!" *Yes, I'm listening!*

"Okay . . . harrumph!" He snorts as if in exasperation. "Truths . . . life's truths. They're kind of like laws, life laws—like the Law of Gravity is a physical law?" He stopped to regard me in ruby expectation.

Yes, I'm listening, I groaned, my voice gravelly.

"Good! Believe the laws . . . or, don't believe them. Doesn't matter. Break them and life is dysfunctional. Understand them and the light of truth is turned on. You'll need a lot of light to see some of the shit in your life."

I'll do whatever it takes, Mr. Death.

"I prefer to be called Big D!" The glow in his eye sockets seemed to tighten. "Remember it!"

Yes, Mr. Dea—I mean . . . Big D.

"Okay. Now go where I lead, and don't be parroting me. Do your own fucking thinking! Oh, and follow your dreams. Wherever your joy is, there's where you'll go!"

I will, Big D. I will!

"Honesty, truth, courage, following your dreams, your joy. You haven't a fucking clue, but I *will* hold you to your word."

Wednesday, October 7, 1992—2:05 a.m.

"I don't care how well it seems to be working! Get it out of here and have them check it thoroughly. Those readings it was displaying are impossible."

Squinting against the fluorescent light, I opened my eyes to the parting backs of the charge nurse—Nurse Grumpy, I called her—and a technician.

"Mr. Williams, how are you feeling?" For the first time becoming aware of her presence, I recognized the voice of Nurse Fine Ass.

Glancing left, I caught her sunshine smile and returned it before replying, "Okay, I guess. What's going on?"

"Sorry to wake you, but your monitor was acting up and we had to change it." Pulling out the tails of my hospital gown, she flipped it aside and quickly stripped the leads from my chest and side and applied the round, sticky stubs of new ones, then expertly snapped the new wires back on. "There now. Get some more sleep. Do you need a pill?" she asked as she finished tucking the blanket back around me.

Comb Ridge, Utah—Present Day

"Ahhh . . . shit!" My curse comes with the tightening of the final knot on the contraption now holding the bones in my leg from grinding together with every agonizing movement. The damned thing needs to be loosened occasionally and the leg massaged to keep the blood flowing smoothly, what with the swelling.

Damn! There's only so much a guy can do to self-hypnotize this kind of pain away.

Stowing my tool kit back into its leather pouch, I survey the remains of my motorcycle with the front forks removed. Parts of them now cradle my throbbing leg. My hand caresses the dented but still somehow beautiful red paint of its gas tank. "You may yet carry me out of this mess, old girl," I murmur. "A half tank of gas exploding will make a great signal flare."

Now if I can just manage it all without blowing myself up as well. Maybe a carefully cut wick, fashioned of dirty clothes soaked with gas stretched from the opened fill hole of the tank across the ledge. Then when the time is right . . .

But no, there isn't enough space on this ledge to get myself a safe enough distance away. If the exploding gas doesn't get me directly, the pinion pines—even the few on this end of the ledge—are sure to catch fire and will likely roast me like rabbit on a stick.

No, that'll never work. I heave a sigh. *Gotta be a way . . .*

What else can I use for a signal? I have the taillight, with its array of LEDs. That should provide a decent nighttime signal light requiring very little of that precious motorcycle battery's juice.

I look down into the Comb Ridge Wash with its little dirt road, so far down there that it looks like a scratch on the ground, only occasionally seen between the big cottonwoods lining the trickle of water in the bottom. *Fuck! Fat chance . . .*

There is one lone surviving rearview mirror for daytime signaling. *Sure, much of this ledge only catches a couple hours of afternoon sunlight as the overhang keeps it in the shade most of the time. And sure, a protruding wall of sandstone cliff blocks much of the line of sight to the road. And sure, that road is not heavily traveled. But just maybe . . .*

I note each item in my meager inventory as I load them back into my emptied saddlebags. There is my leather coat and chaps. I set them aside. *It does get chilly in the desert at night, even in the summertime, and the summer's almost over.* Assorted clean underwear and clothes—*need those to keep the leg wound clean.* Two Big Hunk candy bars, a large bag of jelly beans, and another of cheesy puffs—*must remember to save a few puffs as bait. A chipmunk or lizard will go a lot farther feeding me than a cheesy puff.* And a large, plastic jar of jerky. *Thank God, I've always loved jerky.* Six cans of soup, a can opener, and an army mess kit.

Lastly, besides the several filled notebooks, there are half a dozen empty ones and three pens. Knowing Big D as I've come to, he may be my mentor and even my best friend, but he is still the Angel of Death! Clearly, my life depends on living up to my bargain with him. And he did ask me to write the second book. He demanded that I write that first one, but with this one, I thought it was only a request, so it hasn't been my main priority—until now. Nevertheless, I am satisfied that it is pretty much done. The ending was a little tricky, but I improvised to where it will satisfy the reader.

My eyes fall on an early written recollection of Big D's words from back then. "Now go where I lead, and don't be parroting me. Do your own fucking thinking!"

Go where you lead, Big D? I call out. *Why did you lead me here to this place of pain and torment?* My only answer is the swish of the desert wind, such a mournful sound for this lonely ledge high up on the rarefied heights of this slick rock cliff.

Big D? Goddammit! Dammit! Dammit! My cry echoes off the canyon walls. *Big D . . . Big D . . . Big D . . .* "Shit." My cry ends with one whispered word.

The wind sighs once more, long and lonely, before ending with the sound much like irritation incarnated very closely behind me. It comes as no surprise when he speaks.

"Not very functional there, Jeff. You want to back it up a few lines?"

What? Turning, I come face-to-face with the Grim Reaper—not my friend, Big D, but the Reaper incarnate. The ruby laser of his unwavering gaze, the purposeful way he clutches his sickle—the steely menace of it carries through in his tone. *W-what?* I repeat aloud, as if that would somehow calm his irritation.

"Back it up to where I said, 'Believe the laws . . . or, don't believe them. Doesn't matter. Break them and life is dysfunctional.'"

I-I'm not following, Big D. My uncomfortable, stammering mind stalls but doesn't gain me any insight into what he is saying, and the edge of his sickle looks so deadly sharp.

"The first of the Spiritual Laws of Life, Jeff. Quickly! What is it?"

I am the Creator.

"Good!" His stare seems to soften to a less lethal burn. "Looks like we need to go back over some basics here, Jeff. What's it mean?"

I-it means that everything in my life is of my own creation. That everything requires an element of my own personal conscious or unconscious creation to exist in my life.

"Right!" There is a certain sharpening to his scrutiny. "Now apply it to this moment."

It means that you didn't lead me here, Big D. I got here all on my own. I swallow and speak aloud as the full meaning of it hits. "Look, I . . . I'm sorry, Big D. Me, of all people, blaming you for my own pain. I know better! I'm . . . I'm really sorry."

"S-okay, relax." His hand clutches my shoulder in a hard, boney grip that is somehow tender. "You *are* in pain. And yes, you are correct about the application of the law, 'at least on this most primary surface level of its meaning.' But for the pain, you are excused its transgression.

"And you're right," he adds. "I have been leading you, but only on your *inner* journey. You—your soul—knows *everything*. I have merely been leading you to *remember* just a little of it. That first Law of Life? You know it well. We have explored this law into the infinity of its truth, but with infinity, there is always more."

Thanks. My throat closes up with gratitude thinking about all he has taught me. *Unnerving . . . yeah. Even deadly. But as a friend, there are none truer.*

"Hell, life itself can be unnerving. And in the end, it's always deadly." Big D's voice adds to my thought, reverberating as it does in those old, familiar bass tones. The glow in one eye socket slowly winks out before Big D, himself, follows.

While I no longer see him, I hear his last question. "As for the book . . . 'improvise?' Isn't that word synonymous with . . . *to lie?*"

Not really, Big D. You see, for the ending, I had to . . . Big D? Big D? Are you still here?

AUTHOR'S NOTE
This book is my story. My life has been an argues experience told using two different timelines. The prologue begins in the present day timeline, Chapters One and Two begin back then in that ICU. Now for the sake of clarity, I need to take it all back to then—back to when I first met Big D.

The experiencing of true love between two people never results in pain. Pain between lovers is always the direct result of fear—the unmet, fearful needs within themselves.

Redneck Spirituality—Book Two

CHAPTER TWO

Masquerading Love

Wednesday, October 7, 1992—6:40 a.m.

My eyes opened to the brightness streaming in between the open drapes in Sunrise Hospital's third-floor ICU. Beyond the metropolitan haze of Las Vegas, the sun's first rays were striking the cliffs of Red Rock Canyon. Above, the clouds reflected with the gold of a new day. There came an ache to the back of my throat as I looked at the scene, now suddenly blurred.

God! When has the beauty in a simple sunrise ever awakened such emotion in me? Is it out of relief to be seeing another day? Shit, that was one weird-ass dream. Big D? I chuckle. *Bad enough to be hallucinating about the Angel of Death, but to even give him a name? Glad all that's over.*

But wait . . . don't dreams usually melt away with the light of day? This one was stuck in my mind as if put there with a branding iron. Briefly, I made a mental note to ask Dr. Laring if blood thinners cause hallucinations. That one was pretty prime.

"Good morning, Mr. Williams. We brought you some new company. Sorry, we don't normally have more than one patient per room in the ICU." Behind the well-rounded curves of Nurse Fine Ass, there was a bed, complete with patient, being pushed into the room. Glancing over, I was surprised to discover that the poor, stroked-out bastard was gone. "This is Mr. Johansen. Looks like he's pretty sleepy. You can get to know each other later."

"What happened to the guy with the stroke?"

"Oh, he's fine," she replied a little too quickly. "We transferred him early this morning. Once he was stable, there was no reason to keep him here in the ICU."

"Does that mean that I'm not stable?"

"Oh no, Mr. Williams." There was that too-quick-on-the-trigger reply again. "Maybe I should have said he was 'no longer critical.'"

"Does that mean he's dea—"

"Oh, look here! Mr. Williams, you haven't filled out your breakfast order form yet." She picked it up from the cart and handed it to me together with a pen. "If you'll do it now, I'll see that it gets to the dietician in time."

Seeing the blush creeping up the back of her neck as she turned to attend to the new man, I shrugged. *Damn but they're skittish about talking reality around here. And, maybe she's just new and doesn't know how to deal with patients like me.*

"Sure, I'll do it now. And hey . . . don't mind me. I was just jerkin' your chain."

"It's all right, Mr. Williams. There's a reason why we usually limit the ICU to one patient per room. But what with two busses wrecking head-on and then the botulism outbreak, all the ICUs in town are full. Look, everyone here has their own way of dealing with it." The smile she flashed was sweet enough, but the way she turned to deliver it was deliberate. Her eyes left no doubt that she was no innocent to this ward. She, too, knew exactly what the "it" was to which she referred. Was it possible that she also had weird hallucinations of specters stalking the night around here?

After she left, I lay studying the plump bundle in the other bed. There wasn't much to see, other than some grubby, gray whiskers and a few equally gray hairs on an otherwise bald head. He lay as if asleep, and the small crowd of family hung back at the door. Yet, I knew he was not asleep. I could feel his fear . . . and something more, something vaguely familiar. Finally, someone in the cluster of relatives outside the door mentioned breakfast. They all took the hint and left. He and I were, for a time, alone. I broke the silence.

"Whatcha in here for?"

"Heart attack." His voice reminded me of gravel slush being dumped from a cement truck.

"With me, it's a blood clot on the lung."

"Look . . . Mr. Williams, was it? I really need to get some rest."

"Sure."

And I'm no hallucination.

"What's that, Mr. Johansen? What did you say?"

"I said I'd like to rest. Now, if you don't mind . . ." The cement now seemed to be running down the chute, and I didn't want to be in its way.

"Sure, yeah. Sorry." I lay there in silent confusion, wondering about my sanity. Last night I could chalk up as a bad dream, but that voice . . . that bottom-of-the-barrel way it sounded. No, it couldn't be. I was still chewing on it when the man's wife came tiptoeing in to sit at his bedside. The look in her eyes touched something in me as I watched her study his face.

God, Meg, where are you? I know you said the house was a mess and that you had massages scheduled today. I know I said it was okay . . . but why couldn't you see?

"Meg thinks she's about to lose all security in life, Jeff. Can you blame her for not wanting to watch you die?"

"Wha?"

"Shhh! It's me . . . Big D."

Oh, Jesus! That weird voice from last night!

I struggled into a sitting position, craning my neck.

"That's right. Now just think what you need to say and I'll hear you. No sense keeping the man up. Didn't you hear? He wants to sleep the last of his days away. I'll be around with the shuttle bus for him soon enough."

Shuttle bus?

"Yeah. He's one of those who has given up on life. Hell, you've seen his family hovering about. He doesn't have the courage to show them his feelings, nor let them help him fight for his life. He knows he's dying and doesn't care. Cowards don't ride in the limo."

What about me? And why can't I see you? Big D . . . it is you, isn't it?

"You've got a front-row seat in this little drama. What more do you need? After I brought the shuttle for you last night, you know about me. But you ordered the limo, and as for that . . . well, that remains to be seen."

But why do you say he's a coward?

"When it comes time for dying, those with any courage at all—and who have time to sense me coming—always look at the bottom line. You did."

I'm not sure I follow.

"C'mon, Jeff! What have you been thinking about almost constantly these past few days?"

Well, about my wife and son, my parents, and the people I've known in life. And I've thought a lot about whether or not I've made any difference in their lives.

"Exactly, Jeff! The bottom line of life is love."

"Love?" I said it aloud, then realized I was staring across the room and into the lady's eyes. She looked from me to her husband, as if seeking his stony advice, and I suddenly became aware of the expressions that had been flowing across my face those past few moments.

I smiled. "Sorry. Gas pains . . . y'know?"

My expression carefully blank, I lay back before continuing. *I don't recall saying anything just now about "love," Big D.*

"Sure you did! When it comes time for dying, the bottom line about life is how much love do others hold for you? And how much of yours did you give to them?"

Holy shit! You're right!

"Course I'm right, if you insist on making everything about 'right' and 'wrong.' Better to look at it as, does it work or doesn't it? Is it truth? Those things that work in the space of love are always the truth of life, which brings me to one of those Laws of Life that I mentioned you need so much to learn—"

A clatter of pans from the hall interrupted him, and Nurse Grumpy sailed in to settle my breakfast tray onto the side stand. I hit the button, cranking my bed into the sitting position as she swung it in front with a flourish. "Eat up, now," she ordered.

Looking under the tin lid, I wondered at the generic ham. Clearly, the powdered scrambled eggs weren't real. I understood why she seemed so curt and kept silent. Obviously, adding my complaints to everyone else's would only darken her day more.

"Excellent choice!" Big D's voice was hearty, and I didn't need to see him to know he was smiling.

You like what I chose for breakfast?

"No, Jeff. I like your choice of energy just now." He chuckled. "You're observing the Law of Thought Energy even before I tell it to you."

How is that?

"Goes like this. **Thoughts are energy and exist in one of only two forms . . . love, or all that is not love—fear.** The energy of love always feels good to the soul and harms no one. Fear, though it sometimes feels good to the ego, always harms your soul, and in your oneness . . . everyone's."

Thought energy? It doesn't sound all that earthshaking. Kinda nebulous even . . .

"Huh-uh!" A steely fist again clutched deep inside my chest, shaking my very world.

"This may be one of the more minor laws," Big D hissed, "but I share it with you. And by God, if you won't hold it sacred, I . . . *will* take you. Right now!"

"Hhhuh . . . hhha!" *Big D, yes . . . sacred. Got it! I'm sorry! Please . . .*

As quickly as it came, the fist went away, leaving me gasping and dabbing weakly at the spilled milk on my tray.

"Sir?" the woman's voice intruded. "Should I ring for the nurse? You don't look so good."

"No . . . it's okay. Just swallowed down the wrong pipe, y'know?" Again, I smiled, though it, too, felt a little weak. *Big D! Please. You don't have to be so harsh. I didn't mean to offend you.*

"It was not about my taking offense. It was about your disrespect for the agreement you made. Don't do it again!"

I won't . . . not intentionally. Just tell me if you think I'm out of line. God! This man's wife must think I'm a gastric basket case by now.

"Ha. You needn't try to divert my attention. You forget, I read your mind. And, it's true," he added, chuckling, "she does."

Big D, I don't know how to deal with you. One minute you're ripping my lungs apart and the next, you're joking!

"Look, Jeff . . . life's too important to be taken so seriously. Lighten up, there. Cuss, fart, be obnoxiously crude around me anytime you want. But the Laws of Life, or the agreements you have made with me—or anyone else in your life, for that matter—those things you will hold sacred!"

I will . . . I will! You have my word.

"Just so . . . be sure you keep it."

With that, there was silence, except for a raspy snore from across the room. The moments ticked slowly by, and I began to wonder if Big D was still there. There was a question . . . oh, but did I really want to know?

"Yes, Jeff, you do. The real question is, do you have the courage to accept the truth? Ask—"

Big D, how well am I loved? I mean, Meg . . . does she love me?

"Perhaps first it would be wise to ask how well you have loved her. Indeed. Do you love her?"

I . . . I'm not sure I know anymore.

"Sure, you know. You are the world's foremost authority on you."

Oh God, Big D, since all this happened, I've come to question everything I ever thought I knew!

"It is well." I detected a slight chuckle in his voice. "The truth is that as true love goes, you, like most in this world, have not done as well as you might think. Your love was more need, a fearful neediness born of your own insecurities."

I don't understand . . .

"Few in this world do. Yes, in the general view of what passes for love between a man and a woman, to hear it, folks would say yours is the most magnificent of love stories. Not even Shakespeare could have written your love for Meg any better."

Are you saying that my life with Meg was like some romantic tragedy?

"Yes, it is that, too."

I don't see it that way. You must mean about Meg, as a young woman, being raped and pressed into prostitution and how my love saved her from that life?

"Yes, there was that, too."

Then . . . are you saying that I did love well?

"No, Jeff. What I am saying is that you never learned your lessons well. Yet, when and if you do, this world will still perceive your love story just so—as a romantic tragedy."

Now I'm really confused, Big D.

"Look, Jeff, it is not that this world generally doesn't know the truth about love and relationships. It's that they don't want to accept the truth. Or rather, they don't want to accept the responsibility."

Responsibility?

"Yes, responsibility." His chuckle seemed to have become more pronounced. "And that brings me to the most important of all the Laws of Life—The Law of the Creator. Most all of the laws hinge on this one, and every dysfunction in every relationship between one human and another, between one country—between one race—and another, is the direct result of breaking this law."

That sounds like the great secret of life. Tell me.

"Indeed, it is the great secret of life, were there to be only one." His laughter was like a static charge of energy. The goose bumps rose all over my body. "Knowing this law, Jeff, requires a sense of responsibility such that few have and you cannot presently conceive. Are you willing?"

I moistened my suddenly dry lips, and my thought to him, when it came, seemed to stutter.

Y-yes.

"Good! You might just be one of the few! Here is the law. Say it after me. *I-am-the-Creator.*"

I am the . . . You? You, Big D, are God?

"Ha!" His chuckle was more of a snort. "No more than you are, and yes, we are . . . Though, while I said 'Creator,' it is just as true to have said 'God.' You will find all this easier to understand when you stop letting every religious bible thumper fuck with your mind."

Are you saying that the Bible was wrong?

"Wrong? Oh, shit! Here we go again with the 'right' and 'wrong.'" I heard his exasperation and cringed, my hand going to my chest.

"Relax. It's only natural for you to have a skewered sense of how and what to hold sacred. The Bible was not written by God, but rather by a bunch of control freaks. Mostly well-meaning ones—true. But the fact remains that what they said of their own personal experience of the divine has been translated several times over, each time by someone saying what they thought was meant, and each one's thoughts being colored by their own wants and needs. By the time it came to be written in English, who's to say what the original authors meant. And then there is what is actually meant in the Bible, as opposed to what yet another control freak is telling you from some pulpit. You get my drift? Use your own mind, and the love in your heart, to discern the truth."

I lay there in the comfort of my sheets, listening to the sounds of Las Vegas. For a man who never really believed all that Mormon religious stuff of his childhood, why did I find it so difficult to let go of the Bible—and for that matter, the Book of Mormon?

"Oh yes, Jeff," Big D interrupted softly. "There is great truth in the Bible. As for the Book of Mormon? Doesn't matter how hinky you think the story, it is patterned after the Bible in its basic premise. There is great truth in what passes for a Bible in most every religion. It is the interpretation, or rather, the 'religion' part that is all fucked up—the *control freak quotient*."

I don't understand what you mean by saying that I am the creator, and especially, that you seem to imply that I am also God. I mean . . .

"Look at the 'creator' part for now, Jeff. Most simply, it means that you create your own life and everything in it. There is nothing in your life that does not require your direct involvement in some way in being created. You can no longer blame anyone or anything outside of yourself for anything in your life!"

You mean if I walked out into the street and got killed by a falling meteor, I created it?

"Didn't you say that you walked out into the street? Could it be that some higher, unconscious part of you knew it was time for you to die?"

Uh . . . but you said the law can also mean that I am God? Didn't God have a hand in creating my life?

"You are God."

No disrespect, Big D, but that's a little hard to swallow. And don't get me wrong! I mean, I do hold your laws as sacred!

"I'll pass by the disrespect this time. It was not intentional. The truth about God has always been confusing to mankind. You insist on placing God as someone or something that is essentially outside yourselves that occasionally touches you inside. Your Bible was very clear— God is everywhere and everything. Literally, you are God. There is no part of God that is any more powerful than the part that is you."

Just seems like . . . well, sacrilege.

"Whoa! There you go again, letting those control freaks fuck up your mind. Religious organizations always tend to place God as 'out there.' Were they to tell you what I just told you, how could they keep their congregations powerless and dependent?"

You mean that all those righteous men of God and their churches are—

"Fucked up? Exactly. Look, consider God in this way. You are like a drop in the sea of God. You are God. The essence and entirety of that drop holds the essence and entirety of all the power of God. You know that every cell in your body carries the same DNA code that determines everything about who you are physically? Spiritually, it is kinda like you possess God's DNA."

Damned if that doesn't make sense! But . . . well, something still bothers me.

"Yes?"

Well, you keep saying the "F" word. Why do you do that?

"Communication, Jeff. It is the wording you most commonly use when you are trying to stress your point. Thirty years in auto repair shops hasn't exactly lent you an academic vocabulary."

Oh, I didn't realize. It just seems so—

"Yeah, but it is an effective way of pointing out the obnoxious. Used between you and me, don't sweat it. Now, how about getting back to the smellier shit of life?"

Smelly shit?

"Yeah, the part about breaking this law in life. When you are holding yourself responsible for being its creator, what stinks in your relationship with Meg cannot really be Meg's fault. Can it?"

No, I suppose not.

"Then it must be about you and your creation of your life. She doesn't create your feelings—you do." I felt a finger poke my chest three times and looked down to where the blanket covered me just in time to see a third dimple magically appear. "She doesn't choose your viewpoints or what you will believe. Your view of your personal world exactly follows those beliefs. All that is in it is what you put there. You—your feelings, your viewpoint, your beliefs, your life. It's all about YOU. Get the point?" I cringed as another invisible finger jabbed my chest.

Then why would I create Ho Chi Minh, Gaddafi, Kim Il Sung, or the Khmer Rouge being in my world?

"Actually, smart-ass, inasmuch as what they mean to your personal world, you did—and you better tone your attitude." There came a twinge deep down inside my chest, just enough to emphasize his words. "For now, we're talking your personal world and those you let into it."

Oh. Well, I can accept responsibility for that, I shot back quickly.

"Good! Pretty shitty to be blaming others for what you create by your choice of feelings, beliefs, and subsequent actions. Bottom line is, relationships are the perfect schoolground for learning about you. More specifically, Meg is in your life to give you the opportunity to learn the truth about your feelings and, hopefully, learn how to love. You've always had a loving soul. Whatever she's done, because you care for her, you've usually managed to deal with your feelings and take them to love. In that, your love was exceptional. That doesn't negate the fact that much of your love has really been nothing but fearful need. You feared you'd never find another beauty like her."

Yes. I shuddered. *That's true.*

"So, in your relationship with Meg, tell me exactly who it is that you are learning to love?"

Well, Meg, of course.

"Eeeeeeeen-t!" Big D sounded off in true game show host fashion. "Dysfunctional!"

Dysfunctional?

"Yes, it doesn't work. Could you have understood me had I said, 'wrong?' The truth is that the viewpoint represented by your answer is the crux of your relationship's dysfunction."

I . . . uh . . .

"You learn by looking in the mirror of another. Should you ever learn, through Meg, to love yourself, then none of your feelings for her would ever be a masquerade of fear and need, but rather, true love. It's one of the laws—***Everyone is but a mirror for one's self.***"

Silence stretches between his mind and mine. I know he sees my confusion.

"Haaaaa!" I hear his frustrated sigh. "Look! Until you love yourself, you cannot love another. You cannot give what you don't have. While you have more than most, self-love was never one of your strengths. None of it is about Meg, y'know?"

When I pursed my lips, dubious in thought, and didn't answer right away, Big D continued. "But then that's the simplistic way of stating it—and the most applicable one for you right now. Wanna hear the full scope of that one?"

Well, I—

"Look, Jeff, clearly the finger of your responsibility still points outward! Maybe you need me to say it this way. Are you willing to live up to our agreement or not?" The tone of his voice left little doubt as to my answer.

Yes, yes! Of course I am.

"I am not going to bully you into living, nor am I going to continually remind you of the stakes. You have full personal choice."

Yes, okay. I understand.

"Good! Now here is a fuller gist of that law. **There is nothing 'out there.' Everything within your universe is within yourself.** The way you choose to view it 'out there' gives you the opportunity to look at what is 'in here'—in yourself—if you have the courage to look. What you dislike in another person you could never have the ability to conceive were it not a part of you that you don't like. Another way of stating it is, **Everything 'out there' is but a reflection, the mirror, for something 'in here.'** How much truth you can see is restricted by the clarity of your insight—and your courage to look."

There was a long silence as I began to digest it. Then Big D added, "Now, do you still need to ask me if Meg loves you?"

No.

"Can you be okay that Meg is afraid to be here with you just now?"

I . . . I don't know.

"Sure you do! The truth, Jeff."

The truth is that, well . . . I looked over at my roommate's wife, to the shine of emotions in her eyes as she gazed at him, to the way she lingered at his bedside, clearly wanting to be there, willing to face whatever came. Mousey little thing that she was, she had a magnificent heart!

The truth, Big D, is no, and I don't want to look at it just now.

"Yeah . . . look at that one then," Big D whispered, his voice becoming thinner. "Confusion is one of your favorite ways to sabotage your life. Procrastination is another. Just don't procrastinate on getting clear about the laws. Learn them as they are revealed to you, and observe them with each day I give you. Right now, they're like the first edging of ice in a deep pond. As your life goes on—*if* it goes on—everything will grow from them and become clear. Eventually, the world of your pond will hold your weight. Perhaps you may even learn what a joy it is to ice skate." His last words seemed to blow across me like a breeze over ice.

"Big D? Big D . . . don't leave me here alone!" My eyes jerk open in frantic search. Across the room, his whole family was clustered around the heart attack man's bed—all eyes on me.

"Uh, sorry . . . must have dozed off. Uh, just a dream."

Yet, from somewhere far away came a chuckle, and I knew . . .

* * *

Mr. Johansen died in his sleep that night. The bells and buzzers and hoopla of the crash team woke his wife as she slept in the chair at his bedside. I watched as Big D escorted him out. He did not so much as glance her way as he passed.

Looking at the empty chair at my own bedside, I knew it would always be empty. When they finally pronounced him and cleaned up their clutter, they let his wife back in. She threw herself across his plump figure and sobbed for an hour before they finally came to remove the body.

I was almost torn by wishing it were Meg and me. Had Meg felt that way about me, maybe it would have been. Or maybe it would have given me all the more reason to live. Funny how we can get so attached to all those *what might've beens*. Mrs. Johansen certainly was.

Comb Ridge, Utah—Present Day

Today is one of pain. Every movement of the leg is agony, and I know that soon I must be about the business of surviving. But Big D cautions me to lie quietly and rest for now.

"It takes strength of character, strength of mind, and even some physical strength to self-hypnotize the pain away." Big D's smile is gentle. "Eat your soup, lie still, and rest."

Wouldn't it be wise to only eat half the soup now and save the rest for later?

"No. You need the energy, as well as rest."

Accepting his recommendation, and with my glove on one hand, I lift the can of soup out from the glowing embers of the small fire of twigs used to heat it. To keep the ashes out, I purposefully leave off running the can opener the full circle and now take the combination spoon/fork from my mess kit, pry the lid on up, then take a slow, cautious bite. The soup is not too hot, which sets me to shoveling it in as fast as I can go. Then, picking up the canteen, I groan. *Oh my God, it's almost empty! Where am I to get more water?*

"All in good time." Big D's voice is calm, unworried. "You still have one beer. Drink it and rest. And save the cans. You're going to need them."

That last remark goes a long way to calm my reservations. *He must expect me to survive, at least for a time.*

Then he gives me one last admonition. "When you're done there, you need to loosen the straps on those splints and lightly massage the blood flow in that leg before you sleep." He sits nearby, dangling his leg bones over the side, watching my weak, fumbling fingers go about the painful task. I don't see him go.

Time? Money? Such excuses are like farts in a hurricane when it is one's life on the line. Funny thing is, when it comes to being someone one can respect, one's life is always on the line.
Redneck Spirituality—Book One

CHAPTER THREE

It's Not the Money, Only the Price

Thursday, October 22, 1992—3:30 p.m.

"What the hell are you doing now?" Meg's voice broke the stillness of my mind as I concentrated on the smooth flow of blood throughout my body. Mindful meditation, the tapes called it. Breathing in deeply through my nose and letting it slowly out my mouth, I gave myself a count up to wakefulness.

ONE—coming up. TWO—feeling good. THREE—rested. FOUR—relaxed. FIVE—calm. I sighed, adding—*no matter what kind of crappy drama may be raging around me.*

"Meditating, Meg. What's the problem?" That my voice is so calm seems to stir her shit to a new froth.

"You!" Meg stands before me, her fists clenched and stuffed solidly against each hip. "You're the problem, Jeff!"

"What do you mean?"

"I mean, you've been home from the hospital almost a week now. All you do is lay around and read or listen to those damned tapes, and now this weird shit!" Meg paced the cool, blue carpet in front of the mess of pillows and blankets surrounding me on the couch.

She stopped and swiped a finger over the TV. It came off clean, as usual. She grimaced, and I knew she would soon be dusting it anyway. "I can't even sleep at night, what with that speaker you have jabbering under your pillow."

"It's called 'sleep learning,' Meg. It just runs for a short time. I turn it on when I'm falling asleep, and it shuts itself off automatically when it reaches the end of the tape."

"I don't care. You're getting weirder and weirder. It's scaring me. And what about the bills? When are you going back to work? No one's paying you to lay around."

"C'mon, Meg, you know Dr. Laring said he wants me to stay in bed for another three weeks. We don't have all that many bills. Besides, your business is doing pretty good right now, isn't it?"

"What! You expect me to use my money to pay the bills?"

"Well, yeah. I thought—"

"Dat's my money! Is you responsibility to pay bills and buy food and clothes. Goddammit! I'm tired of having to fill in when you money not 'nough." Her Korean accent thickened as her voice rose into that 'I want a divorce' tone. My own remained calm.

"I know, Meg. You've always been generous with your money. I'm sorry." I sighed, doing a quick mental assessment. Yeah, I felt pretty good. And Big D? Well, I was doing everything he asked, though he hadn't really been around that much. It did seem somewhat safe now.

I resisted a chuckle, thinking about what Meg would say if I were to tell her about Big D. "You're right, Meg. Look, I'll go back to work on Monday. Hell, it's not like they give a shit about us mechanics. They're not likely to ask for a doctor's release or anything."

Looking satisfied with her victory, Meg began her cleaning rituals. Watching as her supple body moved with a grace of its own, it was easy to see past the minor unpleasantries occasionally dispossessing her. Her natural Asian beauty—so exotic—always seemed to trivialize such things as her viewpoint on money. Besides, hadn't Meg always taken very good care of me and the house? My part was the money. That was part of her culture, the Korean man's and woman's responsibilities. Meg bent to pick up my pen and notebook from the floor, reminding me of what it was I most cherished about her. Ah, yes . . . that body. Most of all, it was her body. Looking at it, touching it, making love to it . . .

Yes . . . *it*. Looking back over our lives together, I could see that I had to say 'it' to stay honest with myself because, as much as I enjoyed Meg's body, no matter how close to her I might feel while locked within her warm depths, I knew it was different. She was never really *there* when we made love. Oh, her body enjoyed it with me—she said. Yet emotionally? Meg was never vulnerable with me in that way. Maybe that was why she could never let go enough to even orgasm.

Yes, I could well see what Big D meant about *love* and *need*. All those years, I loved Meg with a passion that shouted, "I don't want to live without you!" Never mind that we had very few interests in common. Never mind that Meg was unwilling to see, or nurture, my emotional needs—those things of my life for which I held passion, those things that made my spirit soar.

Why should she? After all, *Korean men* didn't have *emotional needs*. No wonder Meg held so little respect for me. But wait. Was my own culture really so different? Yes, Big D was right. My love had always been *needy*.

Oh God. I sighed. *When did it all change? When did Meg last reach for me, actually cling to me, share her innermost feelings, find me amusing, find me lovable?* "Huh-uuuh." I hacked, trying to clear the sudden lump in my throat. *Never? Fuck! When did I become so oblivious?*

From my perch on the couch, I watched her stroke the vacuum back and forth and saw the jiggle of her still-shapely breasts, the sway of her hips, and the suggestive line between the thighs of her tight pants.

Here I sit, lusting after her. When was the last time she lusted for me? Wait . . . was it possible there was never a first time? No, that's impossible. That would mean our life together was all a lie.

A sudden draft of air moved across the back of my neck. Glancing around, I saw nothing out of the ordinary and was about to dismiss it when there came a chuckle close to my ear.

Big D?

"Yes, it's me."

Why are you here?

"You know the law, Jeff. And your concerns . . . are concerning."

Concerning? Concerning what? I don't think I follow you.

"The Law of the Creator, Jeff. How does it go again?"

'I am the Creator.' But what does that—

"Have to do with Meg, Jeff? Exactly. *You* create it. Your life is about *you*. Stop blaming it on Meg."

That wasn't what I was about to say.

"I know."

And, I don't see where I'm blaming my life on Meg.

"You do when you base your feelings on how Meg feels or felt about you, about what's changed or not changed in her mind. That's none of your business."

Meg is my wife. If that isn't my business, what is?

"'What is' is how you feel or felt about her, about what's changed or not changed in your own mind."

Oh.

"So?"

Oh . . . ah, you mean you want an answer? Big D's grunt of exasperation was clear enough. "Ouch!"

The thump of boney knuckles against the side of my head, I felt, was unnecessary.

Meg, still vacuuming, glanced over my way and I quickly ducked my head, pretending to read from the book in my lap.

Shit! That hurt, Big D. Just give me a minute. I'm thinking.

"Take your time, Jeff. Much that is beauty to you is beauty to me. I, too, am enjoying the view. You do, indeed, have a wife whom most men would die for."

I . . . I wouldn't, Big D—die for her. I mean, not anymore. I swallowed against the painful lump again lodged in the back of my throat. *Yes, I was concerned a moment ago about the possibility of my dying for going back to work too soon. And, yeah, I know we have a bargain, and I don't believe I've broken it. But still, I was a little worried.*

"It's okay. In fact, it is good that you value your life. So why are you going back to work? And what does it have to do with changes in how you feel about Meg?" Hearing speculation in his voice, my answer comes quickly.

It's not because Meg feels the money part is all my responsibility.

"Then why?"

Well, it's because I feel like my support is my responsibility. Married or not, I don't want to use her money.

"So how are you *not* blaming your feelings about it on her resentments? You were okay about it before she resented it. What changed?"

I believed, then, that we were in this life as a couple.

"So, then you *are* basing your feelings on how she feels." Now his tone is tantamount to an accusation of lying, and I know what that means.

N-no, Big D, not really. The words fumble out of my mind. *I . . . i-it's more like I see us differently because of how she showed me she feels. I accept it. We are not a couple anymore—not as I believe couples need to be.*

"It's good you finally see that."

And tonight, I'll be staying up, reading. I see why it's almost the norm for me now, why seducing Meg doesn't seem worth the effort anymore. Maybe it has become a harder feat to accomplish these days. Maybe not. But it's a sure thing that it isn't worth the effort expended in the impossibility of getting past her anger, and that is about me.

I thought she'd be happy I survived that ICU—but God, Big D. I run my hand through my hair and fight to stem the tears. I don't remember when her anger started? Maybe it's always been there and I'm just now seeing it.

"It is what it is, doesn't matter the *when*. But seeing it, do you accept her choice of feelings as being her right?"

Yeah.

"Yeah, Jeff, it's true. You do. And so it is, through your acceptance, that you will have the changes you want in your own life, and they will come with far less pain."

Monday, October 26, 1992—1:20 p.m.

Rich, the Mac tool peddler, looked up as I stepped up into his truck. "Jeff, haven't seen you around in a while. They said you were sick."

"Yeah . . . well, I should've stayed sick. Would've, had I known they were going to fuck me around like this."

"That's nothing new for you. So, what are they doing?" Rich's voice was more curious than sympathetic, although I hardly noticed.

"They've raised my bogie. Now I don't start making a commission until I reach twelve hundred dollars. Fucks me out of about two hundred a month."

Now, Rich looked concerned. "How are the others taking it?"

"I'm the only one they're doing it to." I gritted my teeth. "They took me in the office, first thing back, and told me. Said, 'There's the fucking road if you don't like it!'"

"Sounds like they're trying to run you off, Jeff." Rich cocked his head. "Doesn't make sense. Hell, you're the one the other mechanics run to whenever they've got a job that's eating their lunch. Do you have any idea why?"

"Ah, shit. They think I wrote a letter to corporate. Corporate publishes a monthly news rag, y'know? This last one had a letter about how some of their independents are screwing the techs out of schooling. Independent stores have to pay the company schools for tech training, whether anyone actually goes or not. Some are just too damn cheap to pay their mechanics for being there."

"Why do they think you wrote it? Did it name you?"

"Now, would I write a letter like that?" I shrugged, all innocent like. "But this franchise is one of the guilty ones, and I think corporate gave them some heat, y'know?"

"Yeah?" Rich had his head cocked again. "So, Jeff . . . give it up. Why do they think it was you?"

"Just some stuff the letter said." I shrugged.

"Like what?"

"Ah, well, it just said something about us techs being no better trained than the 'average backyard fender lizard.' Talked about this particular independent being too damn dumb to know that while they may sell a tire or two now and then, their main commodity is really the tech's labor. And right now, that's not worth shit. The old man thinks it sounded like me."

"Does sound like you." Rich grinned. "What're you going to do?"

"Shit, Rich . . . gotta have insurance right now." I paused and gazed out at the passing traffic. "But that road? Damn sure looks fucking good right now. I'm gonna give them what they want real soon."

"Damn." Rich shook his head. "Almost wish I was still wrenching. Least you can get another job whenever you want. Me? I'm in too deep with this truck. Company jerks me around all the time. Makes me buy an allotment and won't honor my warranties. And there's not a damn thing I can do about it. And I got a pile of mechanics won't pay their bills." His eyes squinted sharply. "You *are* going to catch up on the weeks you missed today, aren't you?"

"Rich . . ." My eyes traveled the length of his truck and back, over all the shelves packed with tool sets and walls hung heavy with the gleaming chrome of wrenches and such. Prominently displayed was the timing light I'd intended to buy. Glancing back at Rich, I noticed the narrowing of his eyes. Abruptly, I decided against buying. Hell, I could get one just as nice from the Snap-on man, and he never seemed to worry about getting paid. "I'll do better than that. What's my balance?" I asked, getting out my checkbook.

Four Months Later—Tuesday, February 23, 1993—10:05 p.m

"No! I've been telling you for over a month now, you're not going to any silly, damn, five-hundred-dollar seminar. Enough that all my friends think you've gone crazy, leaving a perfectly good job, where you were at the top, to start all over again at some dealership. Jesus Christ! You're not making near what you used to." Meg flopped onto her side, away from me, sending a mini tidal wave across our waterbed.

"Kinda hard to make much fixing car doors and such on light line, Meg. But it won't be long before I'll be doing drivability again. There's good money in diagnosing engine-run ability problems. It'll work out."

"No, I said. That's it! I'm sick of all you ku-raziness—you sitting 'round like zombie, meditating, and you weird-assed frenz, and you stoo-pid self-help books and tapes." She whipped back, face contorted, eyes flashing, punctuating her point. "Now is sem-nars?" She stomped her foot. "No! If you go, I divorce you."

From the thickening of her accent, I knew she was working herself into a real tizzy.

"Ah, but Meg. If you could have just known Rich, back before he took the seminar. Jeez. He was a real asshole. I'd only buy his tools when I couldn't get them elsewhere. Only time we ever got along was when we were having a mutual bitchfest." I took a deep breath and blew it back out. "God! I'm so tired of being unhappy with my life. Rich has changed. I like being around him now. He's happy. Shit, last week he even smiled when I brought him a broken tool to warranty, and—"

"I said, no."

"Meg, c'mon."

"NO!"

I could only stare at her back and ride the next mini-wave. My heart reached for hers in the aching cold of the abyss, and as my courage lagged, my mind began running silent excuses. *I know Big D pointed it out, but perhaps just this one time, just this one seminar. They do it every month. I'll figure a way to do it next month.* Lying beside her stiff form, sleep was a long time coming.

Wednesday, February 24, 1993—4:10 a.m.

I awoke once more to those baleful glows. Again, my hands clutch at my chest, trying to ward off the agony once more within.

Big D . . . no, wait. "Huhhh-aaargh." *Haven't I done all that you asked?*

"Yes, all but this last one. Is your life really held so cheaply?"

Wait! Please, just a minute. "Huhhh-huhhh-uuuuh." My panic escalated with the tightening of his grip. *Look, it's not about the money.*

"Yes, I know. It is the price." The glows of his baleful sockets were now inches from my eyes. "Our agreement remains—honesty and courage, remember? Still, you do not choose to even learn to understand it. Understood or not, it is the price of your life, and you have refused to pay."

Wait . . . please. "Ahhhhh-hah-huuuuh." *Wait! I'll pay it, Big D. Whatever it is, I'll pay.*

"The seminar, Jeff. You know you need it, and yet, you refuse to go."

No, no. I mean . . . yes. "Huu-ah." *The seminar . . . I fully intend to go. I was just looking for a better time. Please . . .*

He paused one ominous moment while the scarlet glows from his empty eye sockets lost their malevolence, then muttered, "Hmm, it's true. You have not yet given up. Procrastination, Jeff . . . could be deadly." Abruptly, his gaze softened, along with the grip within my chest. "You can relax with the fear shit now. Believe it or not, while you still breathe, I am your greatest advocate. And when you go, just know that **it can only be by your own decision**." A bleached-white, boney finger reaches forth from the folds of his cloak to tap me on the chest between where my own hands were still trying to massage away the pain.

I don't understand.

"Either your purpose here will have been accomplished, or you will have given up. Your choice. We've been over all that."

"As for the seminar? Such things are never about the money, Jeff. They're only about the value for which you reach—and the fear of the real price from which you run." His soft chuckle carried with it an eerie echo. "*That* is the fear you must now face, Jeff. Your lack of courage in facing it had you at the point of giving up. *That* is what almost ended it all for you just now—that *and the dishonesty*."

But I have been honest.

"No. You said you wouldn't die for Meg. *You lied*. Just now, you very nearly did." His shoulders seem to shrug once within the smoky swirl of his cloak, which then appeared to melt into the blackness of the night. "Yet, how could I fault you when you have never experienced such courage and therefore don't know how?" All that remained now was a tight reminder in my chest and his final words. "Courage and honesty. Learn, Jeff . . . learn."

—10:00 a.m.

I stepped up into Rich's truck, eager to tell him about my decision. Before I could begin, he said, "Jeff, the seminar starts tomorrow evening. If you could go for free, would you?"

"Damn straight!"

"Well, there is a woman who took it, then later bought a ticket for her husband. The husband wouldn't go. Now they're divorced and she wants to scholarship the ticket to a man who will appreciate it."

"That's five hundred bucks worth." My words gush with incredulity. "No strings?"

With a quick cock of his head to the side, Rich answered, "No strings—none."

"She's found a man who will appreciate it," I said, feeling a sudden new conviction in my words.

Rich gave me the number to call to find out if it was still available. Clutching the number in my sweaty and strangely shaky hand, I dialed it. A woman's voice answered.

I broke into my fumbling request. "I . . . well, I was told you have a ticket for tomorrow's seminar to give away. Is . . . is it still available?"

"Yes, it is, if you *really* want it."

I was on it. This duck wasn't missing this June bug. This, I figured, would even make Meg happy. "I do. I *really* do.

—6:00 p.m

"Free? I don't care if they're paying you. If you go, I won't be here when you get back."

I'd not told Meg about Big D or the choice presented me. Somehow, I knew I never would. Nor, I decided, would I tell her just yet that I would be attending the Empowerment Today Seminar. Suddenly, it seemed almost as if it were no longer her business. Instead, I changed the subject.

"Meg, I saw Dr. Laring this afternoon. It's not as bad, but the clot has come back."

"Course it's back, you silly shit! What'd you expect? They told you to never stop taking the Coumadin." Her words were somehow surreal in their implications.

"He wanted me back in the hospital—"

"Now what are we going to do? You lost our insurance when you insisted on changing jobs. Jesus! This will wipe us out."

"It's okay, Meg, I refused. Said I'd take it easy a while and get back on blood thinners. He didn't like it, but then, with no insurance . . ." I shrugged. "Well, he took my seventy-five bucks and wrote the prescription."

Thursday, February 25, 1993—6:15 p.m.

Meg was silent, her face a frozen, unreadable mask as she watched the last of my hasty preparations for the seminar from her chair at the kitchen table. Last night's sleep had been fitful, and work at the shop this day, endless. I was at the door, pulling on my boots, when her cold, monotone voice froze my motions.

"I won't be here when you get back."

She said it very calmly, decisively. Her voice carried a familiar, icy essence—something I couldn't quite . . . wait. Ah, yes, I had it. It was like the water dripping off the icicles over the porch of my childhood home in Utah. That same sharp chill, shockingly cold where it lit on the back of my exposed neck to run down inside my collar. Ah, and, too, there was the same threat of frozen daggers poised overhead, waiting to break loose and fall. I shivered.

Yes, I knew that tone well. She meant it, but I'd given my word, sworn my commitment. Goddammit, I *was* committed. This meant change for me. No! I would not die a coward even I despised. On that, I would *never* give up.

My foot stomped into the last boot with more force than intended. I straightened up and faced her. A shaky breath hissed through my teeth, and I realized my jaw was tightly clenched, as were my fists. Silently, I regarded the bitter sweetness of her beauty, my anger evaporating. The time for discussion was past. My reply, too, came quietly, even calmly. "Okay."

Turning, I stepped through the opened doorway.

Comb Ridge, Utah—Present Day

My canteen is empty, and surviving in the desert depends on water. One can survive several weeks without food but only a few days without water.

So, the discovery of the weeping, wet stain on the sandstone up under the overhang comes with immense relief. That it was so near the ruins of that Moki mud-and-rock hut was also a relief. Crawling around with this broken leg is such agony. Until such time as I can deal with the painful prospects of setting up the tent, I need that hut to provide me with protection from the elements.

Using the one solid chunk of river rock I have found on this ledge, I slam it hard into the steel nail once used as a tent peg. Each such hit drives it an almost unnoticeable fraction of an inch deeper into that weeping rock layer, bringing even more weeping, only now it flows out, downward along that peg.

Water seeps slowly through sandstone. The layer underneath is one impermeable to water and forms a slight fold just below this spot. That's something I need to thank God for—that one Great Intelligence of the universe. It is his/hers/its Laws of Physics at work here.

"Yes, Jeff, life has little meaning without gratefulness." Big D speaks. "Oh, and by the way, it's that Indian's mate whom you need to thank for the stone. That hollowed chunk of sandstone upon which it was found was where she used it to grind her corn. You might want to think on that one sometime."

What does he mean by that? But I dismiss asking the question. I'm just too tired to think right now. "Big D, I swear, sometimes it's really hard to understand you."

Picking up my empty canteen, I glance over at his smoky swirl. "Grateful? That's right, and I have much to be grateful about to you—especially for leading me to that seminar." I set the canteen carefully in the sand beneath the slowly dripping faucet of the tent peg.

His hollow, bottom-of-the-barrel chuckle is all that he leaves behind as I lie down to sleep.

Sometimes in life you get to touch a stranger in such a loving way that it makes a difference to their entire life, giving them something they could never have had without you. Sometimes they honor you for it in their heart. The highest award one can receive is to be cherished in someone else's heart forever.

Redneck Spirituality—Book One

CHAPTER FOUR

The Finger of God

The woman clutches my arm as she glides through the doorway of the Enlisted Men's Club. While I am aware that the eyes of the other G.I.s are appraising her, it does not matter. She seems to see only me, and I wonder if she, too, has looked forward to this meeting throughout the long hours of this day. My friend Gerky, and his girl, Suki, are with us, but my mind wanders from the conversation while my eyes engage in a dance of stolen glances with Meg's.

Will she? Please God . . . will she?

Soon the meal is finished, and Gerky and Suki leave to play slot machines. We are alone. Does she see my heart through my eyes as I finally broach the question? "Miss Pak, would you like to be my Yobo? I will pay you thirty M.P.C.s"—military payment coupons.

She looks down, a slight frown wrinkling her forehead. My God, is it not enough? Everyone said it would be. What if she thinks I'm cheap? My mouth opens, about to raise the amount, when her eyes rise to meet mine.

"Koo-ray." Her face is again calm. "Yes . . . I wan' be you steady gorl."

* * *

We sit on the porch of our rented hooch drinking Korean

champagne and enjoying the warmth of the spring sun. My hand creeps, as if on its own accord, tickling slowly up her far side, and she responds by pulling on my nose, eyes twinkling in time with the music of her laughter. It has been such a struggle to get back. But here I am, now discharged and with a job stateside. I am back in Korea. Sure, the job's one of torturous labor, and though thirty pounds lighter, it is with the unfailing strength of a hero that my arms open to enfold my new wife.

* * *

An expanse of starched linen surrounds her. Face drawn with fatigue, hair still plastered tight with the sweat of her efforts, she reaches for the child. As she holds him close and peels back the blanket to my eyes, her own shine with an unconquerable joy and pride. Softly, I reach out to touch my son.

Friday, February 26, 1993—2:00 a.m.

"Wha' . . . lemme alone, goddammit!" Shrugging my hand roughly aside, she continued. "Ja-heez! It's 2 a.m. You think we're just going to make up?"

The sweet nectar aftereffect of my dream dissolved quickly. "Uh . . . sorry, dear. I was dreaming. Didn't mean to wake you."

"Like hell. Only time you come to bed anymore is when you want some." In the dark, the blanket was jerked half off me, and air bubbles roiled within the disdainful tidal surge of our waterbed mattress. "Well, just forget it! And if you go to that seminar again tonight, you can forget it forever!"

I did not answer, and after a minute ticked by, she added, "I mean it! You hear me?"

"Yes, Meg." I breathed in deeply and felt it whoosh back out. "I know you do."

Friday, February 26, 1993—7:00 p.m.

The chairs were close, and strangers were pressed against me on both sides at the Enlightenment Today Seminar. Such, it seemed, was always my lot in life. At six four and two hundred forty-five pounds of mostly solid, work-hardened muscle, the chairs were always too small for me.

Jim Weenan, the facilitator, began going over some of the rules established the previous night. Why, I wondered, did they actually think we needed a reminder? As he ticked the points off, I could fairly well hear the army officer he had once been.

"No side talking. No gum, candy, nothing in the mouth. In your seat when the music finishes. Confidentiality—you may talk generically, but you will not divulge specifically anything you hear or see, nor identify to anyone outside the seminar the particulars about anyone. And you will not divulge the particulars about any of the exercises you will be doing here. Someday, that person may also experience this seminar. You would not want to *take* from their experience, now *would you?*"

Yes, 'experiential learning,' he'd termed it. Whatever it was, I was sure I'd never forget any of it. Jim had a way of holding one's interest, tickling their curiosity when he spoke, although little of the seminar was delivered in the form of lecture. Mostly, it was one exercise after another—people doing, saying, and experiencing things together. The lectures were only to clarify, and much of that was precipitated by our questions. The idea, Jim said, was that we learn by what comes in through our senses. Hearing is only one sense.

Funny, yesterday, I disliked Jim almost immediately. That, it was now obvious, was compliments of my army experiences. Yes, and where else did my past still now run my present? Back then, officers were not to be trusted—egotistical bastards, every goddamn one! They'd do you in, if they could. It was an officer who had, through Meg, given me V.D.

Sure, I'd forgiven her. But him? I still took it out on people like Jim. I made it clear that first night that I didn't like him, but somehow my sentiments warmed when I discovered that Jim didn't give a shit.

This second night was over too soon. Again, I went home, my head swimming with new concepts and understandings about myself and my world. And, too, humming John Denver's song, "It's About Time," played in the seminar, a song he had written as a tribute to his own experience here. For the first time, I realized that I could have everything or be anything I wanted in life. Such was the true connection and power of my own spirituality.

At home, I slipped quietly between the sheets of our darkened bedroom. "Oh no you don't!" Meg's voice was one of chipped stone. "You're not sleeping with me ever again!"

I sighed, considering how to break the news to her. "Meg, you might want to rethink that one. I'm not going anywhere, and that couch out there isn't all that comfortable. I know from recent experience."

Meg's breath hissed, but she made no comment as she stomped out to discover that truth for herself. Watching her go, I now knew how

Meg was merely playing out her drama for control. I knew also that I didn't want to continue playing my old part.

Saturday dawned bright and beautiful and strangely refreshed, despite so little sleep. I watched the sunrise, then, as was the norm of late, made my own breakfast. Meg stayed on the couch, glowering, as her share of the eggs and bacon were getting equally cold on her plate.

"If you go, you'll find your shit out in the yard when you come home."

I paused a moment, wondering if she would change the locks. To ask her I knew would be to step into her drama. And my stuff? I doubted if she would throw out anything very expensive. Besides, like she said, it was only 'shit.'"

That day at the seminar, we played a stupid game, an awesomely stupid game. In it, I discovered exactly how I did life—or rather—had done. In that moment of learning, I changed. Later in the day, we learned about goals. In a very simple, yet embarrassingly hard exercise, I learned how to attain them. I left that evening high on life, again singing the songs they played and laughing insanely all the way home. Meg ignored me as I tripped past her couch.

Somehow, the alarm didn't go off on Sunday morning. I got up late to find Meg fixing me breakfast. She was dressed up—or rather, undressed—in a see-through slip and panties, talking cordially as she slowly mixed the pancake batter. The coffee was hot and the orange juice cold. I gulped both in my hurry to leave.

"Slow down. Breakfast isn't ready yet," Meg murmured, her voice strangely husky. "Besides, I thought we could just stay home in bed this morning"—her words ended with a whimsical promise—"making love?"

Picking up my boots, I headed for the door. "Can't. Got a seminar to go to."

She was on me before I reached the door, clinging suggestively, touching as she never touched me before, even kissing me passionately. I was surprised at the transparency of her ploy. Meg initiating sex?

"No, you're not going to stop me." My voice was firm, though inside, something felt very surreal with the situation. Still, she clung, begging me for sex. Sickened, I implored, "Look, you've nothing to be so afraid about. I will always love you!" Still, she clutched. "Meg, let go!" I shoved her roughly away and, boots in hand, ran for my truck. Little did I realize how far I'd missed the mark—how determined Meg was to make her fears real.

The E. T. Seminar was a turning point for me, one of those times when one knows all life thereafter will never be the same, like a light had been suddenly turned on in my life and everything was illuminated differently. Though I wasn't sure what it was, clearly, I'd gotten something I needed. When it was over, that Sunday evening, I met the woman who'd given me such a precious gift. Standing there, bathed in the music of Aaron Neville and Linda Ronstadt, face-to-face, I reached out and hugged her to me. Cheek to cheek, I thanked her with my tears and was acknowledged with hers.

She was a lovely woman, a young, blonde, blue-eyed beauty, nearly as attractive on the outside as Meg. But it was something on the inside, something I saw in her and wished were in my Meg. And I know that as she gazed at me, she saw something inside me she wanted—no, needed—something that was surely lacking in her own man.

In this woman's gift, there was no ulterior motive. She asked nothing in return. All she wanted was for me to accept it, get what I needed, and allow her to feel good about herself in the giving—and perhaps in the simple purity of my loving her for it. With its legacy, she had changed a piece of the world and made it a little better.

We shared an intimacy together that night few ever know, one far beyond anything sexual. We came together as strangers, and as strangers we parted—strangers who touched one another with the finger of God, for in that touch was the purity of love. The song that was playing said it all . . . *I don't know much, but I know I love you* . . .

At home, Meg was again a pair of silent, glowering eyes without any other voice.

"Meg, I know that couch is uncomfortable. Why don't you come to bed?"

Silence.

"I won't bother you—promise. I'm too tired anyway."

Silence.

I left her then and slid alone between the sheets of our bed. My head barely touched the pillow before I was asleep.

* * *

The abyss yawns before me, strangely familiar and real, though something tells me it is but a dream. A chill breeze whines through the empty branches of the pinyon pine and cedar trees behind me. I notice only a few tufts of needles here and there to mark the existence of life still within. Across a canyon shrouded in dust, I can barely make out the dark drapery of manganese stains on the nearest cliff wall.

Wait! I know this place. It's located in Southeastern Utah, near the confluence of Fry and White canyons. I spent many hours here as a child. It is an ancient place of great power—a place where the Native Americans sat with their spirits and made arrowheads. The profusion of flint chips scattered about is what tells that to me.

But my memory of it includes the warmth of a springtime sun across my back while sitting on this rock ledge. And later, the cooling shade, drying the sweat on this same back while sitting on the fuzzy, blackened moss capping the lumps of powdered, red sand beneath that nearby cedar tree, a cool respite from the worst of the summer's heat. But back then, those sandstone cliffs across the way were cream and orange where the fingers of black manganese stain did not touch—not gray and colorless as they appear now. And the cedar was alive and green.

Why does everything here now seem so dead?

"It's time you saw some things correctly, Jeff. Things you cannot change."

"Big D!" *I whirl, for the first time aware of his tall, smoky-black presence.*

"Yes, Jeff, observe." *His cloaked arm sweeps outward, and though the gray overcast remains, the scene is now in black-and-white clarity.*

"Big D, it's Meg!" *On the far side. I see her.*

But wait! She is no longer a figure of willowy grace. Her gaunt form moves stiffly as she bends to sit on the porch of a Korean hooche. It looks to be the same one where once she plied her trade—back before she met me, and even for a time more. Though at this distance her figure is small, I can see the bitter lines of her face.

"Meg! Meg!"

"You waste your breath, Jeff. She chooses not to hear you."

"But Big D . . . I must get to her or bring her here with me. Can't you see how she needs me?"

"What she needs, you have long been offering." *His head swivels left and right slowly, sadly in the negative.* "She does not want it from you."

"Goddammit! Can't we get a rope and throw it over? I could shinny across and—"

"Aren't you afraid of heights?"

"Doesn't matter! I—"

"No." *He says it softly with a sincere overtone of sadness.*

"But..."

"Jeff, listen. To bridge this abyss you would need, at minimum, someone willing to tie the rope. All functional relationships are a function of two people doing for one another, meeting each other's needs."

"Big D, I thought we discussed all that."

"We did, but you have not yet seen it clearly, nor applied the law."

"You mean Meg doesn't love me?"

"In what passes for love in this world, Meg does indeed love you—loves you fiercely. Ah, but does she meet your needs? Haven't you discovered a little about the truth of it? Your own love for her, for all its fearful needs, has long been honest and true, especially of late. With hers, she cannot see past her fear. Why do you think she has found yours increasingly unpalatable?" He ducks his head and seems regretful for his next words. "Her view of love carries the image of an unfulfilled martyr who only wants some sort of security, some sort of control. With her, you need no control and there is no suffering, save the suffering involved with you ignoring the truth."

"I can give her the security of my love."

"No, Jeff. You did that. You met that need for her. But security is only a lie—you know that—a lie she equates with control. That also is a lie. How many years have you already spent endeavoring to give that to her? Now, she has reaped the truth."

"But—"

"Didn't Meg demand a divorce every time she felt her control threatened?"

"Yes, but—"

"And didn't you always beg her to stay?"

"But I had to!"

"Did you now?" The glow of his eye sockets has sharpened. "In fact, Jeff, do you? Do you right now?"

Taking a long breath, I stop, then let it out slowly, remembering the events of recent days. "No, Big D, you're right. I have stopped playing out that drama with her. I did it nearly every month for the last twenty-five years."

"Why have you stopped?"

"It's not honest. I know it's what she wants—needs—but it's not at all loving, for me or her."

"Exactly! It's the law, Jeff. Remember—**What you concentrate** *your energy on, be it your fondest dream or worst nightmare, is what you create."* Big D plants the butt of his sickle on the ground before him, and with both sets of boney knuckles grasping its shaft, he leans deliberately forward. *"So . . . when will you be leaving her?"*

"No! Oh no, Big D. Please don't ask that of me."

"A mere speculation—for now, Jeff. Any action demanded must come later." From beneath his darkened cowling, I hear a note of amusement. *"Besides, Meg has more yet to teach you, much of it regarding the true depth of the meanings concerning the Law of the Creator. And for now, where it concerns the truth of your own selfishness."*

"Selfishness?"

"State the law, Jeff."

"I am the Creator."

"Is it true?" The casualness of his question belies what I know must be my answer.

"Yes, Big D. I am sure it is."

"Is it limiting?"

"No. I think it is just the opposite."

"Ah, but there's where the selfishness comes in, Jeff. **It is limited to the creating of your life—only.**"

"Oh, I get it. It's all for yourself. Does seem kinda selfish."

"No, Jeff, just the opposite. What's selfish is you trying to create in someone else's life—trying to make their life go the way you want."

"But sometimes they don't see what we see."

"Children, yes. It is your duty to teach your child. But another adult? No. **You have not the right to determine the lessons another's soul has deemed necessary, nor the process by which they are taught.**"

"But don't we all affect others with our own lives? Can't we do that deliberately for their good? What about the woman who gifted me the seminar?"

"It was required that you ask for and want it—and, in fact, need help getting it." I am sure I hear his chuckle now. *"Such is the only way a loving act is performed, a true gift given. All else is selfishness. Though called 'giving,' it is really 'saving,' for it is from a place of superiority that it comes. Worse, it is a 'taking' from that other person's ability to create and thereby to grow."*

* * *

From somewhere barely within my range of consciousness, there comes a snort followed by a snore. I roll onto my side. I only snore when on my back.

Seated on the side of the bed, Big D stands and pauses a moment to look down at the sleeping figure now settling into his new position. "Sleep well, Jeff." He picks up his sickle from where it leans against the wall. "You will not forget this conversation."

Comb Ridge, Utah—Present Day

I shake my head at the memory of that dream of things long past, just as Meg, too, is now in the past, then set the notebook aside to massage my leg. The straps holding the fork tubes that stabilize the whole affair must be periodically loosened and the circulation massaged as best it can be. I wouldn't want to die of gangrene. *Gruesome shit!*

The swollen, red hotness to it, of late, indicates infection, and the pain has changed mostly to a deep, dull ache, except when being prodded, like now. My breath produces only grunts and hisses to the rhythm of my hands.

"Leg is not looking so good, Jeff." I glance up to note that Big D has joined me and sits. His boney heels begin knocking in rhythm against the sandstone where his legs dangle over the edge. "But the writing, though a little disjointed, is excellent."

Disjointed? In reading it, I've not noticed. Sometimes it is hard to keep focused, what with the pain and the fever.

"Then focus on this, Jeff. What specifically is the law that I was teaching you about back then?"

The law?

"Yeah, Jeff. What was the law you wrote about and just finished reading? State it clearly."

"Oh, umm." I pause. *Give me a second.* With a sigh, I gather up the notebook and steel myself to concentrate. The page blurs slightly for a moment, then clears. *That would be about the law that goes,* **One gets to create one's own life only—no one else's**.

"Excellent! And what of the derivative laws? We've talked about them in the past."

"Uh." *Yeah.* Again, the sigh. It seems so easy for my mind to wander of late. *So hungry—must check the trap for chipmunks.*

Let's see, that would be . . . I shake my head, searching for a clarity that doesn't seem to exist. *Oh God, Big D, it is so hard to concentrate. Help me out here. Just tell me.*

"No. You can do it. Use the technique. Go to level."

Taking a deep breath, eyes raised under closed lids, and holding my thumbs to the tips of my first two fingers, I breathe out long and slow, counting down as my body relaxes and my mind whispers, *Three . . . Two . . . One . . . Clarity.*

Then, again I scan the last few paragraphs, feeling free and in control once more. *Ah, yes, that would be—*

He interrupts me. "It's in this chapter but not spelled out as being a law. And you skipped right on by it. I want your mind clear before I point it out." He pauses, giving me time, then continues when I nod. "In the format of a law, here it is—***Helping is really taking when it is saving others from doing something they have the ability to do for themselves.***"

Oh my God! My head reels with the realizations, thinking of the times I did just that— helped people who didn't need it, didn't want it, and didn't appreciate it.

"Yeah, big one for you, isn't it?"

Just one thing, Big D.

"What?"

Why did you have me revisit the most painful part in my life, and what's your point now in the applications of all this to it?

"You don't see it yet, do you, Sir Galahad?" His mocking grin carries with it the stink of fish bait. "You just don't get how breaking this law is what fucked-over your marriage. Saviors *always* get crucified."

His grin seems wider and his eye sockets fairly glow with a sort of merriment as he adds, "Oh, by the way, it's roasted lizard tonight, if you can get to him before he jumps out of that trap. He's a big one. No thanks necessary for the help—you *do* need it. I know the jerky is tempting, but you must ration it closely."

Shaking my head, I grab up the sleeping bag cover. It's now a catch bag for emptying the simple jump-in-and-trip-the-lid trap made from a plastic-lined saddlebag. With multiple grunts of pain, I hasten my laborious crawl.

Sometimes in life you must face death in order to truly live. But always—always!—you must face your fears if you want to live in respect . . . your respect.
                              Redneck Spirituality—Book Three

CHAPTER FIVE

Ten Thousand Feet

The air seemed to swirl and converge with a flapping of midnight-colored robes into a familiar boney form. Yet the peace of this, my special nature spot in the meditations of my mind, was not in the least disturbed. *Big D . . . you came.*

"Yes, Jeff. From within your meditations, you can always call on me."

I didn't know. Why didn't you tell me?

"You might say it is one of the rules. You are given what you need, when you need it. No more, no less. Besides, self-discovery is always the most effective way."

What I need, when I need . . . hmmm?

"Let's just say you *will* be needing me. And now that you know how to lower your mind's vibrations, to go to a level *outside* of normal meditation techniques, you can call on me anytime you choose."

You mean the 'Silva Method' technique I've been studying? The three-second thing?

"Just so."

I thought it only worked as a way of centering one's thoughts and energies.

"Oh no." Big D's smokey robes roiled with his chuckle. "Going to level is so much more than you know. It is like a switch connecting your consciousness with your higher unconscious self." He paused, and his grin seemed to widen as he added, "And more."

More?

"Yes. So much more that I require you add it to your repertoire of what you hold sacred, for this switch connects you with all the power of the universe."

You mean like prayer?

"Oh no. More literally so." His chuckle sounded serious this time. "But it is not some 'gimme this' or 'gimme that, please, God' sort of thing. Don't be so frivolous with your meditations. Be sure about what you want in them. Whatever that is, you need to be coming at it in the energy of love. Sometimes it is best simply to tune into the energy and let it uplift you."

Yes, Big D. I have felt it.

"And Jeff"—his gaze seemed to harden sharply—"when you call on me, be sure you can accept the truth. Now, what do you want?"

Well, I just wanted to tell you how much the seminar meant to me.

"That, I already know. But do you?"

I'm not sure I follow . . .

"Tell me what has changed, Jeff. How are you living your life any differently?"

Well, I choose consciously how I want to feel about things now.

"Like how? Give me an example."

Well, for instance, at work, the day after the E.T. Seminar, I was called to the office. The secretary informed me that the service manager had to give away an hour of my labor to satisfy a customer. She added, *'You won't be getting paid for it . . . but we'll make it up to you.' Now this sort of thing has happened many times before, and the service manager never comes through. But . . . well, this time something was different about me. This time, I noticed how her jaw was set, sort of grim, like she was ready to do battle with me.*

"Okay, that'll work," I told her cheerfully, then turned and walked away. Course I hid my amusement. The expression on her face alone was worth an hour's pay."

"So, was that why you gave in?"

Big D, I don't see it as 'giving in.' It's simply that . . . well, it's like a part of the job. It was just going to happen. The management has always fucked-over the help rather than have the company take it in the ass. It always has. Hell, I've moaned around and bitched her out several times before for the same kind of shit. Obviously, it would continue. I also saw how instead of resisting what I couldn't change, I could look for solutions that would be a win/win.

"So how was this a 'win' for you?"

Oh, it wasn't, but she was offering to make it one. I'd never taken her up on it before. I wanted to see if she'd make good on her offer.

"And . . ."

Well, about an hour later, she approached me. It was the first time I'd ever seen her out in the shop. "Mr. Williams," she said, her voice sounding almost friendly, "you've made a mistake on this repair order. You need to correct it or it will cost you two and a half flag hours." That's hours of pay billed.

"So, you think the principles they taught in the seminar about 'win/win' work?"

Yes, Big D, but this one wasn't about win/win so much as about trusting other people. She has never given me reason to doubt her personal word. Now the service manager . . . he's different.

"Oh, so Jeff, how are you different? Wouldn't you have bitched him out?"

Would have before, not anymore. Don't need that kind of energy. But I have since had the courage to be honest when he promised me something that I knew he had no intention of delivering.

"How so?"

I told him that if he didn't make good on his word, it would cost him an employee.

"How is that not 'bitching him out,' or at least threatening him, Jeff?"

The energy, Big D. I wasn't holding any fear energy. There was no resentful bitching. That kind doesn't feel good. And no, it wasn't any ego kind of threat. That only seems to feel good. No. I was only telling him the facts.

"He will fire you, soon as he can find an excuse, Jeff. You know that."

Yes, and I know I don't want to be working for him anyway.

"And your wife, Jeff?"

Meg? I shrugged. What about her?

"Do you have the courage to tell her honestly about how you now see her and your relationship? Do you think she won't then make good her threat?"

Ah, Big D . . . surely you don't expect—

"That you live your life in honesty?" Big D's smokey robes seemed to expand as the ruby glow coming from his eye sockets became a sudden beacon. "That is our agreement, remember?"

Yes, but—

"And courage."

But—

"But?" He paused to stare, bathing me in the redness of his sight. "Yes, I can see you need to learn more about courage."

What do you mean? How so?

"Oh, you will know, Jeff." With a swish of his sleeve, Big D swirled into a tornado of blackness that quickly thinned out to nothingness, leaving only his final words. "Go back now—back to where your perceived cowardice began. Then, when you return and again open your eyes, you will know what you must do."

* * *

The sun bakes my back. Yet, it is a cold sweat I feel as—like a spectator in my own body—I cling, quivering against the face of the cliff. Below, perhaps fifty feet down, I see the red of the dirt on the boulder-strewn, steep talus slope of the Frying Pan, a mesa in Southeastern Utah's canyon country. Again, I am that nine-year-old boy, trying to follow his older, glory-challenged, teenaged brother and that brother's wild pair of friends, climbing barehanded up the sheer, sandstone wall.

Up ahead, the ledge narrows to less than four inches where it rounds a bend. Beyond, I see the others some hundred feet ahead and fifty feet higher. With their backs against one side, their feet against the other, they are shinnying up a cleft in the sandstone that leads the last fifty feet to the top.

Oh God! I don't have their strength. Even if I manage to get that far, I'm sure to fall. Inch by cowering inch, I begin my way back down.

* * *

With a start, my eyes flashed wide.

Uh, Jeez. I've fallen asleep meditating. Big D?

Still, it was all so vivid, so real, both the conversation with Big D and the reliving of my disgrace. Dreams aren't usually this clear. But wait! Big D said I'd know what to do when I again opened my eyes.

My eyes traveled the darkened living room, over its white walls, cathedral ceiling, past the gold, gilded frame of the heavy mirror adorning the wall, the TV console, the expanse of light-blue carpet, the pastel-pink, plaid love seat, and on to the matching couch upon which I was sitting. I shook my head.

Know what?

Everything was in its perfect, pristine-clean, and orderly shape, all as Meg insists. Then I saw *it*. The newspaper lay sprawled across the couch next to me, opened to the entertainment section.

I don't remember seeing that.

An advertisement near the bottom of the page caught my eye. My palms began to sweat as I read the main caption, 'Skydive Las Vegas, Inc.' Accompanying it was the picture of two people doing a tandem jump.

Sunday, May 2, 1993—12:30 p.m.

The wind whipped by the opened door of the plane. The chilly, eighty-mile-per-hour wind seemed somehow strange, as into my mind flashed the memory of still, sweltering air and the desert sun, how it had cooked this plane's aluminum skin, frying my fingers like so many strips of sweaty bacon. Cursing and blowing my scalded digits cool, I entered that door just fifteen minutes before—an eternity ago, or so it seemed—as now I looked down . . .

My God! What am I doing here?

Down through ten thousand feet of open air, the desert floor seemed so . . . so very far away. Fear clutched at my heart, and that old, familiar paralysis began creeping over my arms and legs once more. My hands were stiff and inadequately weak where they clung to the doorframe. Left knee trembling against the patterned, aluminum floor, I extended my right leg out into the wind. For a long moment, it was whipped about clumsily before finding a solid purchase upon the step.

Even as my body questioned, *Can I do this*, my mind answered, *You have no choice. You must!* I'd set myself up well to win this battle, knowing I had to subdue this dragon, this fear of heights. As Big D said, "Fear, given into, is a dragon where it needs only be a little lizard, sent simply with a message of protection."

I'd even told all my friends at work about this skydive. One was down there watching, marking the deed, evaluating my word. Like him, my wife's business partner at the massage parlor, Sook Ja, had come, she said, to keep Meg company.

Meg, oh God, Meg. Since the hospital, it seems that to you, I'm some kind of lunatic, especially in this. Sook Ja is only here to see me fail. But Meg, can't you be here to see me succeed, to see the integrity in me? Can't you see me as a man of courage, a man willing to face whatever he fears? Our future together is at stake. Why can't I be a winner in your eyes . . . just this once?

And yet, still . . . looking down, feeling it, I somehow knew. Still . . . it was still a choice. Could I—no, *would I*—do this?

Strapped in front of Michael Hawks, the owner of Skydive Las Vegas, Inc., kneeling here in the open doorway of his plane at ten thousand feet, I was very aware that I didn't even have the parachute. He did.

Was this Big D's way of telling me I also had problems trusting people? It was true. Trusting other men was something I didn't do well, certainly not with *my* life. Hell, I had great difficulty even trusting *myself* with that. Why else would I be afraid of heights?

Looking down through all that empty air at the desert floor, so very far below, it all came back all the fear, the near paralysis of it.

Goddammit! This is my life, and I'm not going to disrespect myself by not taking this next step. Dying a coward is not an option. Nor was that other thing—the urge I was suddenly feeling to shit myself.

Now positioned in the doorway, a chilled wind ripping around me, my foot out on the step, I felt Michael's hand slap my shoulder. It was the signal to let go of the doorway, cross my arms against my chest . . . and fly.

As we launched, I was dimly aware of our cameraman, Mark, simultaneously letting go of the wing strut from which he'd been hanging. It cost extra to record this event, but I wanted to have pictures and video, something I could look at, to remind me about this as often as needed. Never again would I let my mind tell me, *You don't have the courage to do this*. I planned on putting those pictures right above a framed quote from someone I'd never met, but who'd touched my life forever.

* * *

Be present at your own life, live dangerously, take risks. Cultivate eccentricity, which means getting closer to being yourself. This will give you a life worth living, and of which you can be proud.

Thomas D. Wilhite

* * *

Thomas was later killed in a plane crash, but there is one profound thing I know about him—he was a man who truly lived, just as I was determined to be as well.

* * *

Our bodies did a slow somersault. I kicked my heels back up between Michael's, just as I'd been taught. We stabilized with our backs arched and our stomachs thrust out toward the lowest point. The world was open all around, above, and below me. Nothing but open air. Mesmerizing. The wind was picking up, ripping straight up from the earth and into my face, chilling me and dragging the very breath from my chest.

I felt Michael's hand tug at my arms, which I realized with a start were still crossed against my chest. As I unfurled them like the wings of an eagle, I heard Michael's faint, garbled shout over the shrieking of the wind, "Look up!" I did and saw Mark zooming in toward us with his cameras. He was busily clicking away with his 35mm while the eye of his video leered at me from his helmet.

From somewhere came the clear, calm voice of Big D. "You'd best smile. Do you really want to look at these pictures and see yourself looking this scared?" As I pasted a phony grin across my face, the reality of the situation hit me. Here I was at ten thousand feet, streaming earthward at about one hundred forty miles per hour, and the Angel of Death was mentally telling me not to look afraid.

The thought so amused me that, in that moment, I no longer felt any fear. Rather, I found myself enjoying the wonder of it all. Yes, in that moment, the smile became real. I was grinning with stupid delight at the cameraman, only a few feet away.

Michael's hand again slapped my shoulder.

What is he trying to say? I don't remember this signal.

Then his hand wrapped tightly across my forehead and his body jerked with effort. Realizing he was pulling the ripcord, resentment flared across my mind.

No . . . don't! I'm supposed to do that. And it isn't time yet. It can't have been forty-five seconds . . . maybe ten. Dammit! Just a few seconds more.

With a rumble and a flap, the chute opened and we seemed to stop. Mark, with his cameras, appeared to accelerate down and away. My body tried to follow but was brought up short—violently—by the straps on either side of my crotch.

Ye-outch! Damn, that hurts.

The shock of it was harsh on my slightly beer-pregnant frame. I remembered the standard-issue, Skydiver Ken jumpsuit Mike offered, how it was way too tight. Thank God I refused. Singing soprano with Barbie was not on my to-do list.

Now drifting effortlessly, peacefully, hanging from a seriously sore crotch at four thousand feet, the air no longer shrieked. Michael spoke, sounding surrealistically calm in my ear.

"Bend your legs up and hook your heels on my toes."

I did.

"Now, hoist your weight up by these straps while I loosen us up."

Again, I did. With the tandem harness no longer binding us so tightly, my 'nads were no longer an issue.

Michael's voice again spoke calmly, almost dreamlike, next to my ear, "How're you doin'?"

My initial inclination was to say a macho, "Great! Yeah . . . just fine," but the honesty in my next words felt vulnerable and true. "I'm feelin' kinda weak and shaky. And my arms are tingling."

"That's just the adrenalin leaving your system," he explained, then went on to teach me the use of the steering straps. Guiding me through a couple of 'lazy S' turns, we lost more altitude as we lined up on the abandoned racetrack, which was to be our landing field. A couple of old shacks drifted by below.

Hmmm . . . this is just like looking out the window of a small plane, only slower and without the plane. I wonder how hard we'll hit?

Presently, Michael tapped my shoulder. "Okay, hold your legs out at forty-five degrees."

From the lesson, I knew that this was in preparation for touchdown and that at fifteen feet, he'd again tap my shoulder. This was to be the signal for me to haul back on both steering straps and flare the chute.

We came in lower—too fast it seemed.

Lower still. *Has Michael forgotten to tell me?*

Even lower.

He must have. In panic, I flared.

He hadn't.

My landing was a perfect two-pointer—on both buns. Dazed, I looked up at Michael, squatting behind me, undoing the snaps holding us together.

"Hot damn! Hope I haven't hurt that rock." I grimaced. "Probably the only one on the damned field." Michael chuckled. Rubbing my wounded butt, I struggled to my feet and looked numbly about. With a grin, he stuck out his hand.

"You did it," he began as I grabbed his extended palm and pumped it wildly.

"Goddamn . . . I did, didn't I? I really did it."

His grin widened.

I couldn't hold back. Jumping into the air, I slapped my fist into my opened palm.

"Yessss!" I shouted, arms out, head back facing the sky. There was a sense of weightlessness, as if a great weight had been taken from me. And alive . . . I felt more alive than I've ever felt in my entire life.

Meg arrived from across the field, and I grabbed her up in a bear hug, whirling her stiff body around, all the while grinning stupidly and laughing insanely. Planting her solidly back on her feet, my heart felt nurtured by her slight smile, regardless of what thoughts gave rise to its inception.

"You friend, from whork." Meg's accent always sharpened with anger, excitement, or just when she hung out with her Korean friends, like Sook Ja. "He said he had to go now."

Taking it as excitement, I grinned, my heart suddenly warm. "Railroad Pass Casino is just a couple miles up the road. Let's go eat."

"Ku-ray," Meg replied in Korean. *Let's.*

Leaving Michael collecting his chute, we went for a bite of lunch. Sitting there, between the Korean chatter of my wife and Sook Ja, I took a deep breath, unfocused and raised my eyes slightly, and with my first two fingers and thumb touching, a signal to my soul, I relaxed, letting my breath sigh to a mental count. *Three, two, one . . . Big D?*

"Yes, Jeff, I'm here. But it's more than me you feel here, isn't it?"

Ah, Big D, I can almost feel my brother, Mike, now close to thirty years dead.

"Almost? Trust your intuition. Speak to him, Jeff. Guaranteed, he'll hear you. And you never know. He might just answer."

Ah, Mike. This was something you'd really have gotten off on. All your bravado—all those crazy, insanely dangerous things you dragged me into doing. I never knew it could be so . . . so invigorating!

"Invigorating? Perhaps." Mike's laughter is low. His voice comes clear, so familiar, even after all these years. Yet, it sounds so young. "But the truth was that I did those things to make me feel alive. Unlike you, Jeff, I was so shut down, afraid of life. I used to envy your courage."

My courage? I was scared shitless with all those things I followed you in doing.

"Yes, I know. I envied your courage in walking through so much fear."

But, Mike, I never knew this vigor I now feel. Not like you must have. I only felt the fear. Hell, I think you lived more in your short twenty years than I have in over twice that time.

"No. You've long known it, Jeff, every bit as well as I. It was just not so strong for you as today because it didn't involve heights. I was afraid of life, and I never had the courage to step through that fear and just go for it, y'know?"

What?

"Jeff, you dork." I could hear Mike's familiar jeer. "Climbing heights to me was like you riding motorcycles—neither of us felt our respective joy all that strongly. It didn't involve stepping through much fear. Oh, climbing cliffs always got my blood pumping, gave me an endorphin high, but not near so much as you in those times when you almost shit yourself climbing with me. Face it, you stepped through a buttload of fear."

Really?

"Really. And, for us both, in following our joys, we have lived. But me? I never lived well enough to have much fear to step through. That was my problem. Yours? You just never saw the fun in climbing cliffs, nor saw that it was courage making you do it."

Ah, but Mike, I have stopped riding since we moved here to Las Vegas.

"Why?"

Well, I just thought my Honda 350 Enduro was a little small to be running around in traffic. Besides, drivers in this town are absolutely insane. And off-roading? The desert around here is not all that interesting.

"Maybe, then, a big bike is in order."

A big bike.

My palms strangely began to sweat, yet the thought was appealing. But then there was Meg. She'd never accept my buying a big, expensive road bike.

"Jeff... Jeff?" I looked up to see Meg and Sook Ja both eyeing me closely. On Meg's face was one of those looks that was becoming so common for her of late, and I realized I'd been chuckling.

I waived my hand and shrugged. "Private joke, Meg, never mind me." With a shake of her head, and a disgusted grunt, Meg went back to her discussion with Sook Ja.

"So, Jeff." Big D broke in. "What do you think it is that Meg sees as so unsavory about you these days?"

I'm not sure. Maybe it's always been somewhat so. I don't think Meg's ever looked at me as being much of a man.

"No, it has changed slightly. Perhaps it might have something to do with what you got from the seminar. You know, you've neglected to discuss it in your journaling."

There is my agreement—the rule about keeping the confidentiality of the seminar.

"I'm not suggesting you tell all, only one small part. It is important, if you are to understand your relationship with Meg. So, what part do you think it'd be?"

Oh God, Big D, that's a hard one. There were so many things, realizations about myself, about the truth of life, about my whole damned world.

"Let me help you."

Instantly, I found myself back in the seminar, holding hands with a woman I didn't know from before, sitting, facing her, our knees touching in the darkened room.

Jim Weenan's voice booms out over the speakers. "Now person 'B,' begin."

My mouth opens and the words tumble out, describing the picture in my mind, describing it without even being aware of what I will say next.

"I was four. It was the first time I'd ever been alone, away from everyone I loved. I would wake up screaming from the nightmares. I guess they don't like kids waking the whole orphanage in the middle of the night—at least not at Sunny Hills. They strapped me down with wide, tight, leather belts where I could barely breathe, then stuffed my own dirty socks into my mouth. Do you know how dirty a little kid's socks can get in a week's time?"

Other than her tears, the woman doesn't answer. It is part of the ground rules for the exercise. Yet, seeing those tears touches something within me. The words come with difficulty when I continue. "I don't know how I survived those times, what with the straps, the gag, and all that snot in my nose. Usually, I passed out, but eventually, I learned what was meant by 'the silent tears of an orphan.' That was when I hid my inner child away to protect him from my world."

* * *

"So . . ." As the seminar room evaporated with Big D's word, I found myself frozen, my coffee cup still halfway to my lips. The china rattled loudly as I set it down carefully, glancing quickly at Meg to see if she'd noticed my momentary lapse. "Never mind her, Jeff. When I take you somewhere, you are on my time. Not one second has passed in this world. Even now, your world's time interacts with you only when you choose to be aware of it." I hear the humor in his words as he continues. "Just keep your wits, no matter how startling the thing is I show you."

I will, Big D, but . . .

"So, what did you surmise from that exercise?"

Well . . . I paused to collect my thoughts. *Everyone in the room seemed to have some experience to relate. Obviously, we all, at some point, must have suffered some traumatic experience that caused us to stop being children and start being adults.*

"And . . ."

We hide our vulnerable inner child away for its, or rather, our protection.

"And so, what are you doing about it?"

Well, I've been letting mine come out and play. God, it is so great to be able to act childlike and just have fun.

"And at what price?"

Price? While I couldn't see him, I could feel Big D's attention sharpen, as if he was leaning in close. Other than that, he made no answer. *Oh, you mean that some people—Meg especially—seem to think I act childish?*

"You got it." The feeling relaxed as if Big D had drifted back a bit, removing himself from my personal space. "It's sad that so few of you know the difference. Childish—childlike. There is a world of distinction between the two."

Yeah, I know.

"No! You don't know shit." Again, I felt Big D, as if he had once more moved up close, into my face. "But in time, you will."

What do you mean, Big D?

"Describe 'childlike.'"

Well, mainly it means to have fun.

"And . . ."

And what, Big D?

"*Tsk, tsk.* Jeff, sometimes your head can be bonier than mine." Perhaps it was just the rattle of plates, but in my mind, I could almost see Big D's knuckles extend from within his smokey sleeve to rap against the ivory of his skull in emphasis. "The child you were back then, Jeff. Was he brave?"

Oh, yeah. He wasn't afraid of anything.

"What else?"

Well, he had this quality . . . a great appreciation—no, more like a wonder—of all things new. Life for him was a journey of curiosity, wonder, and excitement.

"Is yours, Jeff? Is your life a 'journey of curiosity, wonder, and excitement?' It was so today, but are you willing to be truly childlike forever? Even in front of Meg? You know what silliness she considers this skydive to be. Will you pay Meg's price tomorrow, and then again the next day . . . and the next?"

Comb Ridge, Utah—Present Day

Setting the notebook aside, I take a deep breath and pause, holding it, remembering the awesome feelings of that day and what it has meant to my life. Since then, I've not even thought about that coward I once believed myself to be. Courage has become an integral part of me. The awesome wonder of that child within me, even given the current circumstances, is a part of who I am now.

Then it comes to me—the feel of that parachute, of both Michael and me tied together, both cradled in its straps. The whole world is open all around us. I glance out over Comb Ridge Wash at all that same open air between me and the cottonwoods way down there at the bottom. If I had a parachute right now, no doubt, I'd base jump. This fucked-up leg wouldn't stop me from riding these canyon air currents, just me and my inner child once more.

I'm okay—you're all fucked up. **Such seems to be the lowest common denominator in the minds of many.** *In my life, I am better than you!* **Perhaps we, in all our relationships, simply need to take another step in conscious evolution.** *I'm okay—for me. You're okay—for you. And, I see the love in you.*

Redneck Spirituality—Book Two

CHAPTER SIX

Like a Steer on the Kill Floor

Saturday, October 2, 1993—6:30 p.m.

Whitney Houston's song wailed bittersweet and strong, tugging at the deepest, most painful truth of my life. The lights along West Charleston flashed by in a blur. For once, I was glad to have Meg driving.

"I know you don't care for Sook Ja, Jeff, but she's my friend. And . . ." Meg glanced over and abruptly broke off her discussion. "Oh, shit! Now what's wrong?"

I looked at her through a blur. Clear sight was not necessary for my mind's view of her timelessly perfect, petite body and the curl of shimmering, black hair framing her beautiful face with its dark, red-brown, exotic, Asian eyes. Indelible. No. It didn't require clear eye sight to see what now marred that beauty. I could hear the disgust now gleaming, sullenly there.

"That song, Meg," I croaked, my voice cracking through the lump in my throat. "That's us!"

"What? What song?"

"The one on the radio, Meg. The song from the movie *The Bodyguard*. That's us."

"Oh, shit!" she repeated, her disgust now turned up a notch. "I don't need this in my life!" And on the radio, Whitney's voice seemed to paraphrase, ". . . we both know, I'm not what, you-hoo-oo nee-ee-eed. . . ."

I sighed. No. I was no longer Meg's bodyguard. She no longer felt safe or comfortable with me. And she . . . hell, was she what I needed?

"How can I take you to dinner with my friends with your eyes all red like that?" Meg grunted. "They already think you're *chun-chee*!"

'Chun-chee'—not all together there upstairs! The meaning of her remark echoed in my mind. "Ah, Meg, I don't care what you tell them. In fact"—I sighed—"screw your friends!"

Meg huffed two or three times before speaking. When she did, her accent was back, thick as ever. "I wan you show respect my friends."

"Haven't I always, Meg?"

"You not show right now. I no understand why you don' likee hor."

Noting Meg's growing agitation, I conceded an explanation, though I knew she wouldn't really understand.

"It's not about Sook Ja having money, or rather, that the decrepit, old, ex-Nazi she's married to has money. It's not even because she's the money behind your business, or that she'll have a lot more any day now, soon as he dies. It's about the authority it gives her in your life—and mine."

"What! You call dat respect?"

"Meg, it's not that I respect them. But they're your friends. Any respect I show is the respect I have for you."

"Look, Jeff. You jus' be nice."

"Aw, c'mon, I'm always nice." Again, I sighed. "Maybe that's my problem."

"What you mean?"

"I'm just wondering why I'm wasting my time on people I don't connect with, especially when the one person I love the most is drifting away."

"What? Who?"

Oh crap! "You, Meg! I mean you."

"Well, if you don' spend all you time scribleen in dose notebooks—up till all hour of night . . ."

"You don't even know what I'm doing, do you?"

"You nebber tell me."

"You don't ask."

"Okay, smart-ass." I look over and note how the muscles in her jaw are quivering with the gritting of her teeth. "I asking now."

"I'm writing my life's story."

"What?" Her voice rose to a derisive note. "Why?"

"Someone very knowledgeable once told me I needed to."

"Needed to? C'mon, Jeff. You don nebber believe everting other peebles tell you. Besides, who would ebber wan read it?"

"Meg, I believe this guy. And even if no other person in the world ever reads it, I need to write it! Look, pull over into that parking lot—there in front of Arizona Charlie's Bar. We need to talk."

Meg did as I asked, grumbling. "Just don' make us late." Once stopped, she slapped the gearshift into park, folded her arms, and looked expectantly at me.

Taking a deep breath, I began. "Meg, we need to get our lives back on the same page again."

"Same page?"

"Yes, we don't seem to connect anymore. Look, I think it would help you in understanding me if you were to go to the Empowerment Today Seminar."

"Oh no you don'!" Meg's voice rose to border on a scream. "We been all over dees before. I-will-nebber . . ." Some guy walking by on his way into the bar stopped alongside the car and bent to look into the window. I held up my hand, finger splayed out, and waved a peaceful 'it's all okay' signal. He walked on. Meg, seeing the exchange, stopped and took one long, calculated, slow breath before continuing in stone-cold, quiet deliberation. "I will nebber go to dat crazy, damn seminar. Just you fooget it!"

"Okay, okay. Forget it. Then let's go to a marriage counselor . . . together."

"Heh." Meg snorted. "I'm okay. You da one whooz all fucked up!"

"Okay. If I have to, I'll go alone." I ducked my head, shaking it slowly from side to side, then looked up directly into her eyes. "Look, Meg, haven't I always supported you in the things that were important to you in your life?"

"What? Like what?"

"Well, just recently, didn't I support you in your massage school training. Didn't I pay for it, and didn't I help you girls remodel your shop when you started your business?"

"Yes, you did, but I still not going no seminars." Her hands gripping the steering wheel shook, knuckles white. "And I no going to no shrinks!"

"Okay . . . look, take tonight. I'm going to dinner with your friends, not because I want to. I'm going because it's important to you. And yes, it is only a little thing."

"Okay, Jeff. So, what you wan' from me?"

"I'd like you to support me in some of the little things, too. Things like not grumbling when I spend time writing or meditating." I paused, eyeing her. "Small things like that."

"Okay. I can do that."

"And Meg, I want to be a writer!"

"So, write. I no tell you *no can-chana*. You can write—"

"A published writer!"

"You? Published?" There was that derisive smirk again.

"Yes, I want to publish that book I've been writing, and I don't want you giving me a hard time about buying a computer to write it with."

"How much?"

"Fifteen hundred."

"What? You don't got dat kind of money."

"I have lots of credit."

"Fine. I'll buy you dat computer wit' my own moneys."

"Aw, honey, that's not what I meant."

"You not charging any more on doz credit cards!"

"Okay, Meg." I shrugged, wondering what kind of payback Meg would extract. "Okay. I can accept that. Thank you."

Wednesday, October 13, 1993—8:45 p.m.

I'd listened to the others now for nearly two hours. Now it was my turn. They were so open and honest with one another, their tears flowing freely. Did I have the courage to let my own feelings show? It was, after all, my first time to the group, but I felt comfortable with the therapist, Karen Moore. I chose her because she'd also been through the E.T. Seminar.

"Jeff," Karen began, "what's up in your life today?"

"It's my wife, Meg . . . she asked me for a divorce today." My tears began. *Well, that was easy.* "I don't think she's going to stay this time."

"This time?" Karen said. "You mean this has happened before?"

"Yes." I noted the hands now covering the smiles on some of the group and realized that I looked as foolish as I felt. "About every four to six weeks or so."

At that point, all six women present started laughing openly. Confused, I looked to the only other man present, questioningly. He shrugged.

"Do you know why they're laughing?" Karen asked. "It's not about you, you know."

"Wa . . . why, then?"

"Does anyone want to answer that?" Six female hands shot up. Karen chose a pretty blonde. "You, Pam."

"I've done that . . . a lot!" Pam's eyes twinkled. "We all have."

"You see, Jeff, that's just something we women do with men when they don't do what we want." Karen continued. "It's called a control drama."

"I know it's a control drama. Hell, I've long since stopped begging her to stay." I sighed, gathering my thoughts before stumbling on. "B-b-but still . . . I know she means it. I can see it in her eyes—every time! She wants to leave me." I finished with an embarrassing quake. "It . . . well, it hurts."

"I didn't say she was consciously trying to control you, or even hurt you." Karen's voice was soft and nurturing. "And she doesn't want to leave." Her hand reached out across the circle to touch my knee gently. "She only thinks she does"—Karen's eyes latched and held onto mine—"just right now."

Wednesday, February 9, 1994—7:00 p.m.

The woman's name was Chris. It was the first time I had ever seen her at group. Karen seemed to know her well, a fact that marked her as one of Karen's rich, one-on-one clients. Chris was fighting for her life. Diagnosed with bladder cancer, she was leaving the next morning for California to have her bladder removed and to undergo chemo.

In her work with Karen that night, she was dealing with all the repressed anger and guilt she'd stored in her body over the many years since she'd given her child up for adoption. These negative feelings, she now believed, were manifesting themselves in 'dis-ease'—that is, in her cancer. During her interchange with Karen, she dealt with it on a deep level, and with such courage and determination that I was astounded. This was a woman whose natural physical beauty had nothing to do with my attraction. For her, I felt great admiration and wished I knew her. Hell, I wished I were more like her.

When eventually she was done, it was then my turn. Somehow, I felt a sense of shame and embarrassment as I started into my prattle. Well, Meg's doing this and that . . . she never listens to me . . . doesn't matter how I feel . . . it's just not important to her . . .

Karen listened to me silently for a moment or two, just letting me dig myself into my story, nice and deep. She'd heard it repeatedly for over nine months. Then, *wham!* She hit me with a two-by-four, right between the eyes.

"So . . . Jeff, does this woman nurture you?"

I just sat in dazed silence, like a steer on the kill floor just before it drops. In interrupting my story, Karen had simultaneously put up her right hand, palm out toward me, as if to say, "Stop this story and listen!" Then, after delivering her two-by-four of a question, she reversed her hand to face back toward herself. It was characteristically Karen, her body language way of saying, of reinforcing, the fact that she wanted, and expected, my honest answer.

"N-n-no. I guess she doesn't nurture me."

"Don't guess!" Karen chided sharply. "Does she, or doesn't she?"

"No!" I said with more authority.

"Has she . . . ever?" Again, the signals.

"No."—Firmly.

"Do you think she ever will?"—Gently.

"N-n-no."—Reluctantly.

"Well, then . . ." Both hands were now on her hips, waiting. "What are your options?"

For just a moment of long, pregnant silence, my mind went to confusion, then cleared. "I can accept her exactly as she is . . . or, I can leave her."

* * *

By the time I reached home, I'd made my decision.

"Meg, I want a divorce."

She didn't say much, just smiled and went along with the 'game,' even humored me by setting plans to move out of our house and into an apartment. I don't think she believed me until the next morning when I arrived home, my pickup loaded with empty boxes from the grocery store.

For me, it was at the gas station that morning when it really hit me. Standing there waiting for the gas to feed slowly through the nozzle, I was idly watching traffic over the mound of empty boxes in the bed. It may have taken thirty seconds, or only three, before I realized what it was my eyes were resting on. A very attractive woman was waiting in her car at the light, and she was looking back at me—looking with obvious interest.

My God! It won't be long and I can... Will it really be this easy to release Meg? It's been nearly twenty-five years.

At home, Meg stood by silently, watching me unload the boxes. When it was done, she began, "Jeff, I made coffee. Come in and let's talk about this."

Inside at the table, we were both silent as she poured. I watched the creamer dissolve into a dark tan under the swirl of my spoon. "I've been thinking." She continued. "Maybe you're right. Maybe we should see a marriage counselor together—but, I'm not going for any of that weird group stuff. That one time you took me, that thing they did. What did she call that?"

"A rage process, Meg, that—"

"Yeah, that was some coo-wazy shit."

"Karen does have one-on-one sessions, y'know."

"Karen's weird. I don't want to go to her." Meg's hand sliced out as if clearing scum from the surface of a pond.

"Sure, Meg. I just thought Karen would be best, seeing as how she knows me pretty well. Been going to group for what, more than six months now? But, suit yourself. I'm willing to try anyone you want."

* * *

Surprisingly, in the end, Meg chose Karen. After two one-on-one sessions between Karen and Meg, and two hundred fifty dollars later, we were there, having our first private session together. Seated on her over-stuffed, floral-patterned, wicker-framed couch, gingerly at the edge, I felt out of place in such feminine surroundings. It was my first time in her private office.

"Jeff"—her expression seemed to say, 'now's your chance'—"I want you to tell Meg everything about her and your marriage that you don't like." Karen's request did nothing to put me at ease.

"Sure." I gulped, and turning to Meg, began. "Meg, I don't like it when you show me disrespect. Or that way you have of turning your brain off and not listening whenever you don't agree with what I'm saying. And... I really wish we had some things that we enjoyed doing together." At this point, I paused for a long moment, suddenly aware that although these things were important to me, still, there wasn't much that I didn't absolutely adore about Meg. Almost as an afterthought, I added, "And Meg . . . I don't like it that you've only had an orgasm but once in all the years of our marriage, or that I have to seduce you every time we make love."

Meg's switched-off look during the bulk of my dissertation was suddenly switched on, as if zapped by a live wire. Vaguely, I wondered why. This was nothing she hadn't heard before. She stared in disbelief during the silence between us. Disquieted, I chose not to elaborate but ended lamely, "I'm finished."

Karen turned to Meg. "It's your turn now."

We sat there in silence for a few moments, Karen and me looking expectantly at Meg, Meg looking back and forth between us. Did she suspect some sort of conspiracy against her? Finally, her answer came.

"I got na-ting to say." Yes, there was that accent and that all-too-familiar, closed finality in her tone.

"Meg, if you're here to work this out with Jeff, now is your opportunity to really let him know how you feel," Karen pointed out.

Meg remained mute, and not being one to stroke people's resistance, Karen moved on, working with me.

"Jeff, how does Meg show you disrespect?"

"Oh, in a thousand little ways." I shrugged uneasily.

"Like?"

"Well, like calling me a slob just because I'm not some kind of clean freak."

"And how do you feel when she does that?"

I shrugged uncomfortably. "So, okay. It doesn't really bother me all that much, except when she says it in front of our friends."

"What do you think about that, Meg?" Karen's tone was light and engaging. Meg's silence was not.

Again, Karen moved on. "Jeff, what did you mean when you said that thing about Meg turning off her brain?"

"Well, sometimes when I'm trying to get her to listen to me about something, it's almost like she reaches into her ear and flips off the switch to her brain," I said with a forced chuckle.

"So, Jeff, lose the bullshit humor and tell Meg how that makes you feel."

With a grimace, I turned to Meg. "Honey, sometimes I just feel like my opinions don't matter to you. Like you think I'm just full of shit, y'know?"

Meg's withering stare was hard to meet, but I did not look away. After a moment, she did. Karen's reminder was soft and devoid of judgment.

"Now's the time, Meg . . ."

Silence.

Awkwardly, I continued to do my best to answer Karen's prods, all the while trying to hide my feelings of disappointment and confusion at Meg's stubborn silence.

Geez, I thought, as we left Karen's office and walked out through the waiting area. *I can see this is going to get very expensive before Meg and I get our act together.*

The outside door closed behind us and we started down the orange, tiled steps. Like them, I, too, began to feel the gentle warmth of the winter desert sun. Then was when Meg finally broke her frosty silence.

"How could you?"

"What?"

"How could you say all those personal things about me? And in front of a . . . a stranger!"

"Meg, why . . . why are we here?" The words fell from my lips simultaneously with my mind's own answer. That sentence started out a true question with energy behind the first words. It ended without energy, in resignation. I knew now why Meg was here.

I paused, watching her stomp down the steps ahead. Again, I placed my thumb and first two fingers together, raised purposefully unfocused eyes, and slid down quickly into level *Three . . . Two . . . One.*

Big D? God, Big D! I think now is one of those times when I need you.

His answer filters down, as if from a great distance. Word for word, the same as he has said it several times before, "All is as it needs to be, Jeff. Have courage."

God, Big D! I'm so confused. Please. Stay. Talk to me!

"I've given you all the tools you need. It's up to you to learn to use them, maybe to dig your way out of all this selfishness and blame?"

Selfish? Yes, okay. You are right. I have been trying to change Meg—at least I did hope she would prefer to deal with things rather than go through with a divorce. But I had to try! Look, can't you give me some sort of direction here?

"Direction?" I hear his familiar chuckle. "Right now, I'd have to say you're moving outward on the limb. You do know that it is going to break?"

Tell me, Big D. Other things in my life now seem so clear, but with my relationship with Meg? I feel like I'm at the end of my wits.

"Ah, yes. War is often like that. Perhaps you might look to your choice of options. What were they again?"

Accept her exactly as she is—or leave. Yeah. I grit my teeth. *I see now how divorce is the way it's gotta be.*

"Is there something, some vital essence, you are missing, maybe from the option not taken?" He chuckles.

Are you saying I'm choosing the wrong one?

"Absolutely not! Taken alone, either can be equally functional." His chuckle comes again. "Interesting that you chose the option of 'doing' rather than the option of 'being.'"

Being?

"Yes. Accepting her would require that you make changes in you. It would require you *being* different—going back to who you were."

Yeah. You mean back when I did accept her, back when she was everything I ever wanted? I can't—

"Good that you can see that. Change is the constant of the universe. You've changed, grown. In fact, you no longer see life the way you did, the way she still does. Do you?"

No, I don't. I shake my head with the realization. *And for the first time, I like who I am.*

"Y'know, Jeff, the law states, **The world is not out there, it's in here. It is composed of every thought, every belief, every feeling you have**."

Yeah, I know that law, too. I nod, wondering where he's going with this.

"Then you must know . . ." He chuckles. "Sheee-tt, son. You don't inhabit the same world as Meg."

Ye-aaaah . . . I'm wondering if it's even the same universe.

Comb Ridge, Utah—Present Day

What Meg would think of my world now? That thought brings up a chuckle and a shooting pain in my leg.

"Shhh-it!" I glance out over the gulf of Comb Ridge. *Fuck! My world now? Hell, I don't even have a clue about what to think of it now.*

For those first few weeks, it looked like the leg would heal, what with all the massaging to keep the circulation going. Big D even had me brewing tea out of pinyon needles—vitamins, he said. That and the fact I was feasting, conservatively, on the soups and beans from the initial hoard in my saddlebags. It actually seemed to work. But now, the soups are all eaten and the infection is back.

Change most often comes on the heels of discomfort or necessity—sometimes, not even then. For some, the game of control is just too strong. It has always gotten them what they wanted of others—they think. They don't see that the game is really one of pretense. And any change from others is also merely a pretense.

Redneck Spirituality—Book Two

CHAPTER SEVEN

Oh, Cheesus!

Tuesday, March 1, 1994—6:35 p.m.

"Another seminar? Oh, Cheesus!" Meg's pronunciation, given her slight Korean accent, would normally have prompted a smile, but there was no smiling in the face of her reaction to the news.

"That's right. Karen Moore is putting on a seminar. She's calling it Inner Quest. It's supposed to be something like the Empowerment Today Seminar—experiential like that, anyway."

"Experiential? Shit! That bitch is coo-wazy." Her accent was becoming more pronounced as her English deteriorated the closer she got to the precipice of her anger. "I had it with all this coo-wazziness! I wan' divorce."

"Ah, Meg." With elbows on either side of my unfinished dinner, I leaned my face into my hands, rubbing at the weariness in my eyes. "You've only been home a week since our trial separation. Please don't say stuff you don't mean."

"Oh, I mean it. You don' tink so?"

"You're right. This is crazy." Looking at the old, familiar set of her face, I knew she meant it every bit as much as she ever had. Her features were twisted with the same inner bitterness that I had witnessed so regularly but had never been able to affect—at least not for the better. "You win . . . I'm tired of it, too."

"Then you're not going to the seminar?"

"That's not what I meant, Meg. I meant you are right about the divorce."

A momentary shadow crossed her face and her mouth fell open with what, shock? Or something else—*panic?* Then the moment had passed, and I was too tired to wish it back. "Good. Yes, I wan' divorce, too." She seemed to need to repeat it.

"Okay, so . . ." I took a deep breath and let it whoosh out. "Do you want to stay in the house or move into an apartment?"

"That will cost too much. We can just liff here together, only haba diffn't bedrooms, seprate lives."

"No, Meg." A picture flashed through my mind of me bringing some other woman home—or of her bringing . . . "That won't work."

Again, the shadow passed. "Den, I leave." She ducked in angry acceptance. "I never likey dis house hany-way."

"Okay, it's settled then." I shook my head slowly. "I'll help you get an apartment."

Wednesday, March 2, 1994—7:00 a.m.

The butter melted as I smoothed it around the pancake with a butter knife, trying also to smooth my uneasiness along with it. "Meg, it's awfully nice of you to still fix my breakfast, what with us getting a divorce and all."

From her place at the stove she turned, her bathrobe hanging unusually loose in the front. So unlike her prim and proper self, she was not even wearing a bra.

"Haven't I been a good wife to you, Jeff? Haven't I always taken good care of you?"

"Yes, you have."

"Then why you want to go? Why you are leaving me?"

"Aw, come on. You haven't been happy in our marriage for a long time."

"How you know that? You not me."

"No, of course not, but last night wasn't the first time you ever asked me for a divorce, y'know?"

"But Jeff, I was just mad all those times. I don't never mean it."

"I know you were mad, but at the time when you said it, I know you *did* mean it. Look." I took a deep breath and let it out with a whoosh. "I've always loved you, and it always hurt, y'know?"

"But Jeff, was just mad . . ." Her voice trailed off and it was difficult to hear her when she continued. "Can you no forgive me?"

I got up and moved close behind to put my arms around her stiff body. "Meg, there's nothing you could do that I wouldn't forgive you. I'm just tired of you being angry with me all the time."

"I'm not angry now." She shuddered as she leaned back into my arms. "I don't want to divorce you."

"Aw, c'mon. In a week—maybe two—you'll be angry again. It's always like that."

"Not this time."

"It doesn't seem like you can stop yourself. You're just not happy with me. And, I don't think you want to be."

"Why you say that?"

"You pretend, but you don't want to do anything to change." I stopped, searching for an easier way to put it. "I want a woman who is happy to be with me." I shrugged. "That's just not you."

"But . . ."

"Meg, you deserve to be happy, and so do I."

"Jeff, no." She turned to face me. "Look, I'll go to your seminar."

"Oh?" Hope flared brightly, and instinctively, I tried to hold it down. "Which one? Karen's or the Empowerment Today Seminar?"

"The one you took . . . E.T. I think you say."

"Look." A grimace crossed my face. "It's not my right to ask you to change, and I don't think you can take E.T. and not change." My eyes locked on hers. "Are you sure?"

"Yes."

"Good. They're having it this weekend. In fact, it starts tomorrow night."

"Tomorrow?" Her eyes slid from my own. "That's too soon."

We stood there a moment, silently, her eyes avoiding mine. "It's okay, Meg. Forget it."

My arms dropped. Turning, I walked to the hallway and lifted my work coat from its peg. "I need to get to work."

"I'll go, Jeff." She sprang into action, running to throw her arms around me. "I'll go."

Holding her at arm's length, I studied her closely. "You sure? You don't have to do this. Once we pay, they give no refunds if you don't go. They only refund if you go and stay throughout—and still don't like it."

"Yes, yes. I'm sure."

Thursday, March 3, 1994—7:00 p.m.

Meg's E.T. Seminar began as had mine before. All those *newbies* in the main portion up front seemed like so many disconnected souls, each trying to keep a maximum distance between themselves and the others. The chairs were set close together for just that reason. Once the participants were herded together and the empty chairs removed by the staff, the seminar got underway.

I sat in the smaller auditor's section in back. E.T. was free to any graduate who felt the need for a *tune-up*. Though I knew only a few, we were like kin and had no such problem with sitting close. In fact, we preferred it so. Seeing Meg with the others, I wanted to whoop like a drunken cowboy. Yet, as the night's exercises progressed, I found it more and more difficult to pick her out in the group. After each break, she seemed to sit in places where I could not see.

On the way home that night, she was silent, aloof. "Meg, what do you think of the seminar so far?"

"I don't know." Her shrug was more of a shudder.

"Is there anything you don't understand? Maybe I can help."

"Lemme alone!"

"Sure . . . no problem." Looking at the back of her head as she stared out the passenger window at the neon façade of Las Vegas, I smiled, remembering my own E.T. Seminar and knowing she, too, had a lot to think about this night.

At home, while I grabbed a quick snack to replace my missed dinner, she went straight to bed. When later I slipped in beside her, she lay on her side, her back toward me, stiffly, silently. I left her alone.

E.T. opened Friday evening with the picking of buddies— someone with whom the participants could go through the more difficult parts of the seminar with, someone to give support. Without waiting, I chose a woman standing nearby. She turned out to be a refugee from a FLDS polygamist marriage. When the choosing finished, there were two left not chosen—an older woman from the auditor group and a scowling newbie, Meg. My buddy made an offer to the auditing woman, and we quickly became a threesome. The significance of my buddy's act of sharing did not register with me until later. Meg, too, after long moments, found acceptance.

As I watched her take a seat, I noticed something. She sat, kind of scrunched, head down, arms folded, not saying much. A chill crept in beside the joy of my last few days.

When the seminar ended for the night, we walked silently to the car. The night air seemed to hold an unusual chill. With a flick of the key, the engine caught, and I let it run a few moments while I adjusted the heater controls, all the while wondering how best to begin.

"Meg."

"Lemme alone!"

"Sure, Meg . . . sure." With a sigh, I dropped the lever into gear. From then on, Friday night became a carbon copy of the night before.

Saturday, March 5, 1994—8:15 a.m.

I was hungry. The bacon and eggs on my plate smelled so good, so normal. What I had to discuss with Meg was neither.

"Meg, uh . . . look. We've got to talk."

"About what?"

I rolled my eyes. *She's got to be kidding.* "Well, about the seminar."

"I don't want to talk about it. It's coo-wazy."

"Maybe so." I sighed, mentally agreeing as well. *Yeah, coo-wazy.* "Look, if you don't understand something, I can—"

"I said I don't want to talk about it." She slammed her hand down flat on the table. "What! You tinky me stupid?"

"No . . . 'course not. I just get the feeling that you're not trying."

"What you mean"—her upper lip kind of curled up as if in a snarl—"*not trying?*"

"Well, you just don't seem like you're open to it."

"Open? How you know? You not in my head."

"Hey, look, even your body language—"

"*Body language!* What kind of coo-wazy shit is that?"

"Maybe if you unfolded your arms and took part in the exercises—"

"That's it!" Meg's eggs went skidding across the table. "I not going."

For a long moment, I looked down at my now-unappetizing food, then rose and brushed some egg from my lap. "Okay, Meg. I'll see you tonight."

"What! You *still* going?"

"Well, yes, Meg. I promised my buddies I'd be there for them." *God, have I changed so much? Was there ever a time when it was okay for me to just shit on my word?* "Didn't you promise yours also?"

"What you tinking? They mean more to you than me?" Meg gaped as if it were something incomprehensible. Or were my thoughts also written across my face?

For a long moment, our eyes locked. *Surely, she didn't wish for that 'old me' to return—that asshole?* Then I addressed my real issue.

"No, it's not about them." I shook my head slowly, sadly. "But it *is* about me. Guess I've changed—gone coo-wazy. My word *does* mean something to me."

"That's it! It all over, Jeff." Her scream of rage followed me out the door. "I be gone 'fore you come back."

All the way to the seminar, I let the tears fall. Looking at my feelings, I realized they no longer included fear. No longer did I even consider asking her to stay. There was only a dark, painful acceptance where the fear had once been.

I was already in my chair when my buddies sat down. Their Arms, all four, encircled me together. "Jeff . . . Jeff. What's wrong?"

"It's Meg. I just lost everything that ever meant anything to me."

"How? Why?"

"Don't want to talk about it. Just give me a hug and be here for me."

So it was for the better part of the morning. Then, Meg came in during the last break before lunch. The support team leader took me aside.

"Mr. Williams, we noticed your wife wasn't here this morning, and one of the team talked her into coming back. But you need to leave and let her finish this by herself."

"But my buddies . . . I promised to support them."

"They've been told and they've released you from your promise. You need to honor her request and leave now."

For a while, I paced outside the seminar building on the University of Nevada, Las Vegas campus. Eventually, realizing what a sorry sight it would present should she see me there during a break, I headed out of town. Dusk found me on a ridge, high on Mount Charleston, meditating.

Meg was in bed when I came in. I thought about joining her but remembered the request and left her alone. In the morning, I watched through squinted eyes from the couch as she made preparations to leave for the seminar, feigning sleep rather than put any pressure on her.

Sunday was a repeat of Saturday afternoon. From my meditations high above the valley, I called upon Big D and received the same answer. "All is as it should be. Be patient . . . have courage." Darkness found me entering the rented seminar building at UNLV.

During the last ceremony, I stood where my unknown benefactor had stood while the facilitator wound down. Most of the lights were off, and the participants were arranged in a circle. All had their eyes closed. I stood inside the circle, facing her, and noted how she looked small, almost defenseless, like she'd been drained by some great effort.

Oh God, I prayed. *Let her finally understand these changes in me.* Then, over the words of Aaron Neville and Linda Ronstadt's music—*Look at this man. I know the years are showing*—the facilitator made his request. "Now, stay as you are but open your eyes."

She did, and seeing me, blinked. For a long moment, we regarded one another silently. My sight began to wobble and blur as I became aware of her tears. When the facilitator made his last request, we were ready. "Okay, now you can move."

I had it all. My world was finally complete! Dangling in my embrace, Meg whispered into my ear, "I thought I had lost you."

Later, at home, we sat together at the table holding hands, my eyes devouring hers. "Look," I began. "Let's not wait. Let's make our plans now."

Meg's eyes turned puzzled. "Plans?"

"Yes, y'know . . . for our future. I am so ready to go for our dreams!"

Her eyes remained puzzled. "Dreams? What are your dreams?"

"Well, I'm not sure what they will be for us together. That's what we need to decide. For me personally, I want to be a writer. And I want to pursue my lapidary stonework and silversmithing. And I want to ride motorcycles again, to feel the wind through my hair . . . go places. But tell me what you want. We need to make it all work together."

"Together?"

"Yes, y'know. Five years from now—or ten years—where do we want to be in life?"

Meg shook her head as if walking through cobwebs. "Oh, I'm fine." She ended with a shrug. "I don't need nothing." Then her head jerked up. "But does this mean you want to quit your job as a mechanic? How will we get by without a regular paycheck?"

"It doesn't have to happen all at once."

She didn't answer, just looked at me. For perhaps the first time, she truly looked at me and seemed to gain some measure of understanding, but what I saw in her eyes now did not feel good. It seemed to be . . . *Oh God, no! What is that behind her fear—pity?*

"Meg!" I unleashed the words that now burned in my heart, words that I knew would carry a penalty—one I'd never before had the courage to pay. "I want a woman who will walk through life *with* me . . . not some kind of steel-ball-closed-up iron woman, chained to my ankle, someone I have to drag around. Someone who stays with me even though she thinks I'm fucking crazy!"

Meg didn't say a word, just stared. Then, as her face hardened, she stood and stalked off. Numbly, I sat, questioning, as the bedroom door slammed.

Big D? Oh God, Big D! Have I fucked it all up again? It was so perfect. Why did I need to say those things?

His answer came from a distance, like a far-off wind. "You needed to say your truth. And it is still perfect . . . just doesn't feel that way when your wants are not the same as your needs."

You mean I don't need to be a writer . . . or silversmith . . .   or . . .

"Wants? Needs? Those wants are yours. You own them." There comes the sound of wind whistling as if around the yucca trees, on the desert, and it was hard to hear his next words. "It is only your wants of others—of Meg—that you cannot always have. But then, you know that, don't you?"

You mean she doesn't want—

"You've got it." The breeze had almost passed and I strained to hear the rest. It came with a chuckle. "Ha . . . Meg doesn't want any part of your 'coo-wazy-shit' life."

Comb Ridge, Utah—Present Day

The leg is worse. Not only has it swelled up and feels hot to the touch, but the wound has opened and the cloth covering it is sopping with pus. Pulling the covering aside, I inspect it.

The wound is oozing copiously and . . . *oh my God! Something is moving within it—maggots!*

"Fuck!" The word rips out of my throat in raw rage, as frantically, I start trying to clean them out. *Big D . . . why has this come to plague me at a time like this?*

"Leave them be!" His answer comes as white-hot words burning into my mind. "I sent them to you."

My hand is busy trying to brush them away as, looking around, I spot him, a smoke-like, darker shadow in the shade beneath the cliff overhang. The red glow of his eyes is sharply clear with distinct, no-nonsense purpose. "I said, leave them be! For the dead, they are nature's way of cleaning the land."

But I still live . . . A chill runs through me at the possible portents of his words. *Don't I?*

"Yes, and for the living, they are nature's way of cleaning out the dead flesh from wounds." I can sense a grin in his words now. "They won't eat healthy, live tissue. Even the most boneheaded Neanderthal knew that."

B-b-but . . .

"When they fly away"—he chuckles—"your wound will be healed."

Relationships are always about needs. For some, their relationships have nothing to do with love, but most would likely agree that relationships are supposed to be about the need to give and receive love. Yet, no matter what the needs may be, for relationships to work, the meeting of needs must exist for both. For when one's needs aren't met, they become the driving force in one's life—the force that drives the relationship apart.

Redneck Spirituality—Book Four

CHAPTER EIGHT

On the Battlefield of Unmet Needs

Saturday, April 9, 1994—1:30 a.m.

I awakened to the ruby gaze of Big D in my night, his fist once more seizing the insides of my chest. His voice, when he spoke, was insistent, holding the same cutting timbre of my old chainsaw.

"Jeff! You continue to resist the price! Indeed, you still don't know what it is."

Bolting upright beside my oblivious wife, I clutched at my chest, choking, my body ashine in a sweaty chill, my mind putting forth a plea. *Big D! No . . . wait! Whatever it is, I don't know, Please! Just tell me!*

His poised sickle was slowly lowered, and I heard a soft clank as it was leaned against the wall. His grip, too, seemed to relax as he settled on the edge of the bed.

"Yes, Jeff. Now is a good time to ask. You are good at following directions, not so good at asking for them."

Shuddering in relief, but with voice still quaking, I implored him. *W-w-what? What do you have to tell me?*

"Your wife, Jeff." The words hung deafening in the silence. He continued, the timbre of his voice at a low idle. "It's about Meg . . . about who she is."

Oh, Big D, I know. I've tried to change her . . . tried to make her be who I needed, Once, I even played her own control drama on her—asked her for a divorce. Unknowingly, sure . . . but I've learned. I've since come to see our relationship honestly, it's not been easy to accept her, to love her exactly as she is.

"So, you think you've accepted her? It is time to stop *thinking* and to *know*."

Know?

"And then knowing, you must take the steps you will then need to take."

What do you mean?

"I mean, in staying with her, are you loving you?" He held my gaze in the brightness of his own burning stare, then delivered his second query, like a one-two punch. "Are you following your joy?"

I love her. How can I not be following my joy?

"Jeff! To bridge such an abyss between two hearts always takes the efforts of both. You are stuck at the edge, reaching. Can your joy be found in a heart that is not reaching back?" He paused a moment to let his words sink in, then continued, his voice now a soft rumble from the bottom of that barrel. "And your destiny. Aren't you stymied? I showed it to you. Did you not clearly see the abyss—so impossible to bridge by only one? Do you see how you again break our agreement?"

Yes . . . but God, Big D! Not my Meg! Oh, how did it all get so fucked up?

"Fucked up? Yes, it is so . . . if you insist." His grin gaped in the darkness close above. I noticed his front tooth is chipped very slightly, exactly like my own. "Perhaps it's time you told me how you got so *fucked up*."

What? If I knew that, don't you think I would change it? I challenged his burning gaze, trying to stare him down. It didn't work. I dropped my gaze. *Isn't that what I've been trying to do these past eighteen months since we met?*

"Change *it*? No. Change *you*? Yes. That's why you must tell your story, the one you've been playing around at writing."

Playing around? What the fuck! I don't see—

"Just finish it and we'll talk. Oh, and our conversations, no matter how they come about, will need to be included as well."

Ah, c'mon. We both know a story's just a story. Everyone's got one. Hell, I've told mine in a thousand ways to as many people over the years. Was a time when no one could talk to me without me dragging out my story and boring them with a piece of it. I've no great need to tell it to anyone.

"It's true. You've no need to tell it to others, especially not about this relationship you have with me." He chuckled. "Ha, many will think you're a basket case. You know that?"

Oh, fuck them. One of the best things you've taught me is not to concern myself with what others think of me. I get it that my concern needs to be about myself, about what I think of me.

"True, but that requires that you know who you are." I could almost hear the chuckle as he let his words hang in the silence of the night.

"Look, Jeff. You remember your scouting days? About reading maps? All you needed was a compass and two pieces of information." His countenance seemed to somehow sharpen with his tone. "What were they?"

Well, you needed to know where you were and where you wanted to be.

"That's right. Now, it's clear you know the *who* you want to be. But *who* are you right now?" The glow brightened and flickered. "How did you just describe that person?"

Well, I . . . uh . . .

"Yeah, that's right. Some nebulous persona called . . ." He cocked his head, and I got the impression of eyebrows being raised. "How was that again? *Fucked up* . . . did you say?"

Yeah. The word dropped out in disgust as I exhaled. *I see your point.*

"Look, Jeff, we're going to retrace your steps—honestly this time. You'll find you will stop stumbling with it. And, oh . . . my sickle? It's just a prop, you know, meant only to remind you of the cost of not being honest with yourself. But that doesn't mean it isn't sharp."

What does that mean?

"Look, considering I'll be your compass, your life is now a joint effort. You might want to factor that into it the cost of not following my guidance." His grip in my chest tightened slightly. "It *is* what I require. Are you saying you have no more need to live?"

My whispered reply was a long time coming. *But my Meg, Big D.* I felt her soft flesh against my leg where she slumbered next to me. *I don't know if I can live*—his grin seemed suddenly to blur—*without my Meg.*

"Yes. That's been the real issue for some time now, hasn't it?" His gaping grin no longer felt anything other than sober. His fist released the last of its grip and then paused just a moment to softly stroke my chin. "Look, Meg has yet to teach you the secret of acceptance and love. Perhaps Karen can help you come to terms with that."

Inner Quest Seminar
Saturday, April 23, 1994—10 a.m.

Karen's voice boomed out over the music, "War! How do I do war?"

The exercise was one of meditation. In the darkened room, I questioned myself. Around me, people were muttering, many weeping, a few even wailing from the agony of their most painful realizations. Me? Their grief seemed something that didn't quite touch me. *Big D? Will it? I'm just not feeling this? Is it because I don't do war?*

There came a touch on my shoulder, like hard ivory, yet softly applied, a gentle squeeze. "It's because you don't want to know. You avoid it like many others here who remain silent."

But Big D, I've always been a peaceable fellow. I don't see where I do war. Does this part of the seminar really apply to me?

The darkness of the room immediately erupted with a kaleidoscope of light. Images in full color flashed before me, each of someone doing something I didn't like. In each appeared the imprint of my twisted features full of self-righteous rage.

There was the boy in the orphanage who mocked me for my stained sheets—again, my hands grind his face into the depths of the sandbox. There was the one in Fry Canyon who'd dared flip me the bird—his nose bled as he ran home crying. And then the boy in the gym, his glasses flying with the smash of my fist—I'd told him to take them off, but he moved too slowly and I unleashed much too soon. Then, the girl in Australia, so much smarter than me, or so she seemed to think—again, her map project ran with the stain of spilled ink. A hundred more images flashed by me like the flipping of the pages on my life. All of them showed me the ugly me, the self-righteous me, the hurtful me, the pain-filled me reacting in revenge.

"You see, Jeff?"

Yes, Big D. My tears now flowed with those of the others. *I see.*

"Ah, but that's just the beginning of you and war. Have you not thought about how the war began between you and Meg?"

Again, the kaleidoscope erupted. Meg, her face sullen when caught dancing at that private party being held at the Miss Kim Club—Korean businessmen only. I cornered her in the back courtyard of the club, sitting silent in the shadows near the club's back door. *Did she think I wouldn't see her there, or did she just not care?*

The row of rooms used by the prostitutes ranged on my left, most of their wood-framed, paper doors dark. I remembered the thoughts that continued to flash through my mind back then. *Oh God, which one was once hers? Was it about to be so again, tonight, but for this intervention?*

So it went, that war of distrust that erupted in my mind back then. *What is she doing here? Why did she have her friends lie to me tonight? Was that her Korean boyfriend she was dancing with? A lot of the girls secretly have one.*

"Meg," I heard myself say, "I don't want to talk here. Let's go home." Again, I felt my frustration at her continued silence as she sat motionless, scrunched up on that chair next to the door.

My ultimatum again sprang forth. "Look, five seconds." I held out five fingers. "Five seconds more and I go out that gate. I love you. I want you go with me. You no go, I never see you again! You, me—*oop so!* No more. *Ah rhee so.* Understand?"

Again came the count. Again, I left, stumbling away in blurred silence, only to come back just minutes later when I slung Meg unwillingly over my shoulder, then carried her away.

At first, she struggled, kicking and squealing as we descended the path between the hooches. As we approached the main street, she said, "P-prease, put me down. I walkee now." Unwilling to lose face, she finished the trip, walking beside me in frigid silence.

I see it now!

"Yes, Jeff? Tell me what you see."

Ah, Jesus, Big D. I set it all up so well. With that broken ultimatum, I gave up any chance Meg would ever see me in control of my life. With that, I gave control over to her. All those demands she had made for a divorce over the years since? They were merely her reminding me of just who was in control. Since then, we have been at war. Control? Is that all war is about—control?

"Yes." His head bobbled up and down within his soot-colored cowling, like the bobber toy that once graced the dashboard of my car.

"It is exactly so." His comment fit, validated it all. "Power . . . money . . . people's lives. War is all about control."

But big D. I stopped a moment and listened to the moans and whimpering of the others in the seminar surrounding me, listened to the raw pain, to the despair. I could almost see the chains locked tightly around us all. *Isn't there some way to break the chain?*

"Yes . . . about time you asked."

He fell silent while the tension, the want, the need to know built within me. *Are you baiting me, Big D?*

"Very perceptive." His gaping grin seemed to further widen. "You're finally learning to use your intuition."

Yes, well?

"Acceptance, Jeff."

Acceptance? That's your answer?

"Yes, it's that simple. Course, you might throw in a little bit of cherish, a dash of empathy, even a lick of passion." I saw his humor flickering in the glow of his sight. "The simple hacksaw that cuts the chain is love. You cannot have love without unconditional acceptance."

I'll do it! I set my jaw, teeth gnashed hard together. *I will accept Meg. Exactly as she is.*

"Seems like I've heard that somewhere before."

I mean it, Big D. I know it now.

"Yes, Jeff, I agree. Still, there's something else you must come to know."

What's that?

"You must know that you can only cut your own chains."

Thursday, May 12, 1994—7:00 a.m.

Over the next two months, I took my acceptance of Meg to the heart level of my being, learned to shift my viewpoint about those things I'd always found difficult concerning her, to look at them from a place of acceptance. Some I even began to treasure as uniquely her. When she became grumpy with me for leaving a mess, I'd smile warmly inside in appreciation for how well her need for cleanliness and order served to bring organization to my own life.

Sometimes, when rattling on about something only I seemed to find fascinating, I'd realize she'd turned off her brain to me again. Stopping mid-sentence, I'd smile to myself in the realization of how important that quality was to her. It served to keep her alive. When she'd been forced into prostitution at fifteen, that ability to disconnect was what saved her sanity. Suicide would have been *proper* according to her strict upbringing.

While her unwillingness to look at any other viewpoint now stifled her growth, I saw it as a sort of quaintness. I appreciated it in the same manner as I did the picturesque unchangeableness of some of the charming little Mormon farming communities of my native Utah. I even found delight in the way her nose crinkled whenever she got angry. It was something I almost came to treasure.

* * *

But this day was special. The table was set to perfection. A single red rose graced the vase in the center. I smiled as I filled our plates, ladling scrambled eggs and sausage from the pan.

Meg emerged from the bedroom, hair disheveled, still in her bathrobe, and plopped into her chair. A slight frown furrowed her brow, and her eyes traveled the length of the table before coming to rest on me. Silently, she picked up the envelope leaning against the vase holding the red rose. She fingered it without opening, eyes again downcast.

"Y'know, sweetheart"—I broke the uncomfortable silence—"the twenty-fifth is called the *Silver Anniversary*. I'm going to make you something out of silver." A slight rolling of her eyes indicated her gist of thought. Hurriedly, I continued. "But you'll like it this time. You get to design it. Anything you want."

My offering hung unacknowledged, not even by her eyes, as her head ducked and she continued to finger the card. Finally, her eyes rose and met mine.

"Are you still going to the seminar tonight?"

"Ye-esss." I spoke the word slowly, feeling an uneasy caution. "Of course. I've committed to being on the support team."

She declined her head again, and through the curl of her beautiful, black hair, I saw a jaw muscle clench. Quickly, I added, "But we can do whatever you want . . . all day."

Not good enough. With a quick flick of her wrists, she tore the unopened card in half, then flung it into my face.

"I want a divorce!" Her face was a twisted caricature now, somehow minus all beauty.

Her demeanor left no doubt . . . she meant it. And her actions with the card said she'd thought a lot about it. For a long moment, I stared, non-responsive. Ah, such drama, such excruciating repetition.

But this time, *I* was different. There was none of the old, familiar fear and panic. Sure, since my time in that ICU, I'd quit begging her to stay. Yet, the fear she'd leave had still been there. But this time . . .

Silently, I closed my eyes, touched fingers to thumb, and with a sigh, dropped into level. *Big D?*

"Yes, Jeff. I'm here."

Ah, shit, Big D! I sighed. *It's over. I know it now. I understand this great sadness, but why do I feel such relief?*

"You've been true to her, Jeff. You've finally come to accept her unconditionally, and in so doing know the true status of your marriage. But you are only now being true to yourself, and so . . . the relief."

I don't understand.

"Karen said it well. 'Does Meg meet your needs?' That is the purpose of relationships, remember?"

But—

"And Meg?" The fire in his eye sockets drew down to piercing pin pricks of laser light. "Did she not say it well—right after her E.T. Seminar—that single look of pity? Remember it? Not only does she not support you in your dreams and aspirations, she pities you for having them."

It wasn't the laser in his sight that now pierced my heart, but rather, the truth in his words. I closed my eyes in acceptance—and also to clear them of the moisture now blurring my sight. Opening them, I was aware that to Meg, my conversation with Big D had all taken place in the time during those two blinks.

"Okay, honey. I think you're right. We do need this divorce." I said it softly, then watched in sudden, silent anguish as she stormed from the room.

For the next few days, Meg was silent, refusing to speak to me while she packed her things into the boxes I'd brought. Most of the weekend, I was away supporting Karen's seminar. It was late in the evening on Sunday when she came to me. I was sitting at the kitchen table, paying bills.

"Look, I think we need to talk!" I glanced up quickly, surprised by the fear in her voice.

Gravely, I replied, "I think so, too."

Stumbling, she haltingly began. "I . . . uhh . . . I don't think I . . uhh . . . really want this . . . uhh . . . uhh . . . this divorce." I watched a tear slide slowly down her cheek.

Looking into her beautiful, vulnerable, pain-filled eyes, her tear was followed by my own. How I'd always longed for Meg to be this vulnerable and honest with me. *Am I mistaken? Has something in her changed? Do we now have a chance together? No!*

Intuition and acceptance said it all. Tomorrow or the next day this would be but a moment of weakness on her part. She'd resume her role as that strong, invincible woman. Meg did not have the ability to feel safe in any other way.

Ah, but those things were all about her. How did I feel? Did I want this divorce? That was her unasked question. Meg deserved my honesty. I felt an ache in my soul that my answer was final—and undeniable.

"Do I want this divorce? I'm sorry, Meg . . . I do."

Comb Ridge, Utah—Present Day

I grit my teeth at the feeling of maggots moving around inside the wound. *Goddamn little bastards are having a feast.*

As for me, I've long since run out of the soups and beans and now have a stash of empty cans to use to heat water. I've found that by cutting up the jerky and soaking it first, it will swell up. Between the chunks steeped in water, I can make a meal using very little jerky—especially if I scrape a little of the inner bark from the pinyon pines. It serves to thicken the broth, just as Big D told me it would.

Looking out over the gulf of Comb Ridge, a breeze passes softly through the little grove of pinyon pines that have managed to take root in this high ledge. I wonder if there will be enough dead wood to cook and maybe even provide a little heat once the season changes. I'm not sure of the date anymore, but I know from experience that the season will definitely change to colder in the second week of September. That will be any day now. By the end of October, the nights will be bitterly cold.

I suck on one of my two-jelly beans-a-day allotment, enjoying it immensely. They provide most of the calories I now get. I shudder at how it will be when the cold comes. Even now, the breeze across my face feels cool. I have always been proud that while I am a big man, most of my weight is solid muscle, very little is fat. I may come to regret that.

And speaking of regrets, I am wishing I'd told a few friends where I was going. *Joy is the only one who knows, and she's . . . well, she probably just wants to forget about me after the way we last parted. Has anyone even missed me yet?*

It is a Law of Life—*We create exactly that upon which we focus our energy and in exactly the same energy focused.* View your children as useless, unworthy, ungrateful? Be assured, they won't let you down. If those are the colored glasses through which you view them, those are the same glasses through which they will look to see you. Is it any wonder why those *ungrateful little bastards* can see so little to find loving about you?

Redneck Spirituality—Book Four

CHAPTER NINE

Flash Floods of Life

Monday, May 16, 1994—3:00 p.m.

Sitting on my waterbed, legs draped over the sideboard, phone to my ear, I took a long breath. On the other end, the connection clicked in my parents' home in Utah and began to ring. God, I don't want to have to tell them this. Ah, but the decision is made, and they deserve to know. Traumas and dramas . . .

Instinctively, I knew my mother would dramatize it all. At least I'd avoided that possibility until now. But now, it was already resolved, the decision solid. Yes, now was the time to tell them about our upcoming divorce. As such, it was a painful time, a time when I needed my family's love and support, and I was glad that Meg, too, had her family here to lean on.

I always thought I had great parents. Sure, maybe Mom was prone to having private rages. Those my brother, Mike, and I took in stride as merely the norm for all families—at least for those whose sons were not so normal like us. But then, they didn't know. Why would people outside our family think otherwise?

And inside, some things were simply not to be questioned. I was at fault, the source of all unhappiness, disappointment, and dissatisfaction in my mother's life. And Dad? One did not question anything Mom said or did—not around Dad. Mike's death left me to deal with it, and that meant all alone.

Yes, I thought my parents to be models of normalcy. Of my father's remoteness, his disdainful distance—even the occasional threat of his callused hands—all of it was my fault. Like all fathers, mine was my own model representing the properties of a real man.

Doesn't matter now. I reminded myself of that as I waited for the phone to be answered. *Big D taught me how the true nature of our species is dysfunction. It is our evolutionary process, the current against which we swim, the current that takes us to where resides each and every lesson we will ever need. Besides, how many years has it been since I've had to deal with Mother's rage, and though it had only been an occasional thing, with Dad's hard, callused hands?*

Mom's voice broke my reverie. "Hello . . ."

"Hi, Mom. It's me, Jeff."

"How can you be so despicable? Aaaaaarrrrrrrgh!" Mom's rage was there, turned up to maximum volume and full accusation. "You know you're killing me and your dad. How can you be so damned selfish? I'm ashamed to call you my son. If my arthritis wasn't bothering me so much, I'd come down there and straighten you out!"

My mouth fell open, but breathing didn't seem to be the issue as scenes from my youth combed through my mind like fingers of feelings through my hair. When I didn't reply immediately, the tirade continued with barely a pause. Her ensuing description of my persona had me resembling something very slimy and without legs or backbone. Clearly, to her I was now something undeserving of even residing in the basement of the ancestral outhouse.

"I wish to hell your father and I had left you and your hoodlum brother to rot in that Sunny Hills orphanage! Just be glad that he's not here right now to tell you what he thinks of you. We're both so ashamed of you." She paused to take a breath and I attempted a diversion.

"I understand, Mom, but when did you start feeling—"

"Not that you or your worthless brother ever cared. I worked my fingers bloody washing your clothes. All those years of taking care of you two. It ruined my health!"

I sighed, remembering her old, roller-type washing machine. I was seven when she bought it. She dragged us all over Salt Lake in search of that old-fashioned contraption. Seemed no one made them anymore. The year was 1952, and for years, it was to be her pride and joy. We weren't allowed to touch it. But the rest of the housework? That was all ours—the endless piles of clothes we ironed, the dishes washed, floors scrubbed, carpets vacuumed, lawns mowed . . .

"Yes, Mom. I always appreciated you doing the laundry. And that you cooked for us, too. You were a good cook." I stopped, my mind searching for other things I could honestly say I appreciated about her. Nothing more came.

"And what do I get?" She continued as if she hadn't heard a word. "Disgrace! Mike disgraced us back then. Got himself killed attempting a burglary—shot a cop even. And now you . . . divorcing Meg, just abandoning her! You're bound and determined to kill us with shame, aren't you?"

I did not answer, thinking of Mike, and knowing Mom had much more yet to go before she wound down. "Took you in and loved you . . . ungrateful little . . . and now, you've taken Meg's best years. Always a taker, don't give nothing back . . ."

Then, as always, her attack shifted focus. "Oh, my rheumatism hurts so bad now, I can hardly get around. And I got bone spurs growing out of my backbone. Doctor says he may have to operate, but what do you care? Selfish little . . ."

This was the point where Mike and I would normally turn on the waterworks. That usually pacified her.

"Mom! Hold on. I understand how you feel."

"Understand? Hell, you can't even begin—"

"Yes, Mom . . . I hear you. I can see why you might feel the way you do about me." Her assault seemed to have lost its momentum. Hearing it was like déjà vu, my insides wanting to lurch their way onto my outsides. For the first time, it was clear to me just how pitiful her existence truly was. Yet, in seeing, did I have the courage to speak of it to her in honesty? Much of what ruined her life was easy now to see, but would she be willing to hear it from me? Given her feelings, it did not seem so.

Besides, did I really need to be this honest with her right now? Oh, she'd hear me if I took the blame, but was she capable of hearing anything else? No. She'd just hear me making her wrong. Or worse, she would twist it all into something that made her right—that made her the victim of me, her son, the slimy monster.

For a while, I struggled with my urge to speak. If I didn't say it, would anyone ever give her an opportunity to see what she didn't see? Still, I hesitated. *God! Her whole drama is so clear, but will she deal with this painful reality?*

The intuition of my heart said, *Say it!* If you love someone, you tell your truth and hold them capable of hearing you. If they won't hear it from someone they love, they won't hear it from anyone. But how to do that?

My voice still calm, I began, "Y'know, Mom, I see something about you that I don't think you see. It's something I believe is destroying your life, something you probably won't like to hear. Will you allow me to tell you what I think?"

"Well, if it's something I don't want to hear, why would I ever say *yes*?" Her sarcasm fairly dripped out of my receiver.

"Ah, Mom. Course you don't have to listen to me. It's just that this is something . . . well, something that's taken me a long time to learn about life. It's something I know you don't see. If you did, we wouldn't be having this conversation."

Her answering snort only denoted ridicule. I took a deep breath and continued anyway. "I care about you, and I really want you to hear me, but Mom . . . I don't really want to say this."

"Oh, hell," she replied in mock resignation. "Go ahead."

I wondered if she knew she really could shut me up with a simple "no." There was a temptation to ask, but I knew it would only stir the drama already in the moment. Taking a deep breath, I bit the bullet.

"Mom, all my life, since I've been with you, you've always been sick. When you weren't feeling good, the rest of us always did things to try to make you feel better or didn't do them so that you wouldn't feel worse."

Only silence answered.

"Mom . . . can you see how you've always controlled us that way . . . and how it's always gained you sympathy and attention?"

More silence.

"And Mom, don't you know that our subconscious minds are naturally set to make us right? Whatever it is we tell ourselves is what we will create in life. Is it any wonder that you were always sick?" This time, I barely paused but grimly pushed on. "Mom, can't you see how if you'd stop telling yourself how sick you are, you'd feel better . . . maybe even get well?"

"Oh . . . bullshit! That . . . that's a bunch of psycho-babble bullshit." Her words burst forth with raw aggravation. 'Hell, damn, and bullshit' were about the extent of my mother's official repertoire of profanity. And 'bullshit' was way out in the family pasture, beyond even 'horse manure.' Clearly, she was pretty annoyed with me.

"Bullshit . . . Mom?" I took a deep breath. Feeling it whoosh out helped me release my pent-up energy and maintain my calm. "Didn't you start this conversation off by telling me that I'm killing you and Dad? I'd say that—"

"That's right! And you are!" With her shriek, I jerked the phone away from my ear.

"No, Mom, I'm not! But if you insist on it being so . . ." I spoke slowly, my voice low, in a calm, regretful cadence. "Yes, I agree with you, Mom—you are dying."

"Aaaaarrrghhh!" Click.

I sat there on the side of the bed for a long moment as the phone went through its paces, first pausing in a lengthy period of silence, then the beep-beep-beeping busy tone, and finally the fast, shrill-repeating screech of a receiver off the hook.

During that time, I, too, went through my own paces—a short period of numbness, another in the resentful anger of a betrayed victim, then one of self-flagellation. Had I been too indelicate? Did I come off as self-righteous? Could I have put it better, maybe been more loving about it? Indeed, was there just a hint of revenge motivating me?

Then I called my dad at his shop and managed to get through. That conversation was much shorter and more to the point—his point. Mine was not even discussed before he, too, hung up.

Something precious was gone from my life. I felt its void fill with a dull, aching pain somewhere above and beyond the physical. A grief that seemed to center in my middle, almost like someone who had been mentally kicked in the stomach, it had that same churning, sick feeling. When I finally hung up the receiver, the tears in my eyes reflected an ache of aloneness that now was my life.

I stood and, for a long moment, leaned against the wall, trying to remain standing. The sideboards of the waterbed were not the most comfortable place to be caught when the torrent of my mother's anger was in full flood. With the needle pricks of returning circulation still stabbing at my legs and feet, I hobbled through the empty house to the living room and sat down in my place of meditation on the couch.

With deep breaths in through my nose and out my mouth, eyes closed, looking slightly upward, I relaxed. Hands on thighs, palms up, and fingers touching thumbs, I concentrated on the separate areas of my body, relaxing each completely as I dropped into level. Becoming intimate with the heartbeat within my chest, I tuned in to the rhythm of my body. Lastly, I made my connection to that part of creation the Native Americans call *Mother Earth*—becoming aware of my weight against the couch, against the concrete of the floor, against the earth beneath. Like sending roots all the way to her core, I felt my own energy fuse with that of *The Mother*. Then, with palms now open, I felt the fresh flow of shimmering, white energy wash back up in a wave of pure peace. Reaching out, I willed my mind to take me to some special place in nature, a place of serenity. I was not surprised to find myself again on the ledge above the confluence of the Fry and White Canyons.

The warmth of the morning sun against my back felt good combined with the cool, desert breeze. I didn't need to see the mud in the wash below to know of the previous day's flood, with its crazy network of cracks curling upward as each checkered section dried. The smell of it all was sharp on the breeze—damp earth, ozone, cedar, sage, and pinyon.

Ah, there's nothing like the desert after a storm. Close by, a meadowlark called out and was answered by the angry, scolding chatter of a chipmunk. Far below, the soft flutter of cottonwood leaves danced in chorus with the whisper of the pinyon pines, cedars, and the swish of Big D's cloak as he sat down beside me. My good friend and mentor, I smiled in appreciation and threw him a thought.

Thanks for coming, Big D.

"Quite the flash flood came through here last night." He adjusted his cloak and leaned out over the edge. "Remind you of anyone?"

Yeah . . . my mother.

"Usually hear a flash flood coming, though . . ."

I know. Didn't hear that one coming.

"Why not?"

I just didn't think that Meg would go to my parents with it. At least, not without telling me first.

"Yeah?"

Well, somehow it just seems kind of traitorous, like being stabbed in the back. I trusted Meg.

"Kinda makes you a victim, doesn't it?"

No. I'd have to see myself as a victim before I can be one. I'd rather get this lesson quickly and move on. She just did what she did. No choice but to accept it. Can't change the past. I just need to know why.

"It's really a no-brainer, Jeff." He turned toward me. The polished ivory of his skull, with its perpetual grin, seemed to grin more widely, mockingly. "But then, you have your own way of turning off your brain where Meg is concerned, making excuses that let her off the hook. What you said about 'no choice' is true. But 'needing to know?' No. Truth is, you don't *want* to know because you *already do* know."

What does that mean?

"C'mon, Jeff! This last year, your marriage has been like a downhill skier. Haven't you noticed how Meg flits back and forth through the gates? Don't you know that's just her game? In life, there are no gates. Unlike you, she's afraid to face the truth head-on."

I'm not sure I follow.

"It is the coward's way to flit around seeking validation from other cowards doing the same thing. When has your mother ever faced life head-on?"

Never. I shrugged. *But my Dad...*

"What about him?"

Well, Meg had to have been talking to him also. It seems he feels the same as Mom, and he's the kind of man who doesn't take shit off anybody. And, maybe he's just playing to her drama.

"How so?"

Well, where it involved me, he seemed all the more to feel a need to defend her. When I talked to him, I perceived only anger and "righteous" condemnation—and testosterone. Although, I've never made any comments aimed at anything other than clearing the air between him and me. The best he called me was "coward," and his most peaceful offer was to "... kick my ass" if I ever darkened his door again.

"Really? Those are tough words." Big D spread his hands wide. "Then why is he such a ball-less jellyfish around your mother?"

Like I used to be around Meg.

"Exactly." His spread palms now clenched up except for the index fingers, which he pointed toward me like twin six-shooters. "Now do you have some small understanding of your Dad, Jeff? Something you might remember, no matter how distant he may remain. He knows. Can you see why he says nothing?"

Yes.

"And your mother? You came into this meditation questioning your actions in how you dealt with her."

I'm not sure that everything I said to her—I paused and ducked my head in guilty admission—*was totally loving.*

"Jeff, you did your best. It is the nature of everyone, sort of a built-in feature. You always do your best, given your current need and want for knowing the truth and your ability to accept it."

Truth? Yeah, I told her my truth, all right. But isn't my truth a little different from other people's . . . from hers?

"Truth is truth, Jeff. Only the understanding of it varies. Yours that you shared with your mother was very accurate, and you said it with pure compassion and great understanding."

I don't get it. I grimaced. *It didn't feel so pure.*

"The first law, Jeff, what is it?"

I am the creator of my life.

"That was all you chose to share with her. Very mature, very compassionate."

Are you putting me on, Big D?

"The laws are sacred, Jeff. You know I would never put you on about them."

Then what do you mean about it being "all I chose to share with her?"

"Did you tell her how unfair she was being in never even asking for your side of things? Did you share that you felt like she was throwing you under the bus? Or maybe more accurately, throwing you out—out onto the icy steps of Bingham Canyon? Ahh . . . you do remember about Bingham, don't you? You wrote about it in your other book, did you not?"

She was only trying to teach me—I shrugged—*or maybe give me incentive to learn to tie my shoes.*

"Teach you? Or kill something in you, something that was long since killed in her? You were only four, remember?"

Oh hell, Big D. I hashed all that shit out while writing that first book.

"Exactly! So why did you not feel a need to hash it out directly with her?"

All that stuff . . . it's about me making myself into a victim. Sure, I was a victim back then but reject it for what it is now.

"Oh? What is it?"

It's bullshit! No one can accept being a victim, not when they are living the Law of the Creator.

"So, Jeff, do you see how mature you are becoming? To cut through all your bullshit and go straight to the pure truth? Do you see your courage in sharing what you shared with her, even though you knew the price you would pay?"

Yes. I rubbed at the weariness behind my eyes, then leaned forward to gaze into the depths at the red trickle of silt-laden water as it flowed down the wash below. *Ah, Big D, it is so peaceful in my meditations. I love coming here. My life out there seems like a flash flood. Hard to think that one came through this peaceful place so recently.*

"This place in your meditation represents nature. In nature, what is, just is."

Ah . . . I gestured with a sweep of my arm out over the abyss, *but a person could get killed if caught in these canyons with no way to get out during a flash flood.*

"True. But do you remember all those times when you, as a boy, braved them anyway?"

Ah, yes.

"Why, Jeff? Why did you do that?"

The adventure, the excitement, the . . . I ran out of words and raised my shoulders before letting them sag in futility.

"The life? Living life?"

Big D, it wasn't as if we didn't know the danger or the signs to watch out for.

"What signs?"

You know . . . the summer monsoon clouds in the distance, the smell of the air, and if one but listened carefully, the echo on the sandstone cliff would telegraph the churning of the flood waters. Besides, the rains rarely came during the morning. For one who knows these canyons, it was relatively safe.

"Ah, that is true, Jeff, but was it so safe while you were learning?"

Okay, you got me there. I raised my eyebrows, cocked my head, and nodded. *We did have to run for it a few times.*

"It is the same with people."

How so?

"Did you not know from long ago the lightning of your mother's anger? Did you not smell the ozone of it in the air? And divorce? Was that a wise place to venture with her on a summer afternoon in life? How accepting did you expect her to be when you were doing the exact same thing she feared her own husband might want to do?"

Oh, I see. I nodded in agreement. Then came his next revelation.

"And Meg? Let's take a hard look at the truth about what I said earlier, about how you didn't *want* to know about Meg but how you *did* know anyway."

What? W-what didn't I want to know?

"Did you not know of the long-ago storm when she chose you among all the men in her life? Men who did not know of one another? Men of whom *you* were simply the least unacceptable—and that only because *you* fulfilled her need for control? That's right . . . *control*, Jeff. Did you not hear the angry rumbling of that coming down, echoing off your years? Did you not know you would have to run . . . or die?"

I sighed, becoming aware that I'd momentarily stopped breathing. *You're right. It was exactly so.* Again, *I wasn't listening. Just didn't want to know the truth.*

"Yet, in the process of it all, haven't you learned some awesome things about the rules of life, about life's truths? Things you would never have known otherwise?"

I heard it in his voice and knew he was setting me up for . . . something. Some ribbing, maybe? *Yes, I have learned much about life and its rules, and whatever you've got that's tweaking your humor, just spit it out.*

"Yes, you know much more than most about life, but you're not above it. Don't let that stop you from being human, from seeking out the love of other women, drinking from the cool springs bubbling up in the shady twilight from deep in the canyons of their lives." A warm glow emanated from the empty sockets of his eyes as his elbow reached out to give my own a boney nudge. "You will need them when the hot winds of your coming sorrow pepper its dust into your eyes and threaten to dry out your soul."

Poetic, Big D, but I'm not sure I know what you mean by all that.

"I mean, right now, maybe you just need to get laid. The winds will come. They always do."

Comb Ridge, Utah—Present Day

Today is the kind of day that makes most people feel good about just being alive. For me, the pain is making that a hard thing to feel. Big D materializes on the ledge next to me. As usual, I can read the looks on his naked skull. What he has to tell me I know will not make this day any better for me.

"Jeff, as you understand life, what part of it do I represent to you?"

Well, you represent my connection to that Higher Power most call God—the highest and best part of me, the part that exists on that higher level.

"So, am I 'The Grim Reaper,' the evil entity that drags people off to hell, or 'The Angel of Death' that takes people to heaven?"

I suppose you would be both those things, were there a heaven or hell outside those that we here create for ourselves on Earth.

"So, in the reality of it, who exactly am I in relation to you?"

Oh my God! This is sounding ominous. I don't know what you're getting at here, Big D. We've discussed all this. There is no heaven or hell aside from what we create here in this life. And the afterlife? Yes, you do escort our consciousness from this plane of existence to the higher realm where we are as drops of water in the sea of that higher consciousness most like to call God, where everyone is as one. So, what gives? Y'know we are getting into that area where most folks run screaming into the night when finding out that their religion is bullshit.

"Ah, Jeff, that is exactly why. Religions are not bullshit. Y'see, this level is where lies infinity—something that is defined on your level but is impossible to 'know' on your side of the veil. What is the first Spiritual Law again?"

I am the creator. *Why do you ask?*

"Religions are the creation of man wanting to use God to control his fellow man—true. But religions are also man's creation on how he wants to see God. Creating on your level is like swimming through the cesspool. It takes time, is a slower process and, for most of you, flat out stinks. Don't cha think that creating on this side might be just a little faster, a little more powerful? On this level, given infinity, don't cha think there just might be a Southern Baptist heaven with a heavy-handed God? Or how about a Mormon heaven with its three degrees of judgmentalism? How about a Catholic heaven, and hell, complete with fiery misery and brimstone? All the energy is here, the positive and the negative. In the infinite bosom of the Higher Power, you always have free agency. On the Earth plane of existence, you know that. Don't cha think it will be the same on this level—times infinity?"

Oh my God, Big D. I don't know what to think of all this. Holy shit! This just boggles my mind. But why are you telling me this?

"What you don't understand, Jeff, is why it is so important to me that you complete your mission." He ducks his head, and his eye sockets burn bright in that way they do when what he is saying is crucial. "Now, time and space are open to me, but the past is set and the future is composed of possibilities. You need to know a few facts, or this won't end well."

I don't understand, Big D.

"Look, Jeff,

> FACT—You are likely going to be here longer than anyone could expect to survive.
>
> FACT—You are in charge of your actions. Among the infinity of possibilities, I can't see your future until you make them.
>
> FACT—Your resources are limited here on this ledge.
>
> FACT—To survive, you must conserve what you have available.
>
> FACT—Your actions must all be made by your own determination. I cannot tell you anything more right now, other than on my side of the veil, you will have all the power you could want . . . instantly!"

With that, he flickers out of sight, as usual, leaving me with eyes bulging and jaw gaping.

F.U.C.K. The word is from an old English acronym—For Unlawful Carnal Knowledge. But in whose mind was such a God-given, natural thing made into something so evil as to be termed carnal? And who was the control freak who made it unlawful? How many minds were damaged by banning such knowledge? Wouldn't it have been so much more nurturing to mankind had the acronym instead been—For Unmitigated Connecting Knowledge? Be that so—or not. And some do claim it is not. But then, they're probably just the down-in-the-mouth fans of the rock group Van Halen.

           Redneck Spirituality—Book Two

CHAPTER TEN

Have Mercy Baby!

Wednesday, June 1, 1994—
After Karen's Group Therapy Meeting

Her voice was husky. "With me? You want to make love with me?"

  "Jackie, you've never made any secret of the fact that you wanted me in that way." I set my wine down on her coffee table. "Did I misread those looks you've been giving me at group all this time?"

  "But we're friends."

  "I know."

  "And you've only been separated from Meg for such a short time."

  "I know."

  "But you're so much older, what . . . seventeen, eighteen years?"

  "I know." I glance around at the opulence of her home, at the little statues and expensive knickknacks gracing the shelves and on the mantle above her grandiose fireplace. *Am I fucking nuts to do this?*

"It would never work between us."

"I know. Look! Did I misconstrue your feelings, Jackie?" I took her hand and looked deeply into her eyes. "Let me lay it out."

"Please do. I'm confused. I know how much you love Meg, and I know you to be honest and honorable. It's true, in inviting you tonight, I did sort of have it in the back of my mind to seduce you. But—"

"But?"

"But . . . well, not like this. In a week or two, you'll just go back to her. I know." Ducking her head, she looked up with raised eyebrows. "Been there, done that."

"Maybe so, except—"

"Jeff, I don't want to end up as some secret memory you need to keep hidden. Someone who the very thought of will bring a sense of shame to all that is honorable in you."

"Jackie, stop." I touched my finger to her lips. "All that you said before is true. It's exactly for those reasons that I want my post-marriage cherry to be taken by you. And while I would never blab it around, it will never be some secret shame."

"But—"

"Jackie, you once said that you saw me as someone strong . . . 'fearless and noble' I think were your words."

"Yes."

"Well, I am none of that. The truth is that I *need* to make love to you. And it is *not* about anything noble . . . or fearless . . . maybe not even sexual." I sighed. "You see, you're damned sure right about one thing. In a week or two, I'll cave and go running back to Meg."

"What?"

"That's right. But if we make love, you and me, I won't be able to. Meg always made a big deal about that. If I ever made it with another woman, she'd never take me back—ever!"

"But, I don't—"

"Jackie, please. I know it isn't fair to you. In fact, I would be using you, but I don't know anyone I would rather do this with than you." I slipped to the floor, kneeled beside her, and buried my face into the cloth of her slacks. My hot breath mingled with the spicy dampness between her thighs.

Her heady aroma tantalized my senses when next I breathed.

"And I want to taste you . . ."

"Oh God!" she groaned. "Karen Moore warned me about mercy-fucking you!"

"Jackie"—my eyes rose to meet hers—"I . . ." *Oh shit! She's a woman. How can she ever understand something so cheesy? Hell, it puts the cheese in machismo.* "That's exactly what I need to move on in my life, and I don't know if there is anything I have to give you in yours."

"You have, Jeff." Something glimmered, soft and loving in her look. "You already have."

Closing my eyes, I again buried my face in the giddy essence emanating from the wet spot between her legs. From above, I heard the soft whispering of her blouse being removed. "Come to the bedroom." She said the words, as if her breath somehow hung in the back of her throat.

At the bedroom, I paused in the doorway as she stepped over to the bed and brushed aside a couple of stuffed toys, then gestured with a sweep of her hand. "Get comfortable . . . I'll need a moment." She stepped to the adjoining bathroom, and glancing over her shoulder, lips curled into one of those inscrutable, female looks, she added, "To freshen up."

Soon naked and in her bed, my eyes took in the splendor of the surroundings. Jackie's bedroom was no less well furbished than the rest of her home. For a single woman, working as a rep for some pharmaceutical company, Jackie did very well. My own mechanic's pay could never handle anything such as this.

Just then, Jackie stepped from the bathroom. My breath caught at the sight of her girlish features and trim, woman's body, and something within me almost wished this could be somehow more lasting.

Joining me in bed, Jackie's lips touched mine with a fierce passion that said it clearly. All her reservations were now cancelled. For long moments we lay there, our bodies, our lips, fully entwined. Our tongues did things together that mine had almost forgotten could be done.

Then mine, flitting out from between her impassioned lips, began its journey down—down to her breasts, to the hard, little nubs of her nipples. Encircling each in turn, it worked its way again and again around the pink of her areola. All the while, a hand cupped the other breast, jiggling it like an inverted bowl of warm, flesh-flavored Jell-O.

With a light pinch of my teeth and a quick but strong suck, her nipple popped free, eliciting a deep, throaty groan. Then again, my lips resumed their downward march, pausing only briefly to nibble and lick at the dimple of her belly button. Then on down—down into the soft tangle of a blonde, thornless hedge, forming a trimmed triangle above her pubes.

Once more, my senses reeled with the renewed scent of her love. Gently, my hands parted her nether lips to give my tongue, like a wine taster, its first gentle sampling—very slightly dry . . . rich bouquet . . . yet full-bodied. My fingers parted her folds to drink her in more deeply.

Yet, much as I resisted, I could not help but compare Jackie with Meg, so much was I struck by the differences. Hell, I'd always had to beg Meg if I were to do this with her. Oral sex was something her traditional Korean upbringing said was sick and depraved. Yet for me, it always felt so natural.

Beneath her sparsely thatched strip of pubic hair, Jackie's vagina was tight-lipped. As my tongue probed and caressed, it loosened up, and the little bud of her clitoris swelled and hardened. Within just a few moments, Jackie was gasping in tiny sobs and squirming in the throes of her passions. *My God!* After twenty-five years married to Meg, I'd almost forgotten women could orgasm—and so easily.

I've often wondered what sex was for Meg, why she *seemed* to enjoy it, yet never climaxed. But Jackie? Jackie awed and even somewhat frightened me. She was very different in the intensity of her response. My own response was equally different—and frightening.

With Meg, and those few women before her, I was like Tarzan of the jungle. My organ was always hard enough to beat out messages on the jungle drums. Yet, with Jackie's orgasm came a sudden awareness—I was not ready for full intercourse, not even close. I hung as limp as the jungle vines. Jackie didn't seem to mind. She took no notice of my limp dick as her passions abated.

She felt smooth as butter to my finger, as gently it probed alone the intimate depths of her sex . . . then was joined by another. Soon, both were massaging gently but firmly at that spot just inside and to the top—the one right behind the pubic bone that some call the 'G spot.' At the same time, I lightly tasted the folds around and over her clitoris. Within moments, Jackie's back arched off the mattress. Her moaning changed to incoherent screams as she came long and hard—and very wetly—then again, once more in quick succession. Still . . . *Goddamn!* I was still soft.

"Jackie, I . . . uh . . . uh . . . I don't know why, but I'm not ready." Jackie glanced down at my stubborn member, then smiled mischievously.

"We'll just have to do something about that," she said, then pushed me onto my back and took me into her mouth. She worked at it softly, gently, and wetly for several moments before I felt a stirring, then several more before I was hard enough to sit up and slip on a rubber.

Facing her, I introduced hers to mine, and for a while, just enjoyed the feelings of rubbing it gently up and down through the warm slickness of her, its head just inside her folds. Nearing full erection, I slipped it in and began a long, slow, rhythmic stroking, in . . . and out.

Jackie came one more time, though not as intensely urgent as before. My own orgasm was not earthshaking. How could it be? A part of me could find no joy in what this event would surely come to mean.

Laying there next to her in that post-sexual la-la-land, I thanked her. "Y'know, Jackie, I think maybe Meg has me pegged right. I'm not a strong man, not someone she can admire. Ripping out my heart and holding it out to her in offering—that's something I've done over and over with her. She doesn't admire the tears of a man. She sees only weakness in them. Admiration is not something she'll ever be capable of feeling toward me. I love her too much to just give up, and I am not strong enough to accept this as just 'what is' and walk away. I needed this from you." I stopped talking a long moment as I gazed into her tear-filled eyes, then finished with my appreciation.

"Thank you, Jackie. I know Karen said not to, but thank you for mercy-fucking me."

* * *

I closed the notebook from which I'd been transcribing. In those early days, I wrote in longhand whenever the opportunity presented itself between car repair jobs at work. Now I save and close the writing program on my computer—the same one Meg had so graciously purchased in her one attempt at support. I shook my head at the sad enigma of it, then recoiled in startled awareness when Big D spoke.

"That's it? That's all you're going to write about Jackie?"

Well . . . yeah. Isn't gratitude where I need to go to bring a relationship to completion? And dammit! Stop sneaking up on me.

"Yeah? Lost on the la-la-land of your sexuality, were you? C'mon, Jeff." He nudged my shoulder with a boney elbow. "She was more than just a quick fuck to you—more even than the 'fuck you' she was meant to be for Meg." Another nudge. "Well, wasn't she?"

Yes, she was. I smiled at the memory. *Though it only lasted a few months, ours was an honest relationship. There wasn't anything we couldn't discuss. In fact, I even shared my concerns about how I'd never had problems getting it up before—well, except that one time with that pregnant prostitute in Nogales. Yes, that part used to bother me a lot.*

"Ah, but you know what that was about, don't you?"

Dunno, Big D. Maybe it was just about a GI who drank too much booze.

"Ever consider maybe it was about me?"

You . . . Big D?

"Yeah, me." The glow from one eye socket seemed to wink. "Me . . . keeping you from getting some cock-rotting disease."

Yeah, well . . . thanks—I think. Is he putting me on?

His only response was that deep, rumbling chuckle that again sounded as if from the bottom of a barrel in which his voice seemed permanently imprisoned.

I shook my head, took a deep breath, let it out in a rush, and continued.

But with Jackie, I think it was fear. Fear does strange things to a man. I knew what to expect from Meg, but from other women . . . hell, that took time. My member, though it never failed to function, never functioned at peak performance with Jackie. She never did get "all the beef," but she did get all the tongue she wanted and seemed to prefer it.

"Yes, Jeff, point is, you did what a man must. You stepped through your fear. Matter of fact, for a time, you and Jackie did a lot of fancy stepping. But what was it she gave you that you needed most? What is it with her that you now need to clear?"

Clear, Big D? Clearing is about bringing my part of a relationship to the space of love. Jackie and I never left that space. I don't see what I could possibly need to clear with her.

"Oh, there is something . . . that last, crucial step to clearing isn't complete."

What's that?

"Learn, Jeff. You must take it to learning."

I'm not sure—

"Look, it doesn't matter how you initially judge your experience of someone, good or bad. Point is, you haven't grown until you've seen clearly how they have served you."

But how does one ever really know?

"You've already said it—gratitude. When you've taken your feelings to 'grateful.'"

Oh? I thought I had.

"No, Jeff. The question is, what did Jackie give you for which *you* feel *most* grateful?"

Well, bottom line, Jackie gave me a warm, beautiful body and a loving heart to help me over the worst of the pain. Just being able to talk with someone who cared was enough. The anguish, the wailing into the night? Those things I saved for when I was alone.

"Oh, gag! Doesn't sound like you were all that sharing, open, or honest."

Jackie seemed to think so. In fact, she once said what I gave her was the experience of an honest man, said she'd never known a man like me, that all those she'd ever known only wanted their own needs met. They didn't want to fill, or even hear, of hers and weren't above any amount of dishonesty in getting what they wanted.

"And you were different?"

Jackie thought so. She told me she'd never known a man who believed in himself enough to show up as he really was or to talk with her from that level of his heart, which she knew in hers to be truth.

"Pretty flowery. So, how did you feel when she said all that?"

So . . . okay. I was flattered.

"But . . ."

But I was not so sure I deserved to be held in such high regard. I couldn't remember anyone ever holding such a viewpoint about me. In fact, my parents, Meg—all those I loved the most—seemed to share views of me that were much closer to how Jackie described those other men in her life. Had I changed? Yes. I took a deep breath and, shaking my head, blew it out. *Maybe. But clearly, Meg never saw me in the light by which Jackie looked.*

"Ah, now you've got it."

Got what?

"Esteem! Jackie was the first to give you that—something no other person you've ever loved has given you. Until her, that meant *NO other person*, including YOU yourself."

Esteem?

"Yes, now you've got it. The reflection in the mirror of her was what was developing in you—*self-esteem*! So, how did it end?"

Jackie soon found the "one great love" of her life, that someone whom she insisted reminded her of me. I raised my eyebrows and cocked my head. *I suspected he was simply young, unlike me.*

"You sound jealous, Jeff."

No, not jealous. Well, except perhaps of their youth. No, I gave her my blessings, simply made love to her one last time, and left.

Comb Ridge, Utah—Present Day

I pull my sleeping bag around me to stave off this cold breeze and remind myself—again—that it is time to put up the tent. I've been holding that off, knowing what a clusterfuck of pain it will mean trying to crawl around setting it up. Such a normally simple task is now complicated by this miserable leg. I force myself to move around. My lack of mobility is becoming the utmost danger to my survival.

Even wearing my leather jacket and chaps, it is becoming hard to stay warm, as gazing out over the gulf of Comb Ridge I become aware of the fog.

Fog? What the hell. Rarely does that happen here in the desert. The air is generally too dry. But there it is, a white vapor swirl that somehow is tinged here and there by violet. My body seems engulfed, floating in it. Surreal, yet the ache of hunger is very real. It twists at my gut with spasmodic demand. And the pain, the ever-present pain, is there in my leg, though thankfully, it is but a dull throb compared to the searing fire it once was. Yet permeating it all is something more, something ever more persistent. What? A longing?

Then from within the mist, something moves. A shape, disturbingly feminine, like my Meg, yet not. The face is indistinct. Try as I might, I cannot make it out, yet I know it is pleasing.

And the eyes . . . I become aware of the eyes. The rest is blurred by the mist, but they are distinct! An odd, beautiful blue. No, more gray than blue, with a silvery sheen. They seem to be searching, and though, somehow, I know they don't see me, there is something familiar about them. Is it only the longing I see reflected there—a longing like unto my own?

Then strangely, I open my eyes to sunshine reflecting in under the overhang from the cliffs around. Big D, sitting at my side, speaks. "How's it feel?"

What? How's what feel? Still groggy from sleep, I screw up my face in confusion.

"Jackie. I'm talking about how she rejected you because of your age difference."

How should it feel? We both knew it wasn't going to work between us. It was just a temporary thing, something we could do for one another.

"A mercy fuck? That's not a 'for one another' thing. Was it really that one-sided? C'mon, admit it. You wished it could have been more."

More, Big D? No, it couldn't be.

"But you wished it could, didn't you?"

Yeah. Sometimes I did.

"Time, Jeff. This life is all about time. It's all you've got. Why couldn't you both have admitted you wanted to be together, even knowing it wouldn't last forever? Would that time together have brought you both joy?"

Well, yeah. I scratch my head. *I can't speak for her, but for me? I suppose it would.*

"Would that have been following your joy, for you?"

My God! I didn't realize it, but it seems I broke my promise to you.

"It's okay, Jeff. I let it slide at the time because you're right." He chuckles. "It would not have been the same for her. But we *will* take this up," he nods down and toward the side, and with his sight glowing purposefully up at me, adds, "later."

What the hell does he mean by that?

I am about to ask but he is gone.

Love? It's not how you feel about someone you've just met, someone with whom you are starting a relationship. The *truth* is about how you feel when it has ended. Doesn't matter what has happened in the meantime—all that, doesn't mean *shit*. Fact is, if you don't love them and wish them the very best in the end, *then you never loved them at all.*

Redneck Spirituality—Book Two

CHAPTER ELEVEN

Wishing You the Best of Times in the Worst of Times

Saturday, June 11, 1994—12:00 Noon

"What did you want to see me about, Jeff?" Meg glanced at her watch. "My twelve o'clock should be here anytime."

My coffee cup made a nervous rattle as I set it on the table. "Look, Meg. I'm not sure now's the time to be discussing stuff, y'know?" The tilting of my head indicated the others in the foyer—Sook Ja and some other woman I didn't recognize. "I was hoping we could go have a bite of lunch. Maybe be alone . . ."

"It will have to be now, unless you want to stop all this coo-wazy shit and let me move back home."

"Why do you always have to see me as 'crazy,' Meg?"

"Well, this separation thing didn't work the first time. Did it?"

"You don't understand. This is not another trial separation."

"Seems pretty much the same to me . . . coo-wazy."

"No, Meg!" I shook my head. "It's not. It's a divorce, and we have a lot of stuff to discuss."

"Like what?" Hand on her hips, she faced me down.

"Well, like who gets what. We have a whole life full of stuff to divide."

"Like what?" She folded her arms across her chest, as if preparing for battle.

"Oh, there's the household furniture, the car and truck, the boat, the tax refund, and money that's in our bank account. We have to come to an agreement on all of it, Meg."

"I already have the furniture I want. And there is no money in the bank."

"Yes, I've become acutely aware of that. I think we need to discuss that, too."

"And the girls say you need to talk to my lawyer about the rest—the alimony and all that."

"Meg . . ." I glanced at the mirrored wall behind her. It revealed Meg's partner across the room behind me, flipping through her Korean magazine without looking at it. In the eyes meeting mine, there was a glint of smug satisfaction. Deliberately, mine returned to Meg. "It's not that I don't still love you. I don't want this to be any harder than it needs to be for you. We can handle this . . . just you and me. You don't need to be listening to other people." Meg glanced over at Sook Ja. The mirror revealed a quick signal, a negative wave of a hand. "Look, we've always been honest with each other. Well, haven't we?"

"Yes," she said, not quite meeting my eye.

"Then listen to what I am going to say."

"I'm listening."

"About alimony—in the state of Nevada, if both parties work, there is no alimony."

"We'll see about that."

"Yes, you check on it. Now, here is our tax refund check." I held it out to her. "It's for twenty-four hundred and change."

She snatched it from my hand.

"It needs both our signatures to be cashed." I pointed a finger at it. "See, it's in both our names."

She looked closely at it. "Well, I'm not going to sign it."

"Huh-mmm." I frowned. "Just hear me out, please."

"I'm listening."

"Since you took all the money in our account, I need two hundred to pay a bill that's due. The other twenty-two hundred you can have. That should hold you until I can sell the boat. It's worth about five thousand. That, too, you can have." Meg's mouth was now open, but nothing was coming out. Now she seemed at a loss. I continued. "Oh, and don't write any more checks. I closed our account."

"You going to give me this money?"

"Yes. Like I said, I want this to be as easy for you as possible." Meg ducked her head toward the check in her hands, her expression suddenly unreadable as I continued. "The truck's paid for, but I need it."

"The car?"

"Is yours. And yes, I will finish making the payments for you."

"What about the house? I suppose you get that?"

"No. You can have it if you want. We just refinanced last year, remember? If we try to sell it now, there won't even be enough to pay the realtor." I shrugged. "But if you want it, you're going to have to make the payments, and it will be all yours. If not, then it's mine."

Her eyes rose to mine, flashing. "We'll see about that!"

"Look, this next part isn't easy. Just hear me out." I resisted the urge to frown. Dealing with Meg's moods was like walking on egg shells. I could already hear them crackling. "Okay, that about covers our assets. Now, we have about twenty-four thousand in credit card debt."

"I told you to stop using those damn things!"

"Yes." Another deep breath in, then out with exasperated force. My sighs were becoming a part of my vocabulary. "Yes, you did, and it is mostly stuff I bought. Give me your cards and I'll pay for it all. Okay, now that should be all of it."

In the silence that followed, we stared at one another. Finally, she began. "I'll need to speak to a lawyer. My friends say—"

"Look," I interrupted. "You and I just need to trust one another here. Lawyers are in business to get us to fight. The more we do, the more they get to take. I have so little in assets to give you, but whatever money I can get, I want you to have. Don't let the lawyers take it all."

She glanced at her friends, and I didn't need the mirror to know their hands were frantically waving in disapproval. I continued. "In the end, if you force it to be decided by a judge, they will take what the lawyers don't, sell it, and split it down the middle. You get half and I get half. That means you will wind up with half the bills."

Her face turned ashen. "But this is so little."

"I know, Meg. I'm really sorry that this is all our life together has amounted to. Please just trust me and sign the check."

"But can't we just go back like it was before?"

"Ah shit, honey. You've been so unhappy married to me . . . I've seen it in your face. Just look through the pictures you took from our scrapbooks—you took every photo that you were in. Was there even one where you were smiling? The only one I remember was of you in our son's arms, being whirled around. I wished it had been taken with you in my arms."

"But—"

"Yes, but it wasn't. Besides"—I gritted my teeth—"it's too late."

"Too late? What you mean, 'too late?'"

"I've moved on, Meg."

"Moved on? What you mean, 'moved on?'"

"Well, there's been another woman." For a long moment, she stared at me. I shrugged in discomfort, and my words seemed somehow lame as I finished, "I don't think you want me now."

Meg's eyes dropped suddenly to the check. Pulling a pen from her apron, and with a deliberate scrawl, she signed it, then threw it in my face. "You bring me back the twenty-two hundred and I give you credit cards. Den I no wan see you ebber again!" Her accent was back, full force and cold. Yet, for just an instant before she turned, I could have sworn there was a flash of something soft and vulnerable. But then, gazing at her rigid back as she stomped away, I knew clearly—she was gone from my life.

Comb Ridge, Utah—Present Day

"The day you filed was Tuesday, August 30, 1994, wasn't it, Jeff?"

Yes, Big D. I grunt in memory of it and I pause, watching the little bats in spasmodic flight against the early evening sky. *We didn't sign the divorce papers until mid-October.*

"And . . ."

Oh, Jesus! I didn't think it would hurt so much! There was plenty of time to get used to the idea, but still . . . I pause to suck in my breath and notice a coolness in the evening breeze—almost cold.

"And . . ."

And by then, I'd done so much personal growth work. Hell, I'd gone to so many seminars that everyone who knew me before thought I'd turned into some kind of seminar junkie.

"So why did you attend so many?" The glow from his eye sockets intensifies slightly.

Well, they were about getting real, about allowing one's true feelings to show through. I pause, remembering what those times were like for me. *The kinds of things . . . feelings . . . well, those things you don't normally let others see.*

"And . . ."

And, well, Karen, the facilitator, was always saying that, "To feel is to heal." I don't know where she got that, but it's kind of the basic theme of her seminars.

"And is it true?"

Yes, you know it is, Big D. But—

"But?" He still sits at the edge of the cliff, his leg bones dangling over a boulder-strewn slope hundreds of feet below in Comb Ridge Wash. Now he leans back comfortably onto his boney elbows, and with his head cocked toward me, he continues his mostly mono-syllable cross-examination. The intense burn in his sight seems to draw me out, to say things I might otherwise leave unsaid.

Certainly, Karen and her seminars were the place to be then, for me. Stuff we did seemed to just reach into one's psyche and rip the guts out for all to see. Maybe it was the open honesty part of it that was needed for me to heal.

"Yes . . . well, it is the normal human condition to seek validation from others." He smiles and there is a certain sadness in it. "Once a person truly loves another, and it doesn't work out between them," he shrugs then says, "don't know how much more alone one can be."

What? What do you mean?

"I mean that those guts . . . they're like a bucket of worms all squirming and slithering around in your head, not in your belly." There is now a little humor added to the sadness of his grin. "They're mostly just a slimy tangle of all the 'if onlys,' and the 'what ifs,' and the 'why couldn't we justs.' They won't leave until you let them out and set them free. You get my meaning?"

Yes, Big D, if only I didn't.

"Ah, and what about when Karen did those 'How Do *You* Do War' exercises in her Inner Quest Seminars? Did they help you to feel and to heal?"

Look, Big D, I know it seems kind of "pussy" of me, but it was dark and most people cried during it anyway. I duck my head, realizing how it would look outside the seminar. *Well, in the seminar . . . it's just . . . well, like kind of a safe place to let out your feelings and be okay with it. Oh, a few referred to me as "the screamer," but no one ever said it in meanness or even to my face. Some have since told me that my example encouraged them to also be real.*

"Real?"

You know, setting your true feelings free. Not so easy in front of others. There is no other place in our society where you can do that, unless you order a padded truck and have your sleeves tied together behind your back.

"That's true, Jeff. Or, you could take it out on the desert—add a touch of your own agony in chorus to the howls of the coyotes."

Yeah.

"And, too, you could just retire to the innermost bathroom of your house to exchange the pain in your heart for the pain of your fists bruised on a tile-covered, concrete floor. Then, bathed in sweat and tears, you could curl into a tight ball, like a fetus rebirthed in pain."

You saw that, too? I close my eyes and, ducking my head, let my breath hiss out while I slowly shake my head. *Yes, of course you did.*

"Of course."

Then why didn't you—

"Comfort you?" He sits up and looks directly at me. The glow of his sight, though directed in a tight beam, is softer as is the impression I receive from his perpetual grin.

Well . . . yes.

"Save you from your pain, as mankind seems to think is such a *loving* thing to do? We've been over that one, remember?"

Yeah, Big D, we have.

"Karen is correct! To feel is to heal! In fact, it is one of the laws."

Laws? I don't remember that one.

"You might call it the Law of the Conduit."

Tell me.

"Simply stated, **The energy must flow**."

Must flow . . . I pause. *Yeah, I do remember something like that. Just didn't think that one was all that important.*

"Oh, it is, Jeff—very. You were not meant to be vessels for holding energy, but more like channels for directing it. All those angry, mean, painful feelings of fear . . . If you don't feel them, acknowledge what they're about for you, and then let them go, they'll stay. And they *will* cause dis-ease. Your pain will do the same." He chuckles. "Ha! If you don't let it go, it will begin eating you alive."

I know, but what about the energy of love? Isn't it healthy to hold on to that?

"No, not really. Even love energy must be given back out in order for more to flow in."

He falls silent, and for a time, I watch the moon where it hangs between the twin buttes of Bears Ears off in the distance. I remember the times poaching deer there with my father during my days as a child in Fry Canyon. *Ah, those good old days, but then there were those that were not so good. Kinda like these days, high up on this ledge—this ledge spatially within sight of those good times. The best of times in my face here, mocking the worst of times. Life's about the lessons, and I haven't a clue about this one.* Finally, the thought that nags at my mind is released.

　　　Big D?

　　　"Yes?"

　　　There are times when we can help someone through their pain without saving them from it, aren't there?

　　　"Yes."

　　　How do we tell the difference?

　　　"It begins when someone reaches out to you, when their pain—physical or mental—is more than they're strong enough to bear. Then, well, you'll feel it in your heart and just 'know.' And you'll reach back, not to save, but rather to add your own strength to theirs."

　　　I see.

　　　"No, Jeff, you don't. It is the same as you did in those seminars—laid your pain out there in truth and honesty. That was you asking and being boosted up by the love of others all around."

　　　Yeah, I never saw it that way.

　　　"Now, here, this ledge is your testing ground. There will be times when you will need to reach out for my support. In fact, you already have." He points a boney digit at my thigh. "That bone . . . who showed you how to set it? Who was it that erased the pain from your memory?"

　　　Reaching out, Big D? How about this? Whatever this fucking lesson is about, I've not a clue. Can you help me with that one?

　　　"I have. So far, you've not been accepting what I've offered. Your lessons are always a matter of self-discovery. The lesson offered on this ledge amounts to everything we both have yearned for throughout this lifetime. No one has the right—including me—to interrupt that process for another. Saving is always about you doing just that. So, no, I won't save you here. Truth is, when you are not selfishly trying to save other people, you are helping one another. For those who have love in their hearts, it just happens, and often you don't even know it."

Uh . . . yeah. I guess.

"Remember the law, ***Everyone in your life is there, bearing you a gift of learning.*** Karen suggested you write the letter—a gift of healing for you to give yourself. You never realized how you were giving it to Meg, raising her energy and that of the whole universe as well. And now with this next chapter, we come to Eve. You helped her, but knowing these laws, you never sought to save her. Big change, and to your credit, you didn't even try."

Sometimes with others, it is not about accepting them or loving unconditionally. It is merely about what is—about what their integrity is. In my experience with them, are they someone to whom I would give my trust? Given my experience of what they want, what they say, and what they do . . . is it all the same?

Redneck Spirituality—Book Four

CHAPTER TWELVE

Is Love Such a Hard Thing to Swallow?

Eve—her name was Evelyn, but she preferred being called Eve. I remember the first time Big D and I discussed her. Sitting on a lawn chair on my patio, I watched the lights of Las Vegas beyond the darker shadow of Big D filling up the other lawn chair.

He sparked the conversation off with a simple inquiry. "Tell me about Eve." As usual, I answered him in the manner we most often conversed—silently, in my mind.

Ah, yes . . . Eve. I sighed. *We met at a Toastmasters meeting one night. Likely, I only noticed her because my mind was preset on search mode. Her features were regular—more cute than pretty—and her figure medium, though slightly robust in all the right places. Still, from a distance, there was not much about her that would normally have put much of a blip on my radar.*

"What did?" Big D's voice floated back, low, but easily heard over the whine of early hour traffic just beyond the cinder block wall.

Maybe it happened because I let my radar be tuned by a psychic, and maybe it had to do with her eyes.

"Yeah?"

Several evenings before, I'd met a friend at a party. I knew him from the Inner Quest Seminar. A psychic, he was there giving free readings. During mine, he told me I would soon meet "the one"—my soul mate. In fact, he described Eve right down to the freckles across the swelling of her ample breasts. But then he mentioned the violet depths of her eyes. Who has violet eyes? Up to that point, his description was so generic, I thought he was putting me on.

"But she was not 'the one,' your soul mate?"

No, not in this life anyway.

"Jeff, you seem to have this one all figured out. So then, who was Eve for you?"

Uh . . . look, Big D. I don't mean to be coming off as some know-it-all. I shrugged. *Everything I've learned just serves to show me how I really don't know shit.*

"Don't worry." The gape of his skeletally fixed grin seemed to widen. "Just knowing that, as a fact, is the first step to true wisdom."

Then you're not going to . . . I mean, sometimes talking with you . . . well, it's like we're water skiing. You give me plenty of rope, and it's then I find the joke's on me. Are you trolling me for alligators again?

"Yes, Jeff. You do have a habit of opening your mouth only to get your own ass bit." Now there was no doubt that his grin was wider. "Congratulations. That only happens to those who are discovering how very little it is they truly know of life."

Uh-huh. And that's supposed to make me feel better?

"Look, Jeff. Just tell me who Eve was to you."

Y'know, Big D, we discussed Eve once back then, when I was writing one of the chapters in my first book. What more is there to talk about?

"Oh, there is more"—he paused, his head ducked slightly, while the twin glows in his eye sockets sharpened—"much more."

I've wondered about that, Big D. Only thing more that seems to make much sense is that Eve was there to open me up sexually.

"Are you saying you think she was some sort of sex teacher?"

Not exactly. It wasn't as if she taught me that much, but rather more like she adjusted my understanding about women.

"Oh? And how so?"

You see, I'd only known a few women back before I settled down with Meg. And Meg wasn't much for adventure—not sexually anyway.

"Yes . . . and?"

Oh sure, Meg was far from a virgin from about a year before I met her. Even so, there was nothing about sex Meg knew that she'd share with me. Perhaps her experience of it had been mostly from other young, near-virgin GIs like myself—wham-bam, here's your pay, ma'am. Whatever it was, sex for her, that is, anything more than straight copulation, held only shame.

"Maybe she wanted to forget those early days when she was pressed into prostitution. You know about her strict Korean upbringing. Don't you think it gave her a set of very rigid ideas about what was proper?"

I know that to the average Korean, any connections to GIs meant shame for a woman. I guess I just expected it would be different with me—somehow, not shameful? Regardless, in the following years together, Meg showed no inclination to grow, to experiment, especially not sexually.

"Did she ever refuse you anything you wanted to try?"

Refuse? No, Meg seldom refused, not after the required seduction, but she never instigated. Sex was a need of mine more than hers, a need that somehow in the end, for me, never really felt fulfilled. For her, I don't know. Sexually, there was a hard . . . well, indifference that seemed to blunt much of the adventure. And yet . . . .

With head cocked to the side and eyebrows raised, I shrugged. "Yes?"

Well, I think that no matter how painful the situation, eventually one learns to feel comfortable, or maybe safe, with it.

"What are you getting at?" Did I hear a chuckle in his voice?

Just that at first, Eve felt different . . . unsafe. I can almost feel that alligator moving up behind me.

"How so?"

Eve . . . with her that first evening, there was a softness, a soft, eager yearning, one that blew my mind, and more. It began after Toastmasters, her second meeting there. The meeting broke up and everyone was headed out the door, including me.

Pulling me aside, Eve whispered, "Jeff, I'd like you to follow me home. Would you?"

"Is anything wrong? Someone bothering you?"

"No, nothing like that. I just . . ." She looked away, her face scarlet, then turned back to face me squarely with those bottomless, violet eyes. "I just don't want to be alone tonight."

* * *

She planned it well, Big D. There was soft music, a soft couch, and Eve's soft, full body in my arms—all the things that should have led to a raging hard-on, yet hadn't. I, too, was soft.

My conscious thoughts trailed off as the events of that evening came back in startling clarity. Big D did not interrupt the flow, although somehow, I knew he was still there, watching, just one alligator chomp away.

"Eve . . ." (kiss) "Uh . . . Eve . . . I . . . ahh . . . need . . ." (more kisses). "Eve, I need to talk."

"Sure . . . uhhmmm . . ." Her tongue slurped across mine. "I'm always open to you, Jeff."

"Uh . . . look, Eve." It took an effort to sit back and hold her at arm's length. "I . . . uh . . . I haven't exactly been a man of steel since my marriage broke up. Do you understand?"

"Do you mean there have been a lot of women?" Her concern referred to STDs and was well placed. In a way, I was relieved she'd asked.

"Oh, no, nothing like that. It's just that since my divorce, my dick doesn't seem to want to get all that hard, and sometimes"—my eyebrows raised and I looked down, unable to meet her eyes—"well . . . it doesn't always jump to as fast as it used to."

The concern left her face. "Oh, is that all? Don't worry about it."

"Well, I do worry about it. In fact, I think that sex scares the shit out of me."

"Well, if it does, we'll just clean it up." She grinned. "Now just lie back and let me handle it."

My pants were soon around my ankles, and Eve's soft, wet lips surrounded my still-soft limpness. It took a little while, but eventually, it wasn't nearly so limp. Eve was good. Though I hadn't been performed on many times, orally—only once during my marriage—this act I knew was good. It deserved, and got, a standing ovation.

"Eve, take your clothes off. Don't you want something in return?"

"Oh, no." She grinned. "I'm enjoying this. And besides, this one's just for you."

The stroking and bobbing, and her swirling, soft, warm wetness, made protest—or even just talking—nearly impossible. The art of her handiwork was having its effect, but not nearly as much as the thoughts that crossed my mind. *My God! This woman was indeed enjoying this . . . this . . . act of servitude.* Along with those thoughts, my dick was standing at attention. And quickly—too quickly—I felt the rising magma of my passion.

As it neared, I gasped. "Stop! Eve, stop. I'm going to . . ." Even I could hear the panic in my voice. I'd only cum in a woman's mouth once. It was the first—and last—time in Meg's. She spit and sputtered in outrage, then rushed into the bathroom for her disinfectant mouthwash. I'd suffered her disdainful silence for days following my despicable act.

But Eve didn't stop. Instead, she plowed on with ever-increasing gusto. Soon I, too, was plowing—with gusto. In fact, with great, foaming gobs of gusto. Spurt after spurt of it went into Eve's eager mouth. Then, passions spent, I relaxed into nerveless contentment as Eve slurped up the last drops and continued on, even then, for several moments more after my erection began to subside. When eventually she raised her head to stare into my eyes, there was a smile of satisfaction. Behind those slightly parted, smiling lips was the obvious evidence of my enjoyment there, within her mouth.

"So . . . err . . . uh." I searched for something to fill the silence while looking around for some sort of hanky. Finding nothing, I finished my lame query. "Do you . . . umm . . . swallow, or what?"

Holding my gaze, a twinkle in her eye, Eve very deliberately swallowed, then slowly grinned.

***

Chomp! A picture of alligator jaws closing upon my naked ass passed briefly through my mind.

God! The honesty of her sexuality, her instigation of it . . . intriguing, and at the same time, frightening.

"So, Eve was a woman who knew what she wanted?"

Yeah, and just then, it seemed she wanted only to be of service. Oh, to be sure, later—many times later—over the few short months of our relationship, she took her own pleasure, even instructed me on how she wanted it to be.

"And Meg, Jeff? C'mon, didn't Meg teach you anything of sex?"

Oh, sure. Coaxing Meg to passion over those many years of our marriage taught me to be a considerate, perhaps even artful lover. I had to be, just to get a semblance of my needs met. Somehow, it never occurred to me that a woman . . . I mean, Eve . . . was a very passionate, caring, giving, and artful lover.

"And yet?"

Yet still, even with Eve, my erections were never all that hard. Eve, too, never got all the beef.

"Why? This skewered you through the very essence of your manhood." His finger bone stabbed forth painfully against my chest. "Why do you try to make light of it?"

"Ow!" *Shit, Big D, take it easy. I didn't know why . . . scared maybe. Inside, I still felt scared—and ashamed.*

"Ashamed of what?"

Goddammit, Big D! I don't know. Ashamed that my dick no longer worked right. It always did with Meg, but even with her, I wasn't man enough to make her love me. And yeah, there's gotta be more to it. But what . . . I don't . . . fucking . . . know!

"Yes, Jeff, fear can make a man blind to the truth. There will be more for you to see about it—later."

Truth? What is the truth, Big D? I said it, asked for the truth, but was not ready for him to tell it to me straight out.

"Truth was, once you started growing spiritually, you became more of what it means to be a man than Meg could handle—or Eve, for that matter. A man's dick has little to do with how much of a man he is."

Chomp, chomp! A vision of that alligator swam through my mind once again.

"So, what happened? How did it end with Eve?" Big D's grin widened, and I had the impression he was silently chuckling.

Uh . . . yeah. I consciously closed my jaw before I answered, and even though my part in our conversation was by thoughts, the words in my mind had a surreal ring. *After only a few months, Eve's job with a rental company took her away.*

"You could have stopped her."

Yes, but letting her go was easy, Big D. She wasn't the one I wanted. I couldn't help but grimace. *Oh, I searched my soul but couldn't see why this was so. It wasn't about her looks, her body, and certainly not about her sexuality. We got along great in all ways. Even still, I wonder what it was about me that I couldn't just love her.* My breath hissed out in regret.

"Ah, but you did, Jeff. You took her exactly as she was and accepted her and loved her. There was just that thing that she did, that behavior—the one you both needed to but she wouldn't, and you couldn't, deal with."

Doesn't sound like I accepted her.

"Again, Jeff, you did. Did you ever ask her to change to suit you?"

No, of course not.

"Why not? That's what most everyone else would have done. It's what you asked Meg to do for so long." His eye sockets glowed bright, almost burning. This time, he didn't bother to hide his amusement. "Hmmm?"

Chomp, chomp, chomp . . . that damned alligator again.

I know, Big D. I looked down at the concrete of the patio, unwilling to meet his gaze. *But I learned, y'know, from the laws, from the seminars, but most of all, from you.*

"What?" The light emanating from those deep sockets up above his gaping grin was like an irresistible demand for my acknowledgment of it all. "What was it you learned?"

That it was not my right to ask her to change.

"Because?" I saw the flicker of humor as his gaze grilled me and I shuddered, knowing that with this truth, I was about to be lunch for his pet alligator.

Because that is the true definition of "selfishness"—asking another to live their life to suit yours, demanding them to be other than they want to be. If who they are doesn't work in my life, then parting is the only answer.

"What was it about Eve that didn't work in your life?"

Eve was an alcoholic. While I never saw her floating tits up in a bottle, the smell was always on her breath. The few times I asked if she'd been drinking, she denied it, even those times when the renewed fumes told me she'd just gone to the other room for a nip.

"That's not it, Jeff. Go deeper."

Deeper? Oh, you mean that it was not so much that she drank, it was that she lied about it to me—and worse, to herself.

"And . . ."

And I could never trust her—I shrugged—*never believe in her because of it.*

"That's right, Jeff. There was nothing you needed to forgive Eve for. There was nothing you judged her wrong about, nothing that required forgiveness, not even her drinking and subsequent dishonesty. You accepted all the silly shit she did."

Then, what?

"Ah, Jeff," he said, shaking his head sadly. "Don't you get it? If you accept that others have the right to be who they are, that leaves only you—*you* forgiving yourself for judging them wrong." He paused to let it sink in, then added, "Judgment . . . and the blame, control, and drama that go along with it. That's not you. That's for those who don't know the simple truths of the Spiritual Laws." He chuckled. "Shit, you merely saw that she lacked something you needed in your life."

Needed? Big D, I know you always say that relationships are about the meeting of needs, but—I wagged my head and looked up into the Las Vegas night sky, washed blank by the bright city lights—*I'm not following you on this one.*

"Integrity, Jeff. You needed someone who possessed as much or more integrity as you, or at least wanted to."

Seems like such a small issue.

"Jeff." Big D's head ducked into the blackness of his cowling. The ivory white of his forehead showed as a dim luminescence, while the glow of his sight looked doubly bright in reproach. "The energy of others does affect you. It either uplifts you or drags you down. If she had wanted it, yours could have raised hers up. But she didn't want it."

The breath I was holding gusted out in regret. *That's true.*

"So, tell me. How did it end?"

Quickly and painlessly. I suppose my own dysfunction didn't work in her life, either.

"How so?"

She seemed to think that I still mourned the death of my marriage—the death of that life I lived with Meg. I shrugged in hopeless frustration.

"Eve was correct. She dealt with her own divorce, finished her own mourning. Do you see how staying together would have only dragged you both down—you, losing ground with your integrity, and she, sliding back into her old pain?"

Chomp, chomp, chomp, CHOMP.

But I was working on getting past my pain.

"Do you think you'd have succeeded if Eve was not there to give you that little shove?"

No. Between her and Karen suggesting the letter . . .

"Ah, yes. There was that goodbye letter to Meg. Oh, I received it, as did the rest of the universe, God, and even Meg's higher self. Here's a copy."

Before me appeared a sheet of paper which, despite a slight breeze, hovered without movement before the deck chair in which I sat. I reached for it and, though it had every appearance of being solid, my hand passed right through. Then, as I read the words, each flamed up turning the paper above into black cinders that blew away on the breeze.

* * *

To my beautiful Meg,

Mere words cannot express what you have meant to my life, or thank you for your loving care and for the gift of our son. You nurtured him well—so much better than I.

Thank you for staying in my life and allowing me to love you, although you were never happy with me. Yes, I know now how my love was something suffered, exchanged for the security it afforded you. I am so sorry if you were cheated. There is no security in life, as I'm sure you now know. Back then, none of it was a conscious thing for either of us.

I now question if I gave you anything of value. Romance, respect, passion, a need to cherish—all things I felt for you and needed in return. But were they things you could give?

Truth was, I could only feel my own feelings, my own love for you, and perhaps lie to myself about yours.

Thank you for allowing me to be there and experience my profound love for you, for a time. Perhaps that was the gift you gave to me. What I gave to you is not for me to know. Can it ever be a gift if it is not accepted? Your acceptance was never for me to know. There is no fault on anyone's part.

Real love is a gift that requires no payback, nor does it carry expectations. Yet, in the end, I had those expectations of you. That lie I held in my heart about you, was it not, in reality, my expectations, kindled by my own feelings? What is, just is—and is the truth. My love for you was never a part in that lie.

In my fear of dying, I yearned for more—some understanding of life—and with my reprieve went searching for the truth of life. Finding it required me to face the truth of my own.

When two people don't grow together, they will always grow apart. I grew apart from you. I have no issue, feel no blame.

I can now express my love for you in honesty and truth, for you have taught me the truth about real love. Though eventually I will die, my love for you will live on within me. Wherever I go, I will always remember you with love—real love.

Thank you, my darling Meg,

Jeff

* * *

Big D was standing beside my chair as the last ash curled up and drifted away on the winds of my memory. His voice, with its unique overtones, was solemn when he continued.

"Like tonight, I was with you, here on your patio, when you burned that letter in offering. The three-a.m. traffic whipping by, like now, was playing a siren song on its own kazoo." The silk of his robe flowed out as he gestured toward the high-back wall alongside the 95 freeway.

"I watched with you as it streamed down the hill toward the lights of Las Vegas, bright in the distance. You wondered if those people, too, felt some sort of pull, just as you always felt when looking at Meg's bright beauty.

"Then, I watched you as you meditated, watched you reach out and sample their energy and felt you discover the truth—how they raced toward the meaningless, bright, frivolous nothings of life, the intangible thrills in the promise of the casinos, the crusty lust that some think of as being the true passions of love. Yet, in the end, they are left with nothing. Oh, they may win tonight, but when their time is all used up, do any really walk away anything other than empty?"

What are you getting at, Big D? I've never heard you ramble this much.

"Hear them? See them? Feel their energy?" Big D's cloaked arm again gestures toward the lines of ruby taillights flowing down the hill. "So many of them are takers! They've no intention of giving anything. I ramble out of the personal disgust I feel when escorting those leaving life, away from this town." He chuckled softly. "And then, every once in a while, there is one who makes it all feel worthwhile—someone like you. Yes, you! With your burning letter, burning with the honesty of your love. An offering to the universe, to God . . . to Meg."

My mind flowed quickly over the years with Meg, over the fullness of them, which her absence now cannot change. *I see what you mean.*

"Yes, and when you lit the letter, its flame against the grandeur of Las Vegas seemed so paltry to you. In reality, it was a shining beacon of love released. And, too, in the flickering flames, the rising pungence of smoke, and the blackened, crumbling ashes—there was healing." His voice paused, and for a brief moment, I again smelled that smoke. "Yes, for you, it was as it needed to be—an ending and a beginning—and all taken at its own perfect time."

I took a deep breath and paused a moment before exhaling. *Yes, I remember how my energy seemed to change. After that, it somehow felt lighter.*

Big D's laughter rang out hearty above the whiz of traffic. "And speaking of the perfect time, when you are not so busy looking to get your chimes rung"—the glow in one eye socket winked—"I have someone I want you to meet."

Who?

"You'll know."

She beautiful like Meg?

"Actually, he is, in his own way. Ah, but you are not yet ready to meet."

Uh . . . Big D. You aren't saying you think I'm gay, are you?

"Nope, but you are a tad bit more humble than you need to be." Big D's head nodded, and again, the fire in one eye socket winked briefly out, then back in. "You'll meet him soon, and in a safe place— one where you can let go of that which your loyalty won't acknowledge about Meg, that which otherwise would hold you tied to her forever."

I'm not following.

"It's about your relationships, Jeff." I heard his chuckle. "Don't you want more than to just get your chimes rung?"

Well, yeah.

"Then there is something you must do."

Comb Ridge, Utah—Present Day

I sit here on my perch over Comb Ridge remembering Eve and all she meant to me. Having her to hold and knowing her acceptance of me—an acceptance I never felt from Meg but which my love allowed me to ignore for so many years—was what I needed most at the time.

Big D sits with me as he so often does here on this ledge.

Did she take that job so far away because it was offered and she wanted it, Big D? Or did she deliberately seek it out because she didn't want to face her alcoholism—to herself or me? I would never have forced her to, and yes, in time would have left. She wasn't the woman I wanted because that would not have worked for me.

"Why do you think that is, Jeff? Doesn't sound like accepting her to me."

C'mon, we both know accepting is just about not trying to change others, that relationships aren't always about love, and the acceptance love requires—

He interrupts my thought. "Y'know, most in this world would disagree?"

I know, but most of this world doesn't follow spiritual law.

"How so?" His grin has practically got a stranglehold on his naked skull now, and I, too, have to grin.

You're right. I was kinda holding myself at fault for not loving her enough and for not even trying to hold her with me. But then, our relationship was not so much about love.

"You didn't love her?"

Yes, I certainly did, but I think that for both of us, we just needed to get our needs met.

"Then why the guilt?" From the intensity of his gaze, I am now aware that he knows, but he wants me to make the point. "What was the need that wasn't being filled?"

I hear you, Big D. Everyone needs to be okay with themselves. Life doesn't work when you're beating yourself up because you don't like who you are and you refuse to face the lie that runs your life. Almost died before coming to accept my own lie. I grin. *But then, you know that, too.*

"And . . ."

And alcohol meant more to her than me—or even life itself. My breath hisses with regret before asking him the real question. *So, how much longer was it before her reset button was pushed?*

He doesn't answer right away, just looks at me, his whole, inscrutable skull oozing with compassion. "About six months. Passed out and crashed her car into a bridge abutment."

Turning away, looking out over the beauty of this world, my sight blurs and glistens with my memory of her and what she gave to my life. *I wonder if what I gave to hers was of equal value?* Big D's boney clutch on my shoulder is a solid comfort.

"More than you know. You offered her the way out. She just wasn't strong enough to reach out and take it."

"Humm-ghhh." My grunt is more of a groan.

"But she loved you and appreciated you for being there in her life. Take solace in that." His grip tightens once more, then he is gone.

Whether it's what you ate, or the feelings you take in of life, such things need nurture, provide growth to one's body or spirit, then pass on through. Shit's shit! And constipation is just not healthy.
Redneck Spirituality—Book Four

CHAPTER THIRTEEN

The Saga of Doc

Personal Quest, Karen's advanced seminar, was barely underway when we were asked to choose buddies.

"As your buddy will also be your bunkmate for the weekend"— Karen grinned—"you need to choose a same-sex buddy this time."

Looking left out past the resort's empty, springtime swimming pool at the wide expanse of Lake Mead, I sighed. *Hell, should I choose or wait for someone to pick me? But no, that scenario usually ends with me standing before the group, head bowed, alone.* Karen's words mock readily from my memory. "So, Jeff, how did you happen to leave yourself out again? Did riding off into the sunset ever get the Lone Ranger the friendships he craved?"

"Hi! Name's Terrance Jackson. Everyone just calls me Doc."

Startled, I glanced up. No one ever picked me. At six four, two hundred forty-five pounds of work-hardened muscle, I seemed to unintentionally intimidate most folks. And then there was the motorcycle.

"W-what?"

"Yeah, you want to buddy up with me?"

Before me stood a good-looking man of maybe thirty-five. About five ten and barrel-chested, he was built solid. His hazel eyes had a powerful feel about them. Vaguely, I remember him from past Inner Quest Seminars.

"Aren't you a minister or something?" I quizzed.

"Yeah, that's me. I'm confirmed. Even got a PhD in metaphysics. That's why they call me Doc."

"Metaphysics? What university has PhDs in metaphysics?"

"The University of Metaphysics, of course." He shifted uneasily, his voice taking on an edge. "So, do you want to buddy with me, or not?"

Glancing about, I realized that most were already paired. "Sure. Why not? Actually, I'm very interested in metaphysics. Oh . . . my name's Jeff Williams."

"Good then! It's done." Doc slapped my shoulder, causing a long, quartz crystal pendant swinging on a leather lace from around his neck to dance across his beefy chest.

"Say, isn't that moldavite?" I gestured at the pyramid-shaped, green stone capping the crystal.

"Yes. How did you know?"

"Lapidary and silversmithing are my hobbies, but I only work with silver. That's nice work," I said, pointing toward the band of gold holding the two stones together and soldered to a U-shaped yoke through which the cord ran. "Custom cast by the looks of it."

"Yeah, had it made special. Cost a bundle."

"Why is it that most of the metaphysical people I've met seem to wear quartz crystal pendants? Is it a fad?"

"No." Doc chuckled. "Quartz crystals are used to channel psychic energy."

"Really?" I cocked my head, eyeing his pendant. "How do they do that?"

"It's because the vibratory rate of quartz is conducive to psychic energy."

"Uh-huh." I grunted.

Doc quickly added, "Are you familiar with physics?"

"Sure, some."

"Then you're probably familiar with the concept that all things are really energy in one form or another?"

"Yeah."

"Well, all energy has a vibratory rate."

When I made no reply, Doc repeated, his voice uncertain. "Vibratory rate . . . you do understand how all energy oscillates in cycles. Sunlight oscillates at a certain frequency, electricity at another."

"Yes, yes. I understand all that. It's just that I've never looked at solid forms of energy in that light—no pun intended."

"Oh yeah." A look of relief passed across Doc's face.

"Look, Doc"—I paused, picking my words—"I'm a mechanic. And like a mechanic . . ." I stretched out my arms, heavily knotted with muscle and crisscrossed by scars, and my palms, perpetually stained with worn-in grease, were held upright. All of it bore the truth of my words. "Hell, I even fucking swear like a mechanic. But *mechanic* doesn't always mean *stupid*." I grinned. "Y'know?"

"Don't take offense. I . . . I didn't mean to imply—"

"I don't take offense, Doc. It just seems that we aren't connecting. Sometimes helps to be up front with people."

"I'm not sure I—"

"It's this way. If I don't understand you"—I shrugged, my smile seemingly putting him at ease—"I'll tell you. Otherwise, if I don't always respond, it's just that I'm making up my own mind about what to believe."

"I knew there was something about you I liked, Jeff!"

"And the moldavite?"

"Moldavite? Oh . . . moldavite is a meteoric, green-glass tektite from a shower that fell many thousands of years ago near the Moldau River in what is now the Czech Republic. Very rare and valuable."

"I know all that. I mean, what does it do?"

"Oh." Doc eyed me closely. "Well, moldavite has a much higher energy vibration. It's kind of like it has the same note as quartz but at a higher octave. It amplifies the energy channeled by the quartz."

When again I didn't answer, Doc continued. "You know, when I meditate, sometimes I can actually hear my pendant singing."

Just then, Karen's voice blared from the nearby speaker. "Has everyone found a buddy?"

* * *

As the seminar progressed, Doc and I soon found ourselves connecting into a true buddy pair. He confided that his male friends never stayed around long, so intimidating was his presence—or so he said. And the females . . . I knew enough about Doc to know he went through them like a bag of pistachios. Still, Doc's big impetus for this seminar was his need to get over losing the one great love of his life. In that, we shared a common need, but my focus was soon toward other things.

* * *

"Jeff!" Karen grilled early the second day. "You've agonized over your divorce through how many seminars now?"

"Quite a few," I conceded, accompanied by more than a few sympathetic twitters from among the female participants. There were few taking this advanced seminar who did not know me well.

"Aren't you getting tired of it?"

"Yes!" I hissed through gritted teeth. "I'm damn tired of it! I just want to move on."

"Where?"

"What?"

"I said '*where?*'" Karen's voice held something very sharp. "My question is, *where* are you going in life? But if you insist, you can have it your way. *What* are you doing with your life?"

"I'm not sure I know what you want to know. I'm getting over my divorce. That's where I'm going *and* what I'm doing."

"Jeff." Karen's look was soft now, as was her voice. "You are going to stay right here in your misery until you look at your joy and get a picture of where that could be taking you"—she paused dramatically—"were you to let go of your pain."

I gritted my teeth but made no reply. Karen continued. "For the rest of this seminar, I challenge you to explore your joy. Make a list of everything that gives you joy—this goes for everyone!" Karen held up her arm, shouting it out, with her index finger outstretched toward the others. "Read your list often and allow it to grow. Touch it, taste it . . . follow it to its farthest reach."

Karen turned back and regarded me solemnly as she continued. "My greatest wish for you, Jeff, is that by the end of this seminar, you will know your true destiny." Karen turned to the others. "That, in case you haven't discovered, is what the ultimate Personal Quest is always about. This seminar is designed to look at your joy and perhaps remove a few of the things blinding you to it."

Glancing back at me, Karen grinned in that secretive way that I recognized spoke of a special plan percolating in her mind. I winced. "Does anyone recognize what it is that is blinding Jeff right now?"

For a long, uncomfortable moment, there was silence. "Anyone?" Karen repeated.

Then, from somewhere in the back, came a small, female voice. I couldn't see whose. "He seems so angry . . ."

"Exactly!" Karen burst out, whirling back to face me, that grin now spread wide. "Jeff, you know what is needed . . . don't you?"

"You mean . . ." I swallowed, suddenly aware of how dry my mouth was.

"A rage process!" Karen finished for me. "The next exercise will be a rage process. Jeff, you're one of the few here who knows what that is. Are you willing to start?"

"Now?" I gulped, remembering how out of it that process could look, remembering Meg. Someone had done one that first—and only—night when Meg had gone to group therapy with me.

"Yes." Karen pointed to the carpet at her feet. "Now."

Laying on my back, arms straight out as if to be crucified, I had only a scant moment for misgiving.

"Charlene, Joyce . . . you two sit over Jeff's legs. No, not *on* them, but *over* them," Karen directed. "Beth, you and Cher each sit over an arm. The idea is not to restrain but to provide a 'safe' cushion around him. Ruth, you sort of kneel over Jeff's chest and stomach."

None of the women Karen chose were lightweights, though the scent of their various perfumes made me acutely aware that Karen had chosen an all-female 'safety net.' Kneeling by my head, her red hair falling around her face, flaming in the rays of sun coming through the bay windows of the room, I could see the freckles through her makeup and was even considering counting them. Yes, if a guy needs to, it isn't hard to divert his attention—but that was before she began.

"Breathe, Jeff!" Karen glanced around. "Everyone, notice how when we try to shut down our emotions, the first thing we do is to stop breathing." Then, with her eyes holding mine, I forgot about the freckles, even the flaming red of her hair that almost brushed my face. Karen began in earnest.

"Jeff, in all the time I've known you, you've freely, and bravely, expressed your pain concerning your failed marriage. You've taken full responsibility for your divorce—as it should be—that is, for your own experience of it. But the truth of relationships is that we each bear a one hundred percent responsibility. Jeff, you have never expressed your anger over Meg's failure to take responsibility for her own one hundred percent. No matter how many excuses you make for her, you know it. And you . . . *are* . . . angry."

"Ah, Karen. I was the one who—"

"Shhhhuuttttt." Karen's tone stopped me cold. "Feel it! Feel your anger. Let it come!"

I only lay there, puzzled, wondering why I didn't really feel anything. Karen continued. Her hand reached out, and like a plunger, she pushed down against my diaphragm.

"Breathe!" —Push— "Feel what it's like when you try to express your deepest feeling to someone you love, only to have them tell you you're 'coo-wazy!'" Karen mimicked Meg's accent perfectly. "And when you write them poems, and they wad them back into your face. Breathe!" —Push— "When everything you say and do is greeted with suspicion and derision. Breathe!" —Push— "When everything about them says that there's something 'wrong' with you for feeling and thinking and loving . . ."

Karen leaned closer, her eyes boring into mine, making the accusations sing with an indefinable power. "What's it like when the one person you love the most—perhaps more than life itself—goes behind your back and turns your own sorry-assed parents against you in her struggle to be right? The very people you thought would love and nurture you . . . help you get through all this?"

"Aaarggghht . . . fuck!" Like a super-heated teacup, the feelings started as an imperceptible seething that frothed, then exploded over with the dropping of the tea bag. "God! Shit! Motherfuuuuuuuuuck!" My body banged and bucked against soft restraints as my words turned unintelligible, then ripped out into a continuous shriek—a shriek that went on and on for an indeterminate time, stopping only when, in the remaining burning croak of it, I no longer felt the need to exchange the pain for breath.

Like a run-over dog, I lay there bathed in sweat and tears, whimpering. "Ladies, take Jeff over to the far wall. And Beth, if you would, just hold him and nurture him for a while," Karen said, her voice quiet in the stillness of the room. Then, she turned to the others. "Now, who has the courage to go next?"

Comb Ridge, Utah—Present Day

Here on the ledge, I pause reading to tap my pen against this chapter's pages with what, embarrassment? No, not for anything I did in the seminar. It was more of a distasteful uneasiness, a kind of sadness, just in knowing what was going through the minds of some of the others. Not because I give a shit what they thought, but it did give rise to memories of Meg. She, like them, was simply unwilling to get real. Like they probably did now, she regarded the rage process—and me—as insanely wacko. When one partner loses faith in the other, the marriage, as such, is over.

"Oh gag! What went through their minds was none of your fucking business. And those who had those thoughts only had them in defense—to excuse themselves for not having the courage to be real like you. Like Meg, they, too, would not let themselves be so vulnerable."

Yeah. You're right, Big D. It's just . . . well—

"You never saw it, did you, Jeff?"

Saw what? He is eyeing me closely and I feel his humor.

"How Karen loved having you in her seminars."

Well, we did have a long relationship, what with the group therapy and—

"Not what I mean, Jeff. You never saw the part you played in her seminars."

I'm not following.

"How it was that she could always count on you to be *real*."

Well, sure, that was what the seminars were about—getting real.

"Jeff, you were the catalyst for her, the one person she knew she could count on to touch that off in the others."

Huh?

"Why do you think she chose you to start off that rage process?" He chuckles. "Unless they actually participated, most would look back at it the same way Meg did. Karen knew she could count on you to do it honestly with an open heart. It took you, or someone like you, to put the magic in her seminars. Don't go getting a fat head. There were others, but you were her star." I get an impression of raised eyebrows on his boney skull. "You have no idea how many people you touched by just being real, nor do you have a clue how many this book will touch just by its reality—your reality. And you thought you had it pretty much done with that one final chapter you wrote."

I was just getting it all lined up to publish when this thing happened, and now I find myself stranded on this ledge. Sure, there are no coincidences, but this? What I have no fucking clue about is why this is happening.

"Yes, that is the question, isn't it?"

But the place I chose to end this book, I think, is perfect. After all those relationships I went through—and then me finding my soul mate. Why is it I feel you're not impressed?

"Maybe because I'm not." He ducks his head and looks up as if to focus my face in the glow of his sight. "Did you ever ask yourself, 'Has this story truly ended? Is this ending real? Is it honest?'"

But . . . but . . .

"Maybe someone's life will depend on it. Just saying . . ."

What . . . what does that mean?

"We have an agreement, remember?" He fades like a mist, leaving me there with my mouth, again, wide open.

Spiritual Law #9—*Others are but a mirror for us to see ourselves.* What we don't like in others is but the reflection of what we don't like in ourselves. If it were not also within us, we could never see it in them.

Redneck Spirituality—Book One

CHAPTER FOURTEEN

Doc's Chicken Exit

Divorced and alone—at least where male friends were concerned—I needed the friendship of Doc. He needed me for the same reasons. Together, we looked into one another's souls, and I saw in his soul the reflection of my own. I saw the loneliness, how he could never keep friends, even as likeable and interesting as he was. And, though I still had trouble admitting it about myself, Doc, too, was a teacher—had been for a long time.

Metaphysics was what he had to share with the world. It's true that we all possess an innate ability of intuition, abilities few see, but Doc was astute and powerful in the use of his. He was skilled in working with psychic energies and personal mind control. There wasn't much about meditation techniques or the astral realms with which he was unfamiliar.

Doc began holding meditation lessons in his apartment, charging a small fee—a donation for his services. I arranged to pay by repairing his car. About a dozen people, almost invariably women, floated in and out of his classes. Only a core of three attended every time—Doc, myself, and Candy, a woman who'd done IQ with us back when.

Doc never met an attractive, single woman whom he didn't try to seduce. He took it as his challenge in life, one he was very good at meeting. Once successful, he'd soon move on. So it was between Doc and Candy, although he'd not told me of his challenge or how he'd met it with her. Whatever sex happened between them, stayed between them. Whatever extracurricular benefits were present in their friendship, they did not benefit mine. Even so, we three were friends.

Doc was someone I came to know very well. I saw how strong his mind was and how sex was a driving force in his life, how it challenged his ego. For a time, I wondered how much of me was reflected by him. Certainly, there was a time in my youth when I'd responded to that challenge, too. Is it a man thing or just a phase? It seems to be much the same for so many.

* * *

After the IQ (Inner Quest) and PQ (Personal Quest) Seminars became ongoing and successful, Karen looked to developing another—a 'next step.' The word went out for volunteers.

Stepping out of the oven of a Las Vegas summer day, I sucked in a cool, air-conditioned breath and found a spot on a couch in Karen's smartly appointed counseling office. Twenty of us were arranged around the room. All we knew was that this seminar would be a huge commitment.

Standing before us, Karen began. "Thanks for showing up, guys." She chuckled to herself. "And I *do* mean *showing up*. This seminar will be called Eagle Quest . . . EQ for short. It will be a challenge, one that will stretch your lives as never before. It'll be five days long and held at an undisclosed place somewhere on the planet. You will not be told the particulars"—she stopped to look deliberately into each person's eyes—"until you show up for the seminar, with your passports."

"You . . . who take this one on . . . are the truly courageous." The cadence of her phrases was clipped—clipped and serious. "You are like an eaglet taking its first flight, stepping off the nest into a thousand feet of open air." Her eyes began to twinkle. "Kinda like doing big things in real life. You'll need to trust—trust in your support system, your facilitators, and in one another"—she paused again to look individually around the table, her look one of challenge—" and mostly in yourselves. You can't accomplish what you're going to do alone." The twinkle turned to an open grin. "And, it will be scary!"

I looked around uneasily at our group. Did they, too, feel this same fear? Karen went on, no hint of humor now showing. "This one requires absolute commitment! Without it, someone could get hurt.

"As for *commitments*, most people have *agreements* mixed up with *commitments*. Agreements are things that if you can't—or won't—

do, you can go to the other people involved and find an alternate acceptable solution." With that, she glanced quickly around, then added, "You know?

"Commitments? Commitments are things that if you find you *can't* do, it's only because you're dead. And even then"—she shrugged—"you'll have arranged to get it done." A tag line like that would seem to demand some sort of chuckle or grin. There was none. "When I point to you, stand and declare, YES, you will commit, or NO, you won't."

Sitting there, my mouth working like a fish out of water, I searched my soul. *Can I make this kind of commitment? Am I willing to jump into this totally blind, to trust in Karen's guidance? And courage? Do I have the courage?* Yes, again my courage was in question. No need to ask. I knew that question came directly from Big D. When my time came, I stood.

"Yes." *Did the fear show?* "I will commit."

There were several who would not. In the end, our number stood at fourteen—Doc, Candy, and I included. Eagle Quest was scheduled for more than two months in the future. Our task meanwhile was to meet weekly for the sole purpose of bonding. We would be trusting our lives in one another's care.

During our first meeting, we were charged to stay clear and honest with each other. Whatever problems or negative feelings coming between us now, or in the future, were to be handled face-to-face and within twenty-four hours. I was voted as counselor for the men. If I suspected or noticed any problems coming up involving any of the men, I was to see they were addressed and dealt with.

Immediately, it became obvious that Doc and two of the women had a clash of egos. All three were deeply into control, and all three needed to be right. At that first meeting, I brought it up. They, all three, swore they'd deal with it. I saw Doc the next day.

"So, Doc, how did it turn out with Myrna and Joanne?"

"Yeah, we talked it out. But damn! Ev-va-ry . . . goddamned . . . time I opened my mouth, that dyke bitch, Myrna, would just jump down my throat. And Joanne? I think she was raised by the Gestapo. I can't stand either one of those bitches!"

"Well, y'know, Doc"—I grimaced—"it doesn't sound like you worked it out to me."

"I did my part!" Doc's scowl was not pretty.

Barely pausing, I continued. "So, when *are* you going to deal with it?"

"Dammit," he snarled, "I am dealing with it. Can't you see that? Is it my fault if *they* choose to dislike me so much? *They* just need to deal with it. *They're* the ones who won't handle it."

"Doc, you can't do anything about their feelings, right?"

He gritted his teeth. "Isn't that what I just said?"

"Yeah, I know. You're right. And Doc"—I ducked my head, eyeing him—"you *can* do something about your own. I see that you're holding on to a lot of energy about them, too." I nodded. "*That's* what I want you to deal with."

"*You* just let *me* handle myself," he retorted, his eyes an icy shade of hazel. "I don't need *your* help with that!"

Clearly, his mind was closed. I'd communicated my thoughts the best way I knew. Further discussion would only be making him wrong in an empty attempt to serve my own need. No, Doc was not ready to see it my way. I dropped it and just dealt with my own mild surge of resentment concerning the tone of his voice, deliberately letting it go. It was no secret how Doc viewed himself as superior, and not just to me—just who he was. It's why he kept no friends. I was determined to be different, so I deliberately chose to accept him as he was.

The problem didn't find its own solution. Myrna and Joanne shared a similar viewpoint of Doc. Of course, they didn't call him a dyke, but a thought had crossed my mind. *Was there a little bit of 'dyke' within Doc's psyche?* He certainly connected with women—those he was seducing, anyway. Like many gay women, was Doc also angry with men? Was this why he had a problem with women who presented themselves like men? And why he only allowed men into his life who would willingly take a subordinate role?

The next weekly group meeting was set up to be a party night at Candy's. As soon as he arrived, I took Doc aside. "This war has to stop. I'm going to bring it up with the group tonight, and I expect you to be open to what they say."

"Don't you dare." He hissed. "Just don't you dare! You'll be sorry if you do."

The meal was unusually quiet. Doc and the two ladies mutually ignored one another, except for a few sideways glances. It seemed as if he was squatted like a gorilla at our table. Myrna and Joanne sat sort of crouched, like a couple of jungle cats.

Finally, I stood up and announced, "We have something I feel needs to be addressed. I'm bringing it before the group as men's counselor since the parties involved haven't been willing to resolve it on their own. I think we all know about the war—Doc versus Myrna and Joanne."

In that instant, I felt a wave of energy wash over me. It hit with such psychic force that I felt my knees would buckle. Speechless, I abruptly sat down. The energy of the whole meeting was shifted. Angry accusations began to fly between Doc and the two women. Justine, the female counselor who was bound by a wheelchair, sought to be the peacemaker.

"Wait a minute! We're all adults here. We don't need to be acting like . . ."

Doc cast one wilting glance toward her and she stopped abruptly. Frantically, she began backing her chair away from the group and into the far corner where she huddled, crying, while two of the women hovered over her, trying to soothe her.

The scene was like a flock of chickens caught on the roadway. The party disintegrated in a cloud of chickenshit and feathers, emotional guts flying everywhere.

Doc turned to me. "Now, see what you've done. This is all your fault. I warned you." He stalked out.

There was a sickening feeling, like a load of buckshot settling in my gut. How do you stay friends with someone who wants to blame you for their feelings, especially when you see the sickness of their drama and feel it with the energy of your very soul? I caught up with Doc on the front porch.

"Whoa there, Doc! This is me . . . Jeff, remember?"

"So?" His single-word reply denied our friendship and the unspoken truth of what we both knew to be. I said it directly.

"Doc." I searched my mind for something, some words he might hear. Nothing came. "Look, I'm asking you to take responsibility for your feelings and for your part in this war you're waging here. If you won't, how can I require that they take responsibility for their own?" His silent glare and the stiffness of his back as he disappeared down the driveway were his only answers.

A lot of Doc's stories I took with an unspoken wink. He told about being in a white witches' coven, how he'd left when they'd started getting into animal sacrificing. Then there were the ones about how they'd tried to kill him several times since. The stories were now suddenly much more believable—except, maybe, the part about the coven being white. The energy I felt from him that night was not positive in any way, and somehow, I knew he'd gone easy on me due to our friendship.

Justine, the woman's counselor, was not so fortunate. More than shaken—terrified—she dropped out on her commitment to Eagle Quest, as did Doc, Joanne, Myrna, and Candy. We all have our chicken exits. This was theirs. Doc's personal psychic attacks that night were real. For the others, they served as self-validating excuses for not keeping their commitment. As for Doc? In bringing up the issue, I'd personally victimized Doc, or so he said.

Going in, we were all clear about commitment. And Karen did warn us about identifying our chicken exits. It seemed I'd helped four would-be eaglets to identify theirs. Having failed in my duties as male counselor, this was not my proudest moment. The drama I helped create that night gave them all an excuse for quitting. The only benefit a chicken exit provides is one of comfort in keeping ourselves stuck in an unhappy, but comfortably familiar place. Change is always uncomfortable.

It was my job to require the participants to work together in simply getting along. Yes, I put Doc's, along with Myrna's and Joanne's, shit in their faces and asked them to deal with it. Even so, the resulting explosion of chickenshit and feathers came as a complete surprise.

Did they not understand the basic concepts Karen Moore was teaching all these months throughout every seminar? A picture of her standing before us, arms out and both index fingers pointing inward, ran through my head. "The correction *always* goes here." Her words screamed in my mind as I watched that party scatter. Didn't they *get it*? We are each responsible for creating *everything* that is in our lives. Hell, it's the number one Spiritual Law—*I am the creator!* Was I the only one who got it?

And what did I create this night? I'd certainly created being a failure as a men's counselor. Was this night something the universe, God, or maybe my soul set up as a lesson for me? Again, there are those Spiritual Laws. *Everything in my life is there as a lesson for my learning.*

Were the other chickens in this seminar also getting their own lessons right then, a prelude required for becoming an eagle? Did they see that blaming others for how one sees and feels about what's happening in life doesn't work? But Doc's chicken exit was way out there as such things go—way beyond getting sick, or forgetful, staying disorganized, or always showing up late.

I should know. I've used most of those excuses at some time myself. No. His chicken exit was even beyond blaming others. His was in creating high drama to get out of doing what he'd committed to do. *That's something I'd never do.*

* * *

Big D's familiar chuckle danced across my mind, along with a sudden mental picture of looking out through a truck's windshield at a rice paddy rushing up at me. *Oh, my God!* It hit me. Yes, there was a time, back in the army in Korea, when I got drunk and wrecked a tanker truck full of diesel fuel. I drove it a hundred yards down a forty-five-degree embankment, through a ditch, and into a rice paddy. It missed the telephone poles and all the randomly spaced trees. At the ditch, defying my expectation, it didn't even jackknife into a crumpled ball of twisted metal and bloody guts. I survived nearly unscathed, an almost impossible feat. Later, the I-Corps MPs at Uijongbu let me off unscathed for driving drunk and wrecking that tanker. The result? I didn't have to volunteer for the Non-Commissioned Officer (NCO) Academy as my commanding officer was demanding.

But wait! That fucker made me an acting jack, a buck sergeant, the NCO in charge of his field showers/radiation decon unit. Was that his way of getting even? Making me do what he wanted? The fact that an acting jack gets little respect, and no sergeant's pay, must have tickled the shit out of that asshole.

Or again, was it by my own soul's insistence in giving me the lessons I needed? That is its job. Fact is, you can *know* something in your mind, but you *don't truly know it* if it's not in your heart. Again, experience is what it takes to move knowledge from the mind to the heart. I learned this from my studies of the Spiritual Laws. The dance of the universe is one of perfection. Everyone gets the lessons they need in the movement of life's moments. Even still, in this present moment, I wasn't sure just what it was I *knew*.

This clusterfuck of a party didn't feel much like perfection. But hell, maybe it was. This seminar? Was it something my soul demanded of me that Doc's didn't from him? Or was my soul just rubbing Doc's chickenshit chicken exit into my face? I suspected he would take it.

Standing that night on the front porch, shaking my head, watching the participants scatter like a flock of frightened chickens, I pondered it all. Car doors slammed and engines kicked into life as the other participants rushed to leave. Despite the heat of this Las Vegas night, a cool breeze blew across my back. I recognized it as the breath of Big D.

"Life is always perfect just as it is. Yes, you're getting it." His words reverberated in my mind. "All is as it needs to be."

Comb Ridge, Utah—Present Day

Sitting here on this ledge, I gaze out across the open gulf of Comb Ridge Wash so far below. The skittering flights of two little bat bodies dance their aimless duet as they scoop up the tiny gnats from the air all around. The day was almost hot, perhaps the summer's last gasp before the change in seasons. In the cooling breeze of the evening air, I put my pen and notebook aside, too dark now to write. Again, a chill rolls across my back and I shiver. Placing forefingers to my thumb and raising my closed eyes upward, I count down to level, making my call.

Three . . . two . . . one. Big D?

"Yes, Jeff."

I see him now, wrapped in his blacker-than-black robes as he squats to sit on the ledge next to me. Only the ivory of his skull shows clearly. The twin fires in his eye sockets appraise me in the calm of the night.

Why, Big D? I groan in exasperation. *Why did there have to be all that drama?*

"Remember how you got drunk and fucked up that tank truck full of diesel, driving it off that mountain road and into that rice paddy?" He chuckles. "You ever wonder why, after all that, they still pinned those acting jack stripes on your arm?"

Yeah. What was that about—that whole acting jack fiasco? Why was it necessary to pin those buck sergeant stripes on my sleeves anyway? I never wanted them, y'know. Why make me a sergeant? I know my commanding officer wanted to send me straight to Leavenworth.

The moment stretches long and silent while Big D appraises me before answering. "I was the one who put the bug in the battalion commander's ear. 'Kick your fuck-ups upstairs' is an old army tradition. Seemed like a good idea to him. And considering all the others who would have taken the fall with you as well, it was necessary." The glow of his sight seems to condense and sharpen, and again, a cold chill crosses my sweating back. I shiver. "Reread what you just wrote—the part about it taking experience to move knowledge from one's head to one's heart in order to truly *know* a thing. We just recently discussed this very concept. Is it really so hard for you to see that it may be your lessons, but it is all aimed at your soul's growth? Your soul knows everything already it just needs to 'know.'"

Okay. And what does that have—

"You remember Mess Sergeant Curtis up at line Pappa in Moonson Korea?"

Yes, of course.

"Then you remember how his kindness to three ragged, Korean beggars was what avoided a second costly Korean War and saved an untold number of lives, including yours?" His gaping grin seems to widen. "And you were there to witness it. You wrote about it in your first book. With the ending of that chapter, I told you what the cost would have been had his choice not been one of love. This reminder now is to place the knowledge—not just of those avoided consequences but of it all—in your heart."

I lower my head in somber realization, remembering the events of that summer. How those three beggars were North Korean insurgents, armed with mortars, grenades, and machine guns. For days, they were sitting on the hill above, starving to death, and were deciding whether to beg for food or wipe out every one of us unarmed American GIs and take the food.

Knowing my every thought, Big D now breaks my concentration to make his point. "You would not have been there to witness it if you were not the NCOIC—Non-Commissioned Officer in Charge—of those field showers, nor would you be here now, were you not there then with Sgt. Curtis. He saw your gentle nature, saw how you picked up your own tray and was about to offer it to them, and was influenced." His gaze now pins me like a bug. "And that doesn't give you the credit. Sgt. Curtis is the one who made the decision. So, just take that mind fart out of your head and put it into your heart."

But what does any of that have to do with me running Doc out of the seminar?

"Look, Jeff, I know you hate to be the leader, the authority, in anything. You didn't want to be a buck sergeant, nor did you want to be the men's counselor for the seminar. But the consequences of you not being there? Do you want to know?"

Yes.

"Well, Doc and the two ladies would have gone. You noticed that all three backed out. One of them would not have survived the seminar. That would have ended Karen's Quest Seminars forever." He stops and regards me, bathing me in the light from his sight while that sinks in. "Do you realize how many thousands attended her seminars over the following years? Can you imagine how much better a place the world has become because of what all those people got from attending? All of that hung on *you* being there to do exactly what you did. Like Sgt. Curtis, what you did you did out of love."

My mouth hangs open, struck dumb in contemplating it all. Then he lays down his zinger.

"And you . . . you have not published this book yet, but you have published your first novel and four workbooks on Spiritual Laws, as well as two volumes of poetry. How many people down through the years do you imagine will learn about Spiritual Law from your books?

"No. Your imagination sucks. Multiply that by a thousand." The glow from one eye socket winks briefly as if in a conspiracy. "Think of how knowing these simple truths, these Laws of Life, have affected your own."

But I—

"Yeah, I know. You self-published. But not before you collected enough reject letters from agents and publishers to wallpaper your house. Still, you felt ashamed to throw your books out there into that great cesspool of self-published, shitty books." I don't need to hear his chuckle to know his humor. I see it in his grin. "Unlike most, you heard what those publishers and agents were saying. Publishers live by society's rules. But you're a redneck—you don't have the fake façade of a 'gentleman.' And while you've taken the time and made the effort to learn how to write, you haven't given up the honesty, crude as it sometimes is. There are those who will value you for being who you are. Thing is, you have something to say, and you don't tiptoe around anyone's fragile, fucking feelings in saying it. Take it from someone who knows. In that cesspool of shitty books, yours will all be the turds that float."

I think the best sex requires an element of love. But let's face it. With many men, it is not their soul, not their heart, not even their dicks, but their ego that does their fucking. I believe it is always so until one learns how to love—and to make love. Until then, sex is just an orgasm of the ego—an E-gasm. Problem with E-gasms? We men are the ones who slime ourselves, and no quick swallow is going to clean up that mess.

Redneck Spirituality—Book Three

CHAPTER FIFTEEN

Shopping at the Meat Market

Looking back, I remember how, after that night, Doc's brand of spiritualism began feeling dangerously close to insanity. For him to feel superior, his natural inclination was always to spotlight others in a light of inferiority. The break in his integrity, on his commitment to EQ, and the fact that I was still going, gave intensity to his spotlight. Ah, the spotlight of one's ego. Sad that he was so blind to its glare.

Again, there is that Spiritual Law—***Others are but mirrors for us to see ourselves***. Doc's reflection in the mirror was not a pretty one. I've often wondered how much of that ugliness was pictured for him in the mirror of me. And how much of him was meant to be a warning for me? For someone who could see the world of metaphysics so clearly, yet be so blind to his own creations in it—yes, heart-wrenching for those of us who loved him, and scary for those of us who know the law.

But why was I getting all preachy about it with my moral judgments about him? Was it jealousy? It's so easy to judge others wrong and blame them for all of one's problems in life, even knowing one's life is totally self-created. I could well see why my soul might rub it in my face, pointing out, by Doc's example, why ***all*** those chicken exits are closed to me. Judgment, shifting the blame, *is* a chicken exit.

Las Vegas was always hot that time of year. Sitting before my computer, all was silent, and although there was no hum from my air conditioner, there was still a cool breeze blowing across my back. *Mirrors—oh my God! Big D, is this your way of pointing out that I suffer the same dysfunction, that I have a need to see myself as better than?*

* * *

Eventually, Doc turned his spotlight directly on me. It happened one night after meditations. Candy and I were the last to leave. During our parting hug, I unconsciously rubbed her back in familiar appreciation of the friend she was. Then I turned and hugged Doc.

"Stay a moment, Jeff," he whispered into my ear. "I need to talk to you." As Candy disappeared out the door, he shifted his eyes back to look directly at me. "Jeff, you gotta stop that. Candy doesn't like it."

"Doesn't like what?" My mouth was hanging open, eyes wide.

"You know, the way you touch her and talk about sex around her. She doesn't like it."

I stared. What was he saying? We three had always been familiar with one another. Joking openly about sex was one of those things I liked most about our relationship—the three of us. Was he saying I was only an intruder in their relationship?

"Doc, what do you mean by, '. . . the way I touch her?'"

"You know, the way you rubbed her butt just now. She asked me to speak to you about it."

"Doc, I didn't touch her butt. And if I had, how could you see? You were standing behind me." I pointed a thumb over my shoulder.

"Well . . . doesn't matter." He grimaced. "She just wanted me to tell you. She sees the way you look at women, how you use Inner Quest as your own personal meat market, and she doesn't like it." I looked at him steadily, and his eyes didn't slide from mine. Whatever he was saying, he felt it was the truth.

"I'll speak to her. This is just a misunderstanding."

"No! Don't do that." The words fairly tumbled out. "Can't you see you'll just embarrass her?"

I could see that, *if* it were true. But how could it be? There was an honest friendship between Candy and me. Nothing else.

"Yeah, all right. I'll think about what you've said." There was little else on my mind until I ran into Candy two days later at Karen's office. I drew her aside.

"Candy, there's something I need to ask you." Her smile was warm, carrying no hint she might be uncomfortable with me.

"Sure, Jeff, what do you need?"

"Uh . . . Candy, I don't quite know how to say this. I guess I just need you to give me some really honest feedback as a woman 'cause I'm really looking at some things about me as a man."

"Sure, Jeff," she repeated, eyebrows furrowed in concern.

I took a deep breath in, then blew it out. *Shit! Might as well face it.* I began.

"Candy . . . umm . . . have I ever come across to you as some sort of sexual predator?" Her mouth fell open and she stared, wide-eyed. "Have you ever felt I was being overly familiar or taking liberties with our friendship?"

Before answering, she shook her head slightly and seemed to become aware that her mouth was open. "What do you mean?"

"Well . . . y'know I joke around a lot about sex with the ladies. Have you ever felt offended by it? Have I ever touched you in ways you don't like?"

"No! Absolutely not! Your open sexuality is one of the things I like most about you." Her hand went out as if to touch me, then stopped and twisted, palm up. "What brought all this on?"

"It's just that Doc had a word with me the other night." I turned my head slightly away, suddenly unwilling to meet her eyes. "He said I use the Quest Seminars as my own personal meat market, that I turn women off by coming on too sexual."

"No, that's just his own stuff. What else does he say?"

"Well, he said I was being too familiar with the way I touch you, that it offended you. He said you asked him to tell me to stop."

"He what! No, Jeff." She paused, shaking her head. "You gotta understand something about Doc and me. We had a thing—just once—way back several months ago. But now that he's had me, he's lost all interest and hasn't touched me since." She smiled grimly. "Oh, I'm gonna straighten him out about this!"

"Candy, I didn't bring this to you to cause trouble. I'm really looking at these things about me. I do look at the women at IQ." I kept my head down, studying a crack in the tile floor. "And I know some have taken offense with me about my sexuality. I don't want to think of myself as a predator." I looked up and paused to take a deep breath, then again blew it out in disgust. "And, maybe I am."

"No, Jeff. Any woman who takes offense with you about this just has a sexual stick stuck up her butt. You just give them an opportunity to see it." She chuckled. "To accept you, they'd have to pull it out."

Candy was telling me her truth. Yet, I knew that predatory part had once been in me. Back in my youth, there was a time I looked to women for sex without much of a care for anything else. I'd been dishonest—not overtly, but covertly. I once allowed one woman to think my feelings for her were stronger than they were—marriage strong—just for the brief opportunity to make my dick feel good. Only recently, in writing about my life, did I look at it honestly. It was a sickening thing to admit about my past. I wanted none of it in my present.

My inquiry did not stop with Candy. I put similar questions to several more women, even one with whom I'd had a relationship. All it left me with was that the only person in the world who could validate the truth about me *was* me.

Hell yes, I wanted a relationship, one with someone who connected, someone who thought like, understood, and accepted me. I didn't just want sexual escapades, though the sex part was great, too. I wanted her to be as open and appreciative of sex as me. What Doc accused me of was indeed true—I was searching the seminars for a mate. And yes, I did enjoy the sexual part of my search. Even so, there was no dishonesty about it.

Explaining this to Doc only seemed to enrage him. It wasn't so much that his ego said he was *right*. Everyone's ego says that. What always tripped him up was that his ego said everyone else was *wrong*. For Doc, friend or foe, *everyone* else was wrong.

Then, when I mentioned my conversation with Candy, his eyes blazed. We were standing in the living room of his apartment.

"Didn't I tell you not to talk to her?" His voice now carried a louder, harsher note, one I'd never heard from him before. It reminded me of my mother's rages, only in a masculine way.

"Doc, it's about honesty for me." Then I added in afterthought, "And I don't always do what others demand."

The blow came out of nowhere, a violent, more numbing than painful blow that landed against my left cheekbone and sent me immediately to the floor. In a flash, I rolled and was back on my feet, a dizzy ringing in my head.

Doc was, I knew, well versed in the martial arts. His real job was working the bars, both as a bartender and bouncer. He moved in with confidence to finish it. His stance was one I recognized immediately from my own karate training in Korea, now thirty years past. Doc didn't know about Korea.

His next two blows, though cobra swift, were blocked equally quickly, and without thinking on my part—a left, then right. When they failed to land, I saw the quick shift and slight outward thrusting of his hip that signaled a reverse roundhouse kick. I knew instinctively it would be a right heel and aimed at my head. Butter smooth, it flashed around. Instead of moving back, I took half a step forward and caught the fleshy, softer part of his calf in my armpit. Wrapping my right arm over and then back under his knee, I locked it with my left hand and stepped quickly back while giving his knee a fast, upward jerk.

There was no popping crunch signaling a broken bone, though his quick intake of breath told me clearly that it had been effective. He must have felt it coming, for he yanked his own body out straight and parallel with the floor. It was the only thing that kept his leg from breaking. Falling face down, his breath whistled out in agony as my left foot landed solidly into his nads.

I hadn't fought or even practiced karate in all those long years since Korea. Often, I wondered why I never stayed in training or, in fact, why I took it in the first place. Standing back now, I knew why and felt no need to continue, though I also knew he'd not have given me this same grace.

For a time, he just lay there, curled on his side, with only his injured right leg sticking out straight. The only sounds were his low, guttural grunts of pain. Then, finally, he seemed to catch his breath and rolled over, his arm outstretched to me.

"I guess I deserved that, Jeff," he groaned, his voice husky and unnaturally calm. "Give me a hand up, old buddy."

Something, some inner feeling, told me not to take it.

"Doc," I said with real regret, "you're too dangerous a man for me to want to reach out to again." I walked away and left him then—left him hobbling around on his injured leg, cursing my back.

"Come back, you chickenshit bastard. Come back and fight!"

In leaving, it crossed my mind, *Will he press assault charges against me? No, Doc won't want anyone to know he'd been bested by me.*

I never went back, and Doc never again showed up at IQ. Doc has everything he wants in life. We all do. Bottom line—*If I'm not sure about what I really want, I need only look at what I have. Then the only question I need ask is, "Why do I want this?"*

Just like my mother, outwardly, Doc was a loving, caring person, constantly putting himself out to and for others. Inwardly, like my mother, he was mean. Eventually, in his mind, they all—every one—betray him. Why? Because Doc wants to be a victim. What better victim than a martyr? Martyrs always get to be better than those who betray them.

I could never change Doc. Only he can do that. He doesn't, as yet, want to. I could only be an honest friend—and I was. Doc, given what he wants in life, wasn't listening. Sometime maybe he will . . . sometime when he wants a friend more than he wants to be superior.

Comb Ridge, Utah—Present Day

Indian summer is over. I'm surprised it has lasted so long this year. At an elevation of nearly six thousand feet, it has been surprisingly warm.

But last night was an arctic hell. I've been putting off setting up the tent, but with the chilling rant of last night's winds, it is now a necessity. Huddled into the back corner, the Moki dwelling didn't provide sufficient protection. Although clothed in leather jacket and chaps, and wrapped in my sleeping bag, still, I was awake and shivering all night.

First light saw me at the end of the ledge, untying the tent from the wreckage of my bike and dragging it behind on my painful way back to the Moki hut. After laying it out from my prone position, painfully, laboriously, I insert the first sectioned fiberglass rod. Then, with a grunt, I roll over, the distance just right to insert the other.

From there, it is a matter of getting the pain back under control. Then, worming my way around to the back side, I align the ends into the pockets made for them and come back around to the front. Holding the tent floor steady, I slowly bend the first rod into a bow and hook its end into the front pocket. The second somehow has come out of the back pocket. Gritting my teeth, I bulldoze my way through the pain and reset the back end. Pushing off with my good right leg, I hobble on one elbow back around to repeat the process with the second stay. *Thank God this fucking tent only has the two.*

Sweating profusely and shaking almost uncontrollably, I fumble the zipper open and, from my seated position, literally fall through the opening.

It is dark when I wake. The temperature is up several degrees from last night and no wind chill. Wearing my leathers, I'm almost comfortable. Sitting up, I hold my arms wide, as if to embrace all of Comb Wash—or maybe the whole damned universe—and shout, "Thank ya, God. I needed that." The echoes come rolling back. *Thank ya, God . . . needed that . . . needed that.*

"He, or rather, We, know you do." I look up into the warm, red glow of Big D's eyesight. "You also need to get some food into your belly. You're pretty run down and you're going to need it."

Thanks. It's a good thing I had the presence of mind to set the saddlebags and sleeping bag so close to the entry. This fucked-up leg has taught me to think things through before I do them. Notice how the doorway has a good view down into the canyon. If I can catch a vehicle down there on the road at night, I can use the LED taillight to signal.

The way this ledge curves around the part that catches sunlight is a jumble of pinyon pines, but there's an outcrop that cuts the view into the bottom. Daytime signaling with the mirror is pretty much useless.

I reach out and drag my sleeping bag, then the saddlebags, into the tent. Getting the canteen out, I take a long swallow. Then I remove a stick from the jerky jar, now numbering only five. Pulling my knife from its sheath, I start to cut a third off.

"Naw, Jeff, just eat the whole stick. You're going to need your strength for tomorrow. Don't worry about cooking up the pine bark gumbo. Just chew it slowly and let it mix and swell with your saliva." He nods his head, and one red glow winks briefly out. "I think there's a jelly bean left to celebrate the occasion, too."

What in hell are you talking about, Big D? You were explicit about making this jerky last. But it's almost gone. What can possibly be so special about tomorrow?

"Pinyon pine."

I huff a deep breath and shout it aloud. "Pinyon pine—what?"

"Tomorrow's the day the pinyon pines give up their nuts. What? You don't remember letting the Navajo collect them on your land when you lived over near Durango?"

Oh my God! I'd forgotten.

When you give of yourself to someone, you are the one who gets the gift.

> Redneck Spirituality—Book Four

CHAPTER SIXTEEN

Eagle Quest—
In the Tent and in the Can

I parked my truck under a spreading cottonwood. Stepping out, I sighed in the welcomed shade it afforded. The weather here still sweltered under the September desert sun. Toquerville, a green spot in the canyon on the road to Zion National Park, was the site of the seminar.

This was the first Eagle Quest, and I shivered in anticipation of what I was about to face. Again, the unknown is always scary.

The rough-cut lumber of the main building was gray with age. I knew this site was normally used for helping troubled teens and smiled. *Know I'm late, but I'm here to deal with the same.* Troubles are always troubling.

I stepped through the entrance into the main classroom, the last to arrive. Only fourteen of us would take this challenge. None of us had a clue as to what we would be doing here.

Karen's grin was alligator wide as she welcomed me. "Good to see you, Jeff. We're all here now. You will notice the bucket sitting before you on the table." Her grin became somehow even wider. "It's there for you to put your car key in. Everyone—put 'em in there." For a moment, we all looked at one another dumbly. Karen added, *"Now!"*

Mine were the first to drop. Their startling, loud jangle broke the sudden silence of the room. Karen continued as, one by one, the other keys followed. "Now you will note the plastic Ziploc bags in the pile before you. Janie, please pass them out." Karen paused a moment until we were all in possession of a bag, then handed a magic marker to Janie.

"Pass this around, and everyone write your name on the outside of your bag."

Once it was done, she continued with a chuckle. "Okay, smokers, put all your cigarettes in your bag." Again, she paused while it was done. "That takes care of nicotine. Now, caffeine, candy, gum, aspirin, antacid—any non-prescription drugs—in the bag. These, folks, are your crutches, the ones you've always used to treat the symptoms of all the dis-eases killing you bit by bit every day. Now, put your bags in the bucket."

"B-but the keys," Dan began.

"Are not taken to imprison you, but rather, to protect you. It is required for you to be clear mentally, should you choose to leave. Eagle Quest is just that—a quest. We don't want anyone running off, screaming into the night. Ha, you just don't know." Karen ducked her head in merriment. "Panic and drama are just two more of the crutches people often use to avoid facing the real issues of their lives. Eagle Quest will set you up to win. Not one of you will ever again be able to say, *I can't*. That, too, is only a crutch we all use to avoid the responsibility of saying *I will* or *I won't*."

* * *

Being the first Eagle Quest, there wasn't a support team. We had to do our own cooking and cleaning, even laundry. For all that, it made for long days and short nights. The food was clean and free—meat free, processed sugar free, caffeine free . . .

The change in diet made for some rather free bowel movements—irritatingly, frequently free. Our bodies were being cleansed of the toxins we all insisted on stuffing them with. The latrine facilities were in a two-room shed that housed the showers on the women's side, the laundry on the men's.

Although our two-toilet stalls had closed-in sides, the front gaped open. I found it very embarrassing to be on the pot when the women would come in to do laundry on the men's side. They never knocked. And, too, they seemed to feel it was their right to use the men's toilets whenever theirs were in use. There were only two men and twelve women in the seminar, and still, I felt resentment rising at each embarrassing interruption. And the laundry machines? Why is it that women have to wash clothes so often? Dan, the other man, didn't seem to mind, but he did have a problem when I took to locking the door.

The second day in, I addressed the issue. During one of the exercises, I found myself standing on a platform above the group. Their eyes were all on me. I didn't miss the opportunity.

"Ladies . . . while I have your attention, I have something I need to say." They all perked up expectantly. Part of the quest is about learning trust and support, and this platform was used for *trust falls*.

"I just want you to know that I get really pissed when I'm interrupted on the pot—trust me. That may be the place to do my pissing, but would you knock before you enter the men's shitter from now on? *Please!*"

There were some red-faced giggles, but everyone agreed that my request was reasonable. A half hour later, I was just sitting down for my first comfortably secure dump when the door burst open and one of the women walked in. My mouth hung open as she breezed by in front of me.

"Hey! Do you mind?"

"Oh . . . it's only me," she said, as she exited with her laundry.

I sat there on the pot, my pants around my ankles, my jaw still hanging. *What the fuck does she mean . . . it's only me?*

Then it struck me. There were two teepees as sleeping quarters and two bathrooms. We shared it all between two men and twelve women. In our tent, there was Dan and me and four lesbian women, one of which had just left with her laundry. *Holy shit! I get it. It's about the energy—male and female energy.* Suddenly, I carried a whole new viewpoint about lesbians. I had to smile. *Damned if they don't have cojones, too!*

One of the exercises on that first day involved a group activity, which was done blindfolded. Another involved something we did while balancing together on cables stretched tightly above the ground. Both called for group cooperation and mutual support. Later, we viewed the video tapes and were able to see how we did, individually and collectively.

There was a woman there . . . Janie. On the tape, we saw how she kept herself separate from the others and insisted on doing everything for herself. Even during those times when a supporting hand was needed and offered, she refused it, especially when the help offered was from either of us men.

"Are you seeing yourself here, Janie?" Karen stopped the video. "Here, I'll replay it for you." Janie watched it, jaw sagging, aghast in sudden awareness.

"Kind of a loner, are you? Don't like men?" Karen queried her, hand outstretched, palm down. "How long have you been divorced?"

"Uh . . . well, several years." Karen ducked her head slightly, flipped her hand, palm up, and wagged her fingers in an out-with-it signal. "I dunno, eight . . . no, ten years."

Without giving her time to think, Karen's next question was more pointed.

"So, when was the last time you had sex? And I mean in more than a wham-bam-thank-you-sir kind of way? When was the last time you had *any* kind of a close relationship with a man?"

Janie burst into tears and wailed. "But Karen . . . how do I get close? I don't know how to be vulnerable. And I know I avoid men, but I don't know any I can trust!"

"It's easy." Karen ducked her head to look her directly in the eye. "Just pick a single, nurturing man and get honest with him."

"But, how do I do that?" Janie squeaked, her voice more helpless and confused than before.

Turning to me, Karen said, "Jeff, do you see how vulnerable Janie feels right now?"

"Yes." I nodded.

"Would you be willing to nurture her?"

"Sure," I responded, although with slightly more caution.

"Would you be willing to sleep with Janie tonight and just hold her and nurture her in a positively non-sexual manner?" Karen asked.

I gulped. "Yeah, I can do that."

Karen then turned back to Janie, who had turned absolutely white. "Janie, would you be willing to sleep in Jeff's bed tonight and allow him to nurture and cherish you?"

Janie's lips were trembling. "But . . . I . . . uh . . . I don't think Jeff wants to."

"Doesn't matter. It's not about him. He's agreed." Karen paused, eying Janie seriously. "This is about you and you getting your needs met. You need to learn vulnerability." Karen's eyes softened.

"Now, are you willing?"

"Y-yes." Janie was rapidly turning red.

Commitments now made, Karen cautioned us, looking from one to the other. "You both understand that there is to be no sex involved? No wham-bam-thank-you *anybody!*"

We nodded.

"No sexual talk . . . no sexual touching . . . no sex! Right?"

"Right." We responded in unison.

That night, in eerie silence, Janie and I laid our mattresses together on a ground sheet inside the tent. She seemed afraid to speak. And I? I didn't know what to say. We used my sleeping bag on the bottom and hers on top. Then, settling in together, I put my arms around her and just held her. She remained mute for a while, laying stiff and trembling although the night was still warm. Finally, she broke the silence.

"You really don't have to do this." She cleared her throat. "Uh . . . you know?"

"Sure I do," I replied. "This is what we agreed."

"Well, you really don't have to hold me like this—"

"Sure I do," I replied again, cutting her off. "Besides, it's been a while since I held a woman in a non-sexual way. It feels . . . nice."

With that, we both began to relax and talked about Karen's seminars, and our marriages, and a lot of other things we found in common. Eventually, we fell asleep in one another's arms. It was a very healing night for me, and I suspect, even more so for her. Janie was a very attractive, firm-bodied redhead. Although we never had a romantic relationship, nor did we ever have sex, we did have that one night when Janie was nurtured and cherished by me.

* * *

We experienced a lot of events in the seminar—events that, for a long time, I could not divulge to others. To do so might ruin the experience for them, should they go. But Eagle Quest has changed. It is no longer held at the Toquerville site, and nearly all the events are now different. Some of it, I can now discuss freely.

As is true of life, all the events meant nothing unless we placed our own significance on them. Those that required team effort were especially important for me. From them, I learned that, like Janie, I didn't have to do it all myself, and in fact, there is much in life that can't be accomplished without help. I could accept help from others, and I learned women would willingly aid me and were surprisingly capable. Those things that were of most importance to me during our marriage rarely were to Meg. No help there.

Thursday morning was spent cleaning up the facility, in teaching us a lesson in life as it applied to the universal law—**Everything is in change.** We were taught to always leave everything better than we found it.

I was pulling weeds when one of the women, Tess, walked by carrying a bucket of lime-green paint and a brush, having been painting one of the logs used in an event. I'd never really noticed her before, but I did now. It was the paint that drew my attention—not the paint in the can or that on the brush. Rather, it was the paint covering the nipples that jutted boldly through the fabric of her very nicely fitting polo shirt. She wore no bra.

Tess was small and petite, but solidly well built. She was around fifty, about three years older than I, and more cute than beautiful. In one of the exercises, it became necessary for me to stand on her back while she knelt on the ground. It was something I was very reluctant to do—me, six four and weighing two hundred forty-five pounds, and she, five foot even and perhaps one hundred pounds. I was impressed at the ease with which she handled it. That evening, I mentioned it to her and we spent some time together, mostly just talking about me and my life. I was surprisingly comfortable opening up to her.

And her? For some reason, she would not step in close or talk about herself to me. Was it the physical attraction I felt for her—I made it no secret—or something else? And why was it that until those lime-green spots floated before my eyes, I'd entertained no special interest in her. But now that I did . . .

Hmmm?

Is it necessarily a bad thing when something sexual is what first draws a man's attention? Isn't sexual compatibility a necessary ingredient of a completely fulfilling relationship? During our conversation, I asked her if she would like to have coffee or lunch and hang out together sometime. She answered, "Yeah . . . sometime," but there was no commitment in her voice.

The single events, those that had to be done alone, were different. On most, the meanings, the metaphors, placed on them by me, were of getting past my marriage and moving on in life.

Being alone was, for me, fearful, as were heights. The events were all perfect for moving through my fears. Courage is not about having no fear. It's about stepping through it. My skydive didn't cure my fear of heights. It only served to change my mind about cowardice—my cowardice.

The high wire and catwalk were events both done high in the air. Although harnessed to a belay line and perfectly safe, I didn't feel safe.

But the catwalk? That was the hardest for me. It involved climbing a telephone pole fifty feet high. Then quaking, shuddering, and with arms flailing, I crossed over another log bridging some thirty feet to a second pole. The belay line hung from a pulley on a cable overhead. It was kept such that it had very little slack and proved a nuisance. It often hung up on its pulley, which forced me to jerk on it occasionally as I progressed along. I must have looked like a spastic chicken as I fought to keep my balance, especially during those times.

Once I reached that far pole, I was required to turn around and go back to the middle, then lean forward against the belay line. It was then loosened, and my body naturally rotated out horizontally until I literally fell off and was belayed down. That was the only safe way of getting off that log without busted bones or splitting one's head open.

As with most, the meanings I hung on those events were of moving on in my life—away from Meg—but toward what, or who, didn't matter. I was done staying hung up over Meg.

* * *

Eagle Quest culminated on Friday with *the pole*. When my turn came, I looked up the forty feet and thought, *I can do this!* I told it to myself, but where was my conviction?

Giving me no more time on that question, the facilitator hollered, "On belay?"

This is it. "Belay on!" I replied.

"Climb!"

"Climbing!" I chimed back and stepped onto the pole.

I began climbing the little, rounded, metal nubs that stuck out at odd intervals. The higher I climbed, the weaker my body felt until, finally, I found myself out of pole and feeling out of strength.

Pausing there, with the flat, sawed-off top of the pole level with my waist, I caught my breath and summoned more courage. Looking down, I spotted Dan so far below. He had his turn a few minutes before and fell off. Not satisfied, he went back up again, only with the same result.

I can do better.

Still, I was now out of pole. It was time to let go of the thinking and just do. No longer was there anything to grab on to, to pull myself up with. My left foot was near the top on the highest nub, and my right, a long step below. The only next step was up onto the flat, eight-inch disc. *My God, my feet are too big to even fit on the top of this!*

Crouched, doubled over, and stiff-armed at the top, I carefully balanced on part of the ball of my left foot where it gripped the smooth, metal nub, then slowly brought my right up onto the top. That step was the hardest I've ever taken. It was easier stepping out of that plane at ten thousand feet than onto this pole at only forty. The pole not only swayed back and forth, but it shook also. I knew the shaking was mostly from my own trembling body. I started to straighten up and bring my left foot, at last, onto the top.

There was a dizzy whirling and rushing all around as I pitched face-forward off the pole. I ended abruptly in a jouncing, swaying halt at the end of the belay line.

Once on the ground, I insisted on trying a second time. Climbing the pole once more, I experienced exactly the same sensations, only this time, at a much milder level of fear. Again, I took that final step supported again only by my courage—and again plunged off the top.

The idea was to stand balanced on the top, then dive off for the prize in one's life, represented by a trapeze hanging ten feet out in front. It didn't look doable, but it was. Three fourths of the women who went before me did it. After basking in the glow of triumph on the end of the trapeze, they'd let go to be belayed down.

As soon as I reached the ground, I headed back for the pole again. *This isn't going to beat me—not like it did Dan. Besides, how can I live with myself knowing all these women did something I can't.*

Karen's voice stopped me.

"Jeff, hold on . . . let the others finish. Then, if you still want to, you can go again. In the meantime," she added, "I want you to look at what this is for you. To win at this exercise, all you must do is go as far as you can, then take one more step."

"I know, Karen, but I failed! I fell off—twice!" My voice sounded whiny, even to my own ears.

"No, Jeff, you haven't failed. Think about it, then think about what it is that is driving you up that pole again."

It didn't take me long. Of course, I didn't go up a third time—not when I realized it was my ego's sick need to be better than Dan and my shame of being bested by women in something this physically challenging. *What kinda asshole does all this make me?*

Then, as I slipped off the harness, the realization hit. *Wait a minute. This is something I can now see about me. Just a moment ago, I wasn't willing to even look at it.* I felt a thrill of triumph when realizing how few people in this world are willing to be this honest with themselves. I was certainly not better than Dan, yet there was something of magnificence I now saw in me. In that moment, my self-respect stood higher than the pole.

* * *

Eagle Quest . . . five days straight of absolutely impossible events, each accomplished one after another. Each one, breaking through, destroying forever the beliefs holding me a prisoner in my mind—those that said "I can't."
Driving home from Eagle Quest, I left the window wide open. I didn't mind the hot, dry, desert air streaming in around me. While my '68, short-bed Chevy had a ball-buster 350 horse motor, it didn't have air. My sweat dried, keeping me comfortable enough, but more comforting still was that I now knew I was going to write and publish books. Before the EQ Seminar, becoming an author was never something I seriously considered as possible. I didn't give a rat's ass about money or fame, but since my days in that Comically awkward looking, I'm sure, but with only me there to do the laughing, it's a damned sight better to have that option than to not have any option other than grunting in pain while dragging myself around on my belly.

My tent bag cover is wadded inside my sleeping bag cover and now hangs around my neck. Taking a sweet lungful of the cold, morning air, I look out over Comb Ridge. This dawning promises to be a seasonally warm day. Indian Summer is what I think some call this time of year—right after the first frosts of fall, but before the serious cold of winter. It rarely snows in Utah's high desert lands. The air is pretty dry most all the year.

With more jerky in my belly than I've become used to, I'm feeling pretty good. Still, Big D has cautioned me to conserve it because today calls for considerably more exertion than usual. Pine nuts are high in fats, proteins, and fiber. They're high in calories but low in carbs—a perfect survival food. Hell, it has always been a staple for the Navajo, Hopi, and Apache Indians. There was my old work buddy, Jimmy

Begay, a Navajo. Remembering him brings a smile. Good people to know.

As many years as I've lived in this country, I never ate more than a few pine nuts now and then—and then only because they grew on my land near Durango. Here I was, starving, with this food source ripening right under my nose. I've lost track of the time. It's been what, six weeks? Two months?

Arriving at the first tree, I look up and my mouth falls open. Pine cones don't necessarily ripen every year, and some years the crop is next to nothing, but this year, the trees, though small and few, are loaded. The ground is already littered with freshly fallen cones.

All this time I've been peeling a little bark here and there and cutting a few small branches for pine needle tea, even busting off dead branches for cooking fires. I'd not even noticed the pine cones. They were all green and shriveled, like gonads on a cold night. Now they were fat and brown and popping with nuts.

There comes a chuckle from my right. "Don't be gorging. You still need to conserve." Big D is sitting at the edge again with his usual grin across his naked skull. "And speaking of gorges, the view is magnificent from here."

Why? How much longer before they find me?

"Along this time line, almost no one's looking." He shrugs his boney shoulders. "Unless something happens . . ."

hospital ICU, I've learned so much about the real truths of life—things most people never have a clue about. Yes, I now had some things to say, and by God, I knew, without a doubt, I would write these books.

Karen was correct. The "C" word—"can't"—is no longer in my repartee of swear words.

Comb Ridge, Utah—Present Day

Morning finds me humping it over to the pinyon pine just a short distance down the ledge to the south. 'Humping' is how I've come to deal with moving around any distance. It's so much less painful.

From a sitting position, I bend my good left leg up, planting my foot flat on the ground. Then, rocking back on my hands a ways, I can push off with my leg and replant my butt about a foot along my path.

Whaddaya mean?

"Well, don't you have a purpose to fulfill yet?" He chuckles to himself. "You do know that you getting off this ledge alive will depend on it—and on living up to our agreement. You've done neither. How's that for creating your life . . . or death." The impressions I now see across his boney vista send chills down my spine.

If you mean this book, there's nothing left that a couple of days editing wouldn't fix. I duck my head, close my eyes, and rub at the weariness there. *And that should be done by a professional editor. Is there another purpose I am to complete?* I shake my head in confusion. *And our agreement? What the fuck is that all about?*

Looking up, he is gone, but his words seem to hang in the air, sounding disturbing, like mockery, but minus the humor. "Our agreement—you've been breaking that every day over the last few years. You need to discover it for yourself and fix it. Think Jackie."

"Jackie? Jackie? What the fuck?" The words burst out verbally, unbidden.

Unhealthy people fall in love to fill the emptiness—the missing needs that they, themselves, mistake as somehow being not whole. They attempt to find someone "out there" to fill it, for the needs are most always about love. Healthy people are those who have looked within themselves for the love they need and, finding it, filled themselves to overflowing. Once there is such an abundance on the inside, they then look to someone "out there" for whom to give it. When they find someone of equal abundance, only then can love blossom past simple need to the full fruition of a lovegasm.

Redneck Spirituality—Book Four

CHAPTER SEVENTEEN

Single . . . Available . . . Women

She was one of those women other women take to with instant jealousy, and for whom men, too, often harbor hard feelings, but of a different sort. Tall and slender, her figure appeared almost as if poured into her clothes. She was the sort of woman I'd never have approached—not before Eagle Quest.

I met her at a new seminar Karen facilitated some three months later. She called it *Beyond Quest*, or, of course, BQ. It was during one of the potty breaks that I was introduced and really took notice. Her name was Regina.

The seminar was being held in a room originally intended to be a restaurant. It had a tiered balcony overlooking a baseball field. At one point during the seminar, we, the participants, were blindfolded and led off by a support team member. I sat in our self-imposed, black silence, listening as, one by one, those around me were taken, hearing the slight scraping of shoes and swish of clothing amidst the soft, murmured instructions of the guides.

Occasionally, faintly, from somewhere "way over there" would come a quick, strangled, bleating shriek of fear. As usual, most participants in these seminars were women. Idly, I wondered if any of those noises were being made by men. Whatever was happening seemed to happen quickly, though for me, the time dragged and the tension of uncertainty built.

It seemed as if everyone had gone before my turn finally came. When it did, it was with a light touch on my shoulder and a whiff of some unknown but enticingly feminine scent that matched the soft voice murmuring in my ear.

"Stand up." A small, delicate hand took hold of mine. The long fingernails of her other hand against the skin of my arm sent chills up my back as she guided me to my feet.

"Turn right . . . walk forward . . . turn left . . . walk . . . stop . . . step up three steps . . . turn left . . . right . . . ." The directions continued until I was totally lost in my surroundings. Then came instructions that sent my stomach quivering.

"Stop. Now, carefully raise your right foot up about six inches and place it on the plank just in front of you." A picture of this balcony's layout flashed through my mind. *No, surely they wouldn?"*

The voice continued to murmur. "Here, take this guide rope in your right hand. It is only loosely connected and is here just to guide you. It will not bear your weight. Now . . . step up!"

I did, and I immediately felt a sense of vertigo in my black, scary world. "That's good. Just take a step, slow and easy." I did and immediately flung out an arm to balance against the whirling in my head. "Get your balance . . . you can do this." Those calm, encouraging words seemed to drift up from somewhere below.

With the first two fingertips on my right hand forming an "O" with my thumb, I drew in a deep breath. Then, rolling my eyes slightly skyward, I expelled it, feeling the tension and fear simultaneously leave my body. That Silva technique for centering and focusing always worked slicker than KY jelly. In no time, I was over the plank and being guided up more steps onto a table or platform of some kind. From there, I was instructed in a special way of folding and locking my arms in front of myself, then told to turn around.

Oh my God, it's a trust fall! My mind recognized it at once and screamed out, though the words never crossed my lips. I'd done them before, but never blindfolded. And those steps. Clearly, this table had some height—too much height. For a man standing six four and weighing a relatively fat-free two hundred and forty, I was not the bouncing type and had strong concerns about the catchers' abilities. Those times prior, I'd always been able to look into the eyes of the guys catching me and feel reassured.

Oh well, I've done this. I can do it again, blindfolded or not. Taking another deep breath, I again steeled myself and was almost ready when Karen's voice drifted out of the darkness.

"Jeff, you are being caught only . . . by women! **Single . . . Available . . . Women**."

Holy shit! It took all my courage to lock my knees and fall board-stiff backward. The air rushed past my ears in a moment of eternity before being caught—easily—by many pairs of soft, female arms. The first notes of Mariah Carey's song "Hero" broke the stillness just as my blindfold was removed.

Upon opening my eyes, they focused directly on the beautiful, violet ones set in the perfect, porcelain face of Regina. She stood just behind those holding me, connected to me only by the link of our eyes. Obviously, she was my guide. As the song played its way through, I was rocked slowly back and forth, lovingly cradled by a dozen pairs of soft, feminine arms and the words of Mariah's song.

> ***It's a lo-o-ong road . . .***
> ***When you face the world alone. . . .***

Karen set my fall up special . . . the song, the women. Karen knew of my journey. She knew how, of all the principal women players on the stage of my life, none had ever played a supporting role, nor had any stayed—not one of my girlfriends, not my wife. Hell, not even my birth mother or the one who adopted me. Perhaps in her own way, she knew, too. I *didn't* trust women. There must have been a time when she, too, *didn't* trust men. Now, having put my life blindly into the supportive arms of females, it would never again be possible for me to view women in the old, distrustful way, nor could I question their ability to be of support. Sure, I got this same message in Eagle Quest, *but never so strongly given.*

That first night of the two-day BQ Seminar weekend, I thought a lot about the single women there. Several were very attractive. Was it possible one of them might be my soul mate? Perhaps a look into the subconscious knowing of my heart might be in order. I decided to use a pendulum.

The pendulum is simple. After drawing two straight lines on a sheet of paper in a ninety-degree cross, I then aligned the paper with one of the lines running straight toward and away from my body. The pendulum could be anything weighting the end of a string or light chain about twelve inches long. I used my old gold chain and cross. Meg had given it to me one October night in 1968. It was the night before I was to leave her to rotate out of the army. I'd held it in my hand that night in Tongduchon, Korea as I swore my love and promised to return and marry her. Yes, that cross had seen more than twenty-five years of loving Meg while hanging from around my neck. Fitting I should use it to aid in searching my heart for the one I could love next.

Most think the pendulum tells the future. Not so. It only tells what is in your heart. For that, it is very accurate. The *how* of its use is not important. What is important is that it pointed out Regina.

* * *

Later on, that first day of the seminar, Karen asked, as she often did, for all the single and available men to stand. I stood. Then the women. I noticed Regina stayed seated. Yet, seeing the way her eyes followed, was she available . . . to me? I could not discount that unknown, but not imagined, thing that passed between us following my trust fall. And then there was this feeling in my heart every time she was near. It, too, could not be denied. I went to my friend Dave, the one who'd introduced us. He was her buddy at their IQ Seminar.

"No, she's not married. She just lives with some guy, but I know she's not happy. He just doesn't think the same way she does."

Yes, I knew that one, that old "*I'm okay, you're all fucked up*" viewpoint. It was the same epitaph now written on the headstone over the grave of my own marriage. It is the eulogy of doom so often spoken from one mate to the other, spoken by the "normal" one to the "awakened" one.

Oh yes, I knew that one too well and wondered, *Had she also awakened to the same thought system and spirituality as me? Did she, too, now find condemnation—outright rejection—from those she loved?*

A minor shift in one's perspective, and two hearts are reeling off in different directions, one now simply seeing something the other is afraid to look at. So sad because where they are seeing it is only within, and what they are seeing—is truth.

I felt I knew her then, knew something of the way of her life. She, too, was one who had begun to feel and to see the beauty within her heart, to look there for the answers in her life, unlike Meg.

Meg always looked "without," pointing the finger of blame for her pain "out there." And most often, it was sighted in on me. Was Regina's mate like Meg, and Regina like me? Did he expect her to *make him happy*, and did he often point that finger of blame for his unhappiness at her? Intuitively, I knew he did.

That afternoon, I found Regina, off alone, sitting on the floor by herself as if deep in thought. On approach, I felt she somehow was expecting me.

"Hello, Regina. Mind if I sit with you a moment?"

She looked up, and the sun reflected violet from her eyes.

My God, violet eyes—again! Maybe there was some truth in what that psychic once told me back then about Eve. Same eyes, different woman.

"Sure, Jeff. What's on your mind?"

Her gaze followed me as I sank to the floor, legs crossed Indian style, matching hers. I got right to the point and was pleased that my directness didn't scare her off as it had with many. "Regina, I noticed you didn't stand with the 'single and available' women."

She nodded. "Yeah, I have someone . . ." Her voice sounded flat and her statement hung there, as if unfinished.

"I know." I paused, searching for an acceptably honest way. "And I'm not looking to push my way in where I'm not wanted. I just want you to know that I find you very attractive and I'd like to get to know you better. Maybe we could get together sometime—just over coffee or something—and talk." I said it to her directly, looking her honestly in the eye.

"Yes." For a moment, her gaze was locked to mine. "I think I'd like that."

"Good . . . be seeing you around." With that, I stood and moved off, leaving her sitting there, looking thoughtfully after me.

About a week later, I called. We talked for over an hour. It was as I suspected—her relationship was over, and she was looking for an apartment and another woman to room with. Obviously, she was at a very vulnerable place in life. I had no intention of taking advantage.

And, too, I remembered how important it had been to me back then, in that same space, just to have someone to talk to.

Besides, I'd given my word at the seminar. Karen always required it in all her seminars. One of the rules we agreed to was not to start any sexual relationships with anyone we met there for at least thirty days. It was a rule I never broke.

"How about meeting me at Starbucks for coffee?"

She regarded me for a moment, then answered, "Sure, how about on Wednesday? Oh, and will you bring some of your poetry? I'd like to read it."

A small jolt of concern shot through me. I couldn't recall telling her I wrote it. My poetry was never the flowery, esoteric stuff of beautiful, flowing words and rhyme that most people seem to like. I wrote only to express my deepest feelings, to pour out into my consciousness what was really in my heart. My first poem was written and read to Meg during the last days of our marriage.

It just seemed to happen, an appropriate way to speak to her of all the agony and the ecstasy of my soul. I shuddered, remembering her response. I looked at my concern and realized that this was an opportunity for Regina to know me—and she was not Meg. Didn't I want her to know the real me? Since that first poem, my soul has been a very prolific writer.

Coffee with Regina was on Wednesday. Going home, my soul seemed as if it were flying on those newly minted wings from the Eagle Quest Seminar—a whole week of doing things I could never imagine could even *be* done. And now there was Regina, this magnificent woman, interested in joining me in my life.

The next day, I came crashing back to Earth. Meg called with disturbing news—my father was in the hospital from a heart attack. I immediately began preparing to leave, scheduling my departure for the predawn hours of Friday. My parents' home in American Fork was some four hundred miles away. The next Eagle Quest was to begin the following Monday, and I was committed to being on the support team.

I didn't break my commitments, but on this one, my heart insisted. Upon explaining the situation to Karen, she, too, insisted, saying, "Don't worry about it. Go!"

Before hanging up, I asked, "If there is any way I find I can be there—even for the last day or two—would it be okay?"

"Sure, Jeff. Just do what you need to do."

After talking to Karen, I next called Regina. When I told her of my situation, she, too, was supportive. Toward the end of the call, a thought flashed into my mind. It seemed crazy, but my heart said, say it!

"Regina, you're looking for a place to move to . . . move in with me." Hearing the sound of it in my receiver, it sounded even crazier.

"Oh, Jeff . . . uh . . . I . . . uh . . . I don't know." Her reply sounded confused.

"Look, if you'd rather, we can just be roommates," I said. "Pay me something if you feel you need to. You can have your own room and bed if you want. Or, you can sleep in mine. It doesn't matter. There is that agreement we both made at the seminar—no sex for thirty days. I'll be honoring that."

She sounded unconvinced. "Oh . . . I don't know—"

"Look," I interrupted. "It'll give us time to get to know each other. You're looking for a place anyway. If it doesn't work out, at least you'll have time to decide where you want to go."

"Jeff, I'm just not ready to give you an answer right now." There was a yearning desperation now. Clearly, I was pushing her.

"You don't need to decide right now," I said by way of releasing the jaws of my Vise-Grips. "There's a potted plant by my front door. I'll hide a key in the gravel underneath it. You can come by and just look the place over. If you're living here when I get back after next week, I'll feel good about it. If not"—even though I knew she couldn't see me, I shrugged my shoulders anyway—"that's okay, too."

Remembering one of the events from my Eagle Quest, I wrote her a poem as a note of welcome. I left it taped to the living room mirror to await her possible inspection.

Standing there, reading it on that mirror, knowing she'd not done EQ, how could she understand? I almost took it down. Even to me it seemed goofy. Then I chuckled at an absurd thought. *Maybe she's never done Disneyland, either.*

It was honest, it was true to who I was, and it stayed.

* * *

Move In

Oh Regina, are you a woman of my soul?
Will you join this eagle's quest?
Perhaps you already have.
The wire of transformation
with its single-tethered guide,
is it already beneath your feet?
The green slime in the pits of your life
waits below, to greet you if you fall . . .
Waiting there for those without courage enough
to stay the course and cross.
The man to whom you were attached,
no longer provides the support you need.
His rope is played out . . .
Your position is tenuous . . . weakened,
As unstable as is your balance.
Still now, you cling to him.
Does he still have the ability
to nurture you?
Needing more . . . wanting more . . .
you reach out and find me.
Am I the right rope to guide you . . .
lead you . . . support you?
For mine leads in your direction . . .
Willingly . . . lovingly . . . with honesty.
His does not.
Do you have the strength . . .
the purpose . . . the will . . .

> *to make the transformation?*
> *Take my rope . . . move with me . . .*
> *move in with me.*

Comb Ridge, Utah—Present Day

Waking at first light is almost a habit now. There's not much to do in the dark except sleep. For a short while, there is my cooking fire for light. I just wish I could use it more for heating food. I have been existing on very short rations, mostly of jerky. It doesn't do much more than serve to flavor the pine bark, thickened soup.

The hunger pangs are now largely relieved, what with the pine nuts. Still, Big D cautions me to resist stuffing myself. They may have to last me throughout the coming winter. He once explained that my future depends on my actions in the present. So apparently, my life *is* in my own hands. Will that change with the picking of this crop of pine nuts? I don't know if my survival depends more on these nuts, or on the completion of my purpose, or even on settling up any lack of integrity concerning my agreements. I *do* know it hangs on every one of these things. *There is no security in this world.* I sigh. *But at least I have some control over these three things.*

Right now, I'll deal with them in that order, beginning with this harvest. Does my life depend on any one thing more than the others? Dunno. But right now, my hunger screams the loudest.

Gathering up my two carry bags, I begin humping it toward the pinyon pines at the south end of the ledge. The leg is still painful, but the wound is healed and closed. It seems the maggots have done their work well, and now the little bastards have flown away to wherever flies go in the wintertime. That, too, I dunno. While I didn't see them go, I do wish them well and I cannot help but wonder if they, too, have any appreciation of me. I am, after all, now a part of them.

Arriving under the first tree, I follow the same procedure as worked best yesterday. Using the smaller tent cover bag, I begin picking up the cones that were on the ground. The new ones are not darkened like the old. It is the same for the nuts that are dislodged by the fall. That wasn't much of a problem, seeing as most of the old ones were gathered up by chipmunks last year before they rotted.

By the time I reach the end tree on the ledge, the tent bag is full, and I have a good start on the sleeping bag cover. Then, sitting up, I begin to pick those I can reach still on the tree. With both bags full and drawstrings secure, I begin humping my laborious way back to the Moki hut where that Indian's mate graciously left her river rock sitting atop that mortar stone. She used it for grinding her corn who knows how many centuries ago. It gives me a funny feeling knowing that she likely sat in this same space. Did she, too, slam pine cones against this mortar stone to strip out the nuts?

The whole process is time-consuming. Huffing around with a broken leg, still *not* healed enough *not* to be painful, was *not* fun. Way too many 'nots' there for my liking.

Today, I drag my sleeping bag over and mold it flat around the mortar stone in a horseshoe shape. Yesterday, when slamming the pine cones against it, the nuts would scatter into the dirt, making it hard to collect them all.

Your ego's expectations of how it must be for you to get what you want will only guarantee you pain. What your ego wants and what your heart wants are very seldom the same, for your ego has eyes that can only look out. It cannot see your heart within.
                                        Redneck Spirituality—Book Four

CHAPTER EIGHTEEN

Hard Hearts Sometimes Break

It was in the last week of January when Meg called. We'd been officially divorced four months but separated more than eight, twelve months altogether. My parents were at war with me for all that time. In the beginning, all my attempts to communicate were met with outrage.

In the end, I almost wished I'd been raised in some other Christian religion, one where, if a son does not live his life the way he is told, the most they can do is threaten him with later burning in hell.

Mormons don't believe in hell. A Mormon son who dares to live differently is ostracized. People don't see hell as happening *in the now*, but for a Mormon son who doesn't obey, it does. Here, a year later, I was being met with silence—cold silence. Conditional love is the Mormon way, the real hell of Mormonism, and it does happen *in the now*.

My mother did not call me. She called Meg, who then called to inform me that my father was in the hospital. After a minor heart attack, he was having an artery roto-rooted. The attack happened on a Saturday. It was now the following Thursday.

Hearing the news, coming as it did in Meg's so familiar soft, lilting accent, struck a sudden longing in me. Like my parents, when we divorced, she also asked me to stay away from her. "Too painful," she said, although unlike my mother, Meg's asking was in a much softer, non-combative way.

Dad's heart attack was not unexpected, nor was their silence toward me concerning it. Finding no reaction to the raging, righteous rejection, their martyrdom turned to silence. But now? Now they knew Meg would pass the message to me.

At the time, I was working as a diagnostic mechanic in an auto repair shop. My vacation was already arranged for me to be on the support team for the second Eagle Quest Seminar, scheduled to begin that next Monday, again in the wilds of Southern Utah. While It bothered me a great deal to bail on my commitment to EQ, the decision was a no-brainer. My father held a prior commitment in my heart.

Before leaving, I called Mom and was surprised when she answered.

"Don't come. He doesn't want to see you." Her voice sounded old and tired, yet still held a hard-clipped shortness.

"I'm coming—" It was all I got in before the click of a disconnected receiver.

The drive from Las Vegas to American Fork, Utah, was not a short one. It seemed longer still in those dark, early morning hours with nothing on my mind but the memories of my dad.

How is it even possible for our relationship to be so fucked up?

I always pictured my religion as being all about family—that *is* what 'The Church' adamantly proclaimed.

I knew the answer. No secret there, not on my side of it. I divorced my wife.

On their side, I was told not to abandon her but to live up to my responsibilities, be a good Mormon. My reasons were irrelevant and not even to be discussed.

Unlike the lies upon which most base their lives, I now based mine on these simple truths called Spiritual Laws. The 'biggie' concerning my marriage was the one that says—***There is only the energy of love, and then there is everything else (fear)***. I knew my love for Meg was true, but hers for me was all about security (fear). The two energies cannot co-exist.

For Meg, security meant control. When I took my balls away and put them back in my own pocket, the marriage ceased to work. I agree, it was all my fault. I could see why, in her mind, I was all fucked up while she was okay, why I needed marriage counseling—but she didn't. The breakup wasn't over just this last year. There was another year and a half of struggle prior, me trying to get her to see me.

So now, here we were. Me? Pretty much broke and in debt—thirty thousand in debt. I don't know what she did with our assets. Eight thousand and change was little enough to help her begin her new life. She has since remarried another limp dick and is doing well financially. I was just happy that I could help her. I still loved her. After all, true love is a gift, one that can never be taken back. I will love her to my grave, and beyond.

But to stay married? It was what my parents demanded in the beginning. No chance of that now—she's moved on. Ironically, my parents still saw it as 'abandoning' her. I was 'scum' in their eyes. No acceptable explanation could be given, and none were they willing to entertain, even now.

I arrived around nine a.m. only to discover Dad was at Provo Hospital, not American Fork. A half hour later found me standing in the doorway of his room, gazing at this frail, seventy-three-year-old man who looked more like ninety. I almost didn't recognize him. Lying there asleep, he looked like an empty husk, certainly not the strong man I still held in memory.

I stood there a long while, just watching him sleep, then went home to American Fork—home to my parents' house. My mother answered the door. Tight-faced, her mouth formed a grim line that matched the cold glint in her eyes as she spoke in a dry monotone, "Well, you're here now." She shrugged and turned away. "Might as well come in."

* * *

The house was familiar as I followed her in. It hadn't changed, yet clearly, it was no longer home. I sat down on the old, familiar, green couch in the living room, and from her matching chair across the room, she told me about Dad.

"He's okay, now, no thanks to you."

It wasn't her words but how she delivered them that told me the most. The gleam of triumph in her eyes said it clearly. I didn't need to be empathic to hear her thoughts. *See . . . he nearly died, and it's all your fault!*

Suddenly, I realized just where her—where their—commitment was in life. Both were committed to being *right*, and *right* clearly meant that I was *killing* them by the way I lived my life. I felt a sudden pang of anger, but it wasn't directed at her, but rather, toward their church—their 'righteous' Mormon church—the one still nurturing these sick, disservicing beliefs in them, just as it once did in me.

I shook my head. Nothing I could do about it, nothing—not unless I was willing to live my life the way they wanted. My disgust hissed out my nose. I certainly couldn't remarry Meg. That left living by the rules of the church, blindly, the same way they did. They wanted—no, demanded—that I be the next 'them.' In the beginning, it was what I was willing to pretend, but that was back then, before that ICU. Now I was done with living my life in pretense to suit anyone else's feelings. That is something I will never do again.

Then, as usual, she got into the subject of her own health, about how bad the bone spurs and arthritis bothered her, and how she just 'can't seem to hold anything down.' As if to prove the point, she excused herself to go to the bathroom. A moment later, I could hear her gagging.

Afterward, she sat on the couch, talking about the dogs and the weather, relatives, neighbors, etc., talking as if she were bearing her cross with grace when, all the while, she ignored that huge elephant dump of martyrdom in plain sight on the living room floor.

My God! Nothing's changed. She is waiting for words of sympathy. I can't—no, I won't—play those sick, fucking games with her again.

Instead, I broached the subject that was burning in my chest.

"Mom, we need to bring our relationship to love. We need to talk about my divorce, and about you and me, and all that's happened. And we need to get past it—"

"How dare you!" With her face Heimlich red, her words burst out in full, tonsil-bending rage. "How dare you! How dare you come into MY house and just expect me to accept your despicable behavior. Aaaaaaaaaaarrrrrgh!"

Listening to her familiar roar of condemnation, I knew.

No, nothing has changed.

I took a deep breath and let it out slowly, and for the next five minutes said nothing, just watched her spew. Then, when she'd quieted, I distracted her. "I understand how you feel. Let's go to the hospital and see Dad."

We took her car. I drove. It was about ten miles between American Fork and Provo—ten miles of frosty silence. In the hospital, she greeted him with a kiss on his pasty forehead.

I cleared my throat. "Hello, Dad." He glared once at me, grunted his acknowledgment, then pretty much ignored me, preferring to stare at the wall in silence than talk to me. When Mom again went to the bathroom, my words fumbled forth.

"Dad, how are you feeling?"

Silence. His gaze didn't waver from that wall.

"What are the doctors saying? What's the prognosis?"

Silence.

"Er . . . ahh . . . w-what can I do to help?"

Silence.

A few minutes later, we could hear her vomiting. While listening to her in there, Dad looked at me, just once, his eyes accusing, and then deliberately stared back at the wall.

"Dad, we need to talk." Again, only silence answered my plea. I said no more.

Later, two younger cousins came by. I wasn't around all that often over the last twenty- some-odd years and didn't know them. Apparently, they knew of me. Except for my nod, no acknowledgment passed between us.

They were warmly received by my parents. Moments later, Mom again made her visit to the commode. This time, as I listened to the sounds of her heaving, the pattern crystallized.

On the way home that night, I watched and remembered how during our trips, both to and now from the hospital, she seemed unconcerned about her 'queasy stomach.' The possibility of soiling the car, or otherwise hurling along the way, didn't worry her. Nauseated? Not once did she show any sign of it even crossing her mind.

Me? Whenever I'm sick and have to travel, I'm always sure to carry a sickness bag or container. I'm always acutely aware of where the nearest facility might be. Mom was not.

My eyes were opened. For the first time in my life, I was no longer an actor in her play, but rather, a spectator in the audience. I was looking at things I'd never noticed about her before. Most of all, I saw how her interaction with me was an almost continuous control drama aimed at soliciting guilt, sympathy, or an expected action from me. Right then, the action demanded was for me to speak up, to take responsibility for all the pain in her pitiful existence.

But hell, she's always done that.

Always before, I interacted, played my part on that stage, and took on the lie of that responsibility. But the scene was clearer now.

Wait! There's more—something I'm not seeing. But what? Then I saw it. The thing I'd not noticed wasn't about her at all. It was about me.

Oh . . . my . . . God! Just like Meg, Mom carries the balls in this family. It's not just attention she craves, it's control! Why didn't I see this before? I married my fucking mother!

Now with my eyes opened, seeing life from the perspective of those Spiritual Laws, I saw many things clearly about my mother, about Meg, and about me. No one is immune to the truth. Although I loved her, I could not support my mother's sicknesses. I would not give alcohol to a drunk, nor would I give sympathy to my mother—empathy, yes. But to give control of my life to her? No. Twenty-five years of giving it to Meg was enough.

And sympathy? It's a verbal thing, an action word, one spoken by someone who sees themselves as better than you, someone willing to release you from all responsibility in what you have created in your life in favor of blaming you for what they have created in theirs.

But I could empathize. I could connect with and feel for her. Yes, I saw how very afraid she was of death. Their lives were coming to a conclusion. They knew it. I knew it. Now facing death, they were afraid.

I've been there. I've known the presence of the Angel of Death—known it often. So often, in fact, I've come to see him as my friend and teacher. He was my mentor throughout the two and a half years prior, since back then when I spent time in that ICU.

It was he who sent me searching for the truth of life and demanded that I look within myself for the truth of mine. Honesty. Life is never functional if it is based on lies. And we've *all* been taught a buttload of them—enough so that we, in turn, stink up the lives of those we love.

I can't blame my parents for not having the courage to look within for the truth of their lives. I didn't, either, until I found myself face-to-face with Big D. They haven't yet met him, but I'm sure they've felt his presence.

We all live life the very best way we can. It is ours, the *only* thing of importance that we own. No one else has a rightful say in it. It is all ours, our own responsibility. Others will try to convince you that you are selfish if you don't live your life to suit them. Truth is, if you don't live it to suit yourself, you are being a traitor to your soul.

So, what was left for me to do to support and love my parents in a way that would work? Honesty and empathy—and staying out of their war. That was what I saw to be my only functional course of action.

Someone, I don't know who, once said—*Man is like a circle whose circumference is only limited by his own thoughts.* My circle was much wider now than it was before.

Now they wanted me to be there for them, for support, and I wanted to be. Yet, I knew I would not. I could see they weren't willing to accept support in the way I would give it, nor was I willing to give it in the way they wanted. Staying out of their war required my absence.

As I sat on that old, green couch in the living room of my once-upon-a-time home, listening to her spiel about her sad life, I dropped my face into my hands and tried to wipe away my frustration.

This is how it must be.

I would not take responsibility for their lives of pain. The truth of this particular Spiritual Law is clear—**Mental pain is always self-inflicted**. Other people may play a part in the physical, but bottom line, we are the creator of our lives, the true responsible party. Blame is one of society's most insidious lies. It's akin to sympathy, where you try to set yourself up as being 'better than' by taking on the responsibility for someone else's feelings.

The sad truth of our relationship, my mother's and mine, was now clear. I'd always been the dog she flogged with the whip of her anguish. And Dad . . . I felt his occasional boot at those times when I would not take responsibility for her pain.

With me now insisting on living my life *my way*, the truth about selfishness was obvious—*to me*. The concept, the truth of it, is not new. As much as I've repeated it, here it is again.

True selfishness is to expect another to live their life to suit yours. I wondered how much of the world shared a similar, sick relationship with their parents? How many would view it as a loving thing for me to continue pretending to be my parents' faithful dog?

I have never purposely been anything but loving to my parents. And yes, they were now facing death as I once did. Likely, they, too, were getting a sense of how much life they didn't live.

Unfortunately, they saw none of it as their own responsibility. Rather, they were frantically searching for something, or someone, to blame it all on, some dog to whip. I took a deep breath and let it hiss slowly out, shaking my head in the realization.

That dog is no longer me.

* * *

Dad was released from the hospital that Sunday afternoon. In all the long hours I spent with him that weekend, there was only one time when I felt any connection or love from him. At one point in that hospital bed, he held out his hand to me. I took it.

He gave my hand a brief squeeze. Then, as Mom returned from the restroom, once more he ignored me. Was he ashamed of his moment of weakness or just hiding it from Mom—hiding that one moment when he showed his love to me?

At home that evening, as Dad lay in his bed just off the kitchen, my mother and I sat at the table and talked. Somehow, I felt she might be open to me. Again, I tried to reach her, to get past those walls of stone around her heart. If only I could reach back into the past to a time before she built them.

"Mom . . . look, whatever happened in the past, back then, doesn't really matter. I'm okay with it. I just think we need to talk about it, acknowledge it, and get past it so that we can rebuild our relationship."

She turned to me, cold fury burning in her eyes. In a low pitch, her voice strangled out, "I don't know what you think I did. I didn't do anything. It's all in your twisted, little mind. How can you tell me I was wrong? You . . . you've bailed out on all your responsibilities, hurt everyone who ever loved you. You're so damned selfish!" Her voice now was at a shriek. "You make me sick!"

I looked up to see Dad tottering unsteadily in the bedroom doorway. "What . . . what's going on here? What are you doing to her?"

"Nothing, Dad." I jumped up, ready to catch him if he fell. "It's okay. Go back to bed."

We both hustled him back into the bedroom where, eyes glaring at me, he collapsed into his bed.

Comb Ridge, Utah—Present Day

Pine cones ripen continuously over several weeks and fall or are shook out of the trees. Each day, there will be more to gather, and I know I don't want to miss gathering them. I am in competition with those pesky chipmunks. Today, I grab up my bags, ready to hump my way back to gather more pinyon nuts. Outside the tent, as I turn my hump-a-lumping little ass toward the pinyons, Big D speaks, stopping me cold.

"That's it? That's all you're going to say about your parents?"

Looking up, I see him now sitting at his favorite spot, leg bones dangling over the sheer drop. *Aw, shit, Big D. Y'know there's not much more I can say. They wouldn't voluntarily speak to me over the years since then.* His torso swivels, along with his head, as ducking, he looks toward me and gives his head a slow, sorrowful shake. I find myself repeating the point. *There isn't anything more I can say—not without engaging in that game of control that they and most everyone else in this world would rather play than to actually love one another. Besides, Big D, at this point they were still alive. Don't cha think it's a little too early to be jumping ahead to where it all ended with them.*

He just ducks his head and sharpens the red glow of his sight down to a laser-like beam. His voice, for all its weird intonations, is also laser tight. "That is a serious question, and I'm sure that anyone privy to this story will want to know the answer." He wags his head almost sadly but without judgment. "Now, out with it. How did it end?"

Well, they weren't speaking to me, but Meg's family all lived in Salt Lake City, and she usually stopped to see my parents on her way up. She and her second husband still lived here in Las Vegas. Meg also wasn't speaking to me, but she was speaking to our son in Detroit. He kept me apprised of anything he heard.

"And . . ."

And my father only lived a few more years before he died—another heart attack. I grit my teeth and shrug. *I rode up on my bike to the funeral.*

"How'd that go?"

Well, all the relatives were polite, to a point—even Mother—although she did flash around some pointed looks.

"Pointed looks? C'mon, out with it."

Martyrdom. Clearly, she wanted everyone to know that Dad's death was all my fault and that she suffered just letting me be there.

"Was it?"

Was it what?

"Your fault."

That he died? No. That she suffered having me be there? Yes. Not my responsibility.

"What was your responsibility?"

Well, Big D, as you know, her choice of feelings was her responsibility. My own ability to respond lay only in that, by then, I knew all the lies and I am not responsible for anyone's feelings but my own. So, her martyr act didn't work on me. Still, in her mind, and probably some of the others, that made me out as quite the uncaring monster. All I wanted was to pay my respects by being there for him and then to get the fuck away as soon as possible, which is what I did.

"Was that her fault?"

Course not, but it was never healthy to be around her when she was busy blaming me for her feelings. Given my history with my mother, I knew it was especially unhealthy for me. Y'know, when the ones you love are that caustic, they are the most unhealthy people to be around. I groan. *Oh fuck, Big D! My mother held me hostage for every bad feeling she chose to feel—and not just then, but for my whole fucking life. That was who I was to her.*

"And her? How did it end for her?"

My cousin Pearl kinda took over things—moved her into an assisted living home. For some reason, they made it a point to tell me that I had no say in the matter. I didn't argue. I'd seen enough Mormon funerals to know that people's greed comes out at such times. Were there any proceeds left over with the sale of their property? I didn't know, didn't ask, and didn't care. She died a little over a year later. I went to pay my respects then, too. I take a deep breath and let it whoosh out, then stay silent remembering.

After a time, Big D prompts again. "And . . . how'd that go?"

I shrug. *Surreal . . . I'd say that is the only word to describe it.* Again, I fall silent.

"C'mon, Jeff. Out with it."

Her funeral, too, was held in the Mormon Stake House. I was asked by Pearl if I wanted to say anything. The look of relief on her face almost warranted a chuckle when I answered "No." I looked around at all the relatives— people I'd been around and thought I knew. Most avoided speaking or even looking at me. Whoever they were, I didn't know them now. Mormons are supposed to be all about family. After all those years growing up, I now question if I have ever been a part of the family. Clearly, I am not now. A few talked briefly with me and were uncomfortably civil—almost nice.

"Was there any family inheritance due you?"

I didn't ask. Two funerals and a year and a half in assisted living couldn't have been cheap. Maybe they might have needed to chip in themselves to cover any excess. I felt it was none of my business and they seemed to agree. Before I left, Cousin Pearl insisted I look through their stuff she had stored in her garage.

* * *

Standing there looking at that big pile of 'things,' Pearl at my side, I shook my head. "Anything you want, just take it," she said.

What was it I detected in her voice—guilt, shame, compassion? She seemed so eager for me to start loading it all up. I remembered much of that stuff, knickknacks mostly. Some of it was even mine. I chose just one item, then turned to her.

"Pearl, I appreciate all you've done for my parents, things I ought to have done, but under the circumstances . . . well, I'm just grateful you were there." I grinned as I made an observation. "Y'know, Mormon men may hold the power of the priesthood, but Mormon women hold the power of the family."

"Ohhh-ooo," she said softly as she hugged me.

* * *

I left then. Adopted at age four, I went into that family with nothing. I left with only the stuffed, red horse that came with me.

As a surrogate myself, I would ask that if you don't want "THAT child" only for itself, then please—just get a puppy. A puppy will never grow up to know it is not good enough.
Redneck Spirituality—Book Two

CHAPTER NINETEEN

Protecting That Inner Child

I put my dad back to bed that evening as he glared at me in silence, his face cold and stony. If I'd known it would be the last time I would see him alive. Would I have made an attempt to talk to him—probably not. There was nothing more I could have said.

It was now a done deal. I knew what my parents thought of me. I was a son who wouldn't obey. They simply needed that control, and they needed to see it as their right. The Mormon Church is big on family—even bigger on control—but control does not equate to love. I didn't have it in me to play that game—not anymore.

God! Why did I never see this? Is this what I taught my own family as being love? I never considered myself a control freak. Truth was, I never questioned.

Heirloom

I feel the rage burning deep inside,
at something my child has done.
Out of my mouth it bursts . . .
demeaning him . . .
telling him how little he's worth.

These years later, I look inside me,
and see . . .
it was really all about me.
Merely something that he'd done,
that pulled the trigger of my gun.
Pulling it with a finger from my own past.
Back then, when I, too . . .
learned "worthless."
Oh, how I hope that it won't be
the same with his child
and he.
For I've talked with him . . .
told him from my heart . . .
what it's really all about.
Still . . .
I know that he,
like me . . .
now carries the same trigger . . .
on the same gun.
My hope is that he
is much wiser
than me,
wise enough to see . . .
It is only an old family heirloom . . .
worthless . . .
much less . . .
than love.

* * *

Dead beat, now mentally as well as physically, and not wanting to chance falling asleep on the long road south, I went to bed also. Arising just before first light, I dressed and, without waking anyone, took my bag and left the house.

The temperature outside was bitterly cold that January morning as I drove away in my pickup. A gray mist hung in the still air over Provo Lake. It extended to the bench lines against the Wasatch Mountains, behind me on the east. They marked the shoreline of ancient Lake Bonneville, now 14,500 years in the past. They also marked the east side of American Fork—the same American Fork, Utah that, beginning this morning, marked my past.

That coal-smudged mist matched a small spot of bitterly cold, gray emptiness in my heart as I realized that my parents will think I slunk away, tail between my legs like a gutless cur. They choose how they perceive me. It is not possible to change another person's mind. That can only be done by one's self, and then, only when it's what one wants. I was done testing out how my parents felt about me or what they wanted. I knew.

It was no longer possible to go back to my old life, to once again be who I was when I was acceptable. I didn't want to be that 'good Mormon son,' that fake person I so despised when it came down to dying. Will they ever be willing to see who I am now?

No. What they will see is a coward running. They will never see a man walking away, unwilling to continue this battle that no one can win.

My engine was not yet warm enough to turn on the heater. I took a deep breath in through my nose as I drove down the empty, pre-dawn streets of American Fork heading toward the freeway. The memories flooded in with the old, familiar feeling, the pinch of wet nose hairs suddenly frozen together.

"Remind you of anything?" Big D's familiar voice reverberates in my ear.

So close is he that, as I turn, I have to cock my head back in order to focus my eyes. I reply in our old, familiar way, speaking to him in my mind.

Yeah, kinda like Bingham Canyon from way back, when I was first adopted. I could swear I caught a whiff of coal smoke. Heard they closed the old Geneva steel mill, next to Utah Lake to the north. Apparently not. The air definitely has that same gray haze.

"You wrote about Bingham Canyon in your first book. Remember the poem?"

I chuckle, recalling how I'd taken it out of the book, then written around it. *Yeah, it was kinda overkill.*

"I agree." He pauses, his calm voice serious. "It is not so now—now it is closure. How did it go?"

I think on it a moment before answering. *Hell, it's been too long. I don't remember.*

Big D's reverberating tones ring in my ears as he begins to recite it.

Of Shoelaces, Trust, and Self-Esteem

I look down the blue of my corduroyed legs
to the free-flung laces of my shoes.
It is because of me that they swing so free . . .
Yes, they flap with delight, a comforting sight,
for I have a new mommy,
and she will tie them . . . just for me.
My heart is as light as my four-year-old feet,
skipping gaily into your room.
With joy and elation, I pull off my ruse,
"Mommy, Mommy, come tie my shoes!"
Your anger and disgust wither my smile,
as into my face you unload,
"How many more times must I show you?"
Kneeling on the floor, just as before,
again, you do the ritual.
"This over that, you loop this,
you loop that, over and under,
now you're done."
Then loosed with a flick, "Now YOU do it!"

Idly I toy with it, my heart not here,
on this thing I need not know,
You are my new mommy,
you will take care of me now . . .
I know.
Smiling shyly, I look up . . .
Look into your eyes,
your eyes of rage . . . bulging . . .
distended with the furor of your emotions.
I'm shocked at your unexpected fit,
and the spite in your eyes as the words hit.
"Whatever possessed me
to take on such a stupid, little shit?
I should have had my head examined!"
From the closet, my suitcase,
thrown down before the dresser,
my single drawer, jerked open.
All possessions of mine,
all the worth of me.
"Get your things . . . get out!"
Through the blur of tears,
I pack my clothes.
Then out into the hall I shuffle.
My stuffed, red horse,
only friend . . . loyal companion,
tucked safely under my arm.
Together we feel the whoosh . . .
hear the slam of the door,

behind us . . .
The hallway dark . . . old and cold,
of an apartment house
built early in the century.
With the promise of the mines . . .
the boom of Bingham Canyon . . .
like me now, somehow sadly left behind.
Suitcase at the door, reaching . . . struggling,
both hands turning the brass knob.
Its touch is as frigid as this chill in my heart,
like the ice-crystalled glass,
encrusting the pane in the heart
of the door's long center part.
Outside the air is biting,
the sun, a dim disc in a coal-smoked smudge,
breathed in, a grunge on every frosted breath.
At the bottom porch step, we stop.
Huddled together, my frayed friend and me,
I hug him tight, to stop him of his shivering.
Staring down the narrow walkway
of snowbanks cresting overhead . . .
Cold, oh so cold . . . the chill stabs at my nose
pulling tight the ice-choked hairs inside.
How will we stay warm? Where will we go?
Is there a warm place somewhere to hide?
Eternity passes . . . then you come for us.
Taking us back inside,
to the warmth of your home . . .

> and the coldness . . . of your icicle heart.
> Tears you cry, and say you love me . . .
> say you're sorry . . . yet, I question every part.
> Are the tears really for me?
> Are you really sorry?
> Can I ever believe your heart?
> Are your words your decoy,
> when you tell me
> I'm a good little boy?
> And though you say it,
> how will it truly go?
> You say you'll always take care of me.
> Yet, I know . . . in my heart, I know . . .
> that I'm not good enough . . . for you,
> and you won't be there . . . for me.
> Will it always be,
> that the women I love will see . . .
> what you now have taught to me?
> Will my love . . .
> ever . . .
> be good enough?

* * *

Closure, Big D? That is why you want this poem regurgitated now?

"You don't see the connection? You don't see how that four-year-old boy was browbeaten into submission by a cold-hearted mother, bent only on control? Do you think it is still her game now?"

I take a deep breath and blow it out in a cloud of white mist, then answer. *No. I think she wanted control then.* I shrug within the warm confines of my coat. *Now she is afraid Dad will know the truth of it.*

Now? I suck in a lungful of frosty air that matches the chill around my heart. *Now she just wants me gone.*

"That child you were back then, sitting on those icy steps in Bingham Canyon—what did he want to do?"

He wanted to just go. Had he been able, he'd have just walked away, left it all behind. What are you getting at?

I look over toward Big D, expecting an answer. But he, too, is gone, leaving his last words to echo around in my mind. "You are no longer that helpless child, and you are . . . walking away. You don't see the closure?"

* * *

It was a lot to think about that Monday morning as I drove down to the Eagle Quest site at Toquerville, Utah. There it was—my relationship with my mother in a nutshell—and it didn't feel good now that it was cracked and opened. The farther I traveled, the more I found myself looking forward to being on the support team, to being of service. Clearly, being of service to my parents was a lost cause. I heaved a sigh and groaned.

"Oh GAG!" Big D's words carried the chill of ice water poured down the back of my neck. I jerked my head to the side. So deep was I into my misery, that even knowing him as well as I did, that gruesome skull grinning at me still came as a shock—enough to inadvertently change lanes on the freeway.

After a moment's panic in regaining control of my fishtailing pickup, and with heart still pounding, the words burst out. "Goddamn, Big D! You trying to kill me here?" Then, with the realized implications of what I'd just said to the Angel of Death, I started backtracking. "I . . . I . . . I . . . mean—"

"Oh, don't get your bowels in such an uproar. There's no traffic nearby. I wouldn't have startled you if there were. Besides, be at ease. Your life won't end so quickly or dramatically."

"What! H-how will it end?"

"You know I'm not going to tell you. Besides, you are the creator here. Remember that law? The ending of your life would no longer be by your own choice, and it won't be anytime soon—unless you decide to stop honoring our agreement?" The sudden ducking of his head and brightening of the glow emanating up from his eye sockets put a question to his statement.

"Oh, I'll keep our bargain."

"Good, and unless you want to embarrass yourself by talking to someone others can't see, you might want to go back to discussing this in our normal way—in your mind. Oh, and you could speed back up. The traffic back there's coming up fast, and you're about to become a speed bump for that semi. Now there's a driver who needs to stop and get some sleep."

I put more heat to the pedal and was soon cruising at a comfortable seventy-five. The speed demons behind started to stream by, including the semi. I was happy to be behind him.

"Oh, and by the way, Jeff, you may want to turn off that bitching in your head concerning your parents, or turn it around into appreciation."

What's that mean?

"Just means your parents have been incredible teachers for you. Yeah, your *story* may seem so tragic and unhappy—and it is. But those very tragedies are where you will find your greatest, most magnificent lessons. That is, if you are willing to look and learn." With a chuckle, his grin widens, although the reality of it didn't change even one millimeter on his naked skull. Then, jawbones clattering softly in time, he continues.

"Life is not about the *story*, it's about the *ride* and the lessons you get while learning to keep the rubber side down. There are those who never learn, y'know? Sometimes—like now—those lessons are accompanied by the gravel one's ass collects when it is sliding down the highway. You just picked up a buttload of it, son. Time you started picking it out with appreciation."

What? You didn't see that clusterfuck of blame I just went through?

"Yes, I did."

Well then, hey, I know that, according to the laws, there's a gift in all that shit, but—

"Ahh . . . you do know that in the pre-existence, you chose her to be your adoptive mother, fire-breathing, screaming dragon that she was. Well, don't you?"

No, I don't see—

"Oh, you certainly did, and don't fucking try to discredit what I'm telling you! It is akin to breaking our agreement. Back there, in the mists of eternity, you made a pact to give one another these opportunities. '*I am a raging, bitch dragon. I'll be your mother, if you'll learn from it and offer your learning to me. Teach me what loving a son can really mean and hold me capable of learning.*'"

He nods, as if to seal its essential truth. "She may not have learned. But you? You did. And now you will pass on your mother's darkest, most shameful secret to all those other wannabe adoptive mothers. You . . . will make a difference in their world."

Uh . . . look, Big D, I don't mean to discredit what you're telling me, but what deep, dark secret?

"Remember the first time you met her in this life? It was at the Sunny Hills Orphanage in San Anselmo, California in the winter of 1951. She began her teaching then, a teaching you are just now learning—right here, right now. Your brother, Mike, was older. He knew things you didn't, things he refused to look at or accept. Killed him, didn't it?"

But I thought it was the cop that shot him who killed him?

"That cop was only the instrument Mike used in giving up on this life. Mike could have. In fact, several times he wanted to pull that trigger himself. He just lacked the courage. Why do you think he was so pissed when you saved his life that time he tried to hang himself?"

What? What did that have to do with my mother?

"Jeff, it has taken you a long time to realize that your mother never wanted you. Either of you. Mike knew it, you didn't—until recently." He reaches over to tap my chest with one surprisingly gentle index bone and continues. "As to the whys and wherefores, what do you need to say to the women wanting to adopt?"

I drove in silence for a time while I contemplated his request, remembering all those times with her. Hell, I thought it was all about her and her sad, unhappy life. I knew she blamed me for it. Back then, I even accepted it as being my fault but never thought to wonder why. Then, clearing my throat, I spoke aloud the truth of it in a voice full of gravelly emotion.

"It can be more joyous to parent a child who is of your heart than one merely of your flesh. Holding on to the child you can't have guarantees you will never be satisfied with the one you can. It also guarantees that child's life will be devastated."

Big D sits beside me in his flowing, black, silk cloak, silent for a time, then asks, "You don't think a mother can learn to love a child?"

I look over at him and shake my head. *Love is not about one's learning, it's about one's being. You taught me that.*

"That's correct, Jeff. And the best part is, we can change who we are being—change to become loving. Remember, I said you made that agreement with her in the pre-existence. Want to know the bottom-line truth about it?"

Not sure where he is going with it, I go along. *Yeah, tell me.*

"What did I say you were to teach her?"

Well, you said I was to teach her what a loving son can really mean and hold her capable of changing.

"Yes, but this life is about you. What was she supposed to teach you?

Uh . . . I suppose it was the same thing.

"Yes! You've got it. Everyone on Earth has a loving soul. The love's in there. You've both lived many lives here on Earth." His grin seems to exude sadness. "Neither one of you would let the love of your souls out. That is the greatest gift your mother gave you. Unconsciously, you knew you weren't loved by her, and still, you loved her. Even now it is a conscious thing"—he pauses, the glow of his eye sockets solemn—"yet, you still love her. Do you think you could have ever have loved Meg without your mother's teaching?"

Then what I said to all those wannabe adoptive parents?

"Is a load of stinking hogshit—but that's a good thing. It is the truth." He chuckles. "And yes, it will make a few prospective parents get a whiff of who they are being, give them a whole different view of reality. They need to see it before they will let that love that is inherent in their heart flow out. They may have made this same agreement in the pre-existence, but those who are unwilling to follow it through will indeed consider it as hogshit. They will need to learn—or not—the same way you did. Perhaps the child they will adopt made the same pact in the pre-existence that you two did."

The slight hiss of the wind past the gap in the window frame, the rumble of the glass-pack mufflers, and the whine of the tires on the highway for a time were the only noises that disturbed the silence. Then he added his coup de gras in the form of a Spiritual Law. "***All the joy that you will accept into this life is only found through love.*** You learned to set your love free because of your mother."

There followed a much longer period of silence between us, then Big D addresses the present. "Jeff, you are standing at the beginning of a relationship with a woman. Tell me about her."

Ah, yes, Regina. I find myself unconsciously grinning, then realizing it, chuckle. *A wonderful woman who has every quality I felt was lacking in Meg. Don't yet know much about the things she enjoys doing, but she's on a path similar to my own. She supports me in my life and accepts me in hers. Though pretty independent, we can still communicate. But most of all, I find her very attractive. Her hormones howl to the same tune as mine.*

"Ah, yes, watch those howling hormones. Could be they'll bite your butt."

I look closely at his grinning skull but can't decide if he is serious or just joking. I continue, just letting my thoughts tumble around as they would in mental conversation with him.

Even though she seems to have every quality I want in my mate, and more, I've noticed that I hold back from fully loving her. Why? Until right now, I didn't consciously know. Thanks, Mom! You've just reached up from 1951 and given me the lesson I needed to learn to keep my butt out of the gravel on this ride of life.

"How's that?" Big D's question comes out sounding like a chuckle.

I hold back because I haven't let go of my ex-wife. I know I can never have Meg the way that I want her to be, her having all these qualities this new woman possesses. Just as my adoptive mother's holding on to her want of a child of her own body—one she could never have—insured her of pain and dissatisfaction with me. I shrug. *So, too, it has been for me, but no longer.*

I take a deep, contemplative breath before continuing. *Meg is in my past. I'll always love her, but I no longer want her. Regina is a wonderful woman. She's the one I want. Of course, it takes two. I don't know how it will be—her to me. Has she let go of her ex, Jim?* Eyebrows arched, again I shrug. *If not, there will surely be another woman for me. I deserve to have it all. Although she appears to love me with a passion that makes my senses reel, we have not yet consummated that passion.*

"Why is that? Hard to visualize it in a horny dude like you."

As with the fixed frown on a trout, I rise to take his bait. *There is that promise we made Karen at the seminar—no sex for thirty days. You know that!* I say it with a mental grunt. *You don't think I will honor my word?*

"She will not stay long if you are unwilling to give her love in the way she needs it. We both know that."

Yes, but she made Karen the same agreement.

Sitting next to me in the confines of my pickup cab, Big D doesn't answer. Instead his normal countenance, with its fixed grin, silently fades from sight. I'm not sure, but it almost seems as though his grin is mocking me.

Comb Ridge, Utah—Present Day

Setting the notebook inside the tent, I zip the opening closed, not that I worry about thieves. That thought brings a smile to my face. But there are chipmunks who might find enjoyment in chewing on the pages, and here on this ledge, there are occasional, stiff breezes. With the door zipped shut when I'm not in it, the tent is much less likely to be blown about, maybe even over the edge.

The weather this day doesn't seem to be able to make up its mind. One moment the sun is actually providing comfortable warmth, the next comes with a gust of near-freezing air.

Big D hails me from his spot at the edge. "If you expect to shake any pine cones loose, you need to take that branch. The one over there against the wall on your left will make a decent crutch to keep you up on your good leg while shaking the trees."

Thanks, Big D.

"Oh, and it's a good chapter, now that you've finally finished it. Kinda heavy-duty lesson, though, wasn't it? But it's this next chapter about Regina that you most didn't want to write about . . . did you?" He chuckles, and I get the picture of my ass getting chomped on again.

Hard to justify being trolled for alligators, y'know?

"No alligator. This time, it's a great white. The best lessons are also the most painful. You do know that pre-existence pact that we—you and I—have is what has made your lessons in this life so necessarily difficult, don't you?"

I do now. I shake my head.

"That is why accompanying you on your pass through this lifetime has been such a joy to me. Not many make it as far as you."

Oh my God! How does one respond when the Angel of Death says that your life 'has been'—past tense—such a joy for him? What does he mean by that?

I look up, my mouth opening to ask him out loud, only to discover his spot at the edge is now empty.

The highest and best of learning is in experience. It is especially so when such learning for a man concerns women. Sometimes it takes experiential learning—and a pack of condoms. Sometimes not.
              Redneck Spirituality—Book Four

CHAPTER TWENTY

Thirty Days, Babe . . . Thirty Days

The dual ribbons of freeway stretched taut across the desert in front, as if tied to some eternally distant craggy hill. I existed, suspended in time, with only the rush of the wind, the blur of Joshua trees, and the steady whine of pavement beneath my pickup's tires. Once again, the thoughts edged in, and this time, I allowed my mind to dwell on Regina—and on the dreams of how I wanted it to be.

For a time, I forgot the law—*Life is always perfect, right here—right now*.

It is our expectations, our neediness, of how we want it to be that often sets us up to miss the perfection of how it actually is. I imagined Regina meeting me at my door, of opening it to the sight of her beautiful body framed against warm, cozy lights, of her in a see-through, baby-doll negligee, the delicious smells of her cooking mixed in with the perfumed woman scent of her.

Ah . . . *but what if she isn't there?* What if the place is its usual cold, dark emptiness, its silence punctuated only by her absence? When at last I arrived, it was indeed so. Yet, not totally, for inside on the kitchen table was a letter. I'd left my own, along with a sincere, though goofy, poem, taped to the ornate, gold-framed, beveled-glass mirror on the living room wall. My letter spoke to her highest and best, encouraged her decision to move in, and acknowledged her for her courage in trusting me. I signed it off with a simple, "Welcome to my home and into my heart."

One thing these seminars taught me was that integrity was the measuring stick for self-respect. I insisted, from the start, that I not hide anything from Jim. It was important to be honest and open about my interest in Regina. Regina made up her mind to leave him long before I came along. Even so, I was determined not to make any covert moves on her, nor did I feel any need to confront him about anything. Instead, I held him capable of dealing with his own feelings. There was nothing that I did for the purpose of causing their breakup. My integrity was intact.

I felt a connection, told her so, made an offer to explore that connection, and allowed her to make her own decision about it all in following her own heart. I trusted in her own integrity that she'd also be honest with him, that she would be clear with him about her intentions and feelings and end their relationship from a place of love.

It was a testament to how much I'd personally grown. Had any of this happened before the seminars, I wondered if my integrity would have survived the experience.

With shaking hands, I tore the letter open. It thanked me for my thoughtfulness, then explained how she would come but would need more time. Jim would not try to stop her leaving, nor would he help her. It was with joy that I called her that night. Jim answered.

"Hi, this is Jeff. Ah . . . is Regina there?" There was a pregnant silence, a faint grunt, then Regina came on.

"Hello?"

"Regina, I'm back! I was so glad to get your note and to hear that you will move in." It all came out in an excited rush. Her reply was slow in coming. Then, when it did . . .

"Uh . . . yeah, Jeff. I . . . uh . . ."

"Look, Regina, if my timing is not good . . . I mean, can we talk now, or do you need to clear more with Jim?"

"Yes, you're right. This is not a good time to talk. I do have more clearing to do with him."

"Okay . . . well, I just wanted you to know that I'll help you move in whatever way you need me."

"My brother has a truck and has offered . . . We'll see." Her voice now seemed hurried. "I'll call you tomorrow."

A warm glow of anticipation enveloped my body as I hung up the phone. I knew Jim was not taking things very well. Yet, like Meg, he'd made his own decision to follow his life in a different direction than his mate. And too, like Meg, he was unwilling to be honest with himself, that this was his own choice and responsibility. He, too, didn't want to be where she was going. There is a universal truth I termed **The Law of Self-ful.** Roughly stated, it says, **To go where you want in your own life is self-ful. To expect someone else to come along when they don't want to is selfish.** I, too, was selfish with Meg—for a while. Now I'd learned to let go of my selfishness and accept my self-fullness, just something we have to do alone. Likely the same lesson was also his to learn—or not.

As it happened, I did indeed help Regina move out of their apartment. For the most part, Jim sat at the kitchen table, glowering at me as we carried out her furniture and belongings. There were a god-awful lot of them, too.

Only once did it appear that he might come off his chair to engage me. I saw the fear of it in Regina's eyes when she asked me to wait outside while she dealt with him. I agreed, only after she assured me that she, herself, was safe with him.

Looking back, I can see why that was so. Like Meg and me, Regina held the balls in their relationship. She, too, needed that ultimate control to feel safe. In reality, does a bull ever ignore the red cape flapping in his face, or does he just have more balls than sense?

Did I? I was ignoring this red flag.

My first few days with Regina were ones of fresh love. I adored everything I saw about her, choosing to not see the rest—the choo-choo-train smoking, the coffee chug-a-lugging, and the prissy way she had about things being just right.

I felt that connection between our souls and believed it could only mean that we were meant to be together. It was true. Regina was there to give me what I needed just then in my life, and I, in hers.

Lying in bed together that first night, Regina was indeed clothed in a baby-doll outfit exactly like my macho mind dwelled upon these past few days. When my eyes reached high enough and gazed into her own, I was the first to break the silence.

"Regina, I promise you that I will never tell you lies." She'd confided that Jim often did. "Only honesty and truth between us." She smiled and snuggled. Holding her in my arms, I kissed her. Coming up for breath, I added, "You're everything I've ever wanted in a woman."

That's when she started in kissing me. I wanted to know her intimately, yet I'd made that promise—no sex for thirty days. I would not break my oath, and so contented myself, for the moment, with only knowing her spiritually and sensually. I touched her through the thin silk of her nightgown and only stopped after I'd breathed in the heady scent of her sex through the thin fabric covering her nether regions. With her, I found myself hard—rock hard. Along with my own laboring breath, I felt her respond and knew that I'd reached the limits of my resolve, and perhaps, possibly hers.

Even without consummating our sexuality, in those first few days, I felt we were really connecting, building something special together. Then on Wednesday, she informed me that she was having coffee with Jim the next evening. They still had a completion or two to make. I agreed and trusted in her that she'd do it the best way she could, that she would come from her heart and do it with love. She did indeed, only not how I expected.

All that weekend, Regina was strangely removed, unwilling to participate in those wonderfully deep conversations, and she avoided my touch. She began locking herself away for hours at a time in the special meditation room we'd set up for her.

Knowing that she had a lot of time and feelings tied up in her relationship with Jim, I respected her privacy. I'd been there myself and felt that whatever the turmoil inside of her, it also required a completion. I'd walked down my own trail of tears and thought I knew the anguish in her heart. So, I put my own needs on hold, offered my support and love, all the while trying not to push myself upon her. Even so, I suppose any level of intimacy, even non-sexual, was too much. Her trail of tears was not the same as mine.

On Monday, she asked for space, defining it as no touching, no talking, and strict privacy when in her meditation room. What I heard was that this beautiful bird was feeling like she was in a cage and was asking me to leave the door open. I did.

The next few weeks were not a time of happiness and contentment for me, nor did I pretend they were. It was clear that she was shutting me out of her life. While I didn't lay any dramas, blame, or control on her, I would not deny my sorrow. I would not put on a phony happy face for anyone. I knew too well the price it would cost my soul by not being true to myself.

Nor did I choose to find joy in the fact that, for a time, she was choosing to be with me—she wasn't, and I was done with pretense in my life. This, now, was not the relationship I wanted, but was it temporary? Was she still the one I wanted, just confused?

Was I, too, confused? *Most certainly.* **I knew the lying-ass laws of society were saying I was being duped.** For once, I expected society was speaking the truth. But then, I was following the Spiritual Law—**Life is always perfect, right here—right now.** This perfection wasn't feeling so good. It's funny how often the truth doesn't feel good.

Regina decided to do the Personal Quest Seminar. Our thirty days expired just before it was to begin. True to my word of giving her space, I did not mention it. Yet, I'd had enough. I needed my own completion. With the ending of the seminar came the ending of the 'space' I was willing to give her. Wanting her decision, I slipped the following two poems into her bags that Friday evening of the seminar, then wished her a sincere good time. PQ was being held over the weekend out at the Lake Mead Lodge. Regina would be back an eternity later, on Sunday night.

Broken Promises and Lies

Thirty days have come and gone,
unnoticed . . . unmarked . . . by you.
Instead of wearing this horn dog to a stub,
you kissed him on the cheek
as you sailed off to your gym.
I want to be closer
than the sheen on your skin-tight blue jeans,
to nestle with you in the gap of your thighs
where we can glorify our love.
Yet, I just feel alone . . . so alone.
Familiar patterns . . .
Up till three, avoiding that bed.
That bed where I sleep alone . . .
Alone, with you by my side . . .
unapproachably . . . untouchably . . .
unavailable by my side.
In the space of awake,

I'm so conscious of my promise . . .
my promise of space . . .
from conversation or touch.
It binds me from expressing my love.
And in my heart . . . now are tears.
Yet, especially in this, I am bound to silence.
For it would only drag you down . . .
my grief . . . my depression,
smothering you, with me . . .
in unspoken communication, without integrity.
And in an insinuating touch,
my putting the blame of it on you.
I thought soul mates were to uplift one another.
Support in times of need.
Or am I just too needy?
I don't want to be.
I lie here beside you . . .
watching you . . . snoring softly.
Oblivious to me.
I gently touch your thigh, lying to myself . . .
saying the promise is only broken
should you wake.
Quietly, I whisper the contents of my heart.
Perhaps my whisper carries
too much of my energy,
for you feel it . . .
and half-awake, mumble,
"Are you talking to me?"

"No," I lie.
It is number one . . .
The lie I swore I would never tell.
Then, quickly caught, I tell the truth.
"Yes."
Yet, before I blink, comes number two . . .
"It's okay . . .
go back to sleep."
Oh, Regina . . .
I feel my love dying.
Like a captured animal,
bleeding to death . . . in agony.
Caught by the steel jaws
of this trap called promise.
The promise of space . . .
A promise that herein, I break,
with a request for my heart's sake.
Is it really the space you need to take?
Or perhaps . . . a decision you need to make?
The space you request closes intimately,
or widens infinitely,
now.

Carpe Diem

"Good things come to those who wait."
It is a lie. Death comes to those who wait!
Even in their living are they dead.
Carpe diem! Capture the day!

Because the night will always fall
when we are not looking.
I know my mortality . . .
For I've looked into Death's unblinking stare.
Felt his chill fingers within my breast . . .
And know that someday soon . . . too soon . . .
I will come to be just dust and bone,
tumbling . . . floating on the winds of time.
Home again . . .
One with, once more, those shady canyons . . .
the ancient homeland of the Anasazi.
Yet, beside you last night . . .
giving you time . . . giving you space . . .
I felt myself stirring with a need . . . a want . . .
Both from within my heart,
and within my shorts.
So much love and comfort
we could be sharing . . .
Yet . . . are not.
Someday, too soon, it will be
as a widow's tears on the dust and bone.
And dusty bones make such a poor lover.
Carpe diem! Capture the day!
For it is the first, or last . . .
of the rest of our lives,
my love.

* * *

On Sunday evening, as I helped Regina unload her bags, I was aware there was indeed a change in her, a certain sureness that was different. I knew she'd made a decision. She hugged me with surprising warmth, yet there was also an aloofness—a distancing—about her. Somehow, I knew she wouldn't be staying. Whatever the changes were to be in our relationship, I welcomed them.

I joined her at the kitchen table as her words tumbled out about all the realizations and understandings she now held about herself. The seminar had again worked its magic with another willing mind. Her rage process was much the same as mine, only hers centered around Jim, whereas mine was about Meg. But the exercise concerning her purpose in life was nothing like mine. Hers concerned all the things she wanted to do or acquire. None of it was about the 'who' she wanted to be.

We talked for some time before she finally broached the subject about which my own mind had been screaming to engage all along—what about her and me? Where was our relationship at—right here, right now?

"You know, Jeff, I found your poems in my bag the first evening." The upper corner of her lip lifted in unconscious dismissal. "I purposefully didn't read them until this afternoon, when everything was over. I didn't want them to influence my seminar."

My shock must have been apparent because she hesitated briefly before continuing. "I don't want you to feel hurt, but I have to tell you . . . I . . . uh"—she ducked her head and seemed unable to look me in the eye—"I've decided to go back to Jim."

I nodded, saying nothing, but it seemed as though something in my gut, some knot, released. I put them in her bag knowing she'd read them at the perfect time for her to see something about me. I hadn't realized her timing would also show me what I needed to know about her. She went on.

"That night I had coffee with him"—she looked up now as if seeking, what, my approval, acceptance, understanding, what?—"he promised to go to Inner Quest. He's going to change himself." Her eyes dropped, again avoiding mine. "I . . . well, I just can't leave without giving him another chance." The words tumbled out in a guilty rush, a guilt I'd not instigated.

It was at that moment that I realized the true extent of her dishonesty. That was the moment I accepted that whatever connection we had, she wasn't my soul mate—not in this life.
She wasn't just now deciding this. She'd known it all along, nearly from the start.

With that realization came my own private admission of my own dishonesty to myself. My heart had known it, too. My conscious mind and ego wanted it to be otherwise, and so I was not willing to look at it in honesty, coming as it did from a place of neediness. No wonder she didn't accept me.

My calm reply, and relieved self-conscious chuckle, left her mouth gaping.

"Okay . . . when do you want to start moving back in with Jim? I'll help you."

* * *

Yes, Regina taught me much about people, and especially myself. While some—those whom she later told of our sexless relationship—thought me a fool, I admired myself for it.

I kept my word even when my ego, my hormones, and now even society said, "Jump her! Enjoy her sexy little body. Hear her moan in ecstasy!"

I was aware that Regina herself wanted sex with me, even expected it during those first few days of our relationship. Had I fulfilled her need despite our promise, perhaps Jim might not have seduced her away.

That would have been a mistake, one I would have very naturally made had I stayed the person I once was, back when I didn't respect myself or my word. But that was before I began to grow, to become the person I wanted to be. It felt good to see myself as deserving of respect.

* * *

Now, looking back, I recognize the truth and acknowledge a lesson learned. Clearly, this one was in my face, and the Law of Creation states—*If it's in your face, it's either a lesson, a message, or a test, validating and acknowledging your learning*. I learned this law from Dale Halloway, a mentor, friend, and kindred spirit. Thanks to Regina, I have been validated. This one was in my face, and I was okay with it. Unlike with Meg, I accepted walking away from Regina. When, in the end, Big D does take me, I will go as someone I like and respect.

I saw how the dramas Regina and Jim played were much the same as played by Meg and me. She wanted him to change, to be someone he wasn't. His heart knew who he wanted to be, and while he may have made a conscious determination to change, I knew he couldn't—not permanently. For him to make an enduring change, he would have to see something in what she wanted of him that his own heart wanted as well. Meg didn't want to be 'fucked in the head' like me. I doubted if Jim did, either.

With Regina, I allowed myself to be used. When she changed her mind, her demeanor did as well. My heart knew it. My consciousness ignored it.

I wanted a soul mate, but soul mates don't show up among the needy. The relationship an incomplete, needy person attracts will not be someone to fill in that missing piece. Many would view Regina as being that. I see her as a teacher, one who showed me how to fill in that gap myself. It was never about something missing, just misplaced.

Ultimately, Regina came into my life and taught me what my unmet needs truly were. I needed to be okay with myself, and most of all, to value my own company.

Too, she taught me about that predator part that tends to use others for our own selfish purposes. That part we are seldom willing to recognize and so seldom see. Regina validated how it was no longer a part of me.

When she walked out of my life, neither of us held on to any ties. Done deal.

* * *

I didn't see her again for nearly a year. One evening, I was exiting a movie and came across her and Jim in the parking lot.

Her pixie-cut, Barbie-doll hairdo was no longer set in a ponytail of platinum blonde. Rather, it was a brittle-looking, bright, purplish red. She still had a very slim, trim body, only now, it appeared somewhat angular—bulimic even. *Was she this same way before? What did I see in her that so attracted me?*

She drew near and spoke, "Jeff, how have you been?"

As we exchanged the mundane pleasantries, I looked into her eyes and realized the connection was no longer there. Whatever she had come into my life to teach—and perhaps, in turn, learn—was done.

Soul mates 'just are' and are not something to be forced. Yes, I wanted it to be Regina and tried to make it so. Our relationship, on the surface, might seem so useless and senseless for most. For me, it was vital. Yes, there was a connection, her soul to mine. Of that, I am certain. But was she my soul mate, the woman meant to be my partner in life? No.

Those events, as they unfolded, were indeed perfect. I learned a great lesson. Now I pay more attention to how my heart says things are than how my mind wants to say they must be. My heart always knows the truth. This was Regina's gift to me.

That last meeting with her in that theater parking lot was one of validation. I looked into her eyes and no longer felt any connection. Too, there was no longer any physical attraction. Our conversation involved only those inane things of the world, nothing of the heart.

Her excitement in life now centered on her new car.

"Did you see my new Jaguar over there?" she asked, pointing. "Jim bought it for me today. Oh, I'm just so happy!" Her demeanor gushed with it, like . . . like what, *diarrhea?*

That was the word that dropped into my mind just then.

Still, I was happy for her. She was getting all that she wanted in life. I didn't fault her, nor feel superior in my view of how short-lived and small her joy appeared to me.

Still . . . *was there any joy in her heart for Jim—for their love together?*

I glanced at Jim, standing there as if in the background, and saw something about him now, felt it in his energy . . . what, a subservience? I recognized it from past personal experience.

I wonder how long he has before his soul will pull the plug?

I gave Regina a quick hug, smiled, and waved as they turned away to go into the theater. Then, thinking about my memories of how it was for me and Meg back then, I shook my head sadly.

Will Jim take the shuttle, or will he refuse to go? If so, will his price be the same as mine? I hope he gets a reprieve.

As I swung my leg over the padded seat of my motorcycle and cocked my head to the side in buckling on the helmet, my eyes naturally aligned and caught one final glimpse of Regina's back as they hurried into the theater. She was not looking back, and in reality, nor was I. There was just nothing left to see. We were complete with one another, and perhaps I, too, knew the joy of new toys. Mine certainly had been playing a part in my growing and healing.

I started my motor and felt that glow as I listened to the throaty sound of power in the rumbling of my exhaust. Long as I live, I'll love that sound and cherish the joy that riding motorcycles has meant in my life. Just so, I will cherish the love I felt for Regina and the energy between us during the few days when it was reflected back, and later, the lesson she taught me, so critical for me, in order to make the shift away from neediness.

My tires gripped the pavement solidly as I cornered out of the parking lot. Upon straightening, I rolled the throttle and again felt pure joy with the surge of power responding beneath my butt. The rear end squatted as the front forks extended, lifting the front tire just clear of the pavement as I accelerated down the roadway. By the time I stopped for the red streetlight, Regina was out of my mind.

At the moment, I was between women, alone in the world, just me and the bike. And the moment felt right. And yes, perhaps for me, too, such material things can be of some service in filling in the gaps in my life. It is certainly so where it performs such a spiritual task.

Comb Ridge, Utah—Present Day

A cold rain is falling lightly. Big D and I sit under this overhang out of it, just going over the manuscript. As the words and thoughts slide by with the reading of these last chapters, I often hear his chuckle or snicker in the background of my mind.

It is probably the least favorite of the times in my life. Were I to choose a chapter to leave out, this would be the runner-up, and not because it paints me as such a woosy. My life is lived by rules most can't even fathom—rules so far from the norm of society as to lend me the least respect. But to me, the rules this society follows deserve no respect. I guess what I'm trying to say is that I don't give a shit what others think of me. On that score, the only person on this earth whose beliefs about me matter is me.

"Ah, well." Big D chuckles. "You must know that most folks reading this are going to see you as quite the limp dick. You know that, don't you?"

Yeah . . . 'fraid so. But with them, they are unable to see that the shit from between society's ears are the lies that slime up their lives, and they, of necessity, have become immune to the stink.

"Wanna know what I think?"

I take a deep breath and blow it out forcefully. *Sure, Big D, why not?*

"Ah . . . yes, to slip the bone or not to slip the bone? That was the question."

What the fuck? Where are you going with this, Big D? What people will be thinking is pretty obvious.

"That is just the point." He answers my thought as if it were spoken seriously. "Not one person in a thousand will see the truth of it. You handled that relationship with patience and the utmost grace."

Huh?

"Yes, you allowed her to be who she was. Not once did you try to change or control her—even when she fell back into that clusterfuck of control that she and Jim both called a relationship. You just accepted it and even helped her move back in with him. Now *that* was grace."

Actually, Big D, by then, I was very clear on the game she played. For my part, there was no animosity toward her, but I was happy to see her go.

"No animosity . . . *that* is what I mean by grace. And integrity . . . you displayed it, Jeff. But do you get that for all she was, and all she might have become for you, she didn't have the integrity required." His jaw comes unhinged as he belly laughs from a place most would see as being from hell. "It is among the very best chapters you have so far written."

I don't understand.

"Jeff, the promise you made Karen is normally considered a nicety, a pretense of who a man should be, but is not. Just part of the façade of your society."

Huh?

"That's right. Watching you live up to your word—such a fucking, simple thing—has given me great pleasure. You don't realize how rare that is."

We are social creatures. We all need each other. It is the connection itself we need so much to feel. Social creatures don't do life well alone. Yet, aren't we all on that higher, spiritual level of our minds and hearts connected? When one gets past the pain with which we cloud our minds, gets to know one's self fully, then one sees that higher spiritual connection and really feels it. Then is when we need no one, yet connect with everyone.

Redneck Spirituality—Book Two

CHAPTER TWENTY-ONE

Burying the Past

As some would have it, I jumped into sex and other women right out of my marriage. I did—and I didn't. My marriage ended that day in that hospital when those seven little words woke me from my slumber and forever changed my consciousness, the way I viewed my life. They awoke, and they killed, the 'who' I was, both at the same time.

"Why can't you wipe your butt better?" Those seven little words also ended my marriage, for the message they said was more—so much more. With them, Meg's message was also:

I don't respect you.
I am disgusted by you.
I suffer your affections.
I don't want to be married to you.
I give you this sponge bath only out of wifely duty—
But if you die tonight . . . I will be free.

These are but a few of the messages I heard in those seven little words spoken that fear-filled night in that ICU, a night I fully expected would not again lighten for me. Yet, they were my messages, my interpretations, and I could not have heard them unless I, too, was on some level saying them. In the manner I heard each message, there was a kernel of truth also said from me to her. Bottom line, what those words told me was clear—I wanted her to be different from who she was.

Thus, I spent the next year and a half trying to change her. My marriage was over the minute I started. It just took those eighteen months to die, months spent in resistance to what already was and anger for what I could not change.

When we finally parted, I was ready for other women. In fact, I needed other women to fill the emptiness and, eventually, to teach me to be okay with me and to help me get through my sorrow.

Oh sure, Spiritual Laws tell us that we are all connected, and I believe that's true—spiritually. It's also true that one has no ability to give love unless one first loves himself, and I damned sure had a problem in that department. In the face of death, my ability to bullshit myself about anything was shaken. Hell, in knowing Big D, it was destroyed.

Just then, I needed others . . . yes, women. If connecting with them had to start on a sexual level, so be it. I was busy reaching deep, learning about myself, learning to love and respect myself. All those years with Meg . . . yes, I truly loved her. Whatever love I possessed inside was given to her, but at what cost? The control over my life?

Did giving her all that control leave me without self-respect, maybe even self-love? Hell, I didn't know. Had I so little of it that she sucked me dry? Why could I not replenish it by loving myself? And Meg . . . did she ever have the ability to love me, or herself?

God, yes, I loved her! And when drained dry of it, why did I refuse to die?

So, for a while there, I let women into my life who could love, while I searched within myself. How could I have touched Meg's soul when I wouldn't touch my own? Sometimes we hear and see by the reflection, the mirror of others, what it is about us we most need to see. Sometimes we are touched by the mirrors of their souls.

While it is something it helps to be told and to know consciously, it is also something we need not be told. Living *Universal Truths—the Spiritual Laws*—requires only the courage to step past our fear of what it means to be the creator, with full choice and sovereignty over our lives. It is intimidating to accept full responsibility, especially when we have created being this person we don't like. Taking it from our head to our heart is a scary journey.

Grief? Yes, grief is the victim side of anger. In dealing directly with grief . . . well, to quote Karen, "To feel is to heal." But first, I had to recognize and acknowledge it. My marriage was dead. That part of my life, that person I was, died with it. And the dead need nothing. It is the living who need the funeral.

I cried, not for my old life, but for my future, for I knew not its worth—or mine—without Meg. Many times, I locked myself away or took myself alone into the desert to weep. I'd open my heart and let the sorrow and agony flow away. I opened my soul and let it wail.

Meg's leaving left a huge, gaping wound in my life. For a time, I tried to fill it with other women. They were like a healing salve. As for that wound itself? Healing that required love—self-love. Those women showed me the way.

* * *

I suppose that it was our grief that initially drew us together—DeeDee, Chuck, and I. And perhaps, too, it was the fact that we were all growing, dealing with our lives, doing what was necessary to get healthy mentally, emotionally, physically, and spiritually.

We met on the support team of a Vision Quest Seminar. DeeDee was a therapist fresh out of a long-term relationship with the love of her life. Chuck, a contractor in the housing trades, was about to leave his. We, all three, knew that in our growth and healing, our grief needed to be felt then moved beyond.

I shared my experience of writing Meg a goodbye letter, then mailing it in flames to the universe. We agreed that we needed to do something more than just mentally recognizing the end of our individual relationships. We needed something physical, a tangible action of some kind, to step past this place where we all felt emotionally stuck. Between us, we decided that the death of our marriages warranted a funeral—for us, the living.

My task in all this was to choose a site. DeeDee's was to provide transportation. For Chuck, it was the music and champagne. I spent two days driving the backroads of Mount Charleston, just to the north of Las Vegas. I'd park at all likely looking places and hike the ridges, looking for that perfect spot.

Its first priority was to have an unlimited view, which meant it had to be high up on the mountain. Then we wanted a clearing, with soil suitable for digging graves and remote enough to afford us absolute privacy. And, perhaps most importantly, we wanted it open to the first rays of the rising sun. Eventually, I found the perfect spot.

We met in the dark, predawn hours of an August Sunday at Chuck's house in northwest Las Vegas. I parked my bike in his driveway, and we all loaded into DeeDee's old Chevrolet and headed up the mountain. The blackness of night was beginning to give way to blue, and only a few of the brighter stars still shone near the horizon when we arrived at the site. Using flashlights, we went about the preparation, both DeeDee and me each digging individual, small graves. That done, we sat in silent meditation, alone, yet together in our grief.

Chuck brought nothing, as his marriage was still gasping out its dying breaths. He was there to support, play the music, and to stand witness to the funerals.

The mountains along the eastern horizon were rimmed with orange, the sun not yet up, when DeeDee arose and began her ceremony. She first placed her shoebox of personal items into the grave, and with her whole being quavering along with her voice, said a squeaky, quiet goodbye. Then, stumbling back, she sat next to me on the ledge overlooking our makeshift cemetery. Chuck played a tape on his boom box of the song that had been theirs—DeeDee's and her lost love.

I then arose and gently, with great reverence, placed the shoebox coffin of my earlier life into its grave. In it was a marriage certificate and four poems, written, my soul to Meg's. They were the words my heart ached to say, but hers found too frightening to hear. Except for that first one, I would not again ask that of her. That first poem was written in an effort to get her to see who I was becoming. At that time, all she could see in me, she often summed up with two words—*fucked up*.

Maybe she was right. Me, writing poetry! But hell, I'd already tried everything else to get through to her, and I did kinda make a big, fucking production out of sitting her down while I read it.

Sir Knight

Your Sir Knight is dead.
Pierced through . . .
Impaled on a shaft
from the light of consciousness.
No longer to ride to your rescue.

> *To slay the dragons of your mind,*
> *to rescue you from your emotions.*
> *Yes, your Sir Knight has fallen,*
> *taking down with him your shield of security.*
> *And your sword of power . . . of control.*
> *The drama is done.*
> *With what, now, will I replace him,*
> *and give you security from your fears?*
> *Money? I have none.*
> *Social position? It's an illusion.*
> *Power? You already possess all you need.*
> *Wisdom? Again . . . also within you.*
> *I will replace him with that*
> *which I give you freely.*
> *I will replace him with love . . .*
> *Unconditional love.*

She'd stared, her eyebrows drawn down with, what, curiosity? Shock? Anger? Looking deeply into her beautiful, Asian eyes in the ensuing silence, I finally said, "W-well, what do you think?"

"What is this shit? Keep it to yourself." My jaw now hung at the lowest point it ever had. "And don't you . . . *ever* . . . bother me with it again!" My mouth snapped shut as the words began to make sense. Her tone denied there would ever be another time for such sentimental sentiments.

Fitting, to bury those words in this grave, to put to rest the ghost of her words, now bothering me. That first poem was my cry for understanding. But the others? They were not coming from as healthy a space. They were the words of a victim filled with anger and sorrow, saying that her love, *as he wanted it given*, had never been. And his love, *as he wanted to give it*, had never been accepted. As such, they were not the words of love. Rather, they were a forlorn cry for love.

The act of holding the funeral was very healthy—healing, actually—for it was a letting go of those feelings. The truth, were it to be written and buried in that grave today, would simply say, *You were my perfect mate. You bore my progeny and taught me all you had that I needed to know from you . . . and I love you.* But back then, had I read the words of those next poems aloud, I would have wept in agony.

Do Eagles Always Soar Alone?

I see the anguish in your eyes,
and with tears streaking my face,
as the blood from these wounds in my soul,
voice quavering, I say the words,
It is over . . .
I love you,
yet I no longer fill your need
for domination and control,
the foundation and security in your life.
Once your submissive husband-child,
I've grown up . . .
found courage . . .
Courage to step out to the edge . . .
To try my wings and soar.
Your fears will not let you nurture me
or join me in my quest . . .
It is over . . .
and my quest goes on.
Alone I sit at this table,
Where once we ate, laughed, and loved.
Now . . . only loneliness.
Feathers ruffled . . .
mildewed from my tears.

> It is cold in these rarefied heights,
> and oh, so solitary . . .
> Do eagles always soar alone?

Only with the last one did I make the attempt. The clear, beautiful notes of Whitney Houston's song "I Will Always Love You" floated out on the crisp, cool, pine-scented mountain air as I laid the coffin of our marriage away. Staring down into that shallow hole, I could no longer see the box as the first rays of the morning sun refracted through my tears. With my eyes blinded by the light, my heart by the pain, my mind for those few moments of her song knew nothing. When Whitney's last high note echoed to silence, I blotted the tears with a sleeve and began to read.

Dawn

> These arms of mine once held the sky . . .
> embracing love as few men know.
> Then darkness came and we lost the flames
> we shared within our souls.
> One went off to school,
> In another, the passion cooled . . .
> Of the rest we had little common fuel.
> Yes, our fires had dimmed . . .
> And Death found me then,
> no longer aflame . . .
> Just one . . .
> of two bitter victims.
> Now its memory exists,
> ghostly hot within my breast.
> Through the dark of night,
> misty memories
> smolder in lonely fright.

Tis time they, too,
must die.
For it is only in one's night,
can there come such light.
In the break of this new dawn,
night can escape . . . dissipate . . .
expand, and change . . .
as it moves on.
Leaving room . . .
making space,
for a new love to grow upon.
Does your heart, too,
feel this yearning . . .
for a new love
bright and burning . . .
as the new light
of this
new dawn?

Several times I had to stop and again apply that sleeve, nor was my voice clear—or steady—as, coughing and hacking at the burning ache in my throat, I finished. Then, waving a reluctant cue to Chuck, the boom box burst forth with the first piano strains of Aaron Neville and Linda Ronstadt's song. Aaron's clear voice began to sing my own entreating message to a duet with a soul mate, yet unknown.

> *Look at this face . . .*
> *I know the years are showing.*
> *Look at this life . . .*
> *I still don't know where it's goin'. . . .*

There was one more poem remaining. I intended to, but found I could not deal with reading it aloud, nor do I now feel that including it here at this time would serve any purpose other than to keep the pain alive in my heart. And that pain cried out for this death, this funeral. It dealt with Meg and with the reason our life together was now dead.

The reason no longer mattered, yet it, too, deserved its place in this coffin. And I? I deserved to leave it there, unsaid. The title of that poem was, "Forgive Me My Love." It asked for something I knew Meg was incapable of giving.

After folding that last poem of benediction back into the shoebox coffin and closing the lid, DeeDee and I slowly filled in the graves of our lost loves while listening to the beauty of that song. On my knees, alongside hers, I shed healing tears, emissaries of the love so long imprisoned simply because it was never accepted, recognizing, in the dawning rays of that new day, a burgeoning freedom in this, the beginning of my new life. The funeral was private. Except for us three, no one has known of it—until now.

I won't deny it. I jumped into relationships, one after the other, and from each woman, learned, and with each, was healed.

As for those women, was the debt incurred paid for with my love? I like to think it was, because still, I cherish each one.

Comb Ridge, Utah—Present Day

Big D chuckles. "So then, why do you suppose you've been kicked to the curb in every relationship you ever had with women?"

I'm not going to lie. I know it is about no one but me. I shrug. *I guess there is something they see as very wrong about me. I believe the Spiritual Laws—they don't. Or, maybe I'm just not good enough for any woman to love.*

"Ah, yes. Hold that last thought—*or don't!* You need to get yourself right on it if you want to live." There is his grin, as always, pronounced across his face, but for some reason, I can't read the feelings behind it. "But perhaps you framed the issue. There have been a couple who also believe as you do, y'know."

A stiff gust of icy wind screams up out of the chasm of Comb Ridge Wash, hits my back, and fairly rips up under every stitch of clothing I have on, including my leather motorcycle coat. I hug the ground as if to keep myself from blowing off into the abyss. Then, all is silent. The air is still, as if to put a period on Big D's last statement.

I . . . I hear you, Big D. No need to get so dramatic.

"Ah, Jeff." His words rumble out of the stillness of the evening. "There most certainly is reason . . ."

Big D? . . . Big D? . . . I call to him, but this time, he does not answer.

There are certain standards that everyone must have to feel okay with themselves. Sometimes these are things we will never allow to be happening in our lives—sometimes things we must have happening. And as for the standards for those whom we allow into our lives? Sometimes it is about the way they show up—sometimes, the way they don't. We get to create our lives the way we want. After all, we are the creator—always. And always, too, we are the limiter. Our standards don't limit how high we fly, only how low—and who we will fly beside.

Redneck Spirituality—Book Four

CHAPTER TWENTY-TWO

Of Motorcycle Wheels, Macho Balls, and Acceptance

Riding motorcycles . . . ah, yes! That is one of those ultimate ways of living in the present. During the first two years of my marriage, while living in Salt Lake City, I rode a motorcycle, then again later, during the twelve years we lived in the Four Corners—that area where the four states of Utah, Arizona, Colorado, and New Mexico all come together. Those first two bikes were the light 250 to 350 cubic centimeters class, designed for both on and off the road.

At times, I would ride the desert trails, kicking up dust, sliding, jumping, even climbing those steep hills, the kind where there was little doubt that stopping meant instant disaster. Other times, I might be riding the highways, leaning into the curves or mixing with the flow of traffic on those two-lane roads. But always, somewhere in the back of my mind, lurked the sure knowledge that one—just one—tiny miscalculation or inattentive moment could cost me my life.

Yes, though life is always just so, it is especially so when riding motorcycles. The reality is, your life is always in your own hands. It's just that when you're riding, you know it.

Some people just aren't as intelligent as others. Most call them 'stupid.' Some are very intelligent but just act stupid. I never viewed myself as either. When Meg, Shane, and I moved to Las Vegas, I saw how crazy some of the drivers were, or perhaps the word is 'crazed.' Las Vegas was a wild town and could be very dangerous, even deadly, especially so on a motorcycle.

For a time, I gave up on my love of riding, felt it only prudent to bow to the added dangers. The risk-to-reward level here was far too uneven for riding. After the Eagle Quest Seminar, having lost the one main love in my life, I found the scales had slammed over onto the other side. My love for riding now carried more weight—at least equal to the danger. Suddenly alone in life, there was no longer even an illusion of any responsibility to others to weigh, and there was joy to be found in riding. And joy was what I needed in my life, especially now that I lived it in the moment.

The only real responsibilities we bear others lie simply in our personal word to them. And of course, a man is obligated to his family—to protect them and to teach his children until they become adults. But my son, Shane, was now an adult and several years on his own. Since our divorce, the real truth was, it had only been my own fear stopping me from riding.

I never before owned a big street bike, the kind they call a 'cruiser.' It was something I now realized I wanted. After looking at my fears came the time to look at bikes, then to go shopping for *the one*. It turned out to be a Yamaha Virago 1100 . . . burnt-orange paint with maroon markings. Yeah . . . beautiful!

In that showroom, sitting on its cheek-hugging, black, Naugahyde seat, I grabbed a handful of throttle and another of clutch. With my legs wrapped around its gleaming, sleek, powerful form, I felt like Evel Knievel, Marlon Brando, and James Dean all in one—pure bull balls and testosterone.

And yet, it was much more than that macho look and mystique that I was buying. Had it only been so, I'd have gotten a Harley, paid triple for it, and even felt proud of the price. This Virago was lighter, faster, and had a better reputation for dependability than most Harleys. The dealer was in Henderson, a town just to the south of Las Vegas. As I climbed aboard my gleaming new machine, my fear was up. I'd never ridden anything this big, nor with this kind of raw power. Still, bikes are bikes. You can die on any of them if dying's what you're about. Certainly, it was no longer so for me.

Smoothly rolling back the throttle, I swung out onto Boulder Highway. Then it seemed but a heartbeat, a gasp, and the burp of my ass, and I was running with the flow on Highway 95—seventy miles per hour and shoulder to shoulder with the dinosaurs. Yes, I was very aware of the tons of steel moving so swiftly with and all around me, all sharing what seemed to be a greed for speed.

Twenty miles later, still a little shaky and high on adrenalin, I reached home. I'd sparred with the dinosaurs, and this time, had won. Would it always be so?

Pulling into the garage next to my pickup, I shoved down the kickstand with the heel of my boot. Congratulating myself on a job well done, I leaned the bike onto the stand and immediately found myself thrashing about, trying to extricate my left leg from beneath seven hundred pounds of hot metal.

"Owwww . . . Hhooo-Whaaaaa . . . SHIT! Goddamm . . . Muuuh-therrrr Fuuuuuukkk!"

While the pain screamed hotly in my mind, and my skin fairly sizzled, I still managed to keep my vocals to a low but very profane squeal. It took several minutes to recoup my leg and to lift my shiny, new, freshly scratched machine back onto its stand—properly this time. By then, the skin on my face was as red as that on my bruised and blistered leg. Looking quickly about in self-conscious embarrassment, and seeing no one, I breathed a sigh at my good fortune, hit the garage door button, and limped into the house.

I was not so lucky that night at the party. All of my friends were there, including my new girlfriend—Tess with the lime-colored breasts. They were there oohing and aahing as I parked that bad boy. Ducking my head, I pretended not to notice the attention, as kneeling, I ran the security cable through the front wheels and locked it around the forks.

The background music was muted as I wandered around, sipping a beer, socializing. I found myself fielding questions about the bike and hearing, time and again, the phrase, "I just wish I could . . ." Mostly, the women were not so vocal, but with a few, the same question seemed to be running through their minds. From the lowering of their eyelashes and the way they glanced up sideways at me, I was sure the verbiage of their wishes was different.

Yes, motorcycles seem to bring out surprising reactions in folks. I found myself uncomfortable with the notoriety, yet fighting not to act out the impulses of my ego. Afterward, the guys all stood around in obvious envy as I slung my leg over the saddle, shrugged into my new helmet, and hit the starter. The motor burst into a powerful rumble. Relaxing the clutch lever, I sped off into the night—about five feet into the night.

That was how far my macho machine flew before it came to an abrupt halt at the end of that security cable. Throwing me to the ground, it then stomped all over me. After a long moment of frantic fumbling, I managed to hit the kill switch on the handlebar. As the motor abruptly died, I scrambled to my feet. My face would have been a match had the color of that bike been burnt red, not orange. Disregarding the pain from a dislocated thumb, and with a little help from the guys, I set the bike back upright on its stand. They tried hard to hide their amusement as they snickered their concern.

"I'm okay, guys. You can all laugh now—know you want to."

While we were all bent over laughing, I grabbed my throbbing thumb and, holding it against my stomach, jerked it back into its socket. No one seemed to notice my involuntary yelp of pain.

Yeah, sure. I spent a great deal of my time in those seminars, learning to be honest with myself and others. Still, sometimes when it comes to motorcycle wheels or macho balls . . . well, sometimes we slip out of the socket a little, just before we crash and burn on that honesty.

* * *

In the months since Regina, Tess and I made a connection. One evening, after an IQ support team meeting, she dropped by. We sat before my computer while I read her something I wrote. Without a word, she slipped into my lap and, suddenly, we were kissing and cuddling. Soon we were in my bed, consummating our relationship.

Tess was short and slight of build, with an impish character. She, nevertheless, had a classic, hourglass waist between the sensual flair of womanly hips, topped with the silicone perfection of her chest. Her face could not really be classed so much as *pretty*. The more fitting term was *cute*. But her eyes? They were gray, clear, and beautiful, as was, I soon came to know, her soul.

And love . . . Tess loved to make love and did it with great passion. While my heart matched her passion, my dick did not. It still refused to snap as quickly to attention or to hold the salute as rigidly as it once had. Tess didn't mind. In fact, she saw no problem for her on that score whatsoever.

As for me? She nearly had me convinced that there was nothing there worthy of my concern. She said it was just one of those gravity and age things about men getting older—same as gravity on maturing titties. Things like that. After all, I was nearly fifty, wasn't I? But that was all before I went to bed one night with a *pissed-off* Tess.

Like me, she had pretty much given up her need for drama. I can no longer recall what sparked her unusual anger that day, just that it was still flaming as we lay together in bed that night.

Me? I was feeling a familiar need, strangely, much stronger than usual, and wanted to make love. Touching her body, I felt her stiff unresponsiveness as she lay inert in my arms.

"Tess . . . come on, honey. I want to feel you . . . kiss you . . . taste you. Let's make love."

"No! I'm not in the mood," came her challenge, or so it sounded to me.

But I was rock hard. Hell, I hadn't been that hard since my divorce. And so, I reached for Tess, touched her in all those secret, exciting places, and thought I felt her respond. And I kissed her lips, her still-angry lips—sure. So, I moved on down and nuzzled and licked her nipples. Her body seemed to respond, to wiggle around some. Was she merely getting more comfortable, or was she responding? I moved on down farther, tasted a kiss on her nether lips, and nuzzled her bud with my nose. She now seemed so wet. Surely, that wasn't all from my eager drool. And so, I rose up and impaled her on the steel of my stake and rocked her body to the rhythm of my passion. Eventually, when that rhythm became a pounding slap, my flesh upon hers, I shifted to a gentle rocking. My rocket was ready to explode, but it didn't seem hers was even off the launch pad. Her passion did not climb, much less rise, to the pounding as I expected it would. I froze.

"What's wrong? I didn't hurt you, did I?"

"No," came her reply on an even breath, nothing like the panting of my own. "Go ahead and finish."

That evening, I did *not* finish.

Tess, by the simple vengeance of withholding her love, taught me so much about me, my dick, and the twenty-five years of marriage to Meg. About how the eagerness of my seduction, and the submissive message it carried beneath it, always supported Meg in her need to be in control. How sexually, that was my part in the game of control I played with her, and how that control did not come from a loving heart.

Perhaps, like Tess that night, it was also about Meg's revenge. I wasn't the one to whom Meg gave her heart back then before she ever met me, but I was the one who paid the price of his betrayal. She didn't know **hurt** is just the victim side of **anger**, and **betrayed**, the prelude to both. **Revenge** is a matter of collecting the payment, often from the innocent who have fallen victim to and, in turn, betrayed by Meg's anger.

Back then, I was that innocent who paid Meg's price. With Tess, there came a déjà vu and the gift of understanding of Meg and why, without her, my cock didn't want to rock.

Being blamed for another man's betrayal, held responsible because I, too, am a man—isn't that about me being that victim at the end of your clusterfuck of anger? Anger, betrayal, revengeful victims blamed for someone else's poor choice in painful feelings . . . sickening! I had no desire to join her parade of victims. That's the underlying truth why gay people feel a need for parades. How much of it is in true, joyful celebration, and how much is to show you their pain? Could get off celebrating sex—not particularly gay sex. But pain and blame and making others pay? That's fucked up.

How much of that is about blaming others for their pain, and in the end, does the whole fucking world have to pay?

* * *

By that time, Tess and I were several months into our relationship. This event, again, gave pause for me to examine it much deeper than ever before. I thought it was about the great sex, the great friendship, and the great times we enjoyed together. Truth was, it was also about some great lessons.

This one was the last of the two great truths that she was there to teach me. I didn't know what I was for her. With Pavlov's dog, the sound of a metronome, followed by food, taught him to salivate. With me? A leash around my balls, followed by sex, would never again be required to put steel in my dick. Maybe this was the reason why I stayed in the relationship, the last of the lessons Tess came into my life to teach.

* * *

The first was learned in the first few weeks with her. It told me Tess was not *the one*—and why. When we parted, she was still trying to figure out why I was not *her one*. I don't know if she ever found her own truth about it.

For me, the realization came earlier. It was during a relationship seminar put on by Karen. We both attended for the purpose of deepening our budding relationship. At least that was *my* belief. Many of the participants were singles who'd paired up only because there was a price break for couples.

I always made it a point never to discuss my sexual life with others, although for myself, I didn't care who knew. What with all our wild monkey sex, in my mind, I assumed Tess and I were a couple. That is, until one particular exercise began.

Tess and I were sitting knee to knee, facing one another. The object of the exercise was to communicate our feelings for the other completely and honestly, but without speaking. I was first.

Taking Tess gently by the hands, I leaned forward to kiss her. She leaned back. Confused, I leaned forward once again, thinking that she'd misunderstood my intention. Now Tess bent backward again, clear over the backrest of her chair, obviously avoiding my lips.

Ceasing my attempts, I sat back, confused, and I have to admit, feeling those old victim feelings of hurt and rejection. A mental picture of Pepé Le Pew, the ridiculous, amorous skunk from the cartoons of my childhood, drifted through my mind, and I felt as if I'd made some unforgivable blunder, some odorous mistake. I often felt that way with women during my youth.

Numbly, I sat there for a long moment, examining my feelings. Maybe my picture was correct. Was I, like that skunk, acting ridiculous, or did I just have skunk breath?

Then her turn came. She held my hands and touched me warmly with a hint of passion, yet unobtrusively, secretively, almost as if she wanted no one to know. It seemed to suggest that the relationship we shared was something to be kept in our respective closets.

Was I not good enough? Was Tess indeed hiding our true relationship from the others? I'd known that one before, knew what it was like to accept and be held responsible for another's shame. And I didn't like it!

And yet, I'd grown since those days. Sitting there, I looked within myself, aware that I was not responsible for her feelings. But there was an answer for me here. I stopped and took responsibility for my own feelings, doused the fire of resentment starting to inflame my gut, and accepted how my reality of the situation might not be the same as hers.

I wouldn't do this the way I'd always done in the past—take ownership of another person's shame and slink away into the dark. That was the coward's way. No, I'd communicate openly and honestly. There was nothing for which I needed to feel ashamed, nor did I think it even possible that I'd ever again choose such immature feelings. This time, I'd be a man and get a clear understanding of her reality—and do it without drama.

* * *

The opportunity came a few days later during a hiking date at Red Rock Canyon. We followed one of the main trails for about a mile in the blazing, Las Vegas sun. The tightness of my shirt gave little opportunity for it to do other than stick to my back, as sweat ran southward toward the crack of my ass. Tess, too, was sweating. Seeking relief, we made our way off into a wilderness of jumbled rock and sand, speckled here and there with cedar and pinyon pine. Finding a secluded, shady spot where we felt secure and alone, we sat together on a rock to eat lunch and talk.

I could tell Tess was also seeking this time with me. Clearly, there were critical understandings to be made. From the uneasy way she was avoiding my eyes, and the unusual lack of conversation between us thus far, I knew she, too, felt a little afraid of what we were to discover about one another.

The desert around us had a calm, almost spiritual feel, and though reluctant to break its silence, I began. "Tess, we have some things we need to sort out."

Her eyes would not meet mine as I related my experience of her at the seminar, ending with, "Y'know." I grimaced. "It felt like you were ashamed of me, that you didn't want the others to know we were having a relationship. Is that true?"

For a long moment, Tess looked down at the ground as she pushed the sand back and forth with the toe of her hiking boot. Finally, she looked up.

"Yes, I was, but I've dealt with that, and I'm not anymore."

"Ahh," I murmured softly, wishing that just this once, my intuition was not so damned spot-on accurate. An uncomfortable silence fell between us.

"Well . . . what is it about me that you don't accept?"

"It's your clothes." Her breath huffed into an exaggerated sigh. "They're . . . well, they're just so geeky and outdated."

I looked down. They were the sort of clothes I always wore. Levis with a wide belt sporting a big, brass buckle. The 'Snap-On Tools' logo, recognized by all professional mechanics, glinted across its face. There was a plaid, western shirt—nothing unusual there. For this hike, a pair of sneakers replaced my usual cowboy boots. "What's wrong with my clothes?"

"Well," she began, "for one thing, western shirts are no longer worn tight, nor do they use that old, plaid design anymore. Now they're baggy and usually have colored panels or stripes. The belt's okay, and even the buckle, but those sneakers . . ." She paused while her breath snorkeled out through her nose. "No one wears Velcro-tab sneakers anymore."

"At that point, her eyes kind of rolled in her head. For me, it all seemed so incredulous, I almost asked her to repeat, just to verify my reality. There was no need. She continued. "And at the seminar . . . my God, those bell-bottomed, polyester pants you had on." She closed her eyes, tossed her head, and snorted in disgust. "I haven't seen them in over fifteen years!"

I thought back to the seminar. The pants she referred to were the one pair of slacks I still owned. Outside of my work uniforms, I always wore standard blue jeans. Shy of the tux I bought for my son's wedding, I seldom went anywhere that required more. They hadn't been worn more than a dozen times and looked practically new. The material *was* polyester, and they *did* flare at the legs. *They were boot-cut, Levi, dress slacks, for Christ's sake.* I always supposed they were like my other Levis—time-tested and eternally accepted. Mentally, I shrugged. I didn't much care what I wore.

"Geeky . . ." I mused in surprised regret. It would have been so laughable had shame not entered into the equation. I would've gladly updated my wardrobe if she'd only let me know that it meant so much to her. But shame—being ashamed of me? That said something else entirely, and it had nothing to do with clothes.

"Y'know, Tess," I told her soberly, looking her steadily in the eye, "you're just not my soul mate." I sighed. "I know it now."

Her mouth fell open, and her beautiful, gray eyes stared as if she didn't comprehend my words.

"It was all just a mistake! S-surely you won't hold that against me?" Her face broke into a spider web of panic. "I-i-it was how I was raised." Her words ranged upward in scale as she began to hyperventilate.

"No," I interrupted. "I won't hold it against you, Tess. We can be friends. We can even still be lovers." I paused a moment, remembering how much we both enjoyed the one thing I ever actually held against her. "Fact, I'd like that." I grinned, then sobered. "But you're just not *the one*. You're not my soul mate."

Our eyes were locked. I could see in hers she didn't believe, or maybe doubted, I was serious as she gazed into my eyes while swallowing, finally getting her breathing under control. Perhaps my mind's momentary lapse into the sensuous joys of our recent past didn't have a proper place in serious conversation. But then, that was just me.

I went on, my voice flat and quiet, with no hint of malice—only fact. "Tess, I simply don't want to spend the rest of my life with you."

She heard me now. Her tears traced silent paths down her cheeks. I knew she felt a great sense of loss. I felt it, too.

"It was just a silly mistake . . ." Her voice trailed off and she dropped her eyes from mine.

"Tess, being accepted is just that important to me. I've already spent twenty-five years married to a woman who wouldn't accept me. And then there's my parents . . ." I let that one hang. Tess's ridicule and shame held no comparison to my mother's.

She did not answer and, for a time, we both just sat there together, listening to a lone, desert breeze whisper through the pinyon pines and cedars and around the rocks. It ruffled our hair as it passed, then moved ever fainter off into the distance. Something had come into our lives and was now leaving.

"Look . . ." I took gentle hold of her shoulders. "My soul mate? She would never be ashamed of me. It just wouldn't be possible."

A relationship with me demands acceptance. I will not pretend to be different than I am in order to be acceptable. That was it—the first great truth Tess was in my life to teach me. Meg gave me the lesson by demanding a pretense, that I change myself to be who she wanted. Tess rejected me through shame due to my lack of sophistication. I simply wasn't who either woman wanted, but until Tess, I did not see the silly futility of pretense.

As for the second lesson? I'm glad I stayed around. It's so much nicer not to play that game called *seduction* just to put some stiff in my dick. I don't want to ever make love to a woman who doesn't want me—

or one who requires that fucked-up control drama called seduction. Foreplay is an entirely different thing.

I told myself to laugh it off, but goddamn, it hurt! That hurt I knew was a choice I was making. But, fuck me silly, who wouldn't choose pain when someone they love finds them unacceptable? I chose that pain, and although I knew better, I wondered why. It took a while for me to see that the loved one who prompted all that pain was not Tess. It was Meg.

What Tess did demanded a parting. It did not demand anger, revenge, blame, or even pain. Neither one of us needed to be a victim. It took Tess for me to see the stranglehold Meg still had on me.

In losing Meg, I went through a great deal of pain. Tess was merely a revival. I needed that motorcycle more than ever. I needed it to take me away to the solitude of the desert and to the ride. One does not live long if clinging to the past while riding a motorcycle in the present. In the simple joy of the ride, I found the peace I needed to heal myself, to let that pain flow away like the wind through my hair.

Comb Ridge, Utah—Present Day

Ah, the solitude of the desert. I sit on this ledge, looking out over the great panoramic vastness of it. This same view, day after day, but I don't think I'll ever get tired of it. *Sure picked the perfect place to crash my bike and find solitude—a real shitload of it. Will I ever forget the view from here, or is it the last one I'll ever remember?*

"Ah, Jeff. You are so clear about your pain—acknowledging it, getting honest and taking responsibility, even doing what it takes to deal with it." Big D's voice blares directly into my ear from just behind on my right side. I find myself fumbling, trying to hold on to the notebook that bounces and skitters around out of my left hand while the canteen in my right continues to pour.

"Dammit, Big D!" The words burst out verbally, as the cold, pine-needle tea I was sipping runs down my chin and spreads across my shirt. *I almost lost my notebook over the edge.*

"You juggled it well. Too bad you don't have it so together about women. And that fear—the one you have yet to see—the one that has kept your life in unwelcome solitude of late?" He laughs. "Yeah, you couldn't see it before. It was always about those women. But you know the truth now, don't you?"

Not sure I get your meaning.

"What is the first law again?"

*Uh, **I am the creator.***
"What's that telling you?"
That it's not about them, it is about me . . . but how?
"Figure it out, Jeff. It is stopping you from following your joy."
Huh?
"Yeah, your promises—our agreement—remember? The one your life depends on."
But . . . but . . .
"That's right . . . but for your willingness to deal with all the *other shit* that you *do* see, your reset button would have been pushed long ago." While I can't see him, I feel a boney digit push against my forehead, rocking my head back. "Figure it out!"

A Necessary Author Intrusion

Ah, the Inner Quest for Vets Seminar. It was a place where I met a very special veteran. I could allow you to picture Ka-Bar, where he sat across from me in the eight-person group I was charged with guiding through the seminar.

Ka-Bar—big and burly, bearded, and multi-tattooed, looking ferocious to the bone, even to the bolts and screws of the metal brace holding the bones of his leg together. I could show you all the experiential exercises we did together—all the personal things as he talked about them, and the tears we shared together.

BUT I WON'T.

An experiential seminar is a place where privacy is sacred. Each participant needs to go into it alone, without prior knowledge. Yes, I have and will show you minor experiences I've had in the seminars—MY experiences—but I will never show you the experiences of others, nor will I divulge more than just enough to whet your appetite. If you are hungry, you will go and experience it for yourself.

In case you haven't yet figured it out, most of what is in this book actually happened as written. For the anonymity of those involved, the names, sometimes the locations, and even who did what, are changed. However, the following chapter about Ka-Bar has not been disguised in any way. I was not there with him in Vietnam—that part is secondhand—and our experiences together in the seminar are sacred.

Even so, his is a story I feel should concern this entire nation. I will tell it to you in the following chapter, as it was told to me. And I will show you an experience, one special to me, that I had with Ka-Bar after the seminar.

Whereas soldiers returning from Vietnam were spit upon, those returning from the wars spawned by the outrage of the twin towers were treated with patriotic fervor.

Now we have cycled back around. Many in this great nation are now considering socialism as being a good thing. Some even want to trash the Constitution.

Let the story of Ka-Bar—what little of it I can divulge—be your heads-up to the patriotism still felt by us, the fucked-over generation of Vietnam veterans.

We all walk a different path in life because we all have different needs. The parts I need to fill, or the wounds I need healed, are not the same as yours, and we are offered what it is we need to become whole and healed. Yes, it can be seen as a private journey to becoming whole again. And yes, we are offered the truth we need to see about ourselves—truth we don't always accept. Those who do are the courageous ones. Truth is what it takes to become whole and healed. And to know that part of that wounding negated the fact that despite the pain, we were always whole. That higher essence of who we are can never be less than whole.

Redneck Spirituality—Book Four

CHAPTER TWENTY-THREE

And Then Came Ka-Bar

Women? Ah . . . yes! The physical, emotional, and sexual contact of women was necessary for me to heal. And love. All healing is done in the space of love. I needed someone to love. Yet, such was not of the true essence, the highest aspect of love, for it was coming from a place of neediness—and fear.

Truth was, like everyone else, it took the practicing of love to evolve my fear into something that truly was love. It was both a solitary learning and a joint venture. True love must begin with loving one's self. So, while it wouldn't be sexual, it involved learning to love men as well. After all, I am a man.

My motorcycle was also a great source of self-healing, for it provided an in-the-moment, conscious solitude for me. Again, many miles hummed by beneath those wheels as alone—just me and the bike—I healed. At times, I did not ride alone. Ka-Bar, my buddy from IQ, sometimes rode his Harley alongside. He, too, was healing.

Perhaps this is a departure from my story, and yet no, it's not. These men are the same as I went to school with, weathered army basic training with, and lived my whole life with, all the while wondering, *Why did Vietnam happen to them and not me?* But for the grace of God, and the unseen gift in the death of my brother, Mike, they are me.

Back then, they were also the shame of our country. Its bastardly progeny. Spawned of America's multi-national life's blood. Sold in political greed. And baptized in the slimy rice paddies of forgotten Vietnam. Ka-Bar, just so, was orphaned with the death of our country's honor and integrity.

They called him Ka-Bar after the Marine Corps combat/utility knife made by the KA-BAR Knife Company. It was a knife he lived with, his trusted companion for nearly thirty years, the same knife he carried during his Marine days and nights in the country. It was a knife that bore intimate knowledge of the internal workings of numerous men—men whose interests to our living the life we value was contrary to our own.

I was his team leader in the seminar, charged with guiding and supporting the group. He was one of several Vietnam vets there, digging his way out of hell, or perhaps more accurately, his grave, the place he had been hiding in—dying in—since the war.

It's not as if I did all that much. I just stood by him and had his back where his country never did as he dug his way clear from all the feces of his past. Only Ka-Bar himself could do the digging. It is something that everyone has to do for themselves.

He was appreciative of the little I did. It was almost nothing to me, yet everything to him. I simply accepted him, recognized in him the loving, beautiful soul that he is. I listened to him, wept with him, held him when he reached out—so little, and yet more than I knew. It was sometime later before I understood this. Back then, I was surprised by the return of his own acceptance.

My experience of him holds special significance. He possessed that same don't-take-no-shit-off-nobody quality as the adoptive father who raised, but never accepted, me. Ka-Bar possessed that same inner toughness and, at times, meanness that I myself lacked and had once mistaken as cowardice. The truth was, I never allowed myself to be taught such malice by adults. My will was strong enough to resist having my mind bent to their insistence. I had my father's toughness but rejected his meanness. I think Ka-Bar saw this in me and gave me the loving acceptance that my father lacked the ability to give. Maybe he, too, underneath, resisted it. Yes, for me, his acceptance was very . . . very special.

Ka-Bar was a genuine hero—and a genuine killer. Daily and nightly, he put his life on the line for his unit, his country, and mostly his buddies. His job, recon, was one of the nastiest, most hazardous and brutal imaginable. It consisted of clandestine forays into enemy-controlled territory, setting up ambushes and sometimes assassinations.

Twice, he made HALO (high altitude, low opening) jumps over Hanoi. This involved jumping from around 35,000 feet using oxygen gear and skydiving, gliding laterally a distance of approximately five miles, then deploying his chute at about 1,000 feet over the target area—all this in darkness. A mistake of less than ten seconds meant instant pizza. These things he did simply because his country asked him to.

Once he was wounded so badly, he woke up in a body bag, unable to move or even cry out, but very much conscious. For several hours, he lay in the boiling sun, surrounded by the stench of death, just another corpse on the row. Only luck, and an observant medic, saved him. It is a nightmare that haunts his sleep—even still.

All this he suffered for his country. Was ever a nation's son so abused? For when he returned to it—to *The World*—instead of honoring him for his bravery and service, he was spat upon and reviled by the very people for whom he'd suffered. Then typecast as a misfit, he was swept under the rug, thrown out with the trash.

His body in ruin, his soul in pain, the war became private. He took to drinking and drugs, fighting and womanizing. He even rode with a couple of different motorcycle gangs. In one, he was the president of the club. Some would say, ". . . the baddest of the bad."

Ka-Bar found something within himself during his IQ Seminar that gave his life a great deal of peace, something he hadn't known since before the war. And he and I somehow bonded in friendship.

For a time, he was the president of the Vietnam Vets Motorcycle Club in Las Vegas. Since 1987, they'd been getting together on Memorial Day weekend and staging a parade across Hoover Dam to honor those who fought and died at their country's call. When first they asked for permission to parade the dam on their bikes while flying the American flag, it was refused. In true political fashion, the authorities chose to bury their heads in the sand and pretend, once more, that the Vietnam 'conflict' was never a war. And as usual, this only served to expose the butt crack across the mouth from which most politicians spoke.

They were told not only no, but "Hell, NO! We'll run your asses in if you do. Fuck Vietnam, fuck the honor of those dead or missing, and fuck you grubby vets."

Of course, the club did it anyway and has every year since. All the other biker clubs around were also invited, and many came. For the most part, it has become an unannounced, unpublicized, just come-on-down-and-let's-do-it type of event.

That first year I knew Ka-Bar, he asked me to be his guest and to ride the dam with him, a ride that, till then, had happened only eight times. I felt honored. We gathered on the Arizona side, about two hundred riders in all. Long hair, beards, a rough-looking bunch—practically every rebel rider around—and all, it seemed, were on Harleys. Then there was me on my rice burner, Yamaha Virago 1100.

Most wore their club colors on black, leather vests and sported black T-shirts underneath. And again, there I was in my white T-shirt with the IQ logo and the saying across the back, "Miracle—One moment of love without attack."

Yet, I felt perfectly at ease among them. No one, to use Ka-Bar's words, "fucked" with me. They were there, as was I, to honor the dead and missing. Their hearts were all in a good place, and there was beauty in everyone.

At ten o'clock on the Sunday of Memorial Day weekend, our motors thundered into life. For a long moment, they rumbled there on the overlook, two abreast. The vibrations traveled up through my butt cheeks planted in the saddle as I glanced over the barrier and noted the dam spread out far below.

Then, in a column of twos, the Vietnam Vets Club led off, nearly every bike flying three-by-five American flags. Ka-Bar and I brought up the rear. Then one badass club after another, the rest joined us with the din of their own motors. Back then, to be a badass club member, one's motor was a Harley.

Mounted to a three-quarter-inch PVC pipe, my own flag was bolted to my sissy bar with hose clamps and flapped proudly in the wind of my wake, just as did those of the fifty in front and the one hundred fifty or so behind. With a sea of flags cutting through the dry, desert air, we wound down off the mountain on the Arizona side.

Hundreds of tourists were standing or milling around as we rounded the bend onto the dam. With some, their eyes bulged in fright, while others only stood in slack-jawed shock. This was not a publicized event, and very few knew what we were about. A horde of bearded, sleeveless, tattoo-covered vets on Harleys—and one Yamaha—rumbled into their midst, trailing a sea of flags. Could they feel the raw, patriotic essence of it, too?

Apparently so, as a few began to clap and cheer. Soon everyone was. There were tears in my eyes. I looked over at Ka-Bar, and noted his, too. It was a day and a lesson I'll never forget. I learned that no matter how bad the ass, if I choose to look with acceptance, I'll see the gold in the heart. KaBar's heart was pure twenty-four karat.

Memorial Day

Two abreast . . . Old Glory streaming . . .
Rumbling . . . thundering . . .
Reverberating off the canyon walls.
Pulsating the air . . .
Shivering the very concrete of the dam.
Hoover Dam . . .
holding back the mighty Colorado.
Leading off the pack . . .
the unsung heroes in parade,
paying tribute to their long-lost brothers . . .
who died at Charlie's hand.
The Vietnam Vets Motorcycle Club,
proudly flying their colors,
and Old Glory.
Followed up by 150 misfit Harleys . . .
and one lone rice burner.
A salute of honor, long past due . . .
Parading the dam in thundering,
rumbling glory . . .
answered with the crowd's applause.
A memorial to the brave . . .

the missing . . .

those who bled . . .

and the dead.

* * *

Ka-Bar went on from the Inner Quest Seminar to take Eagle Quest, the most advanced. A more physical seminar, much of it involved a ropes course and stepping through one's fear on a physical level. Yet, stepping through the fear, the illusion of mortal danger in the seminar was like kindergarten compared to his Special Forces experiences in Vietnam and vicinity. The toll he was paying on his battle-broken body was just not worth any benefits he could see. He'd stepped through all that fear and pain way back then.

Ka-Bar left the EQ Seminar unfinished, and I believe, rightfully so. If there was a fear he needed to step through, clearly it was not of pain or death. If anything, it was of something he felt more vulnerable to—his fear of love.

For many, the pain of their bodies had sometimes been their crutch for not facing the pain in their minds. For Ka-Bar . . . I don't know. Both were crippled in 'Nam and had been long healing. I wasn't with him there in Eagle Quest—or in Vietnam—although whenever in his company, I'd stood proud, for I'd seen him face that pain in his mind, and I knew he had more, much more, yet to face. And I'd seen his courage. I'd glimpsed his heart. His healing was perfect—for him.

Eagle Quest was not for the faint of heart, those unwilling to face life one hundred percent—something Ka-Bar was not. He had faced life to excess, and death, even more so. Perhaps that was the bond I felt so strongly with him. We had both looked into the mirror of our mortality and had chosen to live. He, during the horror of war and from the inside of that body bag, saw his reflection through a haze of pain and the splatter of blood. Me? I saw mine through the cold, hard reality of a life not lived in truth, honor, or courage.

What we both saw haunted us each in different ways, for we had each known the presence of death intimately, but in different ways. To those he touches, Death offers all the same view from the precipice of our mortality—at least those who, for a time, he passes by.

Comb Ridge, Utah—Present Day

Big D's affirmation interrupts my scribbling account. "This time I've given you is especially precious. Ha!" He chuckles, and that weird-sounding voice of his sends chills down my back. "Given, it is lived in the knowledge of your mortality and the inescapable honesty you've seen, what with death spotlighting it in the light of eternity. Ka-Bar saw it, too. He, too, ordered the limo."

Yes, I know, Big D, but I'll bet Ka-Bar's experience of you was much different. For him, death most often came as something wrenched. Something taken unwillingly from young, strong bodies. Taken brutally in blood and gore and suffering, and hopefully, quickly. Something taken for reasons they didn't understand. Reasons called honor and glory—reasons that in 'Nam did not ring of truth.

"Pretty passionate about it for someone who wasn't there, ain't cha?"

Yeah. It's true. At the time, I was glad I wasn't sent there. I lean back against a rock and stare out over Comb Ridge toward the buttes of Bear's Ears in the distance. The day is cold, but not uncomfortably so. Still, I shiver with the memory of that time. *I didn't know my parents had applied for my sole survivor status—didn't find out about it until later. And even then, didn't know whether to be happy, pissed, or just ashamed. After meeting Ka-Bar, I was ashamed.*

"Ashamed? How so?"

Well, that I'd ever been glad. Hell, I thought I was taking my chances. I lean forward, hands against the sides of my face, studying the ground upon which I sit, aware my face is flaming. *I should have volunteered.*

"And now?"

Now, I'm damned sure pissed at my government and disgusted with my country. Our lives were the coinage—the price—we soldiers paid for some prissy elitist's power and wealth. The honor was only in those forever-stilled hearts, and in some others not yet so. Hearts like Ka-Bar's. They were willing to give their all, but for what? Where was there any glory—or appreciation—or even respect ever given? Certainly, it was never found in being spat upon in airports.

"Yeah, I agree."

What do you mean by that? Were you there in that airport when I was coming home from Korea? Ducking, I shake my head in realization. *Course you were. Did you see how badly I wanted to bash their stupid, fucking faces in? Maybe they, too, saw it because they shied away from spitting on me.*

"Ha!" He chuckles. "Have you considered that maybe it was just my energy—my being with you—that kept you out of jail that day?" He holds me fixed, pinning me like a bug by the ruby laser of his sight for a long moment. Then, ducking his head, he looks up at me and nods. "Makes it kind of hard to react with love . . . even still, doesn't it?"

He pauses a long moment to let that sink in before continuing. "And what of that spiritual truth called the Law of Balance? **Everything exists with equal potential, for the universe always balances. With every sorrowful thing, there is the gift of an equal joy to be found.** Yes, you and Ka-Bar have both known me up close and personal. Never mind what it meant to him. What does it mean for you? Do you see the gift in the reflection of your death?"

I take a deep breath and let it out slowly, giving myself time to reflect. *Ah, I suppose my gift was to truly know myself and those truths of life—the Spiritual Laws. Hell, they're the truth of everyone's life, profound for me. They've always been right there in plain sight for all to see, yet so few are willing to look. I feel privileged that I did.*

"So, Jeff . . . let go of all the flowery bullshit. What's the bottom line?"

Before, my dysfunction was in never living my truth, never being that person I wanted to be. I shrug. *Truth is, that's who I really am and now allow myself to be.* I nod my head to him and add, *This gift is indeed equal to the agonies and sorrows of my divorce and the rejection of all my so-called friends and family.* I take another deep breath and let it relax its way back out. *But you're right—I can't even pretend to know what Ka-Bar's experience of it has been.*

"When I come calling, it is always a deeply personal experience for everyone." His perpetual grin seems to widen. "For those who have the time to see me coming, very few go without regrets. There are fewer, still, who refuse to go—like you and Ka-Bar." He stops for a moment, just leaning on his sickle, then continues. "Your connection with him is special. If you have anything more you want to say to him, say it here."

* * *

Ka-Bar, my friend, my brother . . . a special salute. I know you will read this. While my military service was nothing to compare, you accepted me as your brother. But more than simple acceptance, you respected me, and in that, you have been more of a father than I have ever known, and I love you.

I know you will do what you need to do, for you, and for your relationship with that sweet lady whom you met at Inner Quest and married. You will do it with honor and courage—your way. Once again, I witnessed as you faced your fear. I have seen the love you give to one another.

Someone who coaches me recently reminded me of a certain Spiritual Law. I suppose it is my turn to follow his advice . . . and your example. ***For every fearful thing that happens***—and 'Nam was certainly that for you—***there is a gift of wonder, equal in magnitude.*** I suspect you took that law to heart. You met her at the Inner Quest for Vets. By returning to that beautiful woman, the love she gives you so unconditionally, you now have something—know something—I have never known.

A relationship is really only about needs and learning—each getting their own needs met, and each learning in this great mirror called relationship, looking at them and seeing ourselves. When the relationship is especially good, the needs met include the need to love, and the learning in the mirror reflects the beauty of it. Yet, for each, the relationship provides only the opportunity. It is about more than the giving, for each must also be willing to accept.

                                                     Redneck Spirituality—Book Four

CHAPTER TWENTY-FOUR

Sometimes Life Changes— and Remains the Same

Do you use someone when you stay in the relationship only because they meet some immediate need, given you are honest with them about it? I've been accused of bushwhacking— taking undue advantage when the immediate needs included sex.

      Why is it that so many women, and even some men, look at sex as a one-way flow, a commodity not given or taken, rather purchased from her by him, a thing that, once passed from a woman to a man, requires some sort of commitment or repayment?

      Although this may well be the prevalent opinion, the physical reality of sex is that she is on the receiving end. Her plumbing is a receptacle and receives his seed. This being the case, why don't we see it more as being given, him to her. Clearly, we only see what we choose to see. In fact, it is one of those Spiritual Laws—***Perception is a choice***.

      In looking at sex in the light of self-responsibility, there is no such thing as bushwhacking. Each places their own views and values on sex. Each gives what they want to give with it and receives what they choose to accept from it. If one should feel shortchanged, it is they, themselves, who did it. They could have given more, accepted more, or chosen their partner better. Not everyone lives their capacity to give. Virtually no one lives their capacity to accept.

Tess and I were long since clear that we were not soul mates. We were together still because we enjoyed meeting one another's current needs. I think that by the night of that graduation when I met Cindy, we each were about at the end of our capacity to accept any more.

Like all of us, she, too, was taught from birth to put on a show. The Tess who showed up on the outside was someone other than who she was on the inside. Together we learned the truths that exposed the lies. Her parents were well-to-do, the kind who believed themselves to be upper class. Me? Mine weren't. I was raised on the redneck side of life, the working class.

And then there was Big D. I never told Tess, or anyone, about him but shared freely much of what he taught me. With me, honesty was death's message and life's requirement. We cannot live the reprieve of death without a soul-felt honesty in life.

Tess was one of those other brave souls honest enough to see the lies without meeting Big D. I respected her for that. For a time together, it became a driving force in our lives, the stripping away of those lies until we could see who we really were for ourselves. There were those who thought they knew us, but didn't. Now that we were changing, growing, others often labeled it something else. We were climbing the mountain of our truth, something others sometimes viewed as our chasm of insanity.

Stripping lies is a lot like peeling an onion—there always seems to be one more layer, and often, there are tears. For a time, Tess and I journeyed together, peeling the onion . . . and sometimes crying.

*　*　*

The Inner Quest Seminars, by their very nature of being about personal growth, draw many divorcees and others who, like me, were alone and climbing. As mentioned, Karen, the facilitator, recognized this, and early on began asking these singles to stand and be recognized. She always began with the maxim about how relationships provide the greatest opportunities for personal growth possible. It was an eye-opening part of every graduation.

After being on support for dozens of IQ Seminars, I still went to the graduations to check out the new crop of single women. I looked for one who would understand me, who didn't play those old games of drama and control. I wanted a woman who didn't have a need to make me responsible for her feelings, that old, "You made me feel bad. Now you better make it right!"

In my relationships, it was always clear that my commitment was to being monogamous in sexuality only. Tess, too, always knew I was open to a relationship with someone other than her.

Clearly, I knew a lot of other women—friends only—and hung out with them. No, Tess and I were not soul mates. Were we to find someone who interested us enough to explore on a deeper level, one that included sexuality, then would be the time to tell the other and move on.

Though Tess might be sitting right next to me, it didn't matter. When Karen's voice rang out with, *All those single and available men looking for a relationship with a single and available woman, please stand*, I'd stand. And, I'd do it smiling, arms outstretched, from on top of a chair. I wanted to be seen! Some saw me and commented that I appeared "needy." I didn't care. The woman I searched for wouldn't see me so.

* * *

One graduation, I noticed, among those women who stood, a very striking blonde. She reminded me of the actress who played in the old *Gidget* movies—wide, soft, mahogany eyes, fully pillowed lips, and a pert, little nose slightly turned up at the end. Yes, Gidget, only maturely blossomed, attractive—robustly so.

The vets were always called to the front to be honored for our service. That was something my generation skipped. On returning to my seat, I noticed this woman was now sitting in the empty chair just behind mine. Her interest was obvious and refreshing when she took the first opportunity to introduce herself. I found her directness very appealing.

Her name was Cindy. A widow, she lived alone with her adult daughter. Before the night was over, we were having coffee. Before the week was over, I was interested enough to tell Tess I was ready to move on. I think she was, too.

There was a mature quietness about Cindy, which I found to be very comfortable. I soon realized she was compatible sexually as well. She was a good-sized woman, perhaps five ten or eleven. Her body molded with mine in an unfamiliar, voluptuous way—not fat, just big and curvy. In bed, I found her adventurous and sensual.

Yes, sexually, I liked her just fine, yet there was something that just didn't fit, wasn't quite *there* yet. We had a lot of fun in everything we did together, and it wasn't until later that I discovered what it was.

We were together about six very enjoyable months when a friend lent us the use of a beautiful, A-frame cabin near Navajo Lake in Southern Utah. We spent the weekend there. The last night found us kicking back in wicker chairs on the upstairs veranda, discussing our lives and dreams. All the while, the starry skies and a nearly full moon lit up the pine-frame, open meadows of the valley below. Sipping good, red wine and talking softly in the still silence of the evening, we opened our innermost selves to one another.

That was when that little *off* thing first inserted itself into the ass end of my mind. That was when I discovered she suffered from that fatal disease infecting so many women—fear. For me, it certainly was a mindfuck. That night, it was more like a tickling of her finger in a naughty place, but it was about to be crammed all the way in and it just wouldn't fit.

With her chair up against mine and my arm across her shoulder, she laid her head against my chest. "Jeff, do you ever think about getting married?"

Chuckling, I replied, "No. Marriage is an expression of fear."

"What?" Her mouth hung open as she cranked her neck back to look up. "How do you mean?"

I pulled my own head back to look down at her. *Have I misjudged her? Doesn't she know anything about Spiritual Laws? They're what Karen's seminars are based upon.*

"Cindy, surely you've heard of Spiritual Law?"

"Well, yes. Karen mentions them occasionally." As she leaned back to look up at me, confusion painted her face. "Says how they're the simple truths about life."

"Did you ever hear the one about there only being two basic energies, love and everything that isn't love—fear?"

"Well, yeah. So?"

"Do you know what it means?"

"It's pretty simple . . . self-explanatory, really." Confusion wrinkled her forehead. "What's that got to do with marriage?"

Damn! How do I explain this? I began. "What is marriage?"

"It's just two people getting a license to legally join their lives together."

"Yes." I nodded. "But why?"

"For protection under the law, of course." There were those wrinkles across her forehead again, but now they looked more frustrated than confused.

Taking a deep breath, I pitched in. "Protection? Doesn't that word just ooze of fear?" I grinned. "Maybe like a . . . silent fart."

"Huh? A fart? What?"

I cut her short before she could explode. "Well, doesn't it kinda stink to you when two people in love need assurances? There is no security in life, y'know. People die unexpectedly all the time."

"Yes, but—"

Knowing she was about to take a different trail, I again cut into her thought. "Look, Cindy. Why would either person want assurances that the other would stay with them if there came a time when they no longer wanted to? Would you want to be with someone who didn't love you?"

"No, 'course not!" The wrinkles looked a little angry now.

"Then why would you want to promise you'd be there if, at some point, you didn't want to?"

"That's about commitment—the *through thick or thin* part."

I looked her straight in the eye, and holding her by that connection, offered her my thought. "No, Cindy, it isn't. It's about the *to love or not to love* part, about choosing *love or fear*. It's about a contract made out of nothing but fear. I want to always know that the real reason we are together is only because we want to be—love, and nothing less."

Cindy's wrinkles were gone now, replaced with, what, shock or deep thought? Did the eyes now looking into the mirror of mine see me or herself? Time would tell.

We took turns showering in the mini-bathroom downstairs before retiring to the king-size bed in the loft to make love. This night, our lovemaking, also, seemed just a little . . . *off*. Oh, her body was there in full participation, but her mind—

I'd long since worked out my fear of passionate women, compliments of Tess. My manhood now stood tall and straight . . . well, straight with a slight, right-handed curve. It was only the flagging energy of my body, not my member, that eventually caused me to end our lovemaking that night. With Cindy beneath, facing me, her legs doubled up, knees locked tightly in the hollow between my shoulder and chest, I eventually spent myself. I slammed home, deeply pistoning in cadence to her high-pitched chirping, "Oh . . . oh . . . oh . . . ," which blended into a single squeal as my orgasm spewed out, spurt after spurt, filling her and running out to form a puddle on the sheet. Then, passions quenched, we lay together, our bodies a comfortable, intertwining jumble of arms and legs, knowing in our lovemaking a giving and a receiving equally.

I lay there, my crotch against Cindy's thigh, both still sticky with the remnants of our love. *Cindy is unlike Meg. She doesn't find this repulsive. Shit! She accepts it—just as she accepts me.*

Laying there, holding her and basking in the afterglow of the experience, I was aware that I accepted her. How true that was for her, I could not know.

I enjoyed my time spent with her, cherished these intimate moments, and didn't want them to end. Yet, at the same time, I knew that should she leave, my world would not crumble. She would be missed—and my life would continue. Yes, I wanted her to share my life, but I did not need her.

* * *

On the way back to Vegas the next day, Cindy and I talked and laughed a lot, telling one another those funny and sometimes embarrassing stories from our childhoods. Yet, as the trip progressed, I felt her withdrawing, leaving more and more of the talking to me. Sensing her mood, I eventually fell into silence also. Just past the little town of Mesquite, a brief sprinkling of casinos catering to the gambling appetites of the Mormon communities up north, Cindy got around to expressing her mind.

"Jeff . . . I . . . uh . . . I don't know how to say this . . ." Her voice trailed off, almost with the expectation that I would somehow know what she wanted and save her from having to express it.

I waited a moment, and when the rest was not forthcoming, I prompted.

"Well, Cindy, straight out usually works best for me." I smiled, and there was no ridicule in my response. Sarcasm always comes from attack.

"Jeff . . . I . . . I want something more from you. I don't want to be alone anymore." She ended quickly in a rush, and there was a pleading in her eyes.

"Cindy, you're not alone. You spend most of your time with me at my place, and when you're not there, you're home with your daughter, Mandy."

"Yes, but Mandy's almost married, and besides . . . we don't connect much anymore."

"Cindy, what are you asking? Are you wanting to move in with me?"

"No, I want to get married!" It came out in a rush that ended in a sudden high note of expectation.

"You don't want to move in first? I know you don't care what other people think. That's one of the things about you that I find so attractive. You'd fart in church, if you felt like it." I grinned with the crudity of my last remark, expecting her to burst into her characteristic laughter. Cindy did not even crack a smile. Instead, she turned and regarded me steadily.

"Jeff, I want to get married. If you don't want to, then I need to start looking for someone else."

My smile faded. After a long, searching silence, I asked, "How soon do you need to know?"

"Friday, at the latest. I have a date with someone and I don't know how far I want it to go. Will you meet me for lunch Friday at Burger Barn?"

The remainder of the trip was spent mostly in strained silence, both thinking hard on the subject, and both carefully avoiding all further reference to it.

For one silent, very long hour, we gave one another the space to reconsider. Me? I used the time scrambling my brain for an alternative, turning it over and over, searching for a win/win. *Can there even be one with such an ultimatum? Don't we want the same thing . . . to be together?*

But to shift that from *want* to, to *have* to—from being together in *love* or being together in *fear*—was such an *obvious* difference in my mind. But it seemed an *oblivious* one in hers.

For me, there was the Spiritual Law—***There are only two energies, the energy of love and the energy of all that is not love (fear)***. And then there was Big D and our agreement that I live my life with courage and love, that I follow my joy. There could be no joy being with a woman overshadowed by fear. The two energies do not exist together. And the penalty for breaking my agreement with the Angel of Death? But it was not about that. A relationship based on fear for either was unacceptable.

I remembered how I viewed life before I met Big D, back before I learned these laws, these simple truths about life. The issue I faced with Cindy now would—no, back then it *could*—never have been seen. If brought up, I'd have described it all with two words—fucking insane.

Apparently, those were the words that were now lodged in Cindy's mind about me.

In living the rest of my life married to her, my death could only mean the loss of the unreal reality of security, which would only result in an avalanche of fear. No, the love of my life may mourn, but that would be supported by lifetime memories of our love. There is reality in one's love. There is nothing but imagined possibilities in one's fear.

I looked out the window at the yucca and scrub brush, the tan desert soil, the rocks, and the bluffs across the valley floor. It all marched past alongside the freeway, the same goddamned world it had always been, but this world inside me was different. I glanced over to where Cindy sat, curled up against the far door, looking at her world out there. A tear traced its way down my face with the realization that Cindy did not live in this world of mine. She could change her mind, but would she ever want to? No, I suspected that my world was out there somewhere beyond the reach of her imagination.

* * *

I thought a lot about Cindy that week, about how much I enjoyed her company, her wit, and her body. There was a lot that attracted me to her, and I found I didn't want us to part. And, too, how could I further explain myself to her? I already took my best shot. Could she see how the issue's bottom line was, *to love or not to love*? Did she believe in the Spiritual Laws?

When I walked in the door, she was there at Burger Barn, wearing a business suit that hugged her curvy body, clinging in all the right places. I, too, hugged her briefly and avoided the questions clinging in her eyes as I ordered a burger. Cindy ordered a drink and we settled into our booth. Leaving out the small talk, I began.

"Cindy, I don't want to let you go. You mean a lot to me, and I so much enjoy just being with you. I could see myself spending the rest of my life with you. To me, that means I love you, but I don't want to marry you. Marriage is just not something I see as a healthy institution, at least not for me, and I don't think I'll ever marry again. I want someone who wants to be with me freely, no obligations in any way. I want to always have the same freedom."

Seeing the blank look on her face, I took a deep, futile breath before continuing, my voice now calm. "Cindy, I want a woman who wants to stretch in all aspects of her life. Security is not what I want.

The woman I'm looking for wouldn't chain her dog, wouldn't cage her parrot—and wouldn't marry her man."

Hearing the rising energy in my voice, I stopped. She already told me what she wanted, and she didn't care who the man was giving it to her. Hoping I'd misread her, hoping that she did care, I asked my lame question anyway. "What is it that you want in a man?"

Cindy didn't answer right away. With her eyebrows all scrunched up into the center of her forehead, and jaw hanging, she searched my face a very long time before replying.

"Jeff, I want a man who will commit to me. I want to settle down and just enjoy my life with someone I feel safe with, someone I can count on to be there for me."

I suppose my own expression must have closely matched hers. *Security! My God . . . she's like Meg. She fears life so much that it leaves no room for love.*

"Cindy, we don't want the same life, you and I. We don't even think about life in the same way. What I hear you saying is that you want security—guarantees. I thought we agreed that there aren't any guarantees in life, or security, nor do I want them. I like surprises, a-a-and challenges. Sometimes when life doesn't happen the way I envision, I get really unhappy about it, but that soon passes because there is always something new and wonderful in the experience for me to learn, or do, or become. I don't want comfort. Comfort isn't growing for me, and it gets boring. I want to just love a woman who loves me back, to face life together and soar high up in the sky on the winds of change!"

I ended my little tirade on such a note of passion that her mouth literally fell open. Turning my head, I noted her expression mirrored on the faces of the couple at the adjacent table.

"I . . . I guess I never knew you." She said it, eyes wide, like she was just now seeing me for the first time. "Look . . . you're right. We're not right for each other."

She stood abruptly and gathered her purse and jacket from the seat.

"I have to get back to work." Her eyes avoided mine as she turned to go.

I, too, stood up beside her, wanting all the while to reach out and comfort her, to make it all somehow okay, yet I knew I couldn't. I gave her a reluctant hug and watched as she hurried away. Then, sitting down, I silently finished my burger. No longer hungry, it was tasteless, but it gave me something physical to engage my body while I turned it all back over in my mind.

What is it about me? All those years with Meg, and I still didn't see Cindy's fear—her ultimatum—coming.

* * *

Lost in thought, I stared out the window at the mountains in the distance. A woman walked by, and my eyes rose to meet two startlingly familiar ones in an unfamiliar, Asian face. Suddenly, I realized the answer to my quandary and was struck by the irony of the situation. Like an echo, a chuckle reverberated, as if from the back of my mind. *Big D?*

"All is as it should be . . . you see it now," came his answer as the memory struck home. We, Meg and I, were sitting at this very same table nearly two years earlier. I'd been making other deep understandings and later expressed it all in a poem—a poem now residing in a lonely coffin buried high on a mountainside—waiting, waiting to be acknowledged one last time.

Forgive Me My Love

Oh, so long it has been,
since last I saw you, dear.
Near a year, since we parted . . .
The love I held for you,
still swells within my heart.
Your beauty still, a comfort to my gaze,
across this restaurant table.
Oh, so much I have to tell you . . .
Happenings, since, in my life.
So much growth of my soul . . .
And so much, I want to hear of yours.
Yet you are silent . . . strangely silent.
I ask, gently prodding . . .
with open-ended questions.
Yet, so little will you say.

Then with a start, the answer crystallizes . . .
clearly now, obvious to my mind.
Your life hasn't changed . . .
you haven't changed.
It is only I who has.
You still live that life of quiet desperation.
Seeking only comfort . . . security . . .
where none exists . . . nor ever will.
Walking down that path of living death . . .
Asleep to the ecstasy that could be yours,
should you choose to awaken
to the freedom of your spirit . . .
to the wisdom of your soul.
And inside my breast,
my heart bleeds
great tears of sorrow . . .
For I see how lonely your own must be . . .
I can feel it, from your energy.
You walk your path alone . . .
no company.
Alone with only your memories . . .
No longer do you walk it with me.
Forgive me, my love, for not staying . . .
walking it with you.
An enlightened soul not growing . . .
is dying.
Were it only this body, for you,
a thousand deaths I would gladly suffer.

Yet with my soul?

Not even one.

Forgive me, my love, forgive me.

For my mind tells me I am wrong . . .

for what my heart tells me is right.

And to my soul, I feel the agony . . .

for I know that what is, must be . . .

And what was,

is gone . . .

forever.

Remembering that poem, the one I could not bring myself to read back then, I marveled at how much my life since has again changed and at how it is also still the same. How sometimes, in the love of a woman for a man, a certain fearful neediness resides, a neediness that speaks in denial of that love. Only the faces change. There was a great validation here. Of the neediness this time—none of it was mine.

"There is only the energy of love, and everything that is not love (fear)." The Spiritual Law floated through my mind, a gentle reminder spoken in the deep, resonating voice of Big D. "It takes courage to choose love."

"S-s-s-hit!" I whispered under my breath. *Meg all over again. Cindy, too, only wanted security, a Sir Knight, someone—anyone—to slay all those imaginary dragons of her mind. She was never looking for the last great love of her life. Love or fear . . . she, too, chose fear.*

I felt the tear as it dropped off my nose and heard it splat onto the paper wrapping next to the fries. Using a napkin, I wiped my face dry. This tear was all I had for Cindy.

I wanted her, Big D. I paused a moment to swallow the sudden lump in my throat. *I wanted her love, but I didn't need a woman's fear standing in place of that love—not again. I cried enough for Meg. Love was something neither woman had.*

"Courage was something neither one had." I felt his invisible knuckles nudge my shoulder. "But you do."

Me? I was feeling a need to ride, to have the wind in my face, just my motorcycle and me and the desert sailing by. Something I have learned in this life is that the truly alone is he who seeks the companionship of others, yet refuses his own company. It took time, and the help of Cindy, to see . . . that fool described was no longer me.

Comb Ridge, Utah—Present Day

Big D sits in silence by my side as I rant.

Why ultimatums, Big D? What is it with women? Control and fear? The same shit pretty much every time. Different women, different relationships—same scenario. And now, stuck on this ledge looking back over my story, I know there are more relationships to reveal and even my second marriage. Silly me. The wind whips through my hair as I shake my head and shiver in the darkness of another increasingly chilly night. *Ah, but each woman has given me a gift that transcends the laws of our fucked-up society—some truth about me that I did not see.*

Aiiiiii . . . shiiiiiiit! That thought brings out another pet peeve. *Marriage . . . shit! What is it with these fucked-up lies of society? Why can't a woman just love a man and be there only because that's where she wants to be? Don't women have any courage?*

"Uhhhhhg." Big D grunts. "You're right . . . control and the illusion of security. Some women can't function without it." Then he shuts my rant off short with one well-placed question. "Why is it that some men, when faced with such a woman, just capitulate—give their balls over to their woman's holding? Are they not also being cowards?

Well . . . uh . . . shit! I gotta admit, you're right. That's exactly the way it was with Meg and me.

"And then there's your second marriage. You knew to avoid the fake security of marriage with Cindy." He chuckles, his grin getting seemingly wider, at least in my mind. "Even knowing the truth of it, you, too, found yourself crawling into marriage's bunghole of false security. How could you not see what was coming?

"A façade—a fake, fucking pretense of who you are. Face it, to be accepted, that is what society requires. And Cindy? With her you can add one more title common to society's fakery."

Huh?

"Prostitute."

What? Little harsh, isn't it?

"No, just the truth." Again, he chuckles. This whole situation seems to be tickling his funny bone. "She told you about the other guy and how she planned to wrap her pussy around his dick. It was never your love she wanted, only that illusion of security called marriage."

Yeah, seems so . . .

"And face it—this was Cindy's gift to you. Not good, not bad. It's just what most women do to get what they want from a man. Fucking because they're horny comes in at a far distant second to the payoff they expect to get. Very few have the courage to step out and just love a man, and the payoffs most often come as bullshit assurances, not money."

Oh God, Big D, will I ever meet that perfect woman? Someone who will fuck me because she's horny, love me because she wants to, and stay because it's where she wants to be?

"You have met"—he pauses to wink—"one." Then he fades from sight, leaving me, as usual, with my jaw agape.

Someone I've already met? I don't recall anyone like that so far in my story—or anyone further on along the way? We are talking about my soul mate, aren't we? Big D? Big D, come back . . . talk to me.

Does painting a turd pink add anything positive or make it any more acceptable to others? Is it not still a turd? And what's wrong with turds anyway? Aren't they a necessary part of life—something that has nourished us?

Redneck Spirituality—Book Four

CHAPTER TWENTY-FIVE

Painting Pink Turds

Leasha . . . a short, chunky figure of a woman with an air of lightness and open, earthy humor. Her hearty, full-throated laughter preceded my initial view of her that first night we met. It happened at a party—a high-society shindig hosted by a mutual friend. We both knew our meeting was being orchestrated.

Leasha was one of those dynamic people who, through no conscious effort, could light up a room by her mere presence. I watched her as, led by our host, Sue Anne, she worked her way across the room filled with men in sports coats and suits.

I sat nursing a White Zinfandel at the breakfast bar wearing Levis, boots, and a western shirt. Knowing I was out of place, I smiled with the realization that it didn't matter since I didn't give a shit what other people thought of me.

As an executive administrator in a certain local branch of the federal government, she was well known. Each small group she passed hailed her in eager greeting. I, too, felt a strange attraction that was more than just her personal charisma. It was more even than the figure-enriching cut of her dark blue-and-white party dress with its cleavage-enhancing drop in the neckline.

Beyond that dress, was my attraction sensual? Yes. Strange because it belied my first assessment of her appearance. Sexually, I was not normally attracted to plumpish-looking women. Shortly, she stood before me with our host making the introductions.

"Jeff . . . you big stud." Sue Anne had an anatomy fixation. "I want you to meet my special friend." She winked. "This is Leasha."

I smiled into Leasha's vivid, blue eyes and noted how her pretty face was framed by blonde, neck-length curls. She had regular features with a slight upturn to her nose, but those eyes were her most striking feature. I took her extended hand briefly in mine.

"Do you get the feeling this is a setup? Are we two people about to be saved—*snatched*—from the waiting jaws of loneliness?" My voice took on a note of mock drama with the word "snatched."

Both women exchanged a quick glance and brief giggle. Then Sue Anne replied, her hand airily waving away my unanswered question. "Oh, Jeff, why don't you tell Leasha one of your dirty jokes?" Then she turned back to attend to her other guests. "She'll love them," she added, chuckling back over her shoulder. I watched her go, shaking my head in amusement, then turned my attention back to Leasha.

"Well, do you really want to hear a joke, or shall we crucify our savior instead?"

Leasha cocked her head in mock consideration, then replied, "Well, since we don't have a cross handy, I guess we're stuck with the jokes."

I took a quick appraisal of her. Her eyes sparkled with merriment and she seemed like a fun person. I decided to press the matter.

"Okay . . . charades." I set my wine down solidly and assumed a blank expression. Disregarding the other guests milling around us, I extended my hands, palms cupped outward and about two inches away and level with her ample breasts.

"What am I doing?" Along with my question, I simultaneously began rotating both hands back and forth for a few seconds. Then I dropped my right hand down, palm upward at crotch level, and began making a tickling motion with my fingers. Deliberately, I repeated the process twice more, then stopped and looked expectantly at her.

She observed it all with eyes wide and mouth agape. When I finished, she looked me fully in the face for the span of three seconds. Then something clicked, and flinging her head back, she roared with laughter.

"Ha-ha-ha-ha . . . I don't . . . ha-ha-ha-ha . . . snerrrk . . . ha-ha . . . know . . . ha-ha-ha . . . gasp. What . . . what *are* you doing?" she finally asked.

"Just checking the bath water," I said innocently.

Again, Leasha threw her head back and shrieked in merriment, only this time, she was joined by the half dozen or so people close by who'd been following our exchange.

But not all who'd observed were amused. There were a few who turned sour faces away, obviously offended. Leasha picked up on their disapproval and, with a wink, shrugged at me. Knowing that she, too, didn't give a shit about their judgmental opinions fairly cemented a bonding between us. Before the night was over, I accepted her invitation to another party the next evening, following which, I found myself accepting yet another kind of invitation.

* * *

Lying naked together in her bed, I touched her, stroked her, tasted the exotic muskiness of her most private of privates, and marveled at the transformation. What had appeared a short plumpishness was, in reality, a smooth, firm ampleness topped with the twin pink areolas tipping two perfectly shaped, ample breasts jutting youthfully, all this belying the middleness of her age. That night, we made love with a passion matched only by that with which we both lived life.

A woman of power and affluence, Leasha lived on one of those lush, south end estates, complete with pool, spa, built-in stereo, and intruder alarm systems. Though not quite in the rich-and-famous category, she still lived a lifestyle that was much higher than was familiar or comfortable for me.

Observing her and her rich friends, I became aware that they were really not any different from the way my life was before. They had the same insecurities and dysfunctions that marked the lives of almost everyone.

But for my own life, and those of my other friends also involved with the Eagle Quest Seminar, most of us had a grasp on the Spiritual Laws. Any dysfunctions we had usually boiled down to a condensation of our own unmet needs.

Like most, we all knew what we wanted, but of our needs? Those were but ongoing discoveries—the program of learning set up by our own souls, a program known as life. It was weird to realize just how different that made us.

But in Leasha's world, her friends were well off, having much more money than I. Still, they lived in a reality of scarcity, of *not enough*. But not enough of what? I don't think anyone saw it well enough to consider that question.

Yet, there was a certain sophistication about it all. The more they had, the more they seemed to need to cover up the fact that they didn't think *they* were enough. The façade of lies that society demands each person live behind, for them, was merely called sophistication. The pink paint of their façade was called fuchsia.

And power? Leasha was a woman used to making decisions. In her career with the federal bureaucracy, she wielded power. There were none more powerful in her facility. The power of command was comfortable to her. Yet, with it came a certain paranoia, a cover-your-butt sort of thing. Like a fart in an elevator, no one would ever hear it and know it came from her. While she was outgoing, she was also guarded. If she caused a stink in her day-to-day business, no one would know it came from her. Her openness was not vulnerable.

And control? Leasha never tried to control our relationship or the things we did together, though often she seemed perturbed that I was not like the other men in her past. I did not send her flowers and gifts, clamor for her affection, or try to show her a good time.

We simply spent time together around town or at her place when convenient, and I was always happy to see her whenever she showed up at my own door. Whenever together, doing whatever we did, I had a good time and felt that decision, for her, was hers. For me, what we did meant little compared to the fact that I did it with her.

It was always clear that she did control her own life, and I, mine. Still, there was an uneasy feeling in me whenever exposed to her station in life—the power and necessary control it required. Were she to feel the need, would she make demands of me?

Looking back, I can see some things in common with Meg. Both guarded their hearts, but as for any need to control me? That, I did not see in her.

By asking for a divorce every month or so, Meg regularly demanded control of my life. But nothing of the sort occurred with Leasha, and in fact, I wondered if I was being of disservice even to suspect it.

In reality, such issues are often merely the heat waves over the desert of our insecurities, our own disbelief in self. Vulnerability and control are like a mirage—we think we see something solidly in it and, believing it, do stupid things. Violence or ultimatums were never part of our relationship and vulnerability never crossed my mind. I didn't see it crossing hers—not in the physical matters or matters of the mind. But as to matters of the heart? How would that pan out? Leasha did not know the laws. I did and did not feel vulnerable. Would she?

Lying beside her, turning it all over in my mind, watching her snoring lightly, I smiled. *I've been through enough to know that however this goes, my experience of her will be a positive, healthy one. And I'll do my best to make hers of me just as good. Still, in the end, it is a choice how we each experience the other. Yes, it's concerning that she's so guarded. She just needs time.*

For me, I knew the law, the Spiritual Law of Responsibility. **Other people have no power over our feelings—except what we give to them.** In the world of our feelings, we hold the keys of control. Whatever happened, I would cherish our time together. Hopefully, that would last to the end of my life.

Few in this life ever feel safe enough to reach out with an open heart and touch those of others. We who know this law, do. Most other folks live in fear and imprison themselves. I saw that in Leasha. Despite whatever fear her past inspired, I was determined to reach out and touch her heart with mine and wait for her to grant herself a parole. *She is not Meg. Maybe my love will conquer her fear.*

All this was running through my mind as I watched her sleep. Even so, something inside me said, *Watch out for those silent farts.*

Yet, to pretend love—to do something for the purpose of "making" someone love you—may get them to love what you do, but it will never make them love you. In touching hearts and giving love, only freedom and acceptance works. I knew that and gave that to her.

Leasha decided to go to Karen's baseline seminar, Inner Quest, she said because she was curious about why I was so much different from the other men she'd known. I decided to go as a support team leader. That meant I had to keep my distance—conflict of interest. About halfway through, her team leader sidled up to me.

"Leasha's really worried that she isn't showing up for you. Will you speak to her and set her mind to rest?"

The thought never occurred to me, and I stared at the woman silently for a moment, just getting a feel for the drama of the situation—one a savior, the other, a pretend victim. Then, unwilling to play my expected part in it all, I answered.

"No." Our savior's jaw dropped almost off her face. "I'm here to help those in my group, should they ask, and, of course, to look at and deal with my own stuff. Leasha has the same opportunity, but it would be a conflict of interest for me to interrupt that for her."

"But . . . but, don't you want to help her—"

"Don't you mean, *save her*?" I interrupted with a disarming grin. "No. Leasha is very capable, and I'm open to communicating with her"—I paused, shrugging—"if she wants to make that happen, but I'm not up to playing this silly victim/savior game with her . . . or you."

Our savior left me then, walking off, shaking her head and mumbling to herself. I didn't think she understood me, and like Leasha during the rest of the seminar, she didn't ask.

* * *

I was with Leasha for nearly eight months, but who's counting. I just enjoyed my experience of her during our time together, and the learning and growing. I was done with mourning over Meg. My time now was spent in getting healthy with myself. Our marriage—that dream that never was—now was an accepted fact of the past. No longer obsessed with it, I moved on in life, simply trying to discern the truth of my own.

As each new understanding became apparent, I would often write about it, frequently in the form of poetry. This was during the writing of my first book, *The Courage of a Butterfly*. In fact, it was during the writing of the final chapters—those dealing with dying and the honesty death inspires. After all, that was what set my feet on this weird-assed path in life, this journey to find the truth in mine.

Did I withhold my love for Meg? No. I loved her with my very being. My fear was always that she would leave, discard me like every other woman I ever cared about did. We do, indeed, attract into our lives according to the energy of our beliefs, be it of our sweetest dreams or our worst nightmares.

But wait! *It was I who divorced her. Could it be that she did love me? Was she too afraid to admit it even to herself, too afraid to be vulnerable? Were we both bent on creating what we most feared? It's all a done deal now. How fucked up is that?*

It was on a par with our society's own need to control others. Now, coming from a place beyond all that, I had one of those moments of inspiration—the kind that only comes from that soul level, like a personal *beingness* of God. I often have those moments when I write.

Leasha stopped by that afternoon, and in my excitement over my personal triumph of truth, I was eager to share my writing with her. The poem was aptly titled, "A Limp Dick No Longer," and it was written in longhand on a sheet of paper—the first, and only, copy. It spoke of how I had taken my balls back from Meg and now carried them again in my own pocket. As the final words of the poem trailed from my lips, I looked up, eager for her response. The rage glittering coldly in her eyes set my jaw agape.

"Let me see that," Leasha responded, snatching it out of my hand.

"Your wife . . . your wife." She paused long enough to thoroughly tear the paper into shreds, which she promptly stuffed into her purse. "Goddammit! All I ever hear you talk about is 'Meg this . . . Meg that.' You need to make a decision whether or not you want me!"

She stopped screaming abruptly and waited for my response. I stared at her, my mind busy looking at me. Was it true—these things she was accusing me of? Was I holding on to or letting go of Meg? No, this poem was about moving on. When my answer was not immediately forthcoming, Leasha grunted in disgust, then raged one final time.

"I'm outta here!"

My jaw snapped shut as the understanding dawned. I saw it all! This was the part where I'd always begged Meg to stay, to love me, though in her eyes, I was clearly unworthy. This was Leasha's way of saying, "I want a divorce." It was her demand for control.

Shit! Here it is in my face again—another woman saying she loves me while living, instead, in the energy of fear. The thought was crystal clear. *All my relationships, Leasha now included, were women whose choice of energy insured they didn't have the ability to love anyone. Sure, they all liked me, maybe told themselves they loved me. No, none of them had a clue what love was about.*

And, too, I knew, without a doubt, that a few words of humble begging were all that she required, the simple act of releasing the reins of my life. Clearly, allowing her to stuff my balls into her purse, along with that poem, was what Leasha demanded from me.

But my begging days had ended. In silence, I watched her storm out the door, then heard it slam in finality behind her. In that moment, I knew within my being what her unmet need was, why my thoughts about her were silently screaming, *Power! Control!* It was because I stood somewhere outside of it in her life.

"My God," I wondered aloud. Shaking my head sadly, I silently concluded, *I won't do that one again . . . not ever!*

But that was about her part in it all. How long, I wondered, would it be before I'd changed enough within myself that the women I attracted were no longer Meg—only with a different name, body, and face, but all living in that energy of fear?

* * *

I let Leasha go, without struggle, regretfully, but without much pain. That's how acceptance works. It negates our pain down to an acceptable level. Certainly, I accepted Leasha's leaving without the kind of pain I experienced in letting go of Meg.

Am I now so evolved that the pain of Meg leaving, and now Leasha, too, no longer ravages me? I loved them both.

Now, there came a period of solitude. Often, I would ride—just me, the bike, and the highway. Long, hot, straight desert stretches ticked past beneath my wheels with the steady flash-flash of the broken, white lines painted down the center of the two-lane county highways. Sometimes I would ride the roads of Mount Charleston, cornering the curves, feeling the rush of adrenalin with the centrifugal forces and the intermittent scrapings of my foot pegs, ominously telling me I could bank no harder nor go no faster. Now I rode, not to heal my pain, but for the joy of it alone.

Yet, the solitude was only of relationship—a lack of female connection and a growing closer to myself. I did not so much avoid the company of others, only the sometimes-illusionary intimacy of sex.

Saturdays would often find me at Lee Canyon, enjoying the beat of the weekly rock and roll bands, the fresh, clean, cool mountain air, and the flash of female flesh, checking out the women as they checked me out. Drinking beer with my friends, I looked, laughed, and joked, yet did not approach, knowing I needed this time alone. Night after night, there were parties and meetings. Sometimes we meditated or discussed the wonders of the universe or of "self," just having fun being in the company of like-minded people.

Solitaire was always who I played in the past, a loner pushing others away and being held away in turn. Now something in me was changed. I could know the solitude of my soul, and still, at the same time, enjoy the company of others, being wanted and invited in by them.

An oxymoron? No. While before, as I pushed others away, unwilling to let them see the real me, I also was pushing myself away, unwilling to look at the truth about me. Believing the truth about me would be unacceptable. Back then, before I met Big D, I hid behind a façade of lies. I painted myself with the pink paint others seemed to expect. Yet, inside, I knew myself as a liar, and for that reason alone, I became unacceptable to me and to others in turn.

It is the same with most of humanity, covering with pretense so that others won't know the real person. Truth is, no one is made acceptable by the pink paint of glamorous adjectives—debonair, sophisticated, elegant, refined, polished, savoir-faire, urbane, suave. The list goes on, but the meanings are the same—socially acceptable, maybe, but still just lies and deception.

Often, the lies take the more passive form of hiding out—skulking. This, we dress up in elegance by other adjectives—shy, bashful, mysterious, reserved, demure, diffident, timorous, even modest. And the bottom-line question always needing to be asked? Is being what is not truth ever acceptable to you, much less anyone else?

I found that the one glaring thing about me that is different, then to now, is that I looked inside at the truth about me and found I liked myself. The lies covered up the best of me. They were what was once ugly about me, nothing else.

I show up now as who I truly am, all good, solid nouns—my wants, needs, desires, perfections, imperfections, humanity, sexuality—all of it out there, naked for all to see. I find myself attracting those also **not** hiding out, and it seems I'm only threatening to those who are. Those who cling too tightly to their own lies resent us for discarding our own. It's really okay to be solitary in any manner we want, as long as we're showing up real and open.

Honesty is so much more attractive than pink paint. The pink paint, when one looks at it closely, can be really quite ugly, like a pink-painted turd.

We all—every single human on the planet—have been injured. We all are in the process of healing, and yes, some faster, some slower, but we all are doing it the best we know how.

We help one another to grow and heal. We can't see the good in one another without experiencing the opposite. We see it all by the example—the mirror—of ourselves. Everyone in our lives is there for this very reason. It is one of the Spiritual Laws, remember? Sometimes we learn from the reflection of what is beautiful, sometimes what is not. Pink paint is not.

"Thank you, Leasha, for showing this to me."

Comb Ridge, Utah—Present Day

The pinyon pine nut harvest is a thing of relief. Now, feeling the renewed strength my diet now affords me, I start looking at and dealing with survival. Daytime temperatures seem to be getting colder, and brutally so at night. I've used up all the dead wood on this ledge in feeding my tiny cooking fires. Now I need fire for warmth. The bulk of my time now must be spent in harvesting wood. It is a good thing my hunting knife is large—almost heavy enough to be considered a small axe.

Today, I am busy hacking off limbs and hauling them over near my tent. One pile is of small, needle-covered branches. Another is for smaller limbs, and still another for larger limbs—those that will be fed into the fire from one end, a little at a time.

The leg is healing well, not near so painful. The spot where the bone came through is now a great, healed-up scab. I leave the splints off most of the time, except like right now, when I am moving around. Overall, it's been an educational experience—gotta love those nasty, little maggots. Given a little more time to heal and get back some strength, what with being on starvation rations until now, yeah, I can see myself climbing up that Moki staircase.

Hacking away at the tree limbs, my mind wanders back to Leasha. Oh my God! I spent my whole time in our relationship just being me. I saw, from the start, that she didn't understand me, that I was so unlike other men in her life. Hell, that was probably what made me attractive in her mind.

Her dramatic exit from my life now gives me pause to look at it closer, to ask myself what it was all about. Her own life, with all the power and controlling dynamics required in her job, was something alien to me. In my relationships with other people, didn't I avoid being in control even when the job demanded it—being the non-commissioned officer, the sergeant in charge of my army battalion's bath section (decontamination field showers), and later, being the men's counselor in the Eagle Quest Seminars? Both were a stretch for me. For the first time, I now see how I avoid having any power over others.

And, too, I have to admit that I was so concentrated on getting through my own drama—healing and dealing, getting my own shit together—that I missed the cardinal rule of relationships. They are, above all, about meeting one another's needs.

With Leasha, I was looking to my own without seeing hers. I'm still not sure what her needs were, but clearly, while she did not try to control my life, the bottom line of it was that she had no control over me in our relationship, and that must have been uncomfortable for her.

In my view, control is always about one's own fears, but maybe that is not always so. ***The universe always balances***—it's a law. Doesn't everything in life have its positive side? When the control is only concerned with controlling one's self, it is never a thing of fear.

And then there is the question of one's ego. Doesn't everyone view ego as another negative thing? Energy wise, isn't it always looked at as a thing of fear? But its positive purpose is self-awareness—to look at and to understand one's self. Only in knowing one's self can one have a clear sense of self-worth. No, the ego is not some bad thing, something to get rid of. Seeing who you are is about touching your soul level. That is always a thing of magnificence.

This is Leasha's gift—for me to look at these laws of truth differently, to see that every negative thing about life has a positive side. Those turds society insists we paint pink . . . it's not that they don't look so great, and it's not that they don't smell so great. The truth of it is, no matter how society would have me paint it, that shit is what has nourished my life.

What is it about the hero always riding off into the sunset? I used to believe he was being a martyr, giving up the woman in self-sacrifice because he could not love her well. Perhaps it was really because he needed the time alone to heal his pain from the one who couldn't—or rather wouldn't—love him well. Either way, was he really a hero? Did he have the courage to take responsibility for his feelings?

Redneck Spirituality—Book Four

CHAPTER TWENTY-SIX

Riding a Badass Machine

The twin exhausts rumble a deep-throated burble that is tuned somehow to the very cojones of nearly every male around, a song that is heard to the depths of their primal soul.

"There he goes . . . just another over-the-hill, wannabe stud having an episode of male menopause."

Yes, I've often heard that being said, or left unsaid, by others. Either way, their eyes belied it, speaking rather of their own hunger for the freedom of the road, the mystique of it— racing with the wind, long hair flying, teeth flashing in a grin of personal glory framed by a curly, hormonal growth of beard. Knowing, all the while, the rumble of power between one's legs, the surge of it against one's butt slung low, cradled by one badassed machine, it is as a call to one's own personal glory.

True, concerning the bike, there was all that in my mind also, but in riding, there are other realities as well. When Meg and I divorced, I let my hair grow long, simply didn't cut it, and still haven't but trimmed it now and then. By the time I bought the Virago, my hair was quite long. Nevada has a helmet law, but Arizona doesn't. On my first long trip into Arizona, I let my hair fly with the wind. That evening, I lost half of it, trying to comb out the tangles. For a man approaching fifty, and really beginning to thin, it was a disaster—one not to be repeated.

That doesn't mean I always wear a helmet, only that I ponytail my hair or otherwise tie it now. And also, the flash of bare teeth while racing the wind only invites, in fact guarantees, the splatter and splash of multiple tiny, and not so tiny, bug carcasses inside one's mouth.

That first trip I remember very well. At one point, while passing a tour bus packed full with Japanese tourists fresh from the sights of the Grand Canyon South Rim, I became aware that they were excitedly pointing at me. Cruising past, going downgrade at eighty-five miles per hour, I straightened in the saddle and grinned tightly at them—"tightly" because there was a headwind that literally tore at the skin of my face and neck. I was still clean-shaven then. Puffing my chest, I fairly glowed with the sure knowledge that I must have cut quite a romantic sight to them.

Once passed, I found myself pacing next to a Ford van. Its windows had that highly reflective, mirror-type coating that is so popular in the desert southwest. Glancing over, I caught my reflection. The middle-aged jowls of my cheeks and neck were being drawn back by the wind. That was to be expected. What was not was the way it all flapped loosely, in mad-rippling waves. To those Japanese tourists, it must have resembled Godzilla's gills when blowing his nose. So much for romance and the badassed "Amellican" biker.

Riding that cruiser wasn't all about male menopause. Just being alone with myself on those long rides was therapeutic. Cruising and enjoying who I was, being in the moment and thoroughly enjoying it, was what I most needed. It gave a measure of peace to my soul, a soul wounded by the sorrows of the past.

My marriage and Meg's love for me were only a fabrication of my mind—a dream. My reality of it was much different from hers. Those dreams, and our marriage, were now dead, and for a time, I mourned them. But that time was at an end, for it was now in my past. Riding that bike kept me in the present where there was no pain . . . and where I could heal.

And, too, riding represented freedom, doing all those things I'd not been able to do as a "responsible" adult husband and father. I realized I'd always allowed myself to be tied by other people's beliefs about responsibility. I never felt free, not like I could on that bike. Taking chances with life was just not acceptable for a person of responsibility, or so I was taught and, for a time, believed. Yet, in my heart, I always labeled it as cowardice, while my heart always knew the truth—to never take chances with death is to never fully live. That truth I learned, and have always felt it fully, while riding in the saddle of that Virago.

Of those other men who, upon hearing the call of the bike, feel a yearning, perhaps the reality is, it's not just the call of the road, or even the mystique of a badassed bike. It's more a yearning to be free of other people's responsibilities.

Riding motorcycles indeed means taking chances. On one trip in the mountains outside of Kingman, Arizona, I was passing several semi-trucks on an upgrade. The road was a four-lane separated down the center with only a double yellow line. It was a windy day, with gusting side winds from the right hitting at thirty to forty miles per hour. They were more than a distraction as I cruised by the trucks at seventy-five.

As I crossed the wake at the face of a semi, a gust hit at that precise instant and I found myself scooted sideways across the yellow lines. It was one of those frozen moments of awkwardness when one realizes they are not completely balanced, yet body frozen in fear, one hangs in a limbo, unable to do anything about it.

To make it worse, the grill of a green Bonneville was rushing downgrade directly at me. I looked into the driver's widened eyes as he began his swerve and saw there the certainty of my death. Instinctively, I applied the brakes, only to feel an instant shifting as my rear brake locked in a skid. The bike began going down on its right side. With the bike tilted, slipping from beneath me, I instantly released the brakes and felt it fishtail crazily back upright, then to the other side. Simultaneously, the Pontiac's front fender seemed to flash directly through my leg and left side of the bike . . . but there was no impact!

At our combined speed of at least one hundred fifty, it all happened so fast, and yet, my senses told me we'd hit! My mind pondered it all, incredulously, while instinctively, my butt continued shifting, keeping instant and perfect balance with the wild fishtailing of the bike.

It was all over in perhaps three seconds, and I was again in my own lane, still overtaking the next plodding semi, nose to butt in line. Though traveling much slower, there was no room to get over to stop, so I passed the next several trucks, my body shaking and weak with the subsiding rush of adrenalin. I passed them with a renewed caution and a greater respect of the bike—and of Death. Once again, the Angel let me pass. Perhaps it was only his mocking gesture, humorously meant to renew my humility.

It was with humility that I wondered at the driver of the Pontiac. Did he now breathe just a little more humbly? And did he share my thankfulness for the unsoiled underwear he still wore? And hell, maybe he wasn't as lucky as I on that score.

* * *

The River Run is a big deal with the Harley crowd. Every year, thousands descend on the desert gambling mecca of Laughlin, Nevada. The first year I went was in 1995. It was expected that there would be some twenty to forty thousand bikers in town that weekend, the majority riding Harley motorcycles.

Laughlin is around a hundred miles south of Las Vegas, an easy day trip. I went down on Sunday, figuring that I wouldn't miss much if I caught the last day. Not a mistake, just a lesson. I now go on Saturday. Back then, the impromptu, nude, show-us-your-tits parade happened on Saturday. The next year, they passed another law. Now, anyone getting nippled also gets arrested.

Still, Sunday was incredible. I joined the throng of Harleys cruising up and down the main street. Here and there, I stopped to check out the several flea market-style tent bazaars. Most of the booths catered to the motorcyclist, selling stuff like helmets, riding leathers, motorcycle parts and accessories, and also lots of cheap, gaudy, biker jewelry, belts, riding scarves, and hats. And, too, there were food booths selling gut-greasing tacos, burgers, and beer.

The crowd varied in age, with most being older, middle-aged bikers—balding, graying, long-haired beards striped with white, grizzled-looking guys sporting beer bellies, and hard-eyed women. Yet, for all their rough edges, they were a very mellow, laid-back crowd. Walking past a mirror, I realized . . . Levi's, boots, riding leathers, beard, and long hair. I didn't look any different.

At one point, while stopped on Main Street waiting for a light, there was a man, a really average-Joe-type tourist, standing on the sidewalk next to me, videoing the parade of bikes. I suppose he just wanted some verbiage to go with the scene, so he shouted to me over the roar of pipes.

"Hey! How's it going?"

I wasn't exactly thrilled to be the center of attraction in his home movie and murmured a polite, "Great . . . just great."

"Gawd damn!" Just now noticing that I was astride a rice-burning, Japanese-made machine, the words fairly burst out of him. "You sure gotta lotta balls!"

I grinned and chuckled. As the light changed, I accelerated off, my pipes rumbling just as loud as those of the Harley next to me. Perhaps the Harley carried a certain flavor of 'badass,' but in real life, we both took the same chances—we both held our lives in our own hands and in the roll of our throttles.

Balls? Yes, we men like to think we have big, hairy ones. There is always that testosterone thing going on for most, but do the hormones make us brave or just stupid? Perhaps the truth is, brave and stupid often go hand in hand and are sometimes stuck together by testosterone.

I believe it was so, when initially, I ignored my injured leg, and then later, the symptoms of the resulting blood clot. Back then, it nearly cost me my life. Once again, I felt that same hormonal, slick gob of stupidity, again ignoring the symptoms with which my body communicated.

Since just before my Eagle Quest Seminar, I had a leg ulcer, probably due to the poor circulation arising from that original injury. The calf of my leg was itching, and in scratching, I broke the skin and caused a scab to form. With the unceasing itch, I kept peeling that scab until, eventually, it turned into a hole—a crater-like wound that did not want to heal.

It worsened progressively for more than a year. I tried everything . . . every treatment, ointment, and salve prescribed by a series of a half dozen doctors.

And doctors? After multiple GPs, I tried a dermatologist. No good. Then, a cardiovascular surgeon, figuring he could do something about the poor circulation. He only blew me off to a wound treatment and physical therapy center. By this time, I was bandaging it with wet gauze soaked in saline solution and then taping over it. Of everything prescribed, that seemed to work best.

At one point, I even tried a variation using *Living Water*. A friend of mine who was into homeopathy urged me to try it, saying it was ". . . naturally sterile and full of processed nutrients." She even recommended I drink it as well. But drinking it was where I drew the line—*Living Water* is just a homeopathic way of saying *piss*.

Actually, it worked just as well, possibly a little better than the other things, but I went back to saline because it smelled better. Who wants to walk around smelling as if they just whizzed in their pants?

By then, there were two adjoining holes about the size of a quarter each and perhaps a quarter-inch deep. Although I dressed it twice daily, it was clearly, though slowly, growing larger. Every time I dressed it, there would be a sickening stench of decay, followed by about two hours of mind-screaming pain, before it would finally settle down to a mere burning. It felt as if I were being slowly eaten alive—and perhaps I was.

The twice-weekly visits to the wound center produced no better results. They had me packing the wound with a felt-like material made from seaweed, then covering it with a rubber membrane designed to let air in but not let fluid out. Each time, they portioned me out a supply of these materials, just enough to last between visits.

The only thing they did different in dressing was to abrade the wound. In plain English, that means they would pick out the dead flesh with tweezers. It was kind of like having one's fingernails trimmed with a pair of pliers.

This was where life was when I felt the call of Sedona. It came as many different, small messages, stirrings of my soul. First, a friend mentioned she was going there. Then, it seemed as though every magazine I picked up or wall I passed carried a picture of Sedona. Walking by a group of people in discussion, "Sedona this . . ." or "Sedona that . . ." seemed to float out of their conversation and into my ears. I've learned that whenever I'm getting the same message repeatedly, it means my soul is speaking to me. Not so difficult to see. After all, it is about the law. Remember the Law of Learning? ***The purpose of life is for the lessons. When we refuse the learning, the lessons will just be repeated more forcefully until we get them—or die.***

Sedona is a small town in North Central Arizona. Many believe it to have multiple *energy vortexes* at different sites around and about. Strange, magical happenings are said to take place at these sites of concentrated or converging energy. It is, therefore, a gathering place—a Mecca—for many metaphysical or spiritually minded people. It is also a very popular destination for motorcycle touring, due to the beautiful, red, sandstone rock formations and the winding mountain roads that surround it. I often thought of going for both reasons.

My relationship with Leasha was long since over. I was not only alone, being in between women, but feeling pretty okay with both. I listened to the calling and took the trip.

Coming in from the Flagstaff side, I traveled through relatively flat, rolling meadows and pine forest, then came to the rim where it dropped into Oak Creek Canyon. I followed that two-lane as it switched back and forth steeply, sometimes turning back on itself.

I felt, all the while, the Virago's power as it surged beneath my butt, responding flawlessly to my control. The deep burble, and occasional popping backfire of the exhaust, spoke of an engine underload, holding control, descending the heights. That sound spoke almost as a salute to the road and a greeting to the canyon, one power to another.

For I could also feel the presence of Oak Creek Canyon, a majestic, stately, almost solid presence, one acknowledged from deep within my gut.

Then the canyon opened up. Sandstone cliffs and monoliths stood in grandeur all around, marred only by the buildings, the assumed ownership of mankind, owned only in the ego of his mind. In the middle of it all, the town . . . Sedona.

Rows of quaint shops, a forced quaintness—artificial. I parked my bike, still slightly numb, dazed from the buffeting of three hundred fifty miles of wind. A part of me was eager to see, to explore the shops. Another part was angry.

Like Jesus in the temple, that part wanted to drive out this greed, to rub clean this mar to perfection.

For a while, I wandered. Then, getting late, I stopped for gas and asked of a place to camp. In my mind, a KOA camp—showers, amenities . . .

"Hey, buddy," I called to the attendant who was busy ogling a couple of ladies. He seemed a little pissed that I interrupted his endeavor. "Where can I find a place to camp?"

"What?" The man's face scrunched up, as if he smelled gas much worse than the cheap, alcohol-laced shit now gurgling into my gas tank. "You can't just camp . . . you gotta use a camp park!"

What the fuck? I quickly shut my sagging jaw. *Am I a scourge, some kind of a louse upon this land who cannot be left free?*

"Sure. Oh, and by the way, bikers are not lowlifes." I winked real friendly like, then added, "Unless, of course, you chance to offend one." Nodding my head and looking him dead in the eye, I noted it was now his turn to hoist his sagging jaw.

He served to show me how I could expect to be treated by the locals. It was just as well. It changed my mind about that KOA. Motoring west on Route 89A, then turning south, I found a trail off into the trees beneath one of those orange, sandstone cliffs draped with black, manganese stains. A private spot, hidden away.

I pitched my tent and grabbed a snack, then found a spot by the side of a wash beneath a cedar and sat upon a rock. Counting down, I relaxed, edging Alpha to Theta, grounding myself with Mother Earth. Reaching out mentally, I felt the energy, the flow of it through me, and I asked the question.

Why, Sedona . . . why did you call me? The answer came from deep within, like an unconscious plea from between my cells.

To heal . . . it is time to heal!

I thought of the sore upon my leg . . . stinking . . . burning . . . oozing. I sometimes screamed out in pain. But no, that was just a symptom, the outward sign of the one upon my heart—the one I came here to heal.

* * *

The next morning, motoring back into Sedona, I felt an urge to seek out the spirituality of the place. Wandering the shops, I suddenly realized just how few there were that truly centered around anything of a spiritual nature. By far, most were simply selling tourist junk—T-shirts sporting the name 'Sedona,' trinkets, and the like.

I had coffee and an Egg-McWhatever at one of the local fast-food establishments and marveled at how, even here in Sedona, there flourished this mass-produced, stamped-by-the-same-cookie-cutter restaurant. It seemed almost like it had been dropped here in this part of the Monopoly game.

After breakfast, I bought a map of the vortex sites and started on my own pilgrimage. The map was very general. At each site, there were never any signs indicating the exact place where the vortex could be found. It was quite early in the season and there weren't a lot of people around, certainly none who knew any more than I.

Was it simply a look-for-it-yourself, and then, "Oh, yeah . . . that's it! Feel it? Must be! Yeah, you've found the right spot!" sort of thing? I supposed this was how it had to be. After all, like anything else, if you don't recognize it, you ain't found it.

At one of the more remote spots, I hiked up onto a ridge. Finding myself alone and feeling a connection with the natural beauty of the place, I sat down on a ledge to meditate. I felt no wonderful swirling of energy, saw no visions of Atlantis, or heard no communications from extraterrestrials. I simply had a very relaxing meditation.

Refreshed, I motored back into town and bought a few snacks at a convenience store for camp. By then it was late afternoon. There was a cantina next door, and I decided to drop in for a beer and to check out the bar scene.

The place was far enough from the attractions of town that the only patrons were locals. Perhaps a dozen in all, they sat around in small groups of threes and fours, discussing the weather, old man Johnson's new bull, and some 'slut' named Martha, who apparently ran off with the postman. Hearing this, I hoisted my beer in silent salute—good for her. Was she following her heart or just her hormones? Who knows or cares? Point being, she wasn't buying into the shit her society expected of her. I liked her for that.

Alone at the bar, I sat sipping my suds, relaxing, and idly contemplating the old-time wagon wheels and horse collars making up the western motif decorating the walls. The bartender's voice broke my reverie.

"You comin' t'the dance t'night? Gotta band comin' in from Prescott."

My gaze took in his balding head, graying, muttonchop beard and mustache, and noted the Harley-Davidson motorcycle on his belt buckle with the slogan, "*Live to Ride—Ride to Live*" lettered across the top and bottom. I recognized that he, too, rode and that, in this crowd, I was the only one with whom he connected.

"Be lottsa wimmin' . . ." He left it hang hopefully with a familiar wink.

Draining the last of my beer, I set the glass down deliberately while I considered it. Yes, I was between women—again. Well, wasn't I? And I could not deny I felt drawn to come here. Was there a woman I'd been attracted here to meet?

Someone who liked polishing gemstones and the fine sheen of a well-crafted silver piece? Or perhaps, also, she'd like long motorcycle rides and meditating and communing with nature? Maybe she'd even like sharing a cold beer now and then? Then there were the real issues. Would she share the same thought system as I? After all, people around these parts were considered to be spiritually kinky.

And speaking of kinky, what about sex? Certainly, she'd like sex. She'd be the kind of woman who'd slide naked down my body and leave a wet streak from my eyebrows all the way down. I took that moment to contemplate it all and then looked the bartender in the eye. Expelling a long, regretful lungful, I gave him my answer.

"No, bro . . . that's not what I'm here for." My grin was wistful. It had been a while. "But thanks anyway." Standing with a chuckle and a matching wink, I turned and walked out the door.

* * *

Back in camp, I dressed my leg, sickened by the smell of dead, decaying flesh in the confines of the tent. Then, laying back, I relaxed, purposefully focusing my mind on the sounds of nature all around me and on visualizing the burning pain of my leg just evaporating off into space. After a time, it did, and I dug into my new groceries for the evening meal—a Heath bar, twinkie, and a coke.

My favorite, the Heath bar, was saved for last. Taking my time worrying the chocolate away from its buttery, hard center, I allowed my mind to wonder just what it was that I was here to do. I knew I needed to heal these wounds but didn't feel I had any answers as of yet.

Weird as it might seem, that candy bar was the focus of this very real meditation. So it is with all meditation, one must provide the conscious mind something to focus on while relaxing into a connection with one's subconscious higher self. Everyone meditates, but most call it daydreaming.

My mind touched on that bartender and his suggestion. Was he there to tell me the way? No doubt there would be a woman there, and I certainly could have gotten into the exquisitely sensual crudity of that wet streak. Yet, however much my hormones might protest, the reality of the two of us in this tent—and me, with my leg rotting away—much as I might enjoy it, there would be no wet streaks tonight. Something deeper and more powerful told me clearly that one more woman was not what was needed now for my healing. Perhaps that *hog-herding* bartender's message was there to point that out, to help clarify my mind.

My meal over, I thought to read a little but found myself too restless to concentrate. I itched to do something, but what? Crawling out of the tent, I stood and looked around. There were red and orange sandstone cliffs rising several hundred feet high a short distance on my right. Looking at them with their familiar, black stains streaking down here and there, I felt their majesty. Before me stretched a pinyon pine and cedar forest, interspersed with sagebrush meadows. A couple of country homes could be seen off in the valley, on the far side of which were more sandstone cliffs and buttes.

Again, I asked myself, *Just what am I here for?* A slight wisp of wind bearing the sweet essence of burning sage was my only response.

One of the so-called landowners must be clearing some ground somewhere off in the distance. Yet, it was not this vision that sprang so strongly to my mind. Instead, it was one of an old, Indian medicine man, holding up a wad of smoking sage and using an eagle feather to fan-clean the sickness from someone's spirit.

It was a scene typical of spiritual healing. I'd often done it myself to clean my own aura before meditation. But what was the message in my vision, for I knew, for sure, it was a vision. Was it just that my spirit needed cleansing? Yes . . . that was a given. But what of the medicine man? Did it mean I needed a healer—or to become a healer? The truth, in the end, was both.

I started walking. A lizard burst into frantic activity a few feet ahead, hustling off into the sage. A couple of desert buzzards followed each other in lazy circles far overhead. As I continued to walk, I found myself attuning more and more to the desert and to its creatures. Ahead, there came a flash of white from the tail of a cottontail rabbit as it ran between some sagebrush.

Then my eyes fell upon a chipmunk, sitting frozen upon a cedar log. The naked wood of its surface was weathered—twisted, all knurly and gray. About ten feet away, it sprang to life, raced down the log, and out of sight. Was it my awareness of its presence that prompted its mad dash? Did it read my mind or just my eyes? And, if it were my mind, what did it deem so scary?

What was it about me that everything ran away? Habitually, animals run from man because man is a taker. He takes their homes, their habitats, their food, and even their lives. Were they reminding me that I am a man—a taker?

Was I a taker in the lives of the people I knew, giving back little or nothing? Yes, I served on the support teams in Karen's seminars, but then, didn't I also grow in that process? What could I do to serve better, to serve . . . more?

Finding myself in the same nameless draw in front of the same rock upon which I meditated the evening before, I again sat down. Then, closing my eyes, I called silently to the spirit of Sedona. "Why am I here? What is it I need to see? Or is it something I need to do?"

* * *

The sun was just rising as I tied my sleeping bag and tent to the seat above my saddlebags. I gave the load a couple of hard shakes to test the grip of the bungee cords before mounting and heading south on

Route 89A. After stopping to eat in the town of Cottonwood, two hours later found me climbing the steep switchbacks leading to the old copper mining town of Jerome, high up on the flanks of Mingus Mountain.

Jerome, it turned out, was a turn-of-the-century collection of houses and shops, built mostly of rock and bricks, all clinging vicariously to the steep sides of the mountain. They were reminiscent of the Bingham Canyon, Utah home of my early childhood. I didn't live there long, only long enough to leave a goodly measure of my innocence. Like Bingham, here and there—and pretty much everywhere—were tailings piles from the long-abandoned mines. They jettied out high into the spectacular void above the Verde Valley.

In its heyday, Jerome supported a population of some fifteen thousand and was famed to be *The Wickedest Town in the West*. Now it was an artist community of quaint shops, hotels, and restaurants. I passed a pack of eight or ten Harleys parked out front of one of the restaurants. The owners, a rough-looking bunch, were just preparing to ride. In fact, I soon found them close on my pipes as I negotiated the hairpin curves and straightaways of the mountain.

Out of nowhere, a green Kawasaki crotch rocket screamed past. He laid hard into the next corner, shifting his weight off the bike and low to the inside of the curve. His knee fairly kissed the pavement as he whipped around the arc at a dizzying clip. I shuddered at the thought of what his experience would be, were there even a small rock laying on the blacktop.

As his bike again righted coming out of the bend, his already-whining motor fairly howled as he dropped down a gear, and his front tire lifted clear with the sudden acceleration. It was only a moment more before he disappeared around the next ridge.

His riding ensemble was a matching green with white highlights. I chuckled to myself. Crotch rockets, with their pregnant-looking gas tanks, low handlebars, and foot pegs that sit far to the rear, require the rider to fairly lay across the gas tank. This guy reminded me of a tall, skinny, green grasshopper fucking a very angry frog.

He sure was in a hurry to get somewhere—perhaps a funeral or something. It didn't bother me at all that he would be getting there first. I wondered if the two age-challenged citizens in the Dodge Aries I passed a while back were thinking the same thoughts about me. Is it about age or about death? Does some inner prompting make the young hurry to catch up with life? Or is it that, with a little age, the living is stronger when life is closer to death?

There are those who hunger to live close to death, while others spend their energies pushing death away. It seemed a long time since I lived in the camp with those pushing. And then there are those silly youngsters, like my brother, Mike, and that frog-fucking grasshopper, who seemed to possess an insane hunger for inviting death.

Thirty miles down the road, at the crossroads to Prescott, there was a stop sign. The Harleys caught up. They clustered alongside me on the left as I waited for the traffic to clear. We nodded and grinned, and I brushed away a bug that was still alive and wiggling from my beard. Then they pulled out left toward Prescott and I turned right. I'd enjoyed the race during this short stretch of our lives and was again reminded, in the end, we each must go our own way.

I made a decision back there in Sedona, a decision to heal my heart. Oh, sure, I accepted long since that Meg and I were over. I already let go of all that painful mental bullshit, but it was not so with my heart. This leg wound was just the symptom of the festering, stinking wound on my heart. It was as if I'd lanced that wound back there on that rock in that wash, bled it of the pus that was eating at my soul. Once back in Las Vegas, the healing of my leg followed almost effortlessly.

At a party at Karen's house that next weekend, I met another Eagle Quest grad—a nurse working with wounds. She virtually took me by the hand to a doctor friend of hers. The doctor knew what to do. He explained how the wound couldn't heal because the swelling caused a layer of water underneath that prevented the blood from supplying the proper nutrients. He prescribed an ointment and had me fitted for a Jobst stocking. A Jobst stocking is nothing more than a knee-high, heavy elastic stocking with a zipper down the side.

Six weeks later, the wound was healed. So, too, I believe, was the one on my heart. It just took a while longer and the loving medications of one more good woman to show this to me. And perhaps this time with her, the healing was more of me waving a healing eagle feather at her.

What was it, in Sedona, calling me? Was it me—my soul—calling me to a far-off peaceful and spiritual place? One where I could make my decision. My past was rich in every lesson needed for the present. Sedona was the place where the tiger of my could-have-beens no longer ruled or fed on my life—the place I went to put out the kitty, where it could no longer scratch holes in my heart or piss on my life.

My parents both disagreed, but abandoning this kitty was not an act of irresponsible cruelty. For me, it was to abandon my dysfunction and to set that wild cat free. Still, to them I am an unfeeling monster for being capable of letting go of my pain. When you stop playing the game, stop pretending to be who others want you to be. There is a price, but the price is always worth paying.

Comb Ridge, Utah—Present Day

Yes, I let go of all expectations of having intimate relationships with women for a while. Just let my motorcycle and the desert do its magic. What else could I do when all my relationships were with the same woman—just different faces, and breasts, and . . . well, you get my meaning.

I was determined that my next *relationship* would be nothing like the others. There is that Spiritual Law . . . **We, being the Creator, have all the say in creating our own life—no say in the creation of anyone else's.**

So, what does that mean? It's real simple. A relationship is generally two people relating. I have the ability and power to change my part of it, but no ability, no power, and certainly, no right to change the other person's. Changing me couldn't help but change the relationship, but would it be enough to overcome a woman's need for security, and therefore, control?

With Leasha, I never even bothered to look at what her needs were. My next relationship would be one of service—me serving her in getting her needs met. Leasha's gift made quite a positive change in me.

Whenever the shit's in your face, it's either a lesson, a test, or a validation. Lessons and tests are usually given by a teacher. Does this mean that validations are to tell you that you got the lessons, have passed the tests, and are now a teacher? Not really! Truth is, you—that is, your soul—was always your teacher. Others and events are just the lessons your soul prepared. Yes, when not learned and passed, the lessons and tests just get harder. But when passed, the validations? The validations get absolutely orgasmic!
Redneck Spirituality—Book Four

CHAPTER TWENTY-SEVEN

Lessons, Tests, & Validations

Lucy . . . the wound on my leg was finally healed by the time I met her, as was the one on my heart. We first met at Karen's facility. Lucy was supporting the basic IQ Seminar, and I was coaching for an advanced one. Again, a mutual friend seemed intent on our meeting. You know, another one of those people who had a need to save others from their loneliness. Our friend didn't know that, though in between relationships, I wasn't all that lonely. Yet, Lucy clearly was. There was something about her that reminded me of me, back then, when I, too, began life again—alone.

Someone suggested coffee, and we all three met down the street at Marie's Coffee-n-Cholesterol. Our friend quickly and discreetly remembered a pressing engagement and left almost immediately.

The ploy was transparent, but Lucy had a vulnerable quality that suggested it might be her ploy, and I kept silent. I believed in being open and honest, without playing the games, but recognized how most everyone does play them—certainly those who hadn't yet accepted themselves and were afraid of rejection.

For me, a simple, "Hi . . . I find you very attractive. Would you like to have coffee
and get to know me?" would have been preferable. Yet, what I know about life is that it doesn't work to rub a puppy's nose in its do-do. It won't stop them from shitting, and it doesn't tell them anything about where to do it.

I liked her right off. She was small, petite, and very well-shaped. Though I towered over her, dwarfing her like a child, she carried herself with maturity and grace that clearly said it didn't matter. In that, there was much to like.

Lucy had one of those faces that could be termed "cute" in a dark-eyed, dark-haired sort of fortyish way. When she smiled, her soft, brown eyes lit up and her laughter carried a certain bubbly essence. At those times, the "fortyish" vanished, and like a cork removed, the beauty of a pure, young spirit fairly burst through. During our relationship, Lucy was champagne nearly all the way.

We talked for hours and, in fact, closed the place. I learned she'd separated from a husband of some twenty plus years and was only a few months alone. In her eyes, I saw her fear of men, though with me, the attraction seemed to overshadow that fear. There was a fragileness about her, almost like her confidence was stripped away, leaving her naked and alone.

Too, there was a strength in her that spoke clearly of how she made her own choices now, walked her own path, and would not stop her quest, whatever the cost. She looked to connect with friends who were on paths like hers and would accept and, perhaps, give her a hand. Was she unaware the hand she wordlessly asked for just now could only be the hand of a man?

She spoke of how her connection with others, her place in the world, was always one of a dependent gender orientation. She'd never known any life other than one suborned to a man—first her father, then her husband. She'd been a daughter, a wife, and a mother, but never a self-sufficient woman.

I empathized with her. Hadn't I always given my bottom-line control over to the women in my life? Whatever her connection with me, no one would be dependent this time.

Yes, I connected with her closely—knew intimately her feelings—for I once felt them, too. I'd traveled this path and knew exactly how I could best serve her. Though I did not say it so crudely, it seemed she was now needing a little fun, unjudged, connecting kindness. Like Jackie once did for me back then, Lucy now needed someone who would help her to see how she could hold her own power and still be desirable. It seemed she chose me for what I once termed a *mercy fuck*.

We'd been talking a long while and I felt she was comfortable with me when I said, "Lucy, I've told you my story. It's much the same as yours. When I left my wife of more than twenty-five years, I needed to know I could still function with other women again. My wife never really accepted me. I needed a woman who would—one who would be my friend and more. I'd like to be your friend . . . and more. You get to choose how much more and when."

My speech over, I sat quietly, waiting for her answer. Lucy stared at me silently for a long moment, seeming to contemplate the meaning of what I'd said, and was apparently confused. Any answer she may have given was preempted by the waitress.

"It's closing time, folks. Please step over to the counter and settle your bill—and come back soon, y'all."

After we'd paid our checks and stepped outside, Lucy still seemed a little confused. As she turned to me, her voice held an uncomfortable stutter. "L-look, Jeff. You're way ahead of me in your personal growth, and I'm certain you have a lot to teach me about being single again."

She seemed at a loss for words, so I helped her along. "Yes . . . but?"

"Well . . . Jeff . . . I just don't think I should be jumping into bed with strange men."

She said it in a rush, and while I knew she thought it to be true, I, too, certainly knew the needs and wants she was feeling. I also remembered how they clashed with my religious upbringing. And, too, I knew that Lucy's feelings told her clearly that with me, this statement was a lie, and yet, everything in her upbringing said it was the truth. I knew her confusion well.

While very different, the Mormon religion shares a similar stick up the ass concerning sexuality, as does her Catholic faith. Pulling that stick out before she was ready could be traumatic, and it was something that was not my place to do.

Lucy obviously had a ways to go in getting in touch with the truth of her heart. She needed to move herself out from under all those "shoulds." They are the excrements of other people's minds—in fact, probably those of her every ancestor for millennia—and that's a lot of shit.

"Jump into bed with me?" I paused, grinning. "That part's up to you. I'm only offering to help meet your needs." My head was now ducked, and with eyebrows raised, I held the grin. "Whatever they are."

I felt an urge to shake my head. *Why am I propositioning her? I've never propositioned a woman like this before—not even when being prompted by a stiff cock.*

Right now, perhaps for the first time in my life, there was no real want or even need. Since Leasha, I'd spent a lot of time alone—just me and the bike. I'd deliberately avoided sex. It wasn't my way to have it without a more complete relationship. And for the first time in my life, there was no shortage of volunteers. Right now, I was just enjoying the relationship I had with myself—not that it involved all that much sex.

But Lucy? She touched something in me. I'd been given something precious and healing once and now felt the need to give it back. I went on to clarify myself to her.

"I'm not in a relationship with anyone right now, and I'm not looking for another wife. I only do women sexually one at a time, and I don't have to be strange to you. You don't have to go there for me to be your friend"—I paused to look meaningfully into her face—"not if you don't want to."

Lucy's eyes still carried that glazed, incredulous look, telling me I was being more direct than she was used to. Her face flamed bright as her eyes flickered momentarily to my crotch before sliding off to look elsewhere—anywhere except into my face or back at the tent now pitched in my pants. This, and the fact I hadn't been slapped, encouraged me to come to the point.

"Fact is, Lucy." I shook my head. "I'm quite attracted to you," I said, pausing to pick my words carefully, "and I don't ask, or need, to go to bed with everyone I'm attracted to." Again, I paused, studying her. She still wouldn't look me in the eye. "And I want to be your friend, regardless." By now, we were at Lucy's car. Did her continued silence mean she felt pressured? I released any with a shrug. "Hey, you have my number. Call me if you like, and I'll be seeing you around. Let's just see where we go."

Then I opened my hands and arms slightly outward in an unspoken request for an IQ hug. Handshakes just don't carry the quality of acceptance of a hug. As our bodies touched, I could feel a slight stiffness in hers and kept mine neutral, not conveying any further offering, except for a quick pat and pause just before we parted.

Her hug also told me immediately that trust, and possibly respect, must be earned with her. It is not the same with me. I give others the same respect deserving of an equal. Then, in my experience of them, they might earn more or piss away what they have.

Normally, I don't hang around with uptight people, but Lucy's had a vulnerable quality that seemed like a plea for understanding. We all judge from past experience, and being raised a devout Catholic was not so much more uptight than as a devout Mormon. Something, some experience, in her past demanded distrust. Besides, integrity is the cornerstone of trust—not religion.

I wrangled my bike backward out of the parking stall and was about to hit the starter when Lucy pulled up next to me. Leaning out her window, she eye-balled me in mock seriousness.

"Sir, I'd like to know just what your intentions are, here, with me." Her scowl was in
comical imitation of parental sternness.

"Well . . . I assure you my intention is honest. We're on similar paths . . . though, since you've just started your divorce, you might be a little behind. Likely, we've a little healing and learning to do with one another." I grinned rakishly. "In short, I don't exactly see you as my soul mate, and I intend to jump your bones, rattle them around some, and find out who you are to me."

Her bubbling laughter followed the wake of her passing. It was the third time I'd spelled it out. Yes, she obviously liked my spelling.

It didn't take Lucy long to decide where she wanted to go with me. Certainly, our spelling bee had written passion into the script. Passion was something she'd never lived—not the simple passion of lovemaking or of reaching for her dreams. She saw clearly that I lived passion. Hers, long repressed, had been awakened recently, and she chose me to be her teacher.

During our discussion in that restaurant, we both told one another our stories. Born of a good Catholic family, Lucy married the man her family and church all believed to be "right" for her. What did she know? She was a virgin. Everything she'd been taught convinced her he'd be the perfect husband, never mind the feelings. Passion was something good Catholic girls in her family regarded as sinful. She'd always been very careful to repress those sexual urges. This man must be good for her. With no attraction, he raised none of those sinful feelings in her.

The children came quickly—a boy, then a girl—and then the rest of her life just fell into line. She loved and raised her children the best she knew how. They were her sustenance, replacing any passion she might have wanted, yet not quite.

Outside her children, the rest of her life was barren, unfulfilled. Inside, she knew it, and often lashed him verbally as the cause of her unhappiness. Finally, when the children were grown and gone, so, too, was their marriage.

Now Lucy wanted passion in her life and, while she didn't say it, she meant that to begin with her sexuality. That was something she'd never really expressed and didn't quite know how. A week after our initial meeting, she opened herself up to expressing it with me. Yes, "expressing," for passion comes from a place within, never from without. Lucy learned to express it with me. For a time, I was her teacher.

And me? Though I didn't know it at the time, for me it was a completion, a balancing of the universe. I was there for Lucy, just as Jackie had been for me back then when, after Meg, I began my life alone. Now, it was my turn to return the gift. What she needed now was a safe place in me to grow and explore herself—physically, mentally, emotionally, and sexually. Like me, Lucy bore the battle wounds of a loveless marriage. Did he love her as I loved Meg? Did Meg, too, need healing? I didn't know. Nevertheless, Lucy needed healing now. In helping her to start hers, I was completing mine, full circle. Again, we are all mirrors for one another. In Lucy, I was to see the validation of how far I'd come.

I suspect her experience of me must have been similar to mine of Jackie. Mine was one of awe and delight—and also, fear. *Awe* because, unlike Meg, Jackie lusted for me sexually. *Delight* in that such a young, attractive woman would also find me attractive. *Fear* because of the intimidation I felt in being compelled to perform. Jackie required no seduction. The requirement to be ready and able to perform was all mine.

Our first night together, Lucy seemed to be experiencing all of those same feelings, just for different reasons. We undressed together, each eyeing the other. Her dark-blue, silk blouse and skirt slipped off to reveal a black, lace bra and matching panties on a very petite, shapely body marred only by the scar of a C-section. I reached out and gently drew her body to me and felt it tremble slightly when it touched mine. Perhaps my own trembling was in response to hers, or to the rising of my passion.

My shorts, my only apparel now still on, began to tent out with the stiffening of my member. Caressing the smooth skin across her back, I nuzzled my face into her hair and breathed in the female fragrance of her. It tickled my nostrils with the clean smell of scented soap and some unidentifiable flower. We stood there together, just so, for a long moment, then my fingers found the latch of her bra and unhooked it. Lucy stepped away and it fell to the floor, revealing twin nipples jutting out and upward from her still youthfully pert breasts. Lucy, her face slightly flushed, eyed my now distended shorts. Then, mumbling her need to "freshen up," she fairly fled to the bathroom. Clearly, her decision required courage.

Switching off all but one small, bedside lamp, I shucked my shorts and slid between the sheets of the waterbed to await her. For long moments, I lay there wondering, then heard the light switch click off in the bathroom and the door open to reveal Lucy standing there completely naked. The curly "V" on her pubic mound perfectly matched the red/brown tint of her hair, and as I raised the sheets wide to accept her, her eyes sought my own, questioning, then dropped to linger a long moment on my penis, now innocently flaccid once again. A look of relief crossed her face.

We lay together, our naked bodies touching, and I cradled her in my arms. Lucy asked shortly if I would use protection. I assured her that, indeed, I would. It was an opening to the questions we both needed to have answered, and we began telling one another of our past sexual lives. Lucy seemed vastly relieved to hear how relatively few women I'd known since my divorce, how I took the AIDS threat seriously, used protection, and did not do casual sex. Apparently, my reputation belied the truth, with many equating my bedroom as a veritable sexual subway station.

"I've been told a lot of stories about you, Jeff." Her smile told me she didn't set much stock in them. "Some say you use IQ as a female supermarket, but then, others say you are impotent."

Her last statement pricked my ego. "Oh, really? Who said that?" I asked, perhaps a little too quickly, for she smiled and I knew I had taken the bait.

"Marsha." She giggled.

Of course, it would have to be Marsha. My mind retorted, mentally kicking myself over the largeness of my ego. Marsha was Regina's best friend. From the open-ended way she said it, Lucy obviously wanted to hear the story. I obliged, telling her of how Regina once moved in with me, the pact we had of no sex for thirty days, and of how I'd kept my word. There was no breaking of confidentiality there. No sex for thirty days was a standing agreement we all made with anyone we met while participating in any of the Quest seminars. Clearly, some women didn't believe men capable of keeping it.

"I can see why Marsha would think me impotent, given her beliefs about men and given that Regina was living with me."

That thought, verbally voiced, led me to wonder. *Did Regina, too, think me impotent? Did she give Marsha those beliefs? Was this why she'd turned off to me so early in our short relationship?*

I shrugged and, with a sigh, continued. "Shit happens—or not. I suppose Marsha, and maybe Regina, might think it beyond the possible bounds of integrity for any red-blooded, normal man."

Lucy laughed. "You are not a 'normal' man, Jeff." She said it quietly, and I knew it was a
compliment, one she held as truth.

During our conversation, I absentmindedly began touching her, stroking her sweet body with my free hand. She was responding in kind, running her hands across my shoulders and chest. Her touch felt good, and I was oblivious to her fascination with the firmness of my work-hardened body, so unlike her soon-to-be ex—or so she later told me. My body was something I took as normal, never realizing how the rigors of my work as a mechanic had provided such an added benefit for my attraction to women.

Nevertheless, the touching was having its effect, and I soon found one special muscle was, again, very hard. The touching evolved into passionate kissing, which quickly moved from Lucy's lips and neck to her breasts and belly. Soon, Lucy's wetness matched my hardness and the heaviness of our mutual breathing. I was laying above Lucy and between her legs, my weight supported by my elbows. Reaching over, I picked up a rubber from the shelf of the headboard, and raising to my knees, unrolled it to fit snugly over my straining member.

Lucy watched, her eyes wide, engrossed. This was her first time with anyone besides her
husband, and with using a rubber. Lifting Lucy's buttocks up across my thighs, I rubbed my sheathed penis up and down across her wet vulva,

teasing her with anticipation for long moments before presenting it in earnest. Then, lining it up with her folds, it began its journey of ecstasy, slowly sliding tightly within her. Lucy's eyes fairly bugged and her breath hissed a quick, startled intake sharply in my ear. Not yet halfway in, I stopped abruptly, aware I was hurting her.

"Do you want me to take it out?"

"N-no. Just . . . give me a minute . . . to get used to you." She gasped it out between quick, panting breaths. "My husband was not nearly as large, and we didn't do it much these last few years."

We lay quietly together for a long moment and I marveled. I'd been in enough locker rooms to know that mine was pretty much the average. Too, my experience distinctly said she was very ready for me. Yet clearly, to this woman, it was almost as if this were her first time.

"Lucy, I'm not really all that big . . . really. I'm barely above average."

"You're what? But . . . I always thought . . . that is, my . . . husband . . . he always told me that he was average. My God! All those years . . . and he was never"—her voice squeaked between pants—"this hard!" Lucy's words conveyed a growing realization and a conviction, a self-promise I could hear though it was unspoken.

"Lucy, you've quite a journey ahead of you. I'm glad you chose me to begin it with."

I thought of how sheltered her life had been—and how courageous she was now, facing life honestly, breaking from the confines of a zealously religious upbringing and an overly possessive husband. His dishonesty said any smallness of his dick matched only that of his mind. She was as close to a virgin as a forty-year-old mother of two could be.

By now, Lucy had relaxed considerably and was beginning to move on her own accord against me—and with determination. Still, I knew it was hurting her.

"Just take it easy," I told her, "there's plenty of time. It doesn't have to hurt."

"But you can't be enjoying this . . . and I just learned that I don't ever want to be a lousy
fuck."

The words sounded harsh, carrying the self-incrimination for all her years of unenjoyable sex she'd endured. Did she blame herself for her husband's undersized, soft cock? Or did she blame him for his dishonesty and insecure unwillingness to please and be pleased?

Obviously, he'd buried his head in the sand—perhaps both heads—rather than let it be known how inadequately small he was. With courage, he could have learned to compensate by pleasuring one another in other ways. It need not then have been soft.

"Lucy, if I'm to be your teacher here, then I don't want your first lesson to be one of self-flagellation or blame. Are you willing to change that?"

"Uh-huh." She agreed, her look questioning.

"Good, then here's how it goes." I smiled to reassure her I wasn't putting her down. "You concentrate on enjoying this as much as you can. Hold me capable of doing the same. I'll tell you what I need. You do the same, okay?"

"Okay," she replied, looking thoughtfully. Then, after a moment, she said in a small voice, one clearly uncomfortable with asking to have her needs met, "Uh . . . Jeff? Would it be okay if I were on top? I think I can relax easier if I didn't have to worry that you'll spear me all the way before I'm ready . . . you know?"

Quickly, we exchanged positions and she took hold of me, boldly wrapping her hand around my member as she slowly fed it into herself. In almost no time, she had me engulfed all the way and was riding, her head thrown back, a look of utter delight glowing across her face. Fascinated, I watched as her vagina engulfed me, then retreated smoothly, tightly, the skin of her inner lips clinging as if reluctant to release this most intimate of kisses. Faster and faster she moved, and longer and longer were her strokes.

Soon, it was all I could do to control my own passion, yet, I hung on as she rode me all the way to, and through, the first gurgling gasps of her orgasm. Then I released my flood within her.

The spurting palpitations of my own orgasm only served to elevate hers to a higher place. Long moments we were locked, slowly rocking in the oblivious abandonment of it. Then she collapsed on my chest and we lay contentedly together for a time.

Eventually, the tightness of her vagina and the way it still caressed my softening penis, fairly milked my seed back down the rubber, releasing it out to coat my balls and seep into the crack of my ass.

Idly, I wondered how useful this rubber was anyway. That thought brought me back, with a start, to full awareness.

"Lucy! This rubber is leaking out . . . are you on birth control?"

"Yes," she murmured contentedly against my chest, then quickly sat up in concern. "But what about AIDS?"

"I don't think you're any threat, and I was just checked only two weeks ago."

"Well, then I'm not worried. But there is one thing I need to be sure of."

"What's that?"

"Well, Jeff." Lucy seemed unsure of how to continue. "You said you only do women, sexually, one at a time?"

"That's right."

"Then you're not doing anyone else right now?"

"That's right."

"How do you feel about doing me for a while?"

"Does that mean that you want to be free to pursue other relationships that don't involve sex, and I'm free to do the same? If either of us decides to move on sexually, we'll tell the other immediately before we do? Meanwhile, sex is exclusive in our relationship?"

"Yeah, that's the way I want it," Lucy said. "That's what I heard about you that most attracted me. I know what to expect from you. You're truthful with women."

"You got it, babe." And Lucy returned my grin.

* * *

We dispensed with the rubbers after that. Lucy and I spent many months keeping each other company. For a long time, I was not sure just what it was about me with Lucy that I didn't want to spend eternity with her. We had great times, she was fun and delightful to be around, and the sex was always superb.

Yet, there was something about me and her—some little thing I could not seem to figure out—that held me off. True, she was a little behind me in her personal development and healing but was fast catching up. The courage of her spirit was nothing short of magnificent.

Then one evening, I saw it. We were at Arizona Charlie's Casino for their special twenty-four-hour breakfast menu—steak and eggs for $1.99. Our booth was fairly secluded. When Lucy said she thought she'd have a burger instead, I leaned forward and made one of those off-color remarks I so enjoyed making.

"Y'know, if I'd known you wanted that, we could have stayed home." Then, dropping my voice, I finished with a wink. "I'd have fed you a whopper—and served it in bed."

Lucy looked up with a quick grimace, her anger clearly showing.

"You can't speak to me that way. I . . . am . . . a . . . lady!"

I sat back, stunned. It had never occurred to me that Lucy would ever perceive me as not respecting her. My mind flashed back over the innumerable times I'd made off-color remarks and jokes with her.

I was not raised in high society. My private humor tended to be a little coarse, and often, openly sexual. It was just me being me. I enjoyed sex and sexual innuendo. Was this the way she'd always perceived them? Had she been gritting her teeth all along, outwardly tolerating this unacceptable part of me?

"So, have you always felt this way about my jokes?" I asked in an even tone.

"Yes!" Lucy answered, her face red, lips twisted in an ugly scowl. "And it's time I set some boundaries with you! I require respect. I am a lady." She stopped abruptly to glare sullenly.

I sat there for a long moment, just staring at her, sifting through my own feelings. Yes, again I was the object of a woman's disgust—and again, one I cared about.

I let the feeling **flow** through me, a quick **flush** of shame, anger, disappointment, rejection, and abandonment. Once again, I felt the feelings and identified easily where, in my past, each originated. I even experienced the blame of betrayal for the lie of her suffering silence, so typical of my marriage.

It did not take but a moment before I was ready to respond from a place that was here in the present and where I was, again, okay with myself. My tone was neutral—one of acceptance, yet seeking understanding—when I answered.

"Lucy, are you sure you want to do this . . . set this sort of boundary with me?" She just finished a seminar about setting boundaries for one's protection and safety and seemed to think this was a place to set one in her life. "This is not about your safety. Y'know?"

"Yes, it is. I can't feel like a lady when you're constantly making those lewd comments to me!"

"Lucy," I began again, still speaking quietly and evenly, "the lewdness is only your perception—as is the disrespect. It is not the same in my mind." I stopped, but she did not respond. "I've always held you in the greatest of respect."

"Some great way you have of showing it," she mumbled, then lapsed again into frosty
silence. It was the first time she'd ever shown anger toward me. I could accept her being angry with me sometimes, but the message behind this? That, I knew, I'd never accept. It was what I'd known but been unaware of all along. I tried again, more directly this time.

"Look, here is what I'm hearing. It's kind of like . . . you're throwing the egg shells of your feelings at my feet and then making me responsible for not stepping on them. If this is the way it is, then for the rest of our lives, whenever you're near, I'd have to tiptoe around, hoping I don't step on one of them. Do you think I'd ever feel free to be myself with you again? When you make me responsible for your feelings, in your mind, and insist it be so in mine, then it's not about your feelings—it's only about control." I paused, but no answer was forthcoming. "I'm asking you to look at this one."

"Oh no you don't." Lucy's eyes were blazing. "This is not about me! It's about you—and the fact that you don't respect women." She stopped abruptly, suddenly aware that her voice had risen, and we now had the attention of everyone in the restaurant.

I studied her quietly for a moment, letting her words sift through my mind. Was it possible she was correct? I could certainly see why some might think so. But no, it wasn't so. I liked women . . . and I liked sex. Neither was dirty in my mind.

"Lucy, I'm not holding the energy here." My voice was quiet. "You are." I raised my hands, index fingers pointed inwardly, and gently tapped myself on the chest. It needed no saying. The message was clear and Lucy knew it well. "The correction goes here," were my unspoken words. No one got through one of Karen's seminars without knowing this.

* * *

The relationship was over. I knew it. Didn't she know it, too? Lucy also knew the thought system of responsibility, the one we were both sworn to living, the one that said, *I'll be responsible for my feelings and hold you capable and responsible for yours*.

Lucy knew the truth of it in her head but did not know it, or live it, in her heart. Like so many others I'd known, Lucy did not feel safe with me without control. Making someone else responsible for your feelings, telling them and expecting them to take that responsibility, is always about control.

Control of me was something I'd never again give away to anyone—man or woman. Twenty-five years with Meg taught this to me. The penalty of such disloyalty to my soul was death.

Yes . . . I learned that one the hard way. Living my life to suit the feelings of others was a slow death. I was to become someone I was not and a killing off, bit by bit, of who I am. I like who I am.

And then there was Big D and the agreement I made with him in that hospital way back when. No. Break that agreement, and this time, death would not be slow in coming.

Looking back at my relationship with Lucy, I am reminded of one particular law—***If it's in your face, it's a message or a lesson or a test, validating whether or not the message was received and the lesson learned***.

Lucy was a huge validation in my life. I'd received the messages Meg was in my life to deliver, learned every lesson she, and all those after her, were there to provide. In so doing, I'd changed. It was no longer my natural inclination to choose women who needed the security of control and who didn't accept me as exactly who I am. From the beginning of my relationship with Lucy, I knew she wasn't someone I wanted to be with forever. Our agreement was that I would be her teacher. On that score, I failed.

Lucy just set herself against some of the most important Laws of Creation. She required me to be responsible for her feelings and insisted this was how she wanted it to be. Although she never said it clearly before, this, I always knew. Her life with me, or any man, would never really work until she learned the laws consciously in her heart, not just in her mind. Perhaps my relationship with her, when looking back at it sometime, will give her that ability. As it was, just then, she'd made her decision and it was time for me to leave.

Some of us choose our companions in life because they are who we are. For others, it is for who we want to be. In the beginning, Lucy said she wanted to be someone like me. In the end, it seemed that unconsciously, that was a lie. For a time, I was her teacher. She clearly was no longer my pupil.

And me? Well, Big D and I have an agreement. As long as I live, he will be my teacher.

* * *

I did not see Lucy for the rest of the weekend or the next week. She avoided me, and I felt no urge to seek her out. Instead, by the following Thursday, I was feeling only the pull of the road. Riding with a friend, I headed for Farmington, New Mexico, a place I once called home. Though I'd not been back, it had been there in my mind often of late, calling out to me. Now, some ten years in my past, I did not know what it was, what gift would be there awaiting me.

Comb Ridge, Utah—Present Day

My completion of the round-trip mercy fucking of Lucy was a wonderfully fulfilling thing, although the final destination was not anywhere near where I wanted it to be. And who knows? Maybe she'll make the connection somewhere down the road and with someone else. I dunno. That's her life—not mine—and I wish her well.

Here, on the ledge, the days are noticeably shorter, colder, and the nights chillingly so. Today, I am working on a project to alleviate that problem. Pulling my tent a little tighter up under the overhang and digging a hole in front of it, I find that there is a good foot of soft sand over the bedrock.

Making the hole slightly elongated, I line it with rocks, using the sand removed to mound up around the edges. This forms my firepit.

The days don't warrant much of a fire—yet—and I find there is room to sit between the fire and the edge of the cliff and watch for traffic on the lonely dirt road along the wash below. I have seen none.

But the nights are a different matter. After cooking my meal using a small fire on the rocks, I build up a larger fire for a time to keep warm. One side of me is then always burning, while the other is freezing. This keeps me switching between the left and right sides of my fire. That's okay because when it has burned down into a decent bed of coals, I simply push the sand back over them. I find that the battery side cover from my motorcycle makes an excellent scoop for moving the sand. After making sure there are no exposed hot cinders, I drag my tent back over it. If all goes well, the coals will shed their heat into the surrounding sand. And me? For the first time in recent misery, I will sleep well all night long. We'll see.

We all want to have things solid in our lives, just to have something to hang on to. Yet, the only solid thing about life is ourselves—and those beliefs that serve us. As we grow and change, those beliefs often no longer serve. That's the shit that ain't solid in our lives. When our beliefs begin stinkin', it's time to let them go. Everything changes—it is the law of the universe. I guess the trick is just to let those stinkin' things just slide away with their own flow. And the smell... well, perception is a choice. "Shit" is something most view as offensive. The truth is, it is something that has nourished us in our growth, and the smell just tells us to move on.

Redneck Spirituality—Book Four

CHAPTER TWENTY-EIGHT

Once in the Eclipse of a Blue Moon

My muscles quivered from the sustained strain of it all. The rush of wind against my legs insistently forced my knees apart with the constant eighty-five-mile-per-hour speed and the buffeting of the headwinds through which I plowed.

The forward foot pegs I installed were supposed to give a more comfortable ride, but were I to relax under these conditions, there was no doubt that one of my boots was sure to slip off the peg. With the asphalt blurring by just inches below, touch it and that foot would be jerked underneath the bike. What biker would want to be jerked off their bike at eighty-five miles per hour, then experience their own bike run up their leg and over their ass? No, I had to keep my knees in against the bike.

Idly, I wonder how it was for women to sit for extended periods of time while keeping their knees together. Did they, too, have this ache in their crotch? The cool of the early fall air in the predawn hours of this ride only added to the aching in my own.

Glancing over at Dean, my companion, riding his crotch rocket ahead and to my left, I knew he did not suffer like me. Lying forward, chest resting comfortably across his broad fuel tank, legs cocked back, braced by rearward-set foot pegs, he rode in an intimate—almost sexual—embrace of his bike. I regretted letting him set this grueling pace. His was a racing bike, built for comfort at sustained high speeds. My Virago, a cruiser, was not.

We were less than an hour out of Vegas, approaching the town of Mesquite, when I pulled up even with Dean. Pantomiming with one hand, I communicated a suggestion of eating, then pointed toward the freeway exit sign. He nodded, and together we banked our bikes onto the off-ramp.

Dean was just another single man who, like me, rode motorcycles and hung around the IQ Seminar program supporting—and occasionally growing. Strangely, we'd never really connected. We were both divorced and searching, but he was fifteen years younger than I and we didn't really compete. Perhaps our testosterone told us we did. Over my burger that morning, I got to know him better.

He, too, once believed his was a perfect marriage, and too, when it ended, had begun questioning everything in life that he'd always taken for granted. Like me, he discovered how little of his life had been centered around the true joys of his heart. Unlike me, his divorce ended in bitterness, with neither being willing to accept their own part in the creation of their war. Now with Dean, his inner pendulum seemed to have swung over to his spiritual side—perhaps way over.

The week before, when he confided how there was an energy of spirit drawing him on this trip to visit the mountains around Durango, Colorado, I also realized I was feeling the same sort of energy—the pull of Farmington, New Mexico. It was just to the south and now some ten years in my past.

After finishing our McMantit burgers, we talked while I stayed busy with a length of rope, rigging a harness to span my thighs—something to alleviate the constant ache from holding my knees in against the bike. This simple harness would ease the strain of the many miles to come. A simple source of relief, it performed the same purpose for my crotch that the bike did for my life. Whether we are creating strain by going too fast, judging too hard, or just wishing someone or something were other than it is, sometimes we need to also create something to ease the strain, bring our energy back inside, and help us to just be.

The next hours saw us up through St. George, Utah, then east through Hurricane. Skirting south of Zion National Park, we traveled on through Kanab, Utah, across Utah's southern border to Page, and farther through Kayenta, Arizona. Eventually, at dusk, we ended at Farmington, New Mexico.

Sometimes I followed, sometimes Dean, and sometimes we rode abreast. With the wind in our faces, shrieking past our ears, we could not communicate. We rode in a world of our own, yet together, just enjoying the desert scenery and the warmth of the summer still lingering in this early fall.

The warmth lasted until the lofty volcanic spires of Shiprock came into view, then abruptly, the temperature fell a full thirty degrees into the mid-forties as we entered the cold air flow coming off the La Plata Mountains in the Southern Rockies. After a quick stop to don our leathers—the wind chill was below freezing—we continued on into Farmington. A half hour later, immersed in the deepening dusk, the slight breeze now outright below freezing, we pitched our tents at the KOA campground.

I was back again, now camped within an easy walk of the house I'd once owned and lived in with Meg. Why? What was this attraction I'd felt drawing me here? And now being here, it seemed to have deserted me.

The night had fully fallen by the time our tents were up and we'd grabbed a bite. We talked under a full moon as I finished my meal of a chocolate bar and coke. So late was the season that we had the KOA nearly all to ourselves, and insulated as it was by a ridge from the lights of town, it seemed almost as if we were alone with nature.

This night, it seemed, was special for Dean. There was to be a full eclipse of the moon. And further, this moon was the second one of this calendar month, making it an eclipse of a blue moon, something that just, in itself, seemed to be saying, "This moment is special!" We talked for a while, and then, as the event drew near, Dean left me to meditate. He wanted to be alone.

Me? I hardly placed any significance on the affairs of the moon or astrological stuff in general. Never thought much about it, yet this night did feel different, and I also was happy to be alone. Bundled up against the bitterness of the mountain air, I sat cross-legged, Indian style, upon a picnic table to meditate this event for myself. Once sufficiently relaxed, body and mind, into that state many call "alpha," the cold no longer bothered me.

By merely telling myself I was warm while visualizing the sweltering heat of the Las Vegas summer, my body obliged by cranking up its internal furnace. It is just the way our subconscious minds are made. They always make us right.

From that state, I began to explore the meaning of this moon for me personally, allowing my thoughts to float free and be in a state of listening awareness—or "just being." In that mindset, the universe seemed to speak, to bring it all together without effort.

Into my mind seemed to drop the essence of Meg, and with her, the cold reality of the death of our marriage. Here, in the chill of this, our old homeland, lay the bitterness of my sorrow. I saw clearly the barren, arctic death that lay existing in this past.

Now, as I'd been doing in life, with my insight, I gave away my personal power to keep myself in warmth. With my meditative state broken, I found myself shivering.

I stayed for a time in the piercing cold, just feeling it and getting a clear, physical knowing of what hanging on to my past—and Meg—was truly doing within me.

Sometimes one needs to do something physical to put the past away. Not to bed, asleep, but away, never to return. For me, I watched the moon turn dark in eclipse, felt it fully within myself. When the moon was again showing a pearly glow, I pried open my folded legs, hobbled into the warmth and light of the laundry room, and eulogized it in a poem.

Eclipse of the Blue Moon

Las Vegas . . .
up before light and on the bike . . .
traveling throughout the day.
Stopping only for burgers . . . gas . . .
and to empty my ass . . .
'till dusk finds me pitching tent
at the end of the day . . .
back full circle to where
our lives played out together . . . growing apart.
Back once more . . . to Farmington.

Edmond E. Frank

Pitching tent by the light of a blue, full moon.
Yet not . . . For it is shadowing over . . .
bit by tiny bit . . . in total eclipse.
Like our life together . . . our love . . .
slowly dying . . . consumed . . .
Like a dream that wasn't real . . .
or real needs that were never met.
Sitting at this KOA upon a picnic table,
I watch it unfold again . . .
And shiver in the bitter cold as bit by tiny bit,
the moon's pearly glow . . .
the life we knew . . .
is turned to a dull, dim globe . . .
a dull and dirty burnt-orange marble.
Lingering for a time in malevolent glow
that slowly dims near black.
Yes, I watch it all just so,
and shiver in the bitter cold.
The bitter cold . . . like my life this day . . .
its warmth just ebbing away . . .
The dreams . . . the love . . .
the material things . . .
all gone . . . all done
over . . . finished . . .
a shattered crystal vase.
Nothing left but the icy-cold, twinkling shards
of a million tiny frosted stars,
and the cheery flashing of a passing plane . . .

A friend signaling . . .
telling me that life is not gone . . .
Not all is lost . . .
that soon a new moon will be uncovered.
New life . . . new love . . .
And I may use this time
in the clearing of my mind . . .
straightening out my life . . .
making room anew . . .
for a new love's pearly glow.
Yes, how often will the eclipse . . .
the old love . . . old life end?
For me, it happens only once . . .
once in the eclipse of a blue moon.

* * *

The next morning, Dean and I broke camp, strapped our gear onto the bikes, and rode together down to the local Texaco to fuel. His was a burning need to reach Durango without delay.

Me? I wanted to visit old haunts and old friends. We agreed to watch for one another and possibly meet up at the Wahweap Marina in Page, Arizona two days hence—an event that we both seemed to know would not happen. I watched him mount and scoot up Highway 550 and out of my life.

Sometimes life's just that way. People drop in and out, and you don't have to become bosom buddies forever. And it's okay. People seem to think that to be a friend, you must make an effort to stay connected.

Me? I don't see it that way. Hell, to me, that would only be an attempt to force life to be other than it is. I think the real trick to being friends is to reach out to those you are traveling with in life. Then, when in the natural course of things you part, let them go with love, and without asking them to take part in a struggle to stay connected with you.

That way, any future connection will be made from a genuine want to make it happen, not from any expectations. It needn't be about the distance that separates. Friends having shared of themselves will stay connected, even if it's only in the heart.

There is that Spiritual Law—***Everyone in your life has a gift to give you—and you, them***. Once given, why not simply let go with gratitude? They will only be there so long as there is something for them to teach you . . . or you, them.

* * *

Bosom buddies? I was about to clearly see, I had so few, and one of those was a complete surprise. My first stop was to the repair shop where I'd spent over four years of my working life. As I entered the showroom, Sissy, the secretary, looked up from the inside office, then took a quick second take.

"Hi, Sis." I grinned.

"Jeff . . . it's been so long. My God! How are you?" Her face was lit with welcome, her smile warm with delight. *Holy shit! Was I someone special in her life?*

We were busy catching up on one another's lives when Ben, the manager, walked in.

"Hi, Ben. How're you doing?" I reached out and shook his hand. "Is Little Ben working today?"

Ben shook my hand, confusion etching his face, then headed off behind the sales counter. "Fine . . . fine. No, he's off today. Uh . . . can I help you with something?" he ended, obviously at a loss.

Sissy piped in, "Ben, you remember this guy. He used to work here." Ben, his brow wrinkled in confusion, shook his head in embarrassment.

"It's Jeff!" Ben cocked his head and looked me over closely for the space of several seconds.

"No," he finally admitted. "Jeff who?"

"Jeff Williams!"

"Oh." I could tell Ben remembered the name, but the man behind it? He couldn't yet place me as that man.

Just then, Sissy's husband, Jim, the shop foreman, stepped in from the tire bay, spotted me, and hustled over, intent on doing his job.

"Hi . . . you been helped yet?"

"Jim!" Sissy burst out laughing. "This is Jeff Williams. Surely you remember him?"

Jim, his ears turning almost as red as his hair, said, "Oh, sure. Hi, Jeff." He stuck out his hand. "How're you doing?"

Shaking it, I noted the disconnection still in his eyes and knew that he, too, shared Ben's confusion.

We talked over old times for a while—Sissy and I—and gradually, the light began to glow behind Ben's eyes. Then together, we stepped out as I prepared to leave.

As I straddled my bike, Jim seemed to suddenly make the connection. Maybe it was the bike. I used to ride one when I lived here. He asked, "Where's Meg?" in a voice that carried a certain studied casualness.

"We're divorced now, Jim."

"Oh!" Jim's eyes were speculative. I could feel his burning curiosity, which he clearly didn't want to show, perhaps for his wife's sake. His next words also were a little too casual.

"What happened?"

"We just grew apart." I shrugged. "The marriage no longer worked . . . I left."

"You mean after all those years, you just walked out on her?" He blurted it out, then looked quickly at Sissy. Caught in the lie, his entire face joined the color of his ears, now even redder than his hair. Sissy rolled her eyes and winked at me, reminding me of how I'd always liked her easy ways.

Perhaps Jim's remark was a little out of line, but then, I've always known he was attracted to Meg. I never faulted him for it. After all, Meg was a beautiful woman. It would've been a waste of energy being mad at every man who found her so. Still, I didn't see wisdom in telling my deepest feelings to a man who would only look to fault them. Instead, I said, "Jim, would you agree that it takes two to grow together?"

"Uh-huh . . . yeah, I guess—so?"

"Then, how many does it take to grow apart?"

"Whaddaya mean?" Jim's eyes narrowed, never leaving mine. With his lower lip pulled up over his lower teeth, his words carried that certain slur that spoke of a mouth overfull with the slurry of snuff. So intent was he on my answer that he forgot to spit into the empty coke can he carried as a spittoon.

"Kinda depends on who's looking. Blame who you want."

He scowled. "Whaddaya mean by that?"

"Jim, it's great when your relationship nourishes you, but when the nourishing stops, you take your shit and move on." I smiled.

"What . . . you just stopped loving her?" His nose flared and the snuff dribbled, unnoticed, across his hairy chin.

"Kinda depends on who's looking. Blame who you want," I repeated, then shrugged and turned to leave, still speaking over my shoulder. "But relationships are about the meeting of needs. Love's only one—and needs change."

"Splain yourself!" Jim barked, his right fist doubled up while the coke can crinkled in his left.

I looked at Sissy, who stared at Jim. Her mouth hung as if in sudden realization. Then, taking a deep breath, my left leg followed my right on over the seat and I faced him squarely, the bike now between us. Then I told him what he didn't want to know, but what I was now sure Sissy did. *Was this describing their own relationship?*

"I didn't stop loving her. We, neither one, were meeting the other's needs. That's life." I ducked my head down and with one eyebrow lifted, eyeballed him pointedly.

His mouth gaping open, Jim froze. The spit on his hairy chin dribbled down his shirt front as I swung back and sat down into the saddle. My eyes never left his face as I rocked the bike unhurriedly upright, heeled the stand up, hit the starter, slapped her in gear, then turned and rode out of his life.

* * *

My next stop was the local Honda store. The husband of one of Meg's oldest and closest friends ran the repair shop there. His name was Dennis. He must have heard the deep, V-twin burble of my Virago's aftermarket exhausts as I pulled up. When I stepped through the door, he turned from the workbench and, looking me full in the face, said, "Howdy, what can I do ya for? Oh . . . and we don't work on Harleys here, y'know?"

I didn't answer for a second or two. Obviously, he, too, didn't know me. And, too, he'd mistaken my bike for a Harley—possibly because of its sound, possibly because he'd mistaken me for a Harley rider. Always into dirt bikes, Dennis never did think much of Harley riders.

Had I really changed so much? Taking off my riding glasses, I slipped them into my inside jacket pocket and replied, "I know, Dennis.

I was just passing through and thought I'd drop in and see you. How's Kyong Soon and the girls?"

"Do I know ya?" He said it almost angrily, his eyes dark, as if he thought I was trying to put one over on him.

"Used to . . . I'm Jeff." Still no light. "Meg's Jeff?"

"Oh . . . yeah." The light was there now, but no welcome. "How ya doin', Jeff? Didn't recognize ya with the beard 'n all the long hair." I suddenly remembered he didn't like beards, or long hair, either. I wondered just where I now fit into his picture. Was I still among those he liked? I didn't have long to wait in finding out as abruptly, he turned back to his bench. On it was a cylinder head he'd been fitting down over a piston.

"Kinda busy right now. C'n ya come back sometime"—the pause was pregnant—"later?"

"Sure. Maybe I'll just drop out and visit with Kyong Soon and the girls for a while." As a family, we'd spent much time together over the ten years we'd known one another.

"Uh . . . she's kinda busy today, too. Don't b'lieve she be home jist now." There was a nervous coldness in his voice and an avoidance in his eyes that told me clearly all I cared to know. I'd seen it before and knew that whatever his personal feelings might have once been, he'd never counted me as a friend. Too, I suspected his wife, Meg's friend, what with the divorce, also felt the same.

"No problem, Dennis," I said evenly, then turned abruptly on my heel. "It's been real—" The words hung with a measure of regret as I stepped from his shop, mounted, and with a heaviness of heart, clutched the Virago smoothly into motion. There were no friendly eyes on my back this time as I rode away.

At the west end of Farmington, I turned north up the familiar miles of Highway 140. It would take me right past the house that Meg and I built, and also past another old friend, Bart, who owned a wrecking yard. Bart's wife, Soo Ki, was Meg's favorite. Too, of all the husbands in Meg's circle of friends, Bart was the one I liked most.

Pulling into their yard, I was again struck with how nicely kept and neat their house was, compared to the scourge of rusting, old auto hulks in the fields beyond. Yet, even with those hulks, there was an orderliness foreign to most wrecking yards.

True to the weather in this part of the country, thunderstorms the day before had selected this area to piss on. The driveway was graveled, but from where I parked, my boots were caked in those few steps to the concrete walkway. Stomping along, I shed most of the mud before stepping up onto the porch. I rang the bell. Only the storm door was closed. A flicker of motion caught my eye as I glanced in through the plexiglass. It was Bart, ducking out of sight into the kitchen.

"Bart . . . it's me! Jeff . . . Jeff Williams!" Obviously, he, too, didn't recognize me—or had he? Cautiously, he poked his head around the corner, then smiling with relief, came to open the storm door. I saw clearly his smile was genuine. He remembered me.

"Damn, Jeff . . . gave me a scare, what with the bike, the leathers, the whiskers and all. Sorry about that." He began his apology, then left off, realizing, as we gave one another a bear hug, with me, it was unnecessary.

For me, it just felt so damned good to finally see an old friend who still remembered and accepted me. Moving from Soo Ki's immaculate house and over to the shop, where we were both more comfortable, we sat around stoking up on coffee and shooting our shit. It seemed not much had changed in his life, so it was mostly about mine that we talked.

"You remember that last time at Lake Powell? You were pulling me on that ski tube and I took a flip?"

"Yeah . . ." He left it hanging.

"Remember, I mentioned I pulled a muscle, or something, in my leg?"

"Uh-huh." Bart nodded. "I remember telling you to take a break. But you wouldn't."

"Yeah . . . well. I never told you the rest of the story."

"How's that?" He leaned in to pick up his coffee, then with my next words, forgot to take a sip.

"About a week later, I found myself in an ICU—massive blood clot on the lung. Thought it was tits-up for me."

"I remember Meg did tell Soo Ki something about it. The girls here all got together for months talking about you. Alls they'd tell me was that you kinda went nuts." He shrugged. "But I never learned much Korean, so I didn't catch the particulars—and for some reason, they would never say." He set his coffee down, untouched. "Tell me."

"Gone nuts." I mused. "Yeah, kinda did. You ever been in an ICU?"

"Nope . . . never."

"Creepy. Thought I was having hallucinations for a time there." I ducked my head in consideration, knowing I could never tell anyone the full story about Big D. "Thought I met the Angel of Death and bargained with him to give me more time." I had him now. So intent was he hanging on my words that his jaw, too, was hanging free.

"Tell me"—he closed his mouth, quickly swallowing what was pooled there—"what kinda bargain?"

"Oh, it wasn't anything all that out of the normal. Common sense shit—and you got to remember, it was only a hallucination."

"Common sense shit, like what? Tell me."

I was beginning to regret saying anything about Big D, even to him.

"Just promised that I'd face life with honesty, have the courage to step through my every fear, follow my joy. Yeah, common sense shit like that," I answered, trying to shine it off.

"Yeah, I heard you were doing crazy shit, like skydiving."

"Been afraid of heights all my life." I shrugged. "Just never told anyone."

"What else? Was that it?"

"I promised that I'd search out the real truths about life . . ." My voice kind of trailed off as I desperately tried to think of some way to let it slide. I didn't care what other people thought of me, but this shit was sacred, not something I wanted to put out there just yet.

"Did you?" His eyes were big now, and I couldn't help but grin.

"I'm alive, ain't I?"

Maybe it was my grin. He snapped his mouth shut and stared at me for a moment. Then, reaching out, he punched me lightly on the shoulder and chuckled. "Had me there—you did." He chuckled again. "I expect sometime you'll tell me the *real* story."

"I'll write you a book."

"Yeah . . . right." He laughed outright, then added, "You know, Meg's a beautiful woman—real sweet 'n carin' 'n all that." He winked. "You sure you weren't just havin' male man-o-pause?"

"Yeah." I could see his drift. "You might say that. My life damned sure has gone through a change." I winked back, then sobered. "I think I just grew up, and it's been painful. But even in the worst of the pain, I wanted it this way. I'm happier and have more respect for myself than I've ever had before." We sat for a moment in silence. I added, "I guess it just had to be. I am who I want to be—and that's not who Meg wants in a husband. Fact, it never was."

"I kin understand thet."

"Yeah? That's not the shitty part." I dropped my chin to my chest and shook my head. "Shitty part is, Meg's just not who I want my wife to be, either." Then, in afterthought, I added, "Meg's always liked who she was, and it was never really my right to ask her to change to suit me, but I did."

"And . . . did she?"

I looked Bart in the eye and, without expression, questioned, "Would Soo Ki?"

We looked at one another for a long moment. Was he, too, thinking of the hardheaded, I'm-always-rightness so characteristic of our Korean-born wives? It was clearly so, for simultaneously, we both began to grin.

"Shhh-eeee-hittt . . . NO!" we exclaimed together, then laughed so hard, the tears came to both our eyes.

As I was standing to leave, Bart, unwilling to look me in the eye, spoke up. "Uh . . . look, Jeff. It's cold out there. You're welcome to spend the night . . ."

While I knew his offer was genuine, clearly, my acceptance would put him in a bad spot with his wife. I knew she, too, had a big problem with my divorce.

I smiled and gave him a firm slap on the shoulder. "Thanks, Bart, but I think I'll just give Soo Ki a wide berth. Don't think the night's any colder than her feelings would be toward me just now."

He smiled his relief. I did, too. We both knew the price he'd pay for our friendship, had I stayed.

This time, it was the eyes of a friend watching me mount and ride off toward Durango. Though the wind in my face was a few degrees above freezing, the windchill was below. Still, I felt a certain warmth within me that wasn't there before.

Comb Ridge, Utah—Present Day

I wake at midmorning. It is the first good night's sleep I've had in God knows how long. Going outside, I discover the price for being inattentive. I huff around the tent, looking to get the handful of pinyon nuts I normally eat for breakfast, only to discover the sleeping bag sack used to store them is laying nearly empty. Just last night it bulged tight, full of nuts.

"What the fuck." My voice rises in confused anger and some fear. As I pick the sack up, they stream from the bottom back corner. I quickly turn it so the stream stops.

"Fuck! Fuck, fuck . . . fuuuu-ck!" I scream.

For some seconds, the cliffs all around echo it back. *"Fuck! Fuck, fuck . . . fuuuu-ck!"*

Looking closer, I see the tracks in the sand—chipmunk tracks! A veritable fucking super highway of them. The little bastards stole nearly all of my food supply.

"Ah . . . well, you can't blame them. You took it from them first."

Big D, what the fuck?

"What, you didn't notice? This canyon is mostly slick rock cliffs, and this ledge is one of the few places where any topsoil has accumulated. These chipmunks live in practically every little crack and crevice all around here. They count on these pinyon nuts, too—hoard them selfishly. It is the source of nearly all their food supplies, too, y'know."

Oh my God! What am I going to do now? There's only, what, a week or so of food here? If I'm not rescued soon, it's tits-up for me.

"Maybe you need to get busy living up to our agreement then."

But I don't see—

"I know you don't, and life is a matter of self-discovery. Do you really expect me to tell you? Haven't I dropped enough hints over all these weeks since you landed here?"

But—

"No buts! If it comes down to me telling you, then just know—your time is up. Hesitate then, and you will be accepting your death."

But—

"But . . . shiiiiiiiii-it!" Big D draws the word out on one long, exasperated breath. "I'll give you one last hint. You once said you wouldn't die for Meg. Why are you willing to die for Mona?"

Sometimes with the death of one's way of life, there remains a restless spirit—a spirit unable to sleep until it can say goodbye to all it has loved. Such spirits reside in each of us, and to have rest in the new way, each of us must bring them to a loving completion.

         Redneck Spirituality—Book Four

CHAPTER TWENTY-NINE

The Ghost of Durango Calling

Thirty minutes of frigid riding found me pulling off the blacktop and onto a graveled farm road to the east. On my left was the Johnson farm—320 acres of open fields, those closest freshly planted in winter wheat. Only a few relatively flat miles were left between it and the scarp of the La Plata Mountains. They towered majestically in the near distance, and I knew that along their base ran Highway 160 and those last ten miles east into Durango. To the south, on my right, was a dense forest of cedar and pinyon pine with occasional open patches thick with sagebrush and the intermittent, clumpy tufts of summer-dried, wild grasses growing from the alkaline clay soil.

  I felt an old intimacy with this road and with the land surrounding it, for I knew every foot. A half mile in, the road turned right. Just past the curve, I shut off the motor and sat silently astride my bike in the empty roadway, looking at the house I built there and lived in for so many years.

  It looked the same, and yet, much was changed. The grass I planted in the backyard had finally filled in, but the rustic pole fence was gone. I could clearly remember the feel of the chainsaw in my hands—the oily, two-stroke smell and howl of it—as wood chips flew. I cut and notched the poles when building it. For ten years, it stood there in my life, a barrier between our home and the outside world, more visually and mentally than physically protective. Now it was gone, rotted away, and disposed of by some unseen hands in time. The house now sported a new back porch, and aluminum panels replaced the asphalt shingles on the roof. No cars were in the U-shaped gravel drive, and it appeared no one was home.

Long moments I sat there, looking through a blur and feeling the hot tears burning their way across my near-frozen face. The chilled, autumn air was unusually silent yet familiar with the old scents of cedar, pine, and sage, and there was an old comforting and loved ambiance in the very being of the place, a certain wild and free freshness.

From the triple-walled, galvanized, tin smokestack on the roof drifted an almost invisible plume of wood smoke, and I knew it to be from a cedar log, smoldering its last in the big, black Jotul stove within. It stood freely on a huge slab of naturally rust-stained, scenic sandstone. I wondered if the door on the stove would be racked on its rails underneath, with only a fire screen in front so one could see the blaze. I so loved it that way. I'd almost forgotten . . .

An undetermined time slipped by as I sat staring, immersed in my memories. Suddenly, a woman's voice broke my reverie and yanked me back to the reality of the moment. I'd failed to notice as she'd ridden up on her bicycle and didn't know how long she'd been there, straddling her bike ten feet behind, observing me.

"Can I help you?" Her concern was genuine, though her look was perhaps tinged with a little fear for I'd jumped violently when she said it.

"Oh . . . uh . . ." Confused, and not a little sheepish, I stuttered, "Y-you must be the schoolteacher who bought this place." Even to me, the answer sounded inane, a little like a voyeur caught in the act.

"Yes, but that was more than ten years ago." Strange how her ancient history appeared as yesterday to me. "I haven't taught for several years now."

"Yes . . . well, I'm the guy who built this house."

"Oh." Her face cleared and she was openly curious. "Would you like to come in and see it again?"

I didn't answer right away, just took my time and considered her offer.

"No," I said softly, sadly, almost to myself. Then louder, "But thank you anyway . . . I do appreciate the offer. It's just that it's time for me to move on." With that, and a smile, I punched the Virago into life and once again rolled out.

In Durango, I gassed up at the gas station where I once worked. The pumps outside still looked pretty much the same—except all were now self-service and, like the rest of the world, accepted my plastic. Inside, things were different. Inside were only restrooms, fast food, and fast shopping, and I'd always remembered Durango as such a slow and lazy place. It seemed to be bending to the whims of the outside world.

"Jeff! How've you been?" It was Greg, now the manager, who greeted me so warmly. Though I recognized several others in the place, he was the only one who recognized me.

Greg had been one of those nice, Mormon boys hired at minimum wage back then, some eighteen years past. Now, getting reacquainted, I saw he was a man in his mid-thirties. We talked for a few minutes, then he brought out his wallet with his pictures. Married to a plump, Mormon mama, they were raising a half dozen just like themselves. As we talked, I realized a lot had changed, and at the same time, here, too, life was still much the same. The business was still owned by Green Oil, whose offices and warehouse were still in the building behind.

Greg said, "You remember Amanda . . . she still works in the office."

"Oh, really." My tone was nonchalant, belying the sudden leaping of my heart. I winked and said, "Maybe I'll step back there and just say, 'Hey—'"

On the way back to the office, my thoughts were on Mandy . . . her pretty face and her body. I remembered the passion mine once felt when just looking at hers back then. Our passions had always been held in check, something never expressed past a couple of stolen kisses in the warehouse.

Both married, only once had we made plans for more. Meg was visiting her family in Salt Lake that weekend, and I was alone. I'd lain awake for Mandy all night, but she'd not shown. Never being one to handle dishonesty very well, I knew an outright affair would be wounding to my own soul. Secretly, I was relieved. It was difficult enough in the years since just carrying the silent knowledge of such intention. Such a break in my integrity was wound enough. I'm glad our actions made it no deeper.

Clearly, it was always Meg whom I loved. So, what was Mandy about for me? Was she only hormonal? Yet now . . . I'm single. Is she? If so, how could it be with her now?

At the office, I found that most who were there I knew. There was D.P. Green, partner in the firm, Doris, still the secretary, even Bentley, who was once a truck driver, is now the dispatch manager. But Mandy? She hadn't returned from lunch.

I made the rounds, spoke to each one, all the while noting with interest the changes of time written in their eyes and on their bodies. Of those who could place me in their memories, I saw this same deep curiosity toward me—sort of an unspoken gauging and sizing of one another. I wondered if they saw the man I'd become, or just the same motorcycle bum as earlier Dennis all but called me?

Mandy's car pulled up just as I was leaving the office. She saw me through the windshield as she placed it in park and switched off the ignition, but her eyes slid from mine without recognition. She seemed to dismiss me from her mind as she picked up her purse. Opening her checkbook, she began to write an entry. I'd paused as our eyes met through the windshield, then walked the half dozen steps over to her door. Standing there looking at her, while she tried to ignore me, she was still a fine-looking woman who, I noted, had not aged that much. As such, was she just used to ignoring the advances of strange men? I didn't know but felt dismissed and considered taking it as a cue and leaving. I would have once, but now I realized it was just one possible interpretation and might be incorrect.

"Mandy," I called through the window.

She looked up, her eyes asking an unspoken question. Who is this stranger so familiar with her name?

"Mandy," I repeated, "it's me . . . Jeff!"

The truth about our passions—Mandy's and mine—was that it was really only a message. It was our souls crying out to our conscious minds, saying, "Look at this. There is a lie here, a dysfunction in this relationship with the one you are sworn to. This does not line up with the truth. Look at it. Deal with it. Get honest!" Neither Mandy nor I got honest, not back then.

For me? Honesty told of my need to be accepted, cherished, held in special esteem by my woman, even hungered for sexually. These needs felt met when I was with Mandy—never with Meg. With Meg, it seemed the other way around. It was I who held Meg in such cherished esteem, so much so that it kept me blind to the truth. Did Meg ever accept me, cherish me? I was certain she never hungered for my body. I never saw it in her actions, heard it in her words, or felt it in her touch.

No, I was not blind. My heart saw the truth. It just took my mind much longer to recognize it.

For Mandy, I don't know. Looking into her eyes, I saw the lies she told herself in order to stay comfortable, though miserable, in her marriage. Likely, they were similar to my own back then. I thought of the book I'd just finished writing. In fact, I had an early copy in my saddlebags—just a manuscript in a three-ring binder titled, *When a Love Dies . . . or Merely Grows Away*. It was a collection of the poems I'd written and would soon self-publish. In it, I expressed my journey from divorce to healing.

All were about getting naked and honest on the inside. Later, on the cover of its published edition, those poems were expressed—metaphorically graphically—in a picture of me naked, wearing only a cowboy hat. The reason the picture did not show complete nakedness was because, like most of humanity, I, too, hid my socially unacceptable passion.

Yes, the hat was hung on my head, but it did not shade my face. And, too, it hid but spoke loudly of my passion. I felt prompted to give it to her. Did it speak of a passion akin to hers, or did it just tell the truth of similar lies? For Mandy, perhaps my sharing was too honest—too naked. I am not aware of any changes she may have made in her life. I did not stay in touch. Has she, or will she? It was never my intent to change her. But as caring beings, all we can do is share our truths, give them as an offering, a gift to one another.

Gifts, remember, never have any strings attached. Whatever Mandy does with my gift will be what she wants and is okay with me. And, is there really anything "too honest" when we hold others as capable?

Perhaps that book was written for Mandy. It has since been shelved. Although, it was a hit with my friends, and all who knew me, or just knew of me and were curious. For the rest of the world, they seemed to get hung on the same peg as the hat on the cover. When there are enough of the former, perhaps it will again come off the shelf. It is a Law of Creation and my personal belief in those Spiritual Laws. Yes, ***everything is perfect, just as it is***. Perhaps that book's perfection was not premature, but it was written for Mandy and those few who, like her, now have a copy. Perhaps, too, its writing was only for my own healing.

Getting naked, as I did on the inside and the outside, was something no "normal" person would do. It took courage and a dedication to my beliefs to simply do it. Likely, it was only I who needed to get naked, for me, and I who needed to have such courage—and especially, to know it. Except for me, likely there were few who could see its true beauty when looking at my naked butt on the back cover.

Mandy and I had a dance in this ballroom of life. We related for a time. It is clear what her message was to me. I've often wondered what mine was to her. Was she, like Meg, living a dysfunctional thought system that said, *To love, one must suffer and sacrifice*? Perhaps then, her need was also to suffer with the one she had while wanting someone else—someone she couldn't have.

Did her thought system about her world say, *There is not enough—I can't have it all*? Perhaps with Meg, too, there were a few unavailable men to help her suffer in her marriage to me. And maybe they were more available to her than Mandy was to me. I see that possibility now, and it doesn't really matter.

This trip started as a small frolic, a motorcycle tour through my past. It ended as so much more—a resurrected being paying respects to the gravesite of who he was. Yes! I feel as if I've been resurrected. I don't say this to those who would hear it and just squirm on the pointed edge of sacrilege, but rather to those who will open their minds and just look. I say that because that person I was who lived in that past is dead, and the person who started this trip is not the same person who ended it. Have I been resurrected, or have I evolved—or both? I don't know or give a shit. I just know that the person I am now is someone I like.

Comb Ridge, Utah—Present Day

Now too dark to read even with the dim light of my cooking fire, I set the notebook containing this chapter aside. The temperature is dropping quickly as the evening advances into night. Even wearing my riding leathers, it is becoming hard to stay warm. I shiver, and the only word that comes to mind about this chapter is "surreal."

"Ah, yes, you did a ride through your past." Big D chuckles. The harmonics of his voice seem to add another layer of weird to that single word. "Was it a wake-up moment for you, looking at the people in your life who knew you back then—and how many you left so little impression on that they don't recognize you now? Have you changed so much, or did you just not mean anything to them back then?"

Seems not, Big D . . . I hear you. My stirring stick turns the mixture of a few crushed pinyon nuts and some inner pinyon bark now beginning to thicken in the heat of the fire. *I . . . I don't know what to say.*

"You might ask what, if anything, has changed? And why?"

I have to admit that back then, I was a self-centered asshole. I didn't care about anyone else and didn't do much of anything for anyone, either.

"And that has changed?" The red glow of his sight now has a look of intensity, but his grin seems to say he is playing with me.

Yeah, well, I think it has. I've spent most of the last twenty-five years serving others.

"Oh? Who? Name them." Yes, definitely playing with me.

No, Big D . . . I won't. If I did, it would be the same as me demanding recognition for it—like wiping shit on every good thing I ever did. I take a leisurely sip of pinyon needle tea from my canteen, shake my head, and add, *No . . . I won't.*

"I'm real glad you can see that, Jeff. Oh, you still have several chapters to write that cover more than eight years of your life." His grin has somehow sobered. "And you better hop to it. But for the here and now"—the grin is grim and seems to widen—"your shit is about to hit the fan."

We are all unique, and still, essentially the same. It is the uniqueness of our thinking from whence springs creative growth, philosophy, art, poetry, song, dance—all which is of delight to the human soul, one to another. Yet, for so many, 'unique' is labeled 'weird' and considered a source of shame. Only those with the courage to let their uniqueness show really leave much of a mark on this world.

Redneck Spirituality—Book One

CHAPTER THIRTY

Of Moose Milk and Horse Puckies

My mother's words sprang clear in my memory. "Horse pucky! Just a bunch of wackos and weirdoes who don't own a brain between 'em!"

Yes, that's about the best she'd ever said about those I now rubbed shoulders with here at the annual Whole Life Expo—my third attended. Even so, in looking around at the booths, I had to admit, it seemed as if some were indeed trying to out-freak the others. The expo was about opening minds and putting forth the latest information and products concerning the holistic way. True to this theme, all seemed to be presenting a thought system or reality that was slightly different from the norm, and most were quite logical to my own mind. Yet, all spoke of a dire need to purchase whatever techno, spiritually energizing foofaraw was being sold there. And yes, many seemed to be pushing that envelope well past the leading edge of gullibility. Clearly, there was enough moose milk here to flood a Roman bath house.

Still, at many booths, my heart felt a distinct kernel of truth, a seed that, when nurtured, could grow in service to my soul. There is a side to the human psyche that because it has before been impossible to see, it has only recently been recognized, confirmed, and measured by science. The intuitive power of the human mind to affect the behavior of matter on a subatomic particle level is now being explored. Secret government experiments, and use, of out-of-body data retrieval methods for spying are now coming to light. These are just two of the many. I have no interest or desire to discuss them all.

Contemplating science as it relates to government, for me, is an exercise in futility. Government exemplifies the breaking of the Spiritual Laws, not to mention the integrity of our minds and intuitive senses. These are but the tip of the iceberg of our spiritual power, and the icebergs are beginning to melt. How high, I wonder, will the seas of human consciousness rise? How far will mankind then sail on the tides when the winds of spiritual truths are harnessed? Will the change be homogenous, or will it first begin with the masses? It always seems to be that those with the most power operate from the most fear. What kind of world will mankind create when all are fully aware of just how powerful we really are? How we are, indeed, the sole creator of our lives. Yes, there is a Higher Power, and we are included, a part of it all. We really are just that powerful—and more. We are so much more than we can now even conceive . . . while the ice remains.

In one booth, I stopped to watch the computerized aura energies of a man. They were displayed on a monitor and shifted and shimmered with change as several different articles were placed in his hand. The idea was to show which items were nurturing and which were damaging to his personal energy field. Engrossed, I felt a touch on my arm, and a man's voice broke my reverie.

"Hi, don't I know you from somewhere?"

Turning, I studied him a moment before replying. His was the typical look one expected of a spiritual seeker. Long, graying, pony-tailed hair, in his mid-forties, his wrinkled and mustached smile matched a twinkle of fun in his eyes. I knew instantly I liked him.

"Don't know . . . you do look familiar. I'm Jeff," I responded, shaking his hand. "Do you belong to any of the spiritual groups around here?"

"Well, yes. I live out on Lone Cone, and we do hold weekly meditation groups at our place."

The street name was familiar. "I went to a meditation on Lone Cone one time. It was held at an adobe-style ranch house with high walls and a Koi pond in the garden owned by two gay guys."

"Yeah, that's us! My name's Denny." The man's demeanor was warm and open, as was his handshake. There was no hint of resentment over the fact I'd just singled out his sexual orientation as my main identifying factor. We talked pleasantly a moment or two more before going our separate ways. Much later, we met again and he introduced me to his friends.

This was my first meeting with Ramona—Mona as she preferred to be called. It came as a pair of jellied, aqua eyes appraised me intently. Her lovely face was cocked inquisitively to the side and angled upward toward mine in a curious posture I've since come to love as uniquely hers. It spoke clearly of her interest in me.

Our eyes locked in one of those timeless moments wherein one becomes conscious that one's life is about to change. There was no doubt in my mind as her name was presented. This woman would play an important part in my life. The introductions carried on around our small circle. "Willy . . . Sharon . . . Pat . . . ," and I touched each hand in turn. Yet, my eyes kept returning to Mona's.

She was a tall woman—only six inches shorter than my own six four—with the kind of high, wide cheekbones one usually sees on models. Her face angled down to a pleasingly firm jawline—strong, but not at all manly, with a lower lip that jutted slightly full, yet managed to look sensually inviting rather than pouting. Her body was shapely, flaring widely at the hips. Watching her walk away a moment later, I was surprised at the erotic fullness of her behind. Women with big butts have never even listed on my scale for attractiveness. This one somehow seemed to negate the scale.

That night, sleep did not come with its usual ease. Those eyes . . . those inquisitive eyes seemed to hang in my mind. Did they ask the same unspoken question for her as now troubled me—"Who are you to me?"

And for me, they brought up other questions. What was my relationship with Lucy now about? I'd not been dishonest with her. It was always clear that she was not the mate with whom I wanted to spend the rest of my life. Ours was simply a relationship of mutual support and growth with some great sex thrown in. We discussed it in depth, and we both knew eventually we'd take separate paths.

Were we now only marking time together? Stuck? Of late, I did not feel there was much growing going on for either of us. Her angry display when last we met, and its implications, said clearly that we had each served our purpose for the other. That was my feeling as we finished that last meal, both in silent contemplation. Mona's eyes, with their unfathomable question, seemed to be telling me it was so. The only relationship Lucy and I could now have was one of sex. Stuck in sex was not enough.

When one person in a relationship does not want to be there, the relationship becomes dysfunctional. Mona's eyes distinctly told me that I did not want to be with Lucy any longer—and it had nothing to do with Mona. Would her only purpose for me be that of messenger, to tell me these things? I had no intention of seeking her out, and somehow, I knew there would be no need. Regardless, my relationship with Lucy—at least the part that involved sex—would end when next I saw her. The decision made, I drifted into sleep.

Sunday dawned beautiful, a comfortably warm November day on the Las Vegas desert. It was the last day of the expo, and I relished the new thoughts and ideas presented with every lecture. Most were very insightful, giving much to think about, although one was almost comical.

The speaker told of how he'd been involved in a secret government experiment back in the forties, how he was transported into a future time and inhabited the body of a dying child. It was not the implausibility of his story that led to my disbelief, nor the largeness of his ego. I've seen truth proved in many an implausibility. It was the man's energy. There was an almost predatory feel in his neediness for others to believe. It seemed to say that he, himself, did not believe. Those telling the truth don't have such a burning need for validation.

Lunchtime found me buying a veggie burger from a food stall run by a group resembling nonaggressive Moonie types—that one, a rather weird-feeling oxymoron. Locating an open spot at one of the butcher paper-covered tables, I relaxed into my lunch while watching the crowd milling all around. There was a way-out-there feel to the whole place, and I found myself very comfortable in being a part of it. These were just ordinary folks who'd discovered a place where they felt safe to let their weirdness show. I wondered how many had the courage to be this honest every day.

Glancing to the side, I again found my eyes locked with Mona's. Her group sat at a table only twenty feet to my left, and her smile was friendly as she motioned me over. I was welcomed all around as, taking the only vacant chair, I sat down opposite her. The first few minutes were spent fielding questions from the group. They'd seen my self-published volume of poetry and were interested. Though she'd not said much, I was acutely conscious of Mona. She sat studying me, seemingly to be making a decision. Eventually, the conversation moved on. Abruptly, she got up and brought her chair around next to mine.

"I find you very interesting," she began. "What do you do?"

"Well, for now, I'm writing. I was a mechanic for thirty years but took a sabbatical to finish my current book. Don't think I'll ever go back," I added, almost to myself. "I sell my poetry book, do a little silversmithing, and coach part-time for a local seminar company. Oh, and I do personal life coaching as a business."

"Wow! Sounds like you're very accomplished."

"Thanks, but I don't see it that way. I've just had a lot of time lately to learn about myself and life. Some of it stuck." I paused, feeling a little disjointed about the energy that appeared to emanate from her scrutiny. She, too, seemed to find no attraction in my downgrading myself. Why was it so hard for me to accept praise? "I've just done a lot of growing since my divorce." Her eyes lit up, and I knew this last statement was what she most wanted to know. Taking the cue, I changed the subject. I was so much more comfortable when it didn't center on me.

"So, are you single and available . . . and do you like dirty, old men?" I asked boldly, knowing most women were uncomfortable with such open directness, yet was not surprised when she threw back her head and laughed with abandon. Then, still chortling, she replied.

"Yes . . . yes . . . and yes! Well . . ." She paused a moment, then qualified it. "That is to say, I am alone . . . well, in the process of a divorce. We've been separated about a year. Just haven't been in any hurry or interested in anyone." Her pause was pregnant, her smile open, before adding, ". . . until now."

"Oh-kaaay . . ." I said the word slowly, drawn out, also with a smile. "So, what are you looking for in a man?"

"Well, I'm seeking one who knows what he wants, isn't afraid to ask for it, and doesn't play silly games." Now she was grinning. "And I want someone who is spiritual . . . and creative . . . and likes me for who I am—that is, he doesn't have a need to change me."

Her words suddenly ended with silence and I knew she awaited my answer. The conversation around the table, too, had now stopped. In fact, it had slowed and quieted by several octaves from the time Mona moved her chair. Clearly, they were listening in attentively, though politely. They seemed to be hanging on every question and answer almost as much as I was.

"Great!" I paused. "That about covers it . . . well, except for one thing."

"What's that?"

"Do you like sex?" I asked evenly, directly, ignoring her friend Sharon across the table, now frantically clearing mango juice from her sinuses.

"You bet!" she said, laughing heartily. Was her laughter at the question or at her friend? I did not know. "Just haven't had any for a while." She finished with a shrug, obviously acknowledging it as much for herself as for me.

The conversation around the table now picked up again with a few nervous giggles and twitters. I looked at my watch.

"Karen Moore, the woman who runs the seminar company I coach with, is giving a lecture in ten minutes. Would you like to join me?"

"Sure," she said, and standing, we gave the others our leave.

Karen's presentation on personal growth was her usual professional best. Mona and I sat hand in hand until I disengaged mine to put my arm across her shoulder. Then we snuggled together comfortably. There was naturalness about it, almost as if we'd both come home. When the lecture ended, we stood to leave.

"There's another lecture," Mona mentioned, "one on Native American spirituality. It's given by Matal, a medicine man friend of mine." She smiled. "Wanna go?"

"Sure." We soon found ourselves in the theater of the complex, sitting arm in arm.

Science has proven the existence of the human energy field and has indeed recorded it easily for many years with Kirlian photography. Yet, it is something that many seem unaware of or just choose to ignore. I was not ignoring mine. In that theater with Mona, mine seemed to be doing a dance of ecstasy with hers. Not some la-la thing, but rather, it was a clearly felt, very noticeable touching and joining with a harmony of its own. We danced there together, somewhere beyond, but still felt by my consciousness. I didn't say anything until, in the darkened theater, I turned to Mona.

"Do you feel it, too?"

There was a sparkle in her eyes as she nodded her assent, knowing exactly what I meant.

Comb Ridge, Utah—Present Day

"Ah, yes, she was the one. She gave you what you needed—at the time."

Yes, Big D. I take a deep breath and let it back out. *For a time.* A cold breeze stirs my hair as I gaze out over the gulf of Comb Canyon. Somehow, it feels similar to the gulf of my life just now—big, empty, and cold.

"So why did it end? And why did you just stop writing at this point?"

I didn't . . . 'just stop.' I just couldn't find a way to continue and still stay in integrity. The writing of my story—The Courage of a Butterfly—was mostly done during the eight years I was with her, as was this last part covering my life since that time in the ICU.

"You haven't answered the question, Jeff. You *did* stop with the writing of this book—here, with this chapter." He pauses, silently regarding me, and for once, I cannot read his countenance but know his last word comes as a demand. "Why?"

I cannot hide my guilt. *Ahhhh Christ, Big D! I stopped writing because I couldn't see myself as a man if I broke Mona's confidence. I thought to leave it at the place where we were so connected. It seemed like a great ending for this book—much better than the sick, personally embarrassing ending this relationship was headed toward.*

"Would have been a lie . . . wouldn't it? And, as you say, *a sick one* at that." He shakes his head slowly and I can feel his sorrow. "The truth you refuse to acknowledge concerning her is no less life shattering as the one you lied to yourself about for all those years concerning Meg. Do you expect the result to be anything less than the same?"

Lied? Big D . . . I was always honest with her.

"Again! The lie was to yourself. From that night you two first made love, you ceased to be connected. Are you going to deny it to me, too?"

No. I won't deny it. I felt it, too. I just couldn't quite put my finger on it. Still, it isn't plain to me. I mean, I dealt with her about that. I accepted her and made it work.

"Accepted her—that you did. And you didn't lie to her about it. Again, you lied to yourself. You accepted her. You never . . . accepted . . . *it*."

Yes. Again, I sigh and study the panorama of beauty laid out before me. *Is that why I'm here, Big D?* I glance quickly at him, then just as quickly look away. *I know honesty is part of my promise to you, for the reprieve you gave me on my life.*

"That's right." His chuckle this time is sad. Somehow, I am reassured of the fact that I can again read him, but alarmed with the sadness I hear in his words. I swallow, almost afraid to ask my next question, knowing I can do nothing but accept his answer.

So, now . . . is it time for me to be leaving this life?

"You have pens, and you have empty notebooks with you here." Once again, I turn my head, this time to meet his gaze. In the smoldering glow of his empty eye sockets, I note a certain expectancy. "Are you going to finish the story—in honesty?"

Yes, Big D, I will. I swallow to relieve the sudden tension in my throat, then add, *. . . and thank you—again.*

"Don't thank me yet. There are two lies you have been telling yourself. The other one you still don't see." He is fast fading from my sight, and in the end, there are only his words ringing in my ears. "And you won't get off this ledge alive . . . unless you do."

Big D, with the story I have to tell now, it is difficult for me to see any joy in getting off this ledge alive. Were it to involve only me, I wouldn't give a rats ass about telling it. I've taken pains not to reveal the identities of the characters in this book. Even so, they themselves will know. I wish it weren't so. The characters in this book all have their faults, but not one of them is a villain. Have you ever read a book that didn't have a villain? Big D? Are you listening . . . Big D? Goddammit!

As of now, it does have a villain. I don't know if he is listening, but I throw my thought out there anyway. *Yeah, Big D, you're probably busting a ball laughing because the villain of this book now is none other than the asshole telling you this last part of this story—me. Only an asshole would ever tell it.*

From somewhere out there, sounding tinny in the distance, I hear his answer. "Maybe so, Jeff, maybe so. But an honest asshole."

It ain't them that likes me . . . it ain't them that hates me . . . I've touched them—the first in validation and acceptance, the rest in opportunity. The Spiritual Law states, *What we don't like in others is but the reflection of what we don't like in ourselves.* It's really them that don't give a shit who worry me. Either I'm so far ahead they don't connect, or I'm so far behind that were they to fart, I likely, in the mirror of them, wouldn't smell the essence of me.

Redneck Spirituality—Book Four

CHAPTER THIRTY-ONE

Loving Mona

Lucy went quickly, but not easily. I would have liked it to be as a simple shift from lover to friend. That was not the choice she wanted and was, as it must be for her, now. Remember the Law—*I am the creator*? How it means that there is nothing in my life I don't hold a deciding hand in creating, especially concerning my feelings? While Karen's seminars exposed her to the laws, that part she clearly didn't accept. I knew it when she threw those egg shells of her emotions at my feet in the restaurant. Still, somehow, I hoped it was not so.

The IQ Seminar that month occurred on the next weekend following the expo. Sunday evening was graduation. I attended it with Mona. Afterward, some of my friends met to celebrate at a local nightspot. Mona and I were there.

I always had friends while with Lucy, many of them female. She never indicated, nor did I believe, she felt threatened by any of them. Our sexuality was held as exclusively between us. She knew I'd be honest and tell her when I was ready to move on. That night, I did.

Lucy came late. She joined the group at our table, was welcomed, and was introduced to Mona, just as she had been to my other friends in the past. But this night was different. My decision to end our relationship—at least on the sexual level—was already made. I had not seen her in the weeks since that day at the restaurant. This was it, the first opportunity.

Intuitively, I knew she'd struggle with it and did not want it to be this night. Yet, it was not in me to go through a night of pretense and dishonesty. Something had changed with my intentions toward her, and I respected myself, and Lucy, too much not to deal with it immediately. When the others moved off to the dance floor, I took the now-empty seat next to her and leaned close.

"Lucy, I need you to know"—I paused and looked her in the eye to be sure she was listening—"I'm interested in this woman." Her shocked look was clear and it took courage to continue. "Do you understand?" Only silence and a disbelieving stare answered me. "It's time for us to move on. Our relationship needs to change." There was now anger in her eyes. Clearly, she felt betrayed. "Can we stay friends?"

Standing abruptly, she gathered her purse. I rose with her, my hand out, touching her shoulder. She shook it off. "Sure, Jeff . . . sure." But the look in her eyes belied her words. "Have a nice life, *Jeff*." Then turning, she stalked out the door.

Watching her go, I felt an emptiness inside. Our friendship, too, was over. I was clear with her about it back then, when we began. Did she not believe me when I first told her that this was how it would be for us? Obviously, that was only how I saw it in my own mind.

But for Lucy—yeah, sex was involved. Like the rest of the world, she expected to be paid off in what, loyalty? Didn't Lucy understand that the only thing we owed one another was honesty? I'd not lied, then or now. What we had together was a mutually enjoyable thing. In my mind, no one owed anyone anything for it. Honesty is about our own integrity, the important part for we who are sworn to living the Spiritual Laws—the real truths in life.

The eggshells she scattered about in that restaurant said clearly, she lied. In her mind, I was responsible for how she chose to feel about everything. Our relationship had nowhere to go, except to drama and control. That went against everything I now believed. That was about a "normal" relationship—one run on fear, not love. Would I ever find a woman willing to be responsible for her own feelings?

With Mona, I'm going to find out before any sex this time.

Sitting down next to Mona, I remained silent for a time, lost in thought. *Was there a more loving way for me to do this? Could I have been more honest with Lucy—then or now?*

I was at a loss for words, and my throat ached as I turned to look at Mona. "I didn't want it to be this way." She did not hear my exchange with Lucy but saw what transpired, and there was compassion in her eyes.

"I know, Jeff . . . I know."

* * *

Mona and I became constant companions. She virtually moved in with me. Daily, on her way home from work, she stopped to check on her daughters and then came home to me. Both daughters were mature and capable young ladies—one was just finishing high school, the other, well along in a career in home furnishings. They both seemed happy for their mother that she'd found a life of her own—at first.

Though we slept together, Mona and I did not go to sex for nearly two weeks. We spent our time talking, riding the Virago, going to movies, dancing, and in all other ways, getting to know each other.

Breaking up with Lucy was profound for me. I did not want a repeat performance—another sexual friendship going nowhere once the initial learning was complete. It seemed that all my relationships went that way, a few hanging on much longer than needed just because of the comfort, and the sex. It was difficult to see them as perfect and complete. With Mona, I took time first to see if she was indeed someone with similar joys and interests, someone whose passions matched mine, someone whose path in life had the same destination. This time, sex did not cloud my sight, and finally, when it happened, her passions there, too, were a match for mine.

* * *

After years of working as a bakery manager, lifting and stooping with heavy pans and buckets of mix, Mona was a physically strong woman. Her youth spent on her family's Montana cattle ranch assured her of that heritage. Yet, making love that first time, I found she had muscles up in there I never expected. Hands free, she milked me that night exactly like the firm grip of a farm girl milking the family's cow. Yes, sexually, she was a match for me.

Then, after a short period of intimate conversation, I went in for seconds. Beginning with her lips, I allowed mine to flex around, giving them a softer, more active feel, while my tongue ran across and parted her own lips, then danced softly against hers. I was pleased to discover that she did not do that thing where her tongue struggled to rape my tonsil. It seemed many women these days think of that as erotic.

Then, pausing for a few short nips and licks along the side of her neck, I moved on down to the perfect mounds of her breasts, ample but not at all sagging. I licked and nibbled and sucked in the hardened nubs of her nipples. Meanwhile, my middle finger stroked up and down the cleft of her nether lips, sometimes rubbing lightly across her clit, sometimes sinking deep into her chasm. When her sighs changed from throaty moans to shrieks and pants, I quickly slid down, while at the same time, her knees drew up and back, allowing unobstructed access.

It was still slick with the remnants of my own essence. I dearly loved going snorkeling in the cove of a woman's most private place. The few times I'd tasted my own sex there only added to the excitement, just as did the sometimes-strong scent of a woman's sex. But as my tongue sank into her depths, I realized this time, it didn't taste anything near pleasant and that scent was much more than just strong. I paused, drawing back, but from the bucking up of her hips recognized that she was in the midst of her orgasm, so I dove back in until she was finished. With two fingers buried, rubbing the G-spot up inside behind her pubic bone, and my tongue and lips rolling all around and over her clit, her orgasm ended loudly, with gusto.

Later, lying beside her with her head cradled in the crook of my shoulder, she sighed with contentment. But my own feelings were far from content. *My God! What do I do with this? I care about this woman, and in every other way, we are perfect together. Keeping my mouth shut and slinking off into the night is just not an option, but how do I tell her?* I, too, sighed, then recognized the throaty tones of Big D's voice in my ear, as he has often come to me.

"Honesty, Jeff, with honesty—and do it now. It is our agreement, remember?" I knew Mona couldn't hear him, just as I knew that keeping my agreement with him was what kept me alive.

But why does he feel the need to remind me? Surely, he knows I would find a way to tell her in time.

His chuckle in my ear told me that I might once have gotten away with that lie to myself, but not now.

"Mona," I began. "Please don't take this badly, but there is something I need to tell you."

"Oh, God." Her head snapped up. "I didn't think I needed to ask. Surely, you don't have some STD or—"

"What? No . . . nothing like that." I shook my head and wiped my chin. "It's just that . . . well, I don't know how to say this . . ."

She was up on one elbow and stared intently into my eyes. "Just say it, Jeff."

"It's just that . . . well, you're pretty strong down there."

"Yeah, I know." Mona smiled proudly. "I've done a lot of work on my Kegel muscles."

"Yes, you sure have—but no, that's not what I'm talking about. I mean . . ." I paused, then just blurted it out. "It doesn't taste good and smells pretty bad, also."

Her look of concern changed to one of horror as her mouth fell open. "What? How . . . how *does* it taste?"

"Well, a little pissy, but mostly"—I shrugged, finding it difficult to look her in the eye—"well . . . bad." That was the nicest word I could think to use.

Her mouth was still open but worked up and down without anything coming out. I added, "But what do I know. It's probably just some off-strain of bacteria or yeast or something."

That's right, tell her she's got a germy pussy. I almost cringed at the lameness of my words. "Nothing some medicated douche won't take care of." To her look of horror was now added an element of astonishment.

"I don't douche!" There were storm clouds in her eyes. "It's not healthy and it's not natural, but I will go see my doctor about this."

"Look, Mona, I didn't mean to upset you. Just thought you'd want to know." I said it, then wondered if it sounded as lame to her as it did to me. Yes, *lame* was only a poor substitute for describing this whole conversation. She turned away to lay stiff in a fetal position.

"Mona, please look at me." No response.

"Mona, haven't you ever known someone with really bad breath?" Only a slight grunt that sounded like exasperation was my answer.

"As a friend, did you tell them?"

With a quick jerk of the blanket, she drew it closer around herself.

I sighed. "D'ya think maybe it would have been a kindness if you hadda?" With that, I fell silent.

Into my mind came a chuckle of amusement in Big D's standard bottom-of-the-barrel- tinged tones. "You surely didn't expect a better outcome—did you?"

No, Big D . . . and I'm sorry if I didn't tell her just how really rank it was. Have I been honest enough with her? I'd never purposefully break my agreement with you. Do I need to say something more, d'ya think?

"No, Jeff. You did it as gently as possible. It's up to her to be honest with herself."

* * *

Two days later, Mona arrived a little later than usual. At dinner that evening, she addressed the business at hand. "Jeff, I saw my doctor today."

I put down the fork that was halfway to my mouth and waited silently. When nothing was immediately forthcoming, I prompted, "And?"

Mona looked me in the eye, and her next words, when they came, sounded almost like a challenge. "She says that there is nothing wrong—that it is just my natural smell. She says you are just being way too picky."

Now it was my turn to look like a beached carp as I searched my mind for a reply. *Clearly, this doctor person has never munched on another woman's pussy—much less on Mona's.*

Even as I thought it, I realized how that was the least acceptable response I could make. In fact, I realized from her challenging tone that her mind was made up, and any attempt to change that would be the same as trying to change her—rightfully so. There is that law, **Everything begins with a thought—change your mind, change your life.** Me trying to change her that way would be playing the game of control that most "normal" couples played and then called a loving relationship—drama and control instead of real love. And that was something I just didn't do. I wanted more with Mona, more than I'd ever gotten from any of my previous relationships. I thought she was someone enlightened enough to give that to me.

"Mona, this doctor you went to, I know she's a holistic practitioner, but is she a real medical doctor?"

"Real? Damned straight!" Mona's face was getting red. "She's got a wall full of certifications."

"Okay." I spread the fingers on one hand, held it palm out in acceptance, and left it at that. So did Mona.

* * *

It could be that was why, about a year into our relationship, Mona asked me to try out a session with her friend Sharon, a psychic counselor. "She's really good at counseling—very intuitive—and makes a good living doing it."

I knew of those who used their intuitive gifts to counsel others. Some were very good at it.

"How much is *it* going to cost me?"

"Not a thing." Mona smiled. "We're very good friends, and we do each other favors all the time. I just think you will find it a really interesting spiritual experience."

"Spiritual experience?" I squinted my eyes and cocked my head a little to the side. "Is there any other reason for me to go?"

"No . . . no other reason."

Was I right to question her reasoning? I knew of just one point of contention in our relationship—the douche thing—but Mona was right about that and I'd not brought the subject up, not even once. A woman does not want to upset the balance of natural bacteria in her coochie. And here I was, telling her that hers wasn't natural, given the smell.

Ah . . . but then, no matter how badly one stinks, they don't notice it any more than another person might notice when their thinking gets to stinking. Clearly, Mona doesn't know what it should smell like. She's never buried her face in another woman's pussy, much less her own. Does she think my thinking is stinking? Hell, maybe she's right about that.

* * *

It was only natural to think that Mona was now telling me that my thinking was stinking. Did she want me to go douche out my mind? I didn't know, but I was past being that person who would have taken offense, who once saw himself as a victim and never missed a chance to validate it. "Okay." I shrugged, then went along with her program.

Sharon was an attractive blonde of average size and well-shaped. Her counseling was done in her living room, darkened, with only a few candles to light the night. She started by placing a tape recorder on the coffee table between two candles, next to a bowl of tumble-polished, semi-precious stones.

"I always record my sessions, Jeff. Hope you don't mind. If you do, just know that you are the one who gets the tape, and you can do whatever you want with it." It seemed fair enough. I nodded.

"No problem." And with that permission, she punched the tape to life and got down to business.

"So how is life happening for you these days, Jeff? I hear you've been writing a book."

"Yes, I'm self-publishing a book of poems and searching for an agent for the first novel."

"Novel? I thought it was an autobiography?"

"It was, but when you write about the people you've known, sometimes they take offense and want to sue you, so you have to change things, people and places, names, who did what, y'know. And that means it has to be fiction loosely based on a true story. Originally, it was the absolute truth, but now that I'm going to publish it . . ." I shrug.

"You're not okay with that, are you?"

"It has to be. Doesn't mean I can't tell the story truthfully, it's just that I can't say it is. Besides, it's not about the story of my life anymore."

"It's not?" Her eyebrows were knitted together. "But don't you want people to know it's the truth about your life?"

"It's just a story . . . Sharon. Everyone's got one, but the important part of mine is what I learned about life. Not everyone gets to meet the Grim Reaper. Of those who do—and survive—not all have the courage to face the things I've faced or pay the price of learning the things I've learned." Again, I shrug. "Hearing the things I have to say may give them that courage. Will they accept it? Dunno. But change—not knowing who you're going to be—is always scary. It does takes courage, especially when you don't know the price."

"My God!" She is staring wide-eyed at me. "I'm beginning to feel like you should be counseling me."

"Well, I am a personal life coach. But you haven't asked for coaching, so just kick me if you feel like I'm stepping on you. Mona thinks I need your counseling, and me? Well, I am curious."

"Oh . . ." Sharon paused, eyeing me with what seemed to be her own curiosity. "Speaking of Mona, how is your relationship?"

"Great!" I smiled then added, "I was beginning to think I'd never meet a woman who could ever 'get' me, y'know?"

"What about sexually? Does she 'get' you sexually?"

"Hey, you were there at the expo." I chuckled. "You saw me lay the 'sex bomb' on her in front of you and all her friends."

"Yes, I . . . we sure did." Sharon's laughter joined my own. "But what about after? One question isn't a discussion, y'know."

"Ah . . ." *So, this is why Mona wanted me to speak with her psychic counselor friend. Only one way to deal with it—straight on and with honesty.*

"Look, Sharon. Yes, there is one thing that I've obviously been sent here for you to fix."

Caught in the act, I watched it all cross her face in the next instant—shock, confusion, a touch of alarm—but she recovered quickly. "So . . . ya wanna talk about it?"

I just looked at her silently for a long moment, watching the unease build in her body language—a slight stiffening in the movement, or rather the non-movement, of her body and the way her eyes now avoided mine. Then, taking a deep breath and letting it gust back out, I answered, "Sure . . . why not. It's why she sent me." I paused an even longer moment, collecting my thoughts—long enough that she felt the need to prompt.

"And . . ."

"Shit, I can see that Mona feels it is my problem and not hers. And yeah . . . she's right." I paused, reluctant to discuss something this personal. She again prompted.

"And just what is the problem?"

She was asking. I let her have both barrels. Calmly, quietly, I pulled the trigger. "It is just that Mona has the nastiest tasting, rankest smelling pussy I've ever eaten."

"What!" Her mouth fell open, and she appeared to disbelieve what she was hearing. Her mouth remained open while I explained.

"Look, it's clear that Mona has no intention of doing anything about it, so yes . . . it is my problem. A long time ago, I learned the hard way that you can't change other people—not if they don't want to change. I was honest with her, told her about my problem. She saw her gynecologist, who told her it was her natural smell and I was just being picky. It's clear who she believes. So that means it's up to me to change me."

"You? What do you mean?" Her mouth snapped shut.

"Yeah, me. I can change me."

"How . . . what? How—"

"Oh, it's really simple. I have to accept her exactly how she is."

"Huh?" Her mouth was open again.

"My only decision is, do I stay or do I go?"

"And . . . and . . . and—" Mouth still open, she eyed me aghast and was now beginning to sound like a stuck record. I cut her off.

"Everything else about her is perfect. It's a small price to pay. I'm staying."

"But . . . but . . . but—" Again, with the stuck record.

"But?" Again, I cut her off.

"But what about your own needs?"

I chuckled. "Eating pussy is not really a need."

"But . . ."

"Look, neither one of us is a jealous person and we both like sex." I shrugged. "We've talked about the possibility of swinging."

"Who would you swing with?" I had her curious now.

"Well, I don't know. Couldn't be strangers . . . would have to be a couple we both know and like—oh, and of course, trust. But I'm not attracted to any of our friends, except . . ." *Wait! I can't tell her that.*

"Except who?"

Oh God! Trapped by one ill-advised word and my promise to Big D—honesty . . . shit! How can I say this without her thinking . . .

"Look, I am *not* trying to put the make on you, but the truth is, you're the only friend I know who I am the least bit attracted to." I hurried to add, "But seriously, I don't see that as a possibility. Yes, we've discussed swinging, but it's probably not a viable solution. If it is totally—*only*—about me getting a chance to enjoy the taste of someone's pussy, it is definitely not viable."

She seemed to take that at face value and smiled. Then, appearing to realize what I'd really said, she giggled slightly and let it pass.

But I wouldn't let it pass, not without clearing the matter up.

"Look at it this way. As a child, my mother would often feed me asparagus. She loved it. Me? It always gave me the dry heaves and I tried to swallow it down quickly. Not eating it was never an option. She always said, 'It's all in your head. You can get to like it if you try.' Maybe it was the fact that I had no choice because asparagus never got to tasting any better to me."

"But what does that have—"

Again, I cut her off by answering her unspoken question. "Because Mona loves oral sex, I can't, in true conscience, deny it to her. Still, her taste hasn't gotten any better—and I've never said another word about it—but maybe, like asparagus, I've begun to swallow it down a little too quickly as well. Maybe that's why she sent me to see you."

With that, my time was up, more so than I realized. I left her house, tape in hand, and felt like I'd dodged a bullet.

Yes, I had—for eight years. It took that long for that bullet to plow into the back of my head and blow my life apart.

Comb Ridge, Utah—Present Day

The weather now is so cold that I find it difficult to write these words legibly, but I feel I must. What I do with this part of this book is distasteful to me personally, and yet . . . I glance out over the overcast, brooding features of Comb Wash. Is it just my own feelings with what I have to reveal here that causes me to see my world so dark and devoid of joy?

"Kinda feeling like an asshole, are you?" Big D speaks from his spot nearby on the edge.

Well, yeah. Certainly, what I need to divulge in staying honest is something I don't want to even look at. Fuck, Big D. Isn't there some other way?

"You know the Spiritual Laws—those simple statements that always hold true in life. They require honesty." He ducks his head, and the glow of his sight sharpens. "You're sworn to being honest—it's part of our agreement."

This is the first time I've not wanted to be since we met. Wish I could blame someone or something. I had thought to tell that lie of omission—even tried to convince myself it was not a lie. I reasoned that Mona and I riding off into the sunset would make a great ending for this story. After all, we were together a long time.

"Yes, Jeff, for all anyone would know, that lie would have felt good. But honesty often doesn't feel good. Don't cha know that feeling good is one of the biggies why people tell lies?" Looking at his grin tells me that he is enjoying himself with my discomfort. "In fact, *you* and Mona's reluctance to deal with the issue honestly together is why you're on this ledge. Mona told herself that lie, and you let her get away with it. This clusterfuck was not that Mona's coochie stank." His grin appears to widen. "It is really about the lies. You both told them."

What do you mean?

"She told herself that you were just being picky. Your lie was in making her stinky pussy somehow okay with you. It wasn't."

But I didn't want to get into all that drama and control of trying to change her.

"So, you lied to yourself that it didn't matter, that just being with her and loving her made it worth it. And now here you are, getting one of the hardest lessons of your life."

But I didn't want another relationship that was based on fear— one where my love was a struggle against her fear. Christ, Big D! Haven't I had enough of them?

"Well, you certainly don't have one now."

Shiiiiii-it! I sigh. *You're right, Big D.*

"Yeah . . . sucks to be you. But look at the bright side."

Huh?

"You're free." He chuckles. "And there is that Spiritual Law— **There is equal joy to be found in every sorrowful event if we will look for and accept it.**"

You lost me.

"Remember how I told you that you were going against all three things of our agreement?"

Ye-aaaah?

"You've had the courage to be honest, but following your joy is the other, and you don't yet even see it. And you still won't get off this ledge alive until you do."

But—

"Yeah, I know, 'Butt' . . . and you are an asshole." Again, that chuckle. "Cheer up. At least you are a brutally courageous, honest asshole. And that 'equal joy' thing? It could be better than you've ever dreamed possible."

With fingers pointing inward, you say the words, "The correction ALWAYS goes here."

Carol Reynolds—Vision Seminars

CHAPTER THIRTY-TWO

The Correction Always Goes >HERE<

The sun dropped down beyond the rim of the cliffs, leaving behind the orange and crimson of the clouds to belay its now departed sentiments. And belay they did, speaking clearly of the funeral fires still burning with the lingering of this Las Vegas summer. So much has happened since Mona and I first met.

This day, the soapy bubbling of our beers helped us wash the heat away, as sitting atop a picnic table, we watched the beauty of this sunset fade, quietly talking and enjoying one another's company. The overlook here above Red Rock provided us the ideal spot from which to watch the sacred perfection of our world around us.

Gradually, the cars around departed. When the darkness finally fell in earnestness, we found ourselves alone with the silence of the desert. Together then, we touched one another's passions. Laying her across the table, we made slow, exquisite love. There is a specialness to sharing such love beneath the stars, of displaying the clean clearness of our passions before God, nature, and it all, a specialness strengthened only with the ride back . . . us, the wind, and the throaty, satisfying purr of my Virago.

Yes, for me, love with Mona came easily, naturally, not at all as I thought it would be. Certainly, it did not come as some mad infatuation with all the accompanying drama that the world seems to expect. There were none of those insecure questions in my mind, nor did I hear them from hers.

Does she feel about me the same way I do her? What can I do to make her love me more? How do I need to be showing up to be who she wants? Will she accept this or that about me? How can I keep her from finding out my hidden shame, or can I change myself so she'll like me anyway?

No. There was none of that silly shit. Those fear-based, adrenalin-run ways that many viewed as love were absent from ours. I accepted who I was, so did she, and our love developed easily, effortlessly, and quickly.

She was not the small, trim, petite woman Meg was, the one my conscious mind pictured she must be. Those things were all about the "outside." Inside, she was truthful and authentic. As I began to know her for who she was—to let go of my old picture—the picture changed. Her sturdy frame, and the fleshiness of her full behind, became things I cherished. As my admiration for her grew, so did my appreciation for the feel of her strong body in my arms.

And Lucy? Though she dropped abruptly from my life, I still cherish her memory and have always been glad to see her on the few occasions later when accidentally we met.

As for sex with Mona, perhaps my mother was right. Maybe I didn't give asparagus a fair shake. As the years slipped by, the taste of Mona's coochie became a non-issue, especially when coupled with the flare of her passions that munching on her taco meant to her. The experience of her holding on to my ears while screaming in worship—"Oh God, Oh God, Oh God"—non-stop was as an orgasm to my male ego, an amazing experience.

Already an artist in clay sculpture, Mona was fascinated with my silver and stonework. Too, she loved riding shotgun on my bike, and camping turned out to be perhaps her greatest joy. For many years, she'd been spiritual in her intuitive senses, even at times augmenting her income as a psychic channel. The personal growth work I was involved with as a life coach turned out to be her missing link. She eagerly delved into the learning and coaching with me.

After going through the WeCoach program, and in seeking to be my professional best as a coach, I joined the Coach U program and Mona joined with me, a partner in my coaching business. Although it stretched our budget, it also stretched us personally. Coach U is recognized as an international leader in the burgeoning field of training personal and business coaches. Eventually, we graduated, although we didn't stop there.

In her own personal growth work, Mona, like me, has paid her dues. There are no free lunches, remember? There's great joy in personal growth—and sometimes, there's great sorrow. The joy is a given. The sorrow is always optional, a choice one sometimes makes when paying the price. Still, it is best to know the price.

Personal growth is about following one's own heart in consciously living the true joys of life and being exactly who you want to be. Isn't that the natural way to be? That's something that flies in the face of what is considered normal.

For the 'normal' world, this is not how we were taught. Like most, Mona and I were taught to live our lives for our loved ones, that it was admirable for us to live our lives to fulfill their joy. We were not accepted being who we were. Rather, we were required to be who they wanted us to be. Yes, our loved ones had their own picture of how life should be. We were expected to live within their pictures, and for the most part, we did.

But "living the true joys of life and being exactly who you want to be"—that's where the "growth" part comes in. Most people have no clue about their joy, or who they are, much less who they want to be. The growth part is about looking inside and discovering those truths.

And speaking about one's truth, figuring that out requires one to know what the truth is about life, those Spiritual Laws. You can't apply the truth to your life without knowing what the simple truth is about all life.

And that brings us to the Law of Responsibility—***Making someone else responsible for our happiness is never functional, just as taking responsibility for their unhappiness is not also***. But that is possibly the worst lie that we have all been taught.

The lies nearly all of us are taught in growing up in our society, our religions, and the ancient "family wisdom" of our parents is actually the obstacle. Yes, growth is about discerning the truth from the lies.

The lies culminate in drama, and not playing our part in other people's drama almost always ends in us paying the price in our acceptability by them. Sadly, this is why most part company.

For Mona and me, the reward of our personal growth is to live joyful lives that work. The people in our lives accept us as we really are, not just as someone we pretend to be. They are people who dance with us to the song of our souls—no struggles, no drama, no phony acts put on for acceptability. For us, there is often stretching but seldom struggle.

Real acceptability, like love, is a gift. It carries no price tag. While we may think we are giving it to others, in reality, we are giving it to ourselves. Holding others acceptable is a state of grace, effortless, and nurturing to our own souls. Even those loved ones who left our lives and made us unacceptable in their minds can still be acceptable in our own.

Yes, like me, Mona was tuning in to the rhythm of the universe. We quickly created our own song, and it was not one her daughters would dance to. She would no longer even attempt to buy their acceptability, especially when the price they demanded was her life with me. Before me, she'd lived her life for them. Now she lives it for herself . . . with me.

The universe requires no price for the dance. Only we do—we who lay that bill on one another, we who don't know how to love. Mona eventually paid the price with her daughters.

* * *

When one learns a new dance, there is a period of conscious learning and doing before it becomes an unconscious thing to move with the new rhythm one now hears. As Mona began her divorce process in earnest, it began to go the way such things often do. Concerned, she came to me.

"John is getting ugly. He just flies into a rage when I try to talk to him about this divorce." Her pretty eyes were filled with frustration. "He says he's going to take me for everything!" I regarded her a few moments before answering, noting the worry and the anger.

"It doesn't have to be so . . . y'know?" I said it quietly, reassuringly, and perhaps, too, in gentle reminder of how she was no one's victim.

"What do you mean?"

"Well . . . John wants to go to war here with you, true?"

"Oh, yeah . . . big time!" She groaned.

"Then the question is, are you going to war with him?"

Mona sat there, frozen for a moment in realization. "That's true! I don't have to play my part in his war!"

"Exactly!" I prompted. "Now, how can you make it a win/win? What does he need here to feel he's a winner?" I grinned. "Nor do you need to be a loser. What do you need to leave this feeling okay with him?"

"I'll go talk to him," she concluded, "and whatever he says, I won't go to anger and war . . . I'll go to solution. This is going to be fair!" Her voice now carried a note of determination and conviction.

That's exactly what she did. Every time John got angry or tried to bully, Mona calmly restated, "This is going to be fair. Now, what do you need to make this work for you?"

For him, it turned out to be the money. He wanted his freedom from alimony and he wanted his retirement—all of it. For Mona, what was important was her home. They made a trade—her interest in his alimony and retirement for his interest in the house. The bills were minor and soon divided up agreeably.

The divorce then happened quickly. They were in and out of the courts as smoothly as KY jelly, and no one got screwed. There was no war, no court-ordered sell-off of the house, no years of resentment over the forced sharing of his retirement, and no one going bankrupt in an attempt to make the other pay. Best of all, there were no rich lawyers getting richer by feeding on misery and immaturity.

* * *

Mona left the marriage with a new understanding and compassion for John. She is okay with her present relationship with him, but that was something she could not give to him.

"He is so resentful." Her face was wrinkled with worry.

"Why? Seems like you came to a win/win agreement? Wasn't it his initial decision to leave you and the marriage?"

"I think he's just jealous." She shook her head and shrugged. "I have you, and we're happy together. He's got no one."

"And why does this have to concern us?" I reached out, took her face between my palms, and brushed the worry lines away.

She looked up, the worry lines right back as before. "You don't know him. He's vindictive—and he's been talking with the girls."

It turned out there was cause for her to worry. Their minds were, by then, fertile to his brand of fertilizer.

The months Mona spent here living with me in my home were not easy for her daughters, Nanette and Wendy. Mona still bought the food and stopped in frequently to check on their welfare, but she was not often there to cook, clean, and wash their clothes. As adults, those things she now held them capable of dealing with for themselves. Being held capable was not something they wanted. For that, they did not hide their resentment of me.

And me . . . I did not fit their pictures of a responsible adult. I'd left my last employment as a mechanic months before with a clear understanding and determination to no longer spend my life doing work I did not enjoy, just to feed my needs and insecurity. I would meet my needs in other ways. Writing, silversmithing, and personal growth work were my passions and became my pursuits. Regardless of what John told the girls, leaching off Mona was not. But it was what they wanted to believe.

Nanette, the eldest, in her resentment and love of drama, went about getting validation from the old friends in Mona's spiritual group. That is just what we do when we know our views are really not the truth for anyone but ourselves. That's just the coward's way. It takes no courage to blame others, but a lot to face something about ourselves.

When steeped in the drama of trying to control someone else's life, people often feel a need to marshal support. For some, such drama provides the only excitement in their lives.

The message Nanette was giving her mother was clear. "I'm more capable of doing your life than you! I am better than you." It was not a pretty sentiment.

The bottom line for both daughters? Neither was willing to take responsibility for their own lives or hold Mona and me capable of handling ours. In their cry for love, they wanted their mommy back.

While Mona continued to love them, with them, too, she would not do her part in their war, nor would I. Pretending to be other than who I was in a vain attempt to buy their love was not an option, nor would I take responsibility for the choice of their feelings. I simply did not resist them, but instead, acknowledged it was their right to be/feel/think any way they wanted. When their ultimatum—"it's him or us"—didn't work, they both soon left our lives to live with their father up north in Utah, but not before one last salvo, a fuck-you aimed at me.

That old game of control . . . Mona's daughters were experts at it. She didn't expect it when her old friends took her aside and demanded she kick me to the curb. It was painful to discover that the love of her friends came with a price. Real love is always a gift, and control is never love.

It was painful for her to know she couldn't help them understand the game they played, and to know her love for them was only something she felt and didn't transfer into living her life to suit them. Still, not playing their game was easy. Our lives were much richer without all that drama. Mona and I wasted little time and energy resisting. Instead, we accepted the choice of their views. The realities they live under are not for us to choose.

We have other friends, great friends, who love us for who we are and would never buy someone else's stinking fertilizer—certainly not without determining with us the truth of it for themselves.

For me, the hardest thing I've had to do in melding my life with Mona's was to deal with the money. I entered her life broke and in debt, but rich in assets, and juggled some of those assets to pay my bills. My assets included a small amount of equity in my home, two unsold books, a growing silversmith business, a small coaching practice, a host of possessions I no longer needed or wanted, and credit lines built over a lifetime.

* * *

Coaching for me is sacred. One cannot call oneself a coach when there is a dependency on the money it brings. It is not possible to be absolutely honest with a client when one needs that client for one's own survival. A coach who does will not fire a client who is uncoachable. They will prostitute their credibility by withholding, or worse, give them the placebo of an untruth. They will not offer their truth at those times when a client most resists hearing it.   The issue of money was the biggest obstacle in my practice. Several of my early clients were from the seminars and did not pay. But remember the Law of Balance? When something comes at no monetary price, it's hard to see the value. ***In everything, there is equal potential.***

Those pro bono clients were all into personal growth work—they said. The price they paid for my coaching was for them to step out of their comfort zone. Not all could even fathom that as the cost or see the value since most equate price and value with money. My value in coaching them was found in the experience.

Even so, what was I saying about valuing myself? I soon grew to a place where I would not coach for free. The money was nice but was never counted on, or even factored into, my assets.

Still, there were bills, and they presented a huge speed bump to my relationship with Mona. Like all my obstacles, they were self-created by the thought systems of my mind. Where money was concerned, my thought system sucked!

In putting our lives together in the same pot, it was easy for me to meld in all those great things about me that I considered positive. But the others? Liabilities, like debts, I resisted putting into the pot.

Yet, the pot represented our lives together—a joining together of it all. For nearly a year, it remained incomplete, even though I didn't buy into society's laws, lies, or labels. The label marked "LEACH" was the exception.

Truth was, I was withholding my life from Mona, and with it, my heart. Those bills were part of my life. Most represented the cost of my growth. As such, they were aspects of me that she loved, and of which she wanted to be a part. Yes, I struggled with those bills, and she wanted to be a part of my struggle.

It wasn't until I accepted this that our lives really became joined. Together, we rearranged our finances. I sold my home and moved in with her. There was only a little equity coming, but we used it to consolidate debts, sold off things, quit paying for services we didn't need or want, and simplified it all to a place where it worked very well. "Doctor, cure thyself?" We did for ourselves the same things we do for our clients in coaching.

* * *

For recreation, our joy revolved around the motorcycle. Seldom did a weekend pass that there were no runs by one MC (motorcycle club) or another.

Mona and I became members of a one-piece MC—a "family" motorcycle club. Before joining, I brought up the question of also being members of the Star Owners' Association (Yamaha) and was told clearly that yes, that was okay—we just couldn't wear any association patches on the club's vest. Most of the members were also members of HOG (Harley Owners' Group) and attended their events in their HOG vests.

So, I didn't consider it any problem when I convinced the Star Riders to go to a fundraiser in support of an up-and-coming political organization lobbying for bikers' rights. I showed up with my Star group, sporting my association vest—big mistake. The next day, I received a certified letter telling us we were kicked out of the MC club. What with all the staunch HOG members, apparently, they left out the part that we could be members of an association but couldn't wear an association vest.

As for the Yamaha Star Owners' Association, I was the official webmaster. We had links to all the local groups and clubs. Besides official Yamaha sites selling parts, I also had all the aftermarket sites as well. That was when the letter arrived from corporate. I read it at our next meeting. In short, it demanded that we ditch all sites that were not involved with official Yamaha parts and/or other official Yamaha groups. And then came the big "fuck-you" item. If we wanted to ride in any MC events, we had to ask permission. I looked up from the letter to a chorus of "bullshits" and "fuck thems." That was the last meeting we had as a group.

All this happened within the same week. Mona and I were done with the whole association and MC scene. Too much drama.

* * *

Two weeks later, I pulled up at Wally World and parked my bike to the side of the entrance doors. I was approached by a tall, skinny guy who remarked, "I see you're a rider."

"Yup."

"You look like you might be a vet, too."

"Yup."

"You riding with anyone?"

"Nope." *What is it with this guy?*

"Well, I'm with the American Legion. Have you ever heard of the Legion Riders?"

"Yeah, sure. They're in most of the states. Don't think they're in Nevada, though."

"You're right, but a few of us want to start a chapter—fact, the department wants to use the riders to raise a defunct post backup. You interested?"

It didn't take me long to decide. I've always been proud that I served.

We met that night at a private club on Van Der Meer Street. There were only five of us.

Our leader looked us over and blew out a disappointed breath. "I hoped for more, but five is doable. There are five leadership slots that have to be filled in order to start. The department wants me to be commandant."

I stood by and watched as, one by one, all the spots were taken. Then they all looked at me. "It takes a minimum of five. The only one left is sergeant at arms. Are you willing?"

I grunted. "Sure, why not."

That was how I fell into being one of the original five who started the American Legion Riders in Nevada. Been kinda proud of that, too. It's a sure thing that someone would have eventually come along and filled that spot, but the fact was, it was me who did.

With what the Legion Riders have done all over the state since then—things like being a big part of starting the Wounded Warrior Project—yeah, it has been an honor. Then later, when I was asked to be the first state captain for the Patriot Guard, again I stepped up.

None of these things will ever set my name in the annals of history. That was never the point. Hell, it's a question now of how many of the members even know or remember all these years later.

So, what is the point? Just this. My soul gave me the opportunity to make a difference in this world, and I have. That was always a bottom-line reason why I was unwilling to die in that ICU way back when.

* * *

So why am I telling you about it—yes, you the reader—here now, personally? This story is almost at an end, and you may not like how that goes. No one wants to go out with their ass-end stinking, but in real life, people will often release their bowels at the ending of life. In fact, I've already disclosed that I don't like some of what I've admitted to in this book.

Oh, I'm not ashamed of any of it—not now. But back then? Yeah, it was something of a stretch for me—then. And now? Just the fact that I've revealed shit that is none of your fucking business. I've done that only because of my promise to Big D. On that score, sometimes my honesty hasn't always been pretty.

But I wouldn't want your feelings about that to influence what I feel a need to say now. This little author intrusion is because I remember what it was like back then, when I thought my life was over and realized I hadn't done a damned thing that would make any positive difference in this world.

Just consider this. Our souls give us each just such opportunities. Most of us never pay much attention. It is easy to let uncomfortable shit like that go winging on by.

But you? You might just find yourself waiting to die in an ICU, and you, too, might have enough time to remember your life. Will that memory be sweet because you took that opportunity and made a difference, or filled with bitter regret because you didn't?

Comb Ridge, Utah—Present Day

Oh shit—fuck! There are lights coming down the bottom of the canyon. But from the top, I don't know of any roads in from that side. How'd they get past me?

The snowstorm that's been threatening all day is just now breaking in the dusk. Ignoring the weakness that wants to strangle my will, I drag myself over the bare sandstone toward the gas tank at the end of the ledge. Light snowflakes drift across my focused path.

So tired, God! So tired. How long's it been since I ran out of food?

I reach the tank. It's been set up and ready for what, weeks? The carefully cut and twisted cloth of the wick is wrapped into the wires from the wiring harness. The one end will go in at the cap, then is wrapped in with the harness wires tied to the gas petcock at the front of the tank, twenty feet of which is carefully looped to be let down over the edge. The upper end is tied to the brake pedal on what is left of my bike.

I pick up the soda pop bottle that somehow made it to rest on this ledge—thank God for mankind's garbage manners. I keep it full of gas and now pour it over the looped pile of wires and wick. After making sure to soak the end between the petcock and gas tank opening, I empty what's left into the tank. Pushing the tank over the edge, I let it down, hand over shaking hand.

Holy shit! How can a few gallons of gas feel so heavy?

With all twenty feet of wired wick now taut, I take the battery with its readied wires already connected and strike a spark. Nothing.

I strike another. Nothing.

Another. The wick catches fire, along with my one hand. Smothering the flames in the inside folds of my jacket, I grab the battery and begin my crawl.

WHOOOMP!

The fireball rises, fast and intense. From my position twenty feet to the side and five from the edge, my exposed face feels the heat as it passes. Slapping at the singed hair of my beard, I continue to crawl. The taillight beacon is at the overhanging end of the wall.

Reaching it, I peer into the bottom of the canyon. Almost out of sight to the south, the lights have stopped.

With fumbling hands, I twist the positive wires together, then begin tapping out the code using the negative wire. Not much spark that way. The taillight flashes, dot dot dot—dash dash dash—dot dot dot, then repeats, over and over. It is probably only five minutes, but it feels like hours. Then, almost unnoticeable in the distance, comes a tinny-sounding car horn, and the lights move off out of sight.

Is it the adrenalin, the cold, or the hunger that is causing me to shake so badly? Maybe it's just the terrible, constant weakness. I crawl inside the confines of the tent and wrap up in my sleeping bag. Hail now pelts the nylon side, and the tent shudders and shakes as the storm begins in earnest. Somehow, I feel a warmth that is more than physical . . . hope?

Love? It's not how you feel about someone you've just met, someone with whom you are starting a relationship. The *truth* is about how you feel when it has ended. Doesn't matter what has happened in the meantime—all that, doesn't mean *shit*. Fact is, if you don't love them and wish them the very best in the end, *then you never loved them at all.*
                                   Redneck Spirituality—Book Two

CHAPTER THIRTY-THREE

Goes Where?

Eight years flew by with Mona—wonderful years—years I did not think could possibly end. On the winds of love, we rode together in countless club runs, usually with the Legion Riders. We knew the freedom of the ride and the camaraderie of the riders, especially at the Laughlin River Runs. Post 80 became our staging platform. We both loved it so.

The Virago had all the power needed. It just didn't have the size to carry our large booties in comfort. My birthday was coming up, and Mona insisted on buying me a 2002 Yamaha Road Star—ninety-eight cubic inches of beastly torque. But more importantly, it had that kind of Cadillac comfort that only comes with an over eight-hundred-pound motorcycle.

* * *

So it was that our lives mixed and melded and flowed together effortlessly over those eight years we were together. I thought it would always be so until the end.

Then one night, Mona came to me. I could tell there was something she didn't want to deal with from the way her eyes avoided mine. "Nanette had a big blowout with her father and she wants to come home. Well . . . just thought I should run it by you first."

I looked at her and noted the fear in her eyes with what she obviously expected me to say. "Yup . . . well, that would be Nanette—drama queen all the way. But she is your daughter. I would never tell you not to take her in."

"But . . ."

I reached out one hand to lift her face up to where she had to look me in the eye. "You do know you are opening our home up to all that drama again, don't you?"

She nodded her head, as if too embarrassed to verbally acknowledge the truth of it. "And you do know that I will play no part in that with her, don't you?"

Again, the nod.

"That means you will have to deal with her by yourself . . . you do know that?" Again, she nodded. I, in turn, nodded my own head. "Then it's settled."

Not realizing what the cost would be, I could do nothing else.

For the next three weeks, Nanette walked around, avoiding me. Then one day, that all changed. She walked by me with a smirk on her face and a challenge when she eyed me with the same stare I once saw in the eyes of a death adder as a thirteen-year-old boy living in the outback of Australia.

The hair on the back of my neck was standing on end as I sat down at my computer. There, sitting in front of it, was a cassette disk. On it was the notation "Session with Mr. Williams" and a date from long ago.

I knew instantly it was a message from Nanette. Mona would never have even considered invading my privacy. The last time I saw that tape was when I stuffed it in the back of a drawer. Then—out of sight out of mind—I forgot to destroy it.

Mona did not come to bed until very late that night. The heating ducts in the house acted as conduits to bring her conversation with Nanette to me, just as muffled words of feelings. With them, I could hear the tears. The next day, she came to me with a legal form to sign.

"I want a divorce, and I want you to sign this quitclaim releasing any interest in this house." Her tone and her look were bleak.

"You do know that this house has risen in value about a hundred thousand since our marriage, and that half of that is legally mine, don't cha?" She took a deep breath and opened her mouth in preparation for battle.

I raised my hand, palm out. "Hold on. Do you remember our marriage vows to each other?"

Her words, when they came, were low and confused. "What do you mean?"

"I mean, remember how we promised to be there for one another for as long as we both wanted to be?"

"Y-yeah?"

"Well, it appears you no longer want to be. And . . ." I laid the document down on my desk and began signing it. "You've been good to me, even at those times when I wasn't pulling my weight financially. I owe you this, but are you sure that this is what you want?"

"Yes."

"Okay then. But do you mind telling me why?"

"I don't want to talk about it"—the jaw muscles bulged along both sides of her jaw as she ground her teeth together—"and . . . you . . . don't . . . want . . . to . . . know!"

"No." I already knew. Listening to the tone of her voice, I took a deep breath and blew it out. "I suppose not."

The correction always goes here—doesn't matter whose correction it belongs to. If it's fucking up my life, the correction is still mine. Funny how it took so long to come back around to me.

* * *

Taking my shower that evening, I noticed a tube of medicated ointment on the window shelf that hadn't been there before. I no longer remember what it said on the side about how it was the magic cure for Vaginal Rankinitis, or some such shit. I only remember what it said about Mona and me.

To me, it spoke of the depth of the love I held for her. About how, in the bare-assed truth, the result of it in both our lives was simple. That rank-tasting pussy spoke of a disconnect in communication between us. It was a done deal for me—one that did not stop me from loving her.

Still, it resulted in major sorrow because for her, it seemed only to point out her shame—an embarrassment that, at least for her, her love could not survive.

* * *

Mona gave me all the time I needed to get my life together. I found a full-time job driving paratransit busses for the disabled, got myself a one-bedroom apartment, and moved all my personal possessions in. She even gave me enough kitchen utensils and crockery to get me going.

I suppose she wanted all signs of me gone from her house for she took out a second loan to refurbish it, as well as bought herself a new SUV. I'd long ago used the money from the sale of my Virago to pay on the Road Star, so there was not much left owing, but knowing that even that payment would be too much, she paid it off as well as gave me her fifteen-year-old pickup.

It took me two months to get myself gone. Of course, her interactions with me, meanwhile, were cordial, but not loving.

Heartbreaking as it was for me, you have to let other people be who they want to be. What was it that I meant to her? I don't know. ***Was it love, or lust, or just need? Doesn't matter.***

We parted amicably, that being the only thing that told me she'd ever loved me at all. Yes, that is the only reality I can hold on to now of our eight years together that will always say clearly—she loved me.

* * *

The paratransit office and yard were nestled against the east side of the Las Vegas North Airport. I went into the public entrance and was given a name tag with slide bar giving me entrance to the employee side. The HR officer who gave it to me was a short, plumpish woman with a sunshine disposition. I liked her, though I wasn't given any time to appreciate it.

She picked up her phone and said simply, "Send her in." Almost immediately, a woman entered.

Mr. Williams, this is Joy Maxwell, one of our experienced drivers. She has volunteered to ride along with you and get you acclimated to how we operate. Any questions?"

"No."

She pointed to the door. "Good luck."

Outside the door, Joy turned, looked up at me, and remarked, "Yeah, we do have quite a turnover of new drivers, but don't let that bother you." She smiled. "You're going to do just fine." Aside from the fact that Joy was an absolute knockout, I felt relieved. Besides, I personally was swearing off women, and even so, this one was clearly much too young to even be considered.

Being ditched by Mona caused me to seriously look over my whole experience with women. I didn't like what I saw. Every woman I'd ever had a relationship with, it seems, was focused on what they could point to about me that was not acceptable. For me, that reason was usually because I was not controllable. I thought Mona was different.

It didn't seem to matter that I didn't pull the same trick—trying to control their partner—nor did I look for the negative, fearful reasons to leave my relationships. Hell, with Mona, I purposely made her acceptable with what other men would have found unacceptable, and I did it simply because I loved her. Did she never see that love?

Yes, I told Mona my truth about it. And then when she tried to "fix" me, I told her therapist friend the brutal truth as well. That brutality was what bit my ass.

With this new job, I kept to myself. Mental pain is something we do to ourselves, and where women were concerned, I was done with doing it. That meant I was done with women.

* * *

The one big suck in this new job was that if we were to do it well, we were required to come in at least a half hour early to map out our routes. There was never enough time to do it on the fly, and mapping was on our own dime. In the beginning, I came in an hour early to map. Joy's ride-along training only lasted four days, but still, she was always there, doing her own mapping. After a week or two, I only needed thirty minutes, but an hour left enough time for us to socialize.

It wasn't the kind of job where the drivers formed close friendships. We very seldom saw one another while out on route. We were like ships in the night, waving when passing, and it seemed Joy and I both lived solitary lives. I enjoyed her company, so I continued coming in that hour early. I don't know what it was for her—well, other than the fact that she seemed fascinated that I was a writer.

While still unpublished, I'd been writing for some twenty-five years. It was always about all those great truths I'd learned about since that ICU. They were the only thing I had that I felt the need to share with the world.

By then, that included a completed memoir novel and enough material to publish three workbooks. They just needed to be organized. Joy seemed insatiably interested. I suppose it tweaked my ego that she was a fan. I took it to be that she was really getting into the thought system of the Spiritual Laws. It's generally called New Thought. The in-depth discussions we had convinced me she understood the material and was serious about it.

* * *

As time went by, I eventually discovered a country western saloon close by. After a few lessons, I found I enjoyed two-stepping. Joy, too, took an interest and became my dance partner. We were sitting quietly at our table and the band was between sets when I mentioned my plans for my vacation.

"Y'know, Joy, you've read all about my time living in Fry Canyon as a boy, right?"

"Yeah, that must have been an awesome time in your life."

"Oh, it was. Point is, now that I've got a few years in this job, that means two weeks of vacation. I'm going to use that time to take a ride through my past."

"Can I come along?" That question took me by surprise.

"Why? Why would you want to come? Don't you realize that the reason I'm going is because of my relationships with women? Riding motorcycles requires a guy to be 'in the moment.' If he's not, he doesn't live long. Thing about being in the moment is that the pain and regrets of the past are gone and the future is blank. That is why I find solace on the bike—gives me time to heal and get my head straight.

"As for being in the desert? The desert 'just is.' A man can be free of himself and all his bullshit in the desert. Right now, I need some time to get my shit together. My second marriage, I thought we had it all. It . . . well, it fucked with my head to discover we didn't."

"What? Why?"

"Oh, I believe I know why."

"Tell me."

"I didn't plan to ever get married again."

"Why not?"

"Well, because it's about nothing but promises and legal chains that just naturally smack of fear."

"You're talking about the laws—two kinds of energy . . . right?"

"Yeah, I didn't want a relationship based on fear. Leaves no room for love. But then there was her daughter moving back in . . ."

"What did she have to do with it?"

"Hated me. If anything were to happen to Mona, I'd find myself out on the street. Silly me. I was looking for protection under the law—shit! Thought we could ignore the whole fucking fear factor."

"And?"

"We couldn't. Fear's fear."

"Jeff . . . I'm so sorry—"

"S'okay." I cut her off with a raised hand, palm out, waving it in negation. "I thought this time, I'd just stay alone, but the thought of spending the rest of my life alone is depressing. As it is, I can't give my heart to anyone if it is still bleeding."

"Take me, Jeff. I'll help you heal, and I'll never do you that way."

"You?" I sat back in confusion. "How old are you, forty-one—two?"

"Forty-two."

"Oh, honey, I'm over sixty. Why would a beautiful, young woman like you ever want to hook up with an old fart like me? I have a son who's your age."

* * *

The tears were coursing freely down her cheeks when she burst through the door of the dance hall that night. Stunned, I let her go. Then, shaking my head in self-disgust, I went home to pack. *Why didn't I see that coming? Hurting her was the last thing I'd ever consciously have done.* "Shit!"

* * *

I left out as the sun was rising, heading north through St. George. I stopped briefly at Micky D's for a sausage, fake egg, and faker cheese sandwich. Once past St. George, I turned east through Hurricane. Climbing the volcanic scarp on the far side, I broke out at the top to wide, desert vistas and the clean, cool air of the desert morning.

Running east along Utah's southern border, slick-rock cliffs bordered the road as it bounced back and forth across the Arizona–Utah state line. Then I crossed over to Page, Arizona, located at the dam on Lake Powell. It felt so good to again be riding through this red sand and sagebrush with magnificent, sandstone cliffs on both sides—the land of my youth. At Kayenta, I turned north through Monument Valley, an indescribable fairyland of sandstone buttes and monoliths. Farther on, at Bluff, Utah, I pitched my tent at the camp park down by the San Juan River.

Sitting with my back against a cedar, at home once more in Utah's canyon lands, I opened one of the 6% beers purchased in Page, Arizona. The worst abuse the Mormon-controlled government of Utah ever did was to saddle its citizens with all 3.2% beer—Utah piss water. Having spent time in Australia, it didn't matter that it was lukewarm. Sitting there watching the mesmerizing, muddy waves in the flow of the San Juan, I thought of Joy and her strange behavior the previous night.

My God, was she entertaining feelings for me? I always thought we were just good friends. I even tried a time or two to hook her up with a few of my guy friends. After a while, I just figured she preferred women over men in that way. Sure, I thought it a waste, what with her being such an attractive woman, but I never even considered she might find me attractive.

Many were the times, while discussing the ancient wisdom found in the simple Laws of Spirit, it just felt good to have such a like-minded friend. I just figured her sexuality was her own private business. Surely, I never said or did anything to lead her to believe I was interested in her that way. Now she seemed so crushed at my dismissal of her apparent feelings. I shook my head at the enigma of it.

Women. You try your best to love them and believe it is returned, only to find rejection. As in Mona's case—and for that matter, Meg's too—both wives rejected me with great disgust. And now here was Joy, who lived up to her name in every respect, someone I loved just being around, a friend I would never have purposefully caused pain—but did. Did I give her the wrong signals? Oh, I truly do need some time with the solitude of the desert.

* * *

The next morning, I was up with the sun heading north to Shirttail Corner. A glorified convenience store and gas station, it sat at the confluence of Highway 95 just short of Blanding, Utah. I gassed up and went in to see what munchies they might have. It was a pleasant surprise to see a whole display of someone's homemade jerky. I love jerky. And hell, what better munchies to take camping than jerky. It keeps forever, and one stick of it supplies most of the protein of a gentleman-size steak.

I called over to the attendant. "Hey, what's with the jerky?"

Just a pimply-faced kid, he seemed irritated by me interrupting his game on the techno-gizmo he was busy working in both hands. "Oh, it's deer jerky. One of Parley Black's kids makes it."

"How much you want for it?"

"He's asking fifty cents a stick."

Hmmm—must be a high school friend.

I picked up a huge, plastic jar just stuffed with it. I guessed it to be between fifty to sixty sticks.

"Take twenty bucks for the whole jar?"

"Well . . ." The attendant glanced up as if questioning my sanity. "Yeah, sure. Why the hell not."

Putting it away in my saddlebags alongside a half dozen cans of beans and soup, I chuckled. *Always good to be prepared . . .*

I motored west on Highway 95 for about fifteen miles before coming down off the top into Cottonwood Wash. There, I turned north onto Posey's Trail Road. My map said it would take me straight to the top of the old Comb Ridge Dugway. I remembered how I always looked in nervous anticipation to it when traveling to Fry Canyon as a kid. A single-lane road cut into the solid-sandstone cliff. There were only two places where cars could pass along the whole of its length. Far at the bottom of that cliff were the relics of several wrecks.

The last I remembered, the road here to the top was of good gravel. Strangely, now it was just composed of the red, powdery dirt so common in the region. Even that was being crowded in by sage. What did they do, scrape off the gravel and use it elsewhere?

Going up a slight rise, the road sported a mildly washed-out ditch down the center. I rode to the side of it. Then, cresting the top, I looked down a short but more dramatically steep hill with a much deeper, elongated suckhole of a ditch.

At the bottom, it emptied onto a sandstone ledge sporting an alluvial fan of gravel. I knew I should go back, but between the narrow, dirt road with its ditch and the encroaching sagebrush, there was no place to turn around. Backing up old Fu Man Chu—the name I gave my motorcycle—would only land me in the ditch. No, nothing to do but hope I could stay out of that suckhole and make it to that open ledge below to get turned around.

I started down. Several times, the rear tire tried to slip on into the ditch, and I had to gun it to keep to the high side. I sighed in relief as I leveled out on the ledge at the bottom. Turning, I started to come around, but all that pea gravel acted like a thousand little marbles—marbles carrying me sideways toward the edge. Hoping to dig through to something solid, I gunned it once more, only to feel the back end slip over the edge. With no time to jump, I laid it against the near-vertical, sandstone cliff as it gouged and squealed its way down. The bottom came up fast. There was a crack, like a pistol shot, and my world exploded in pain, then dissolved into nothingness.

Comb Ridge, Utah—Present Day

Thank you, Big D. I thought I'd never stop shaking long enough to connect this story completely back to where it all began.

"Wasn't me who steadied your hand, Jeff. That's just how the human body reacts. You stop shivering when your core temperature drops too low."

Ah, I see. Is that why I feel such weariness as I've never experienced before? Lying here on this ledge, surrounded by such magnificence, it does seem a fitting place to die. And still—I'm still not sure what it was about me that I created this.

As if on a journey of its own, my mind wanders back to Mona—she who refused to acknowledge or deal with her stinky coochie. Sure, I told her about my feelings, and still, she chose to blame me for having them. Hell, they were my feelings, and they were my reaction to something that simply 'was'—something that didn't have to be.

"And yet, you still choose to regard her as your soul mate. She wasn't . . . she isn't."

What do you mean, Big D?

"The first time you told her, she didn't believe it from you. It took that second time—that brutal truth of it spoken in confidentiality with a therapist. A soul mate would have believed you. Your word would have been sufficient. She would have taken care of it. Done deal."

So, okay. That was her part in creating the break in our relationship. What was mine? I suppose it wouldn't have happened had I simply destroyed that tape.

"Let go, Jeff. It was never about you or about that tape." He holds me in his gaze, almost hypnotically. "What is it that now you won't accept the truth from me? She . . . wasn't . . . your . . . soul mate! Look . . . how did your marriage vows end?"

Uhhhh . . . whatda y'mean?"

"Errr-umpt!" Big D's grunt of exasperation burst forth. "Look, I know your mind is not thinking all that clearly right now—so I'm going to tell you. It ended with this:

'In the eternity of time

should we part,

your heart from mine,

our parting will be as our starting . . .

in honesty and truth and love.

(Repeated . . .)

(Then repeated together . . .)

In honesty and truth and love . . .

You are free to be YOU, with ME.' "

He pauses with a deep soul-searching stare. "Why did you write it that way?"

Well, I didn't want it to be the prison that conventional vows are. People change and I wanted us both to always have freedom to be and feel exactly who we are.

"Yes! You honored your vow, your way. You'd still be married had she respected your way . . . wouldn't you?"

Well yeah . . . but her feelings changed. I—

"Yes Jeff, exactly! You honored her feelings too." His smile is gentle—devoid of judgment.

I really thought she was my soul mate. But right now, I have to consider her feelings. When this last book is published—

"Yes, and you've done all you could to lose her identity in these pages. But she will know—can't be helped." He shakes his head slowly, sadly. "You could not tell this story without it being true. Everything you are depends on that. Don't you wonder how many women there are who need to hear what Mona refused to acknowledge—and who need to see what the cost has been?"

Me? I still question what I'm not seeing that has led me to being here, maybe to dying here. Is my purpose in this world now completed? Big D, you've assured me that this book will get published. A dead poet—is that what it will take? Me? I haven't given up. But if it is to be, I can die this way. I like who I am. But you said 'two lies.' I still don't see the other one.

"And I can't tell you—not while you are still alive."

I take one last look around at the absolute splendor, now covered with a fresh coating of snow, the first of the season. *Is it Thanksgiving yet?*

"No, Jeff. Yesterday, when you blew that gas tank, it was Halloween. And those in the pickup trucks you signaled to were high school kids out having a woodsy—a drinking and carousing sex party. That is, until the storm moved in. It's just no fun having sex when you've got snow blowing up your ass, y'know?"

I grin at the memories of back then. A woodsy . . . the other guys were all into that sort of thing, even back then, but not that many of them ever got to score. Me, I was never invited. I worked nights at the family gas station. There was never time for girlfriends, and you can't go to a woodsy without one. *Some things you just miss when you have to grow up too soon. Seems like such a silly fucking last regret to have in life.*

Then, too tired to stay open, my eyes close and my world turns black.

For a time, the Angel remains, sitting beside the body. Then, with a sad shake of his head, he murmurs, "Ah, Jeff, you have never faced your fear—the one that keeps you from your soul mate. It is done. Your choice is made."

Your ego's expectations of how it must be for you to get what you want will only guarantee you pain. What your ego wants and what your heart wants are very seldom the same. For your ego has eyes that can only look out. It cannot see your heart within.

Redneck Spirituality—Book Four

CHAPTER THIRTY-FOUR

No Correction Needed

Blanding, Utah, Sheriff's Office—Present Day

Sheriff Daley looks across his desk at the two ladies. The one, Joy, he knew too well. She's in his office every few days whining about some missing biker. And now, she's brought backup.

"Sheriff, this is Mona, Jeff's ex-wife. After you called last night about that report of an emergency signal, I called her. She wanted to be here and drove in last night all the way from Las Vegas."

"Well, you ladies do ree-lize it might not even be him. He's been missing, what, nearly three months? How long d'ya think a man can survive alone in the desert?"

The little one, Joy, curls her lip. "You don't know *this* man, Sheriff."

The other gal, Mona, rocks her rather large butt in the chair as if it itches. "That's right." She nods. "Jeff's a survivor." The sheriff looks at her, at her crossed arms and dour expression. He always had a feel for people. But this one?

Why is she here? Doesn't seem to be out of concern—at least not for her ex. Is she here to be of support for t'other gal? Joy did say they were friends. No, while there's no logic to it, I'd guess it's guilt.

"Well look, ladies. Now that the storm is mostly passed, I got my helicopter out searching. We should know something soon." As if to prove the point, the radio on his desk squawks to life.

"Bird One to Sheriff Daley . . ."

The sheriff groans and snatches up the mic. "God da . . ." Glancing at the two ladies, he takes a deep breath. "Gosh darn it, Jim. This may be Blanding, Utah, an' we may only have the one chopper, but I 'spect you to sound professional—not like some kinda Mormon Barney Fife."

"Well hell, Uncle Hal, iff'n y'all wanna sound all big-city uppity, why don't we just give ourselves another chopper—call in as 'Heads up! Pidgeon Two to Base?'"

"That's enough, smart-ass. When you call in, you *will* say 'Chopper One to Base.' Now whaddaya got?"

"Well, Sheriff, I'm just coming up on a ledge now. There's a huge, black smudge on the side of the cliff, and it looks like pieces of a motorcycle on the ledge. Winds'r a little freaky still. Just easing up. Yiiiiiii . . ." Clunk. Click. Silence.

The sheriff jumps to his feet, mic in hand. "Chopper One, come in! Chopper One . . ." A long, pregnant moment passes while the sheriff takes a deep breath, then speaks slowly and deliberately. "Chopper One, this is Base . . . Chopper One?" Another long moment, then just as the sheriff is raising the mic to his lips, the radio burst in with a crackle of static.

"Chopper One to Base . . ."

"Gotcha, Jim. Y'ain't messed up my chopper, now have ya?"

"No, Sheriff."

"Then what cha found?"

"Sorry, Sheriff, gust caught me. Almost sent me into the cliff. I dropped the mic and . . ."

"And?"

"Well, that's the crazy part, Sheriff. Don't know as I should even mention it."

"Cut the crap, Jim."

"Well, there was this billowin', black, cape-type thing wrapped 'round a skeleton, and it was wavin' the bones of its arms as if to sayin', 'Come here.' That's when the wind gust hit. Well, I'm just glad I don't have to change my shorts."

"Okay, Jim. Y'had yur joke." He sits back into his chair. "Now whaddaya see?"

"Well, there's a tent up under the overhang, and from the way it's bein' blown round by my prop wash, there must be somethin' heavy inside keepin' it from bein' blown over the edge, too."

"Too? Whaddaya mean 'too?'"

"Well, there was that skeleton—"

"I said cut the crap! Now get back to base."

"Ten-four, Sheriff . . . weren't no crap."

"What did you say?"

"Ten-four, Sheriff . . . that's a wrap."

Gritting his teeth, his face red, the sheriff stood up and grabbed his coat.

"Search and Rescue is standing by, ladies. We normally don't take ride-a-longs, but don't want to have to pull ya out of a ditch somewhere. Would ya like to ride with me?"

Comb Ridge, Utah—Present Day

"Come, Jeff."

I automatically reach for Big D's extended hand. Rising up, I'm astonished to realize, *My God! I haven't been on my feet for a couple of months now—and NO pain.* Still crouching, I step out from under the overhang and stand upright.

Turning toward him, my jaw drops. He is again that being, clothed, not in black, but rather in flowing robes glistening with light, like spun spider webs. And his face is no longer a naked skull but one of magnificent splendor, like the face of Jesus from the portrait on the chapel wall in the Mormon church of my youth. But the face is my own. I've only seen him this way once, back when I finished that first book.

Big D gestures with his hand, upward toward the old Moki hand and footholds in the cliff. "Your limo awaits at the top of the hill—as do a couple of your loved ones. You will want to say goodbye."

Standing before that Moki staircase, I note how the sandstone slopes down, then angles onto the ledge before plunging to the depths hundreds of feet below. The remains of my motorcycle are still strewn about at the edge.

I smile, remembering how just such a staircase once scared the be-Jesus out of that child I was. This time, I fairly float up those hand and footholds, effortlessly and with no fear. I chuckle. *Shit, how many times can one person die in a lifetime?* Then sober, I realize the true answer is quite a few—if he is afraid of living, like my brother, Mike, was, or dying, like me.

"No, Jeff." As we start up the old roadway, now covered with an inch or two of fresh snow, Big D walks just behind me. "The truth is, Mike was afraid to love—kinda like you—but he didn't possess your courage to do it anyway. You say I took away all your chicken exits and now require you to follow your joy, to live the life of your dreams? Not so! Let's look at the truth. Your mothers—both of them—set it all up for you . . . not out of meanness, at least not on the spiritual side. You said that one yourself when you wrote in one of your books, 'Life—all of it, from what you eat to what you excrete—is a spiritual experience.' You talk about how you write with honesty. Don't you believe your own shit?"

B-Big D, I . . . I mean—

"Oh, knock it off. We can speak out plainly. No one will see or hear you now. You are on this side of the veil. You already paid the ultimate price." He shrugs. "It's no longer an issue."

I . . . I . . . I'm sorry . . . It just feels more natural, speaking mind to mind. I stop and turn toward him.

"No need to apologize." He gestures almost impatiently for me to continue. "Let's look at the truth about your life. Your mothers started it off. The one threw you away, put you in an orphanage. Your adopted mother didn't do any better with her abuse. But what was the message they both were giving you—the massage you heard? Say it."

Th-that I'm not good enough, not deserving of being loved.

"Exactly. And *you* bought into their bullshit—their *female* bullshit! *You* spent your whole life believing and supporting that lie. *You* supported it with every female you got involved with. *You* created them all leaving you."

I stop, and with my jaw hanging, turn back to face him. *Where is this leading?* He, too, stops and raises his arm out toward me. From within the sleeve of his cloak, a finger emerges and stabs the air before me.

"*You* created it. Not through any abuse of them, nor even from lack of love, but simply by holding that belief, that chicken exit—*your chicken exit*—foremost in your mind. Remember the Spiritual Law, **What your mind dwells upon with energy is what you will create**?"

B-but . . .

"But? But? NO BUTS!" He shakes his head sadly. "I hoped you'd see it in time to live your life—following your joy. Our agreement. Remember? Uuurgh." He grunts his exasperation.

I still don't understand. What are you talking about?

"Huurrrump!" Big D snorts in exasperation. "You'll see."

* * *

My mind is awhirl. With head down into the wind, I slog up the steep hill with its light cover of snow, unaware that I leave no tracks. It is not until the first one passes through me that I notice the EMTs coming down. The next two are carrying a stretcher with all their ropes and gear. The air is cold, though that is not the source of the chill I feel, as shivering, I stand aside.

Trudging on, the landscape seems so quiet and somehow changed with its mantle of fresh snow marred now by muddy tracks. In no time, I find myself in the meadow at the top. Sure enough, there is a limo sitting on the far side, but it is the sight of the two women bundled up from the cold and standing alongside an ambulance that draws my immediate attention.

The one, Mona, stands silently, handkerchief dabbing at her eyes, but it is quickly used to cover her nose and mouth as the supposedly air-tight, zippered body bag is being carried past. The other, Joy, is unfazed by the stench leaking from it. Misery etching her face, she looks up as it passes, and it seems she is looking directly at me. Night has fallen, and the lights above the ambulance doors reflect off her tear-filled eyes. I'm struck by their beautiful shade of blue—no, more gray than blue and with a silvery sheen.

My God! The eyes in the mist! I recognize her then, as they load the body into the yawning ambulance doors and begin to transfer it from the stretcher onto the scissored-down frame of the gurney.

In confusion, I look to Big D. He answers in his own inscrutable way. "Here, beyond the veil, time means nothing. And yes, it's been well over three hours, corporeal time, since we passed them on the hill. You were lost in thought." He looks at me, and I find myself staring directly into my own eyes.

"She loved you, you know." He nods toward Joy. "You wouldn't admit it, but you loved her, too." Big D's voice, with its odd, rumbling intonation, murmurs beside me as tears course down my cheeks. "But you never even gave her a chance, did you?"

Oh Christ, Big D. She was young enough to be my daughter!

"Yes, Jeff, I know—chicken exits." He shakes his head and his next words drip of sadness. "Nevertheless, she was your soul mate."

As they begin securing the body bag to the gurney in the ambulance bay, Joy is demanding, "Let me in! I want to see him."

The sheriff shrugs, and with a sad shake of his head, waves abeyance to the EMT holding her back. As she enters, the one inside puts up a stiff arm, palm out.

"Ma'am, you really don't want to see him like this. Why, the smell alone—"

She gives him a withering look. "If you don't, I'll unzip it myself!"

He tries one last time. "Ma'am, he's dead. He was cold, no pulse or respiration at all when we got to him, and that was about four hours ago."

"I don't care . . . I want to see him!"

With a grimace, he leans forward and unzips the body bag, then quickly buries his nose in the shoulder of his parka.

For a long moment, she stares, eyes pooling, then wrapping her arms around the corpse's neck, she lies, sobbing against the ribs of its emaciated chest—still unfazed by the stench now emanating freely.

During the time it takes her to come to terms and to quiet her sobs, Big D leans toward me and points toward the other woman. "Y'know, they've actually become friends. But it wasn't your own efforts, or any from Mona, that was the catalyst for this rescue attempt." He points toward the broken woman. "When the report came in, the sheriff's mind automatically went to, *'Damn high school kids again, like to rampage and party in the woods—but then, it is Halloween.'* If Joy hadn't been in his face damned near every day over the last two months, he'd have blown it off."

Big D grins in amusement. "And you? You were so busy lying to yourself—trying to deny your feelings for her—that you never saw hers for you. Hell, it's a regular clusterfuck going on here, but for your death on the ledge, it would almost be laughable."

You're right. I duck my head in shame. *And now it's too late.*

"Have you forgotten what I told you about living and dying?"

What? Well . . . yes. I remember you saying that we live until our purpose is finished or we have given up. But I finished this book, and I told the honest story. Isn't my purpose now complete?

"Fuck the book!" He pauses to study me intently. "Have you given up?"

No—God NO!

Big D is silent a moment, his head ducked and I can see his eyebrows, now scrunched down in expectancy. His words, when they come, carry a note of exasperation. "Well . . . what are you waiting for?"

* * *

From inside the ambulance, the woman's head springs up, her mouth agape, she shrieks. "A heartbeat . . . I hear a heartbeat!"

Epilogue

On the deepening dark of the desert night, an angel stands, watching the departing ambulance. Lights flashing, siren whooping, it jostles over the muddied ruts in the fresh snow, a gaggle of support vehicles following. As the eventual quiet settles once more, the luminous glow of the angel's robes seems to swirl together on a non-existent breeze. Then he and his limo are gone.

Long moments pass as the creatures of the desert slowly come out of hiding. A scarred-up, old, male coyote wends a crooked path between the sage to his place of honor on the rise. Circling several times, he tamps down the fresh cover of snow, affording himself a dry place to sit.

Then, outlined by the rising moon, he stretches forth his muzzle and issues a cry. It rises on a ghostly cloud of vapor into the dry, desert air. While warbling with his loneliness, it no longer carries a note of mourning for his mate, lost to a hunter's gun. This time, the tone is one of wanting expectancy.

Then . . . thinly, from a distance, he is answered by one of longing—and heated desire. The tip of his little, red head pokes forth from its warm sheath into the frigid air, sending chills of fresh desire to his core. He rises and trots down the hill.

About the Author

Although I've lived through some interesting experiences, I always thought my life was relatively normal—until, at the age of forty-five, I came face-to-face with death, and life, as it was, came to a screeching halt.

Lying in an ICU with a massive pulmonary embolism, knowing there was little chance of survival, it seemed like a good time to get honest. A personal knowledge of the presence of death will do that, even with someone as oblivious as I.

Truth is, I'd always lived the life others wanted and expected of me—the good Mormon son, the limp-dick, controllable husband, the dependable employee working at a job he hated—but never did I live my own life. Hell, I had no idea what life was about, but now facing death, there came a burning need to know.

With my reprieve, I began a search for the meaning of life, most importantly, of my own. Dying while being someone I didn't know or respect was not an option. This memoir is the sequel to *The Courage of a Butterfly*, which covered the time before that ICU. This book is about what followed—about discovering the simple truths to life that, without exception, always hold true. Some call them Spiritual Laws.

Looking at life in light of these Spiritual Laws, one has a completely different perspective than most. And yes, in living by them, I came to know myself.

There is not much I can tell you about me that isn't covered in these two books. Perhaps leaving you with a thing or two I've discovered about life would be more in order—things, according to these simple truths, that hold true and fit together . . . things I believe and offer up for your consideration. Who I am on that level is the same as who we all are. I offer the essence of me to the essence of you—Namaste.

* * *

I believe our souls are that highest and best of us—the "God" essence where we are all as one. As such, I believe our souls know everything there is to know. Thing is, you can know a thing in your head (consciously), but to truly "know" it takes knowing it from the heart. That requires experiencing it. I believe our purpose in this world is to experience it so that our souls can "know."

Our lives are like pieces of string—**birth at one end, death at the other**. Most everything in this life comes as a duality—good to bad, right to wrong, sweet to sour. You can never know a thing without knowing it from both **ends**, the full gamut. What good is knowing only one end? Can you appreciate the sweet without knowing the sour? Most of the Spiritual Laws mentioned in this book are mentioned multiple times. I've written this book with the intention of giving you their full gamut. But who am I kidding? There is so much more.

Failing that, here are two of these simple truths that I consider to be the most important. If you get nothing more from these writings of mine, get this rudimentary understanding of these two. The first states— ***I am the creator.***

Basically, it means I create my whole world from my perceptions—my thoughts, my beliefs, my feelings, and yes, my experiences. But mainly it tells you is about my responsibility in life— that I don't have the luxury of blame.

I'm very aware that the shit that lies between my ears, is MY shit—not to be blamed on you.

The second truth concerns the energy. There are only two basic energies to choose from when living life. They do NOT ever mix.

There is the energy of LOVE,
and the energy of everything that is NOT love (FEAR).

Bottom line—in every moment of life, we exist in one of these two energies. We may occasionally switch between, but with every single moment, it is our free choice with which energy we are creating ourselves. Do we prefer the energy of love to that of fear— the truth of responsibility to the lie of blame? These choices make up who we are.

These two books tell you about my own choices. In living the from and to duality of my life

—I prefer sweet to sour—
—Love to fear—
And most of all,
—Taking responsibility rather than smearing my shit on you—

Oh, and BTW!
Would someone out there please bring me some damned toilet paper?
'Nuff said.

SomeThingsYou Might Like to Know

Have you noticed the poetry included in this book? If you liked it, you may want to check out a companion book containing all the poems—ninety-two in fact—taken out of the original manuscript. The book is titled *An Eagle's Flight*—IN POETRY by Edmond E Frank. It can be found at Barns and Noble Online or Amazon. It may also be ordered from most book stores. There is also a companion poetry book to *The Courage of a Butterfly* titled *A Butterfly's Transformation*—IN POETRY.

With this being the sequel novel to *The Courage of a Butterfly*, no doubt some readers are curious. Having read this book you are surely aware that this life is a journey.

You might say I met Big D somewhere in the middle of mine—way too young to be dying and not old enough to have a clue about what I have since learned are the simple truths of life.

Having once been a Boy Scout I was familiar with maps. If you have a map you need to know two things—where you want to go and most of all, where you are. I knew who I wanted to be. I did not know who I was.

In that first book Big D and I take a journey of discovery through my early life.

Here is an offering of one sample chapter from that book

Sample Chapter Four
Fry Canyon
* * * *

Often others label us as cowards when they see our fear. The truth is, we are not until we, ourselves, label us so. Every human on the planet has fears. A fear is only an imaginary dragon in our mind. It generally starts as a little flying lizard sent by our higher self out of love to caution and warn us of perceived danger. Then it is blown up large by our conscious mind using the winds of possibility. We believe ourselves cowards, those of us who won't walk the dragon until it is, once again, a little lizard.

Redneck Spirituality—Book Two

FOUR

Fry Canyon

God, how I loved Fry Canyon, wild and remote beyond the imagination of my choicest dreams. Until Mom, Mike, and I arrived, there were no families there, just miners living in scattered trailer camps and shacks—damn primitive.

On the day we pulled in, a late afternoon monsoon shower brought respite from the heat of the summer. A hundred tiny waterfalls plunged over the sheer-red sandstone cliffs, stretching majestically high. The fragrance of sagebrush and cedar floated on the cool, humid, ozone-tainted air. Yes, the smell of the desert after a thundershower was to my young mind unforgettable.

The arrival of our family was like the bringing of civilization. Seeing us take to the primitive life so easily, the other miners' families soon began arriving, necessitating the building of a two-classroom school. Meanwhile, we kids had a nine-month reprieve, which we put to good use.

On long, dusty hikes, we explored the desert. Often braving the threat of flash floods from those late-summer monsoons, we seduced the shady sanctity of the canyons. Should our intrusion coincide with the sudden rage of waters between those smooth, sandstone walls sometimes a hundred feet or higher—though often only yards apart—we could not hope to survive.

In the wash bordering our campsite, we already were witness to those flash floods. They'd come rumbling with the churning of the boulders carried within their muddy froth. Coming, as they did, from miles up the dry washes, a clear sky was no guarantee of safety this time of year. It was with reverence we hiked there, almost as if we were invading the sanctity of Mother Nature's womb. Combined, it titillated a sense of naughtiness well beyond that of normal disobedience to our parents' strict rule of "no hiking in the washes."

I loved Fry Canyon, but of it all, perhaps most appreciated and prized was my growing collection of arrowheads and painted pottery shards. It stretched my young mind to think of how they were so beautifully crafted by ancient hands—hands long since turned to the very dust on which we trod. Fry Canyon was an ancient place. Yet, for an eight-year-old, it was full of fresh, undefiled excitement, danger, and discovery.

* * *

A few miles downstream in White Canyon, just to the north of Fry, we found a Moqui Indian ruin. Tucked in under an overhang on a canyon wall, the only way we could reach it was to walk out about thirty feet along a narrow ledge and then climb down another fifty, using some worn hollows in the cliff face cut there by ancient Indians as hand and foot holds. These ended beside a huge boulder sitting on a ledge. To get to the ruins below, one slid down, around, and under the rock like so many ants under a white sandstone brick. One slip, and it was a very long two hundred feet to the canyon floor. This was something Mike could really get into.

As for me, I sat on top and raged at the sudden, shaking stiffness in my arms and legs and the whirling in my head that threatened to send me skittering into the depths every time I attempted to descend. Below, I could hear the excitement in the voices of the older boys as they explored the mysteries of the ruins.

* * *

It was a wild and rugged place. Here, as in the cowboy movies, danger was a first cousin to death. Like the others, I ran over to witness the hubbub the day the *Happy Jack Mine* caved in. They brought the body down off the rim in the back of a dump truck, arriving just at lunch break, and laid it out on a table in the general store. The store served as a sort of community center and was just across the wash from our school at White Canyon. The body was covered, its outline showing plainly through the sheet, except where the head should be. There, the sheet was oddly flattened and painted in red. Then someone raised the corner for a look. For me then, the Wild West romance of Fry Canyon became sudden, deadly reality.

* * *

Fry Canyon was a huge box canyon about six miles long, varying from a half to two miles wide. All of the more prominent rock formations had names. One, shaped like a chair, could be seen way in the distance down White Canyon. That one was called *Jacob's Chair*. There was another up near the head of Fry Canyon, which was about three hundred feet tall. Its base was cone-shaped, but the top hundred feet or so was a twenty-foot-wide vertical sandstone cylinder. That one was named *Jacob's Peter*. Being completely flat on top, I shuddered, remembering my own experience. It appeared Jacob had been overly circumcised—must of been by one big-assed axe.

Lastly, about midway up the canyon, there was yet another. A free-standing mesa, it was about four hundred feet tall and shaped like a gargantuan pan mounded with food. That one, of course, was known as the *Frying Pan*.

One day, Mike, his thirteen-year-old friends, Willis and Billy, and I all hiked over to it. On the vertical south wall, we located a ledge that varied from a few inches to a foot wide. Angling up the face of the sheer cliff for about two hundred feet, it then entered a crevice, which rose the last fifty straight up.

Last in line, I made it only halfway along the ledge before my heels met only air. The wall was of smooth, orange sandstone with what looked like burnt oil trailers of black manganese stains, running down the sides. My rubbery limbs felt numb, and my head swam with dizziness as that rock face seemed to push the rest of me out into space. To the left and right, my grasping hands met only smooth rock. Glancing below, it looked to be a hundred feet to the boulder-strewn talus slope, though in reality, it was probably a mere sixty. Worse, there was a bend coming up where the rock face turned slightly inward and bowed out even more. Billy was just then humping his body around it.

Up ahead, Mike and Willis were climbing up the crack. Their backs wedged against one side, their feet against the other, they wormed their way up. Only nine years old, I knew I did not have their strength—my God, I had barely enough to remain upright. Backing inch by trembling inch, I made my way down.

Again, I'd stayed back, and I again felt very much a coward for not bringing myself to brave the heights all the way to the top. I would never see the names and dates written on a ledge up there. Some, Mike later said, went back so far as the 1860s. They were the unknown heroes of the Old West, scratched there by their own hands. My own name, borrowed though it was, would never be beside theirs like Mike's now was.

Then it came time for little brother Jeffrey to provide the amusement. It all began with Billy winging a flat chunk of red slate over the edge, arcing it toward me on the slope several hundred feet below. It splattered with a loud crack on a rock twenty feet above and to my right, showering me with painfully sharp shards.

"Oww! Hey! I'm down here, butthead!"

"Hey, look. It's the pus-pus-pussy!" Billy's remark floated down, accompanied by a bigger, more accurate chunk of slate. It narrowly missed as I dived to the side.

"Naw, looks more like a chicken," came Willis' faraway jeer. "Buk . . . buk . . . bu-kuck!"

"Yeah, a chicken," came a new, more hurtful voice. "Let's see if we can chop its head off!"

Then they all got into the act, winging plate-size flat pieces of slate, turning and twisting into weird, unexpected trajectories, bursting explosively all around. They laughed hilariously, prancing and chicken clucking, as I frantically dodged about, slipping and sliding on the sand and rocks of the steep slope.

Next, they began rolling big boulders over the edge. As my panic escalated, I called them every filthy name my fertilized little mind could conjure. That seemed to amuse them all the more, for still, the boulders continued thumping and skidding all around me, often just inches away. Eventually, I tucked myself under a huge rock and waited for them to tire of their game.

The summer sun was hot, and sweat mingled with my tears of anger and humiliation—and something more. "Aw shit, Mike! How could you?" My lonesome moan brought no answer, save for the whump and rumble of yet another boulder careening past overhead, raining me with dust and pebbles.

* * *

The school our fathers built was done up first class. There were separate boys' and girls' outhouses in back, each with three holes. One day during recess, I was taking a leak when I noticed an eye peeping through the knothole in front of me. Shifting my aim, I drilled that hole with a stream of golden quicksilver, honed deadly with circumcised accuracy. An immediate screech erupted from the other side, and I emerged in time to see a girl named Judy stumbling away. Both hands frantically clawing at her face, she tripped and began rolling around, making all kinds of yipes and yowls, like a puppy that had just sniffed up an angry red ant pile.

The whole school gathered around her in amusement. That was the day I became known as **Dead Eye**, a nickname I always felt would have been better applied to her.

As for me, I never again saw Judy's, or any other eye, looking through that knothole. Guess they got my message: You just don't piss around with a straight shooter. Yes, perhaps there can even be a gift in having one's tallywhacker cropped.

* * *

Mike, Willis, Billy, and I liked to play poker in the bed of an old dump truck where we could be out of the wind. We were there one day when Pete—a boy my age whom we all disliked—began teasing Dead-Eye Judy, who's physique indeed resembled that of a very plump puppy.

"Fatty, fatty, two-by-four . . ." Beyond dislike, his voice grated against my concentration.

"Go away, lemme alone." Her whining was even worse. As usual, I was losing. Boosting myself up, I looked over the edge.

"Hey! You guys take it someplace else. We're tryin' to play cards here."

". . . Couldn't get through the bathroom door." He ignored me as he ran circles around her, poking her fat body with a stick. Her whining turned to shrieks as she squatted in the sand, her arms up, protecting her face from the stick.

"Hey! Cut it out, asshole."

Pete paused just long enough to stick out his tongue and wave a clenched fist, but for one insultingly stiff finger.

Reply enough. I jumped out of the truck and stalked over. Still grinning, he raised his fists, clearly expecting an easy victory. Everyone knew I avoided fights and never started them. He'd never seen me fight—but then, he'd never seen me angry.

Drawing near, I saw his mocking grin and didn't hesitate. Charging in, fists swinging, I managed to thump him several times before he broke loose. Raising a cloud of powdery dust, he stumbled to his trailer. Tears streaming and holding one eye, with his nose dripping blood across a split lip, he was no longer grinning. I let him go.

Climbing the steel rungs into that dump truck's bed, I heard Mike's chuckle and felt him slap my back. "Hey, nice goin', Jeff. You really kicked his butt good!" Standing on the clean metal of that bed, its surface scratched bare by a thousand tons of uranium ore, I saw something in his eyes that hadn't been there before.

"Yeah, ya better run home to mommy, ya chicken shit little fuck!" Willis jeered at Pete's retreating back. Almost fourteen, he was the oldest and sometimes used words even he wouldn't tolerate coming from us. "And next time ya bother us, we're gonna sic little Jeffrey on ya again!"

I hadn't realized how there was never really any code of honor that kept the three bigger kids from picking on us smaller ones. And why was it I was the one they would let go hiking with them? They simply were afraid we'd squeal on them to the adults—that is, all the others would but me.

Too, I suddenly understood the thing about the Frying Pan, and even the other time—the time they'd used me for target practice when shooting bird shot from a .22. It was Mike firing, puffing spurts of dust around my feet and off the rocks nearby. They laughed and jeered from the ledge above as, again, I frantically dodged around. I still carry a BB lodged in the rim of my left eye socket that I received as I peeked from around a boulder. *Yeah. They trusted me! They knew I'd never tell.* Suddenly, it didn't seem to matter how that trust might just get me killed.

"Jeff-rey!" It was Mom calling me to our trailer. I was in big trouble now. Pete's mom was constantly coming over, complaining about anything we did—real or imagined—to her "Precious." And here this time, I'd really made a mess of him. I shuffled over, hanging my head in my best "gee-I'm-so-ashamed-of-myself" rendition.

"Here, JW." Mother smiled—JW was what she called me when I'd done something right. She used the name sparingly. "I'm proud of you for sticking up for Judy. Here's a dollar. Just don't tell anyone about this."

I walked away, that big, silver coin riding solid in my pocket. But for its hard, heavy metallic reality as I fingered it, my experience of receiving it might well have been only a dream.

Of course I didn't tell anyone. The dollar remained our secret.

Nor did I tell her the real reason why I'd beaten up Pete. Hell, I didn't know the underlying true source of my anger—how his obvious disrespect was simply saying to me: "Coward! You are no one I need to fear." Does it ever matter what someone else says? The words in one's mind are always one's own.

What I saw in Pete was simply summed up in his grin. It was his red cape in the face of my bull. My bull didn't even think before trampling his ass. Yet, was I like Mike and his friends? In a way, I was accepted. But was I, too, a bully? Inside me, somewhere deep, something about it just didn't feel so good. Yet, for a part of me, there was no denying that kicking Pete's ass felt great! "Coward!" That silent word he screamed at me; was it somehow now negated? No, it still rang loud in my own mind.

Within my family circle, what I'd done was right and condoned, even rewarded. There was that secret dollar, there was that fraternal slap on the back from Mike, and there was that further acceptance from the older boys. I was someone they could bully without fear of being reported. And now, I was someone who would pass it on. *I was one of them now.* Accepted!

But the price? God! Was the price worth it? Mike certainly had a chunk of the bully within his character. I saw it, knew it, didn't like it—and now, it seemed, so did I.

But it was his bravado that scared me. It literally screamed to me of his agony and how he didn't much value life—not his, not even my own—while, too, it whispered, pleading for someone to just cherish him.

Did Mike ever see that there was someone who believed in him, uplifted him, loved him unconditionally—someone who, in the end, could not stop the inevitable. Ah, but back then, at the age of nine, of all this... what the fuck did I know?

* * *

Kicking Pete's ass was the easy way of dealing with those cliffs and with those outside myself who might call me a coward. Inside, it was a different story.

After having failed Mike on the cliff face of the Frying Pan, my nights became even more troubled. Waking with the banging of my head against the ceiling above my upper bunk in that dinky trailer, I'd listen sleeplessly to the silvery desert winds whispering lonesome through the cedars outside.

Except now, beside the gritty stink of sweat-laden socks smothering my sleep, the nightmares now carried a different theme. Helplessly, I would watch from someplace just out of reach, while Mike fell to his death. Or perhaps I would have a hold on him, on a sweaty hand or a ripping shirt. Always, I would be unable to keep the grip. Always, Mike died. Always, it was my fault. And always, sleep would then elude me. Although I knew it was only a dream, I could not rest again, but instead, lie searching mentally for a way I could have saved him.

Almost nightly, I thrashed it out with the walls, ceiling, and bedding. And often, when awakened by a few kicks from beneath—"Hey, dipshit! Knock it off!"—I would promise myself I would never let Mike climb another cliff without me.

* * *

Was Mike ever aware of my silent promise? I don't know. But, for the little time left us in Fry Canyon, Mike seemed to see my fears and looked out for me. Would he do so in Australia? We'd just learned we were moving there.

Kangaroos, wallabies, wombats . . . the outback of Australia would be the next place to where our father's work would take us. Out there in the "bush" were things other than cliffs with which to tempt fate—things just as deadly.

~ *In the Present with Big D* ~

"Well, Big D, am I missing anything?" It's been several days since I finished this chapter and he hasn't come, though now I feel him near. A vague sense of unease seems to surround me, like the darkness of the night—nothing but the embers of my campfire's coals and the desert all around me.

"Yes, it is well—that you feel this apprehension just now, Jeff. You certainly have missed something." Big D shows himself, the dim light off the coals reflecting off his bony skull. He still wears his engineer's cap and carries that same fun-poking grin.

"Okay, then give it up. I'm ready."

"Ha!" He chuckles. "That's what I like most about you. Whatever I request, you are game for it, though I know the sweat coats your palms." He holds his own bare-bones palms out as if they are a reflection of my own. "Still, you are not ready for all of it just yet."

"Is it so bad?" I swallow, trying to moisten my suddenly dry throat, and hear his kind chuckle again.

"Good? Bad? You know about good and bad." His bottomless gaze holds me; the coals in his empty sockets exactly mirror those of my campfire. "The KY jelly coated lies of judgmental minds—minds just spouting their slimy shit to fuck with your head. It could be a matter of the greatest upliftment . . ."—one lidless eye socket seems to wink—"should you choose it so."

God, but he loves the dramatics!

"Yes, I do know that one: **'Perception is a choice'** "—I quote from the laws—"but why won't you say?"

"Cowards? Bullies? Integrity? The truth about real men? Whoa! How about the truth about Mike's love? The truth about *your* love? Indeed, the truth about *you . . . about your whole world?* Yes, you have much to learn."

I can no longer see him and his laughter is fading, seemingly rushing away across the desert like some old western train. "Patience. You're right on track. Keep on a-chuggin, chuggin, chuggin. . . ."

"Wait, Big D! What do you mean '. . . much to learn?' Learn what? Goddammit—wait! Tell me."

His reply seems to mock. A repeat of his own words, it comes floating thinly as if on the wind, like the steam chug of an old locomotive. "Much to learn . . . much to learn . . . much to learn. . . ."

"Wait, come back!" There is now only a thin whistle of wind seemingly rushing through and around the yucca and greasewood of this Nevada desert, nothing more. "C'mon, Big D . . . shit!"

OTHER WORKS

Authored as Edmond E. Frank

The Courage of a Butterfly—THE NOVEL
A Butterfly's Transformation—IN POETRY
An Eagle's Flight—IN POETRY

Authored as E. Egorhh Frank

Redneck Spirituality—THE SERIES

Books One and Two Combined Edition
(In print form only)
Book One
Book Two
Book Three
Book Four
And a soon-to-be-published
Book Five

NOTES

NOTES

NOTES

NOTES

www.ingramcontent.com/pod-product-compliance
Lightning Source LLC
Chambersburg PA
CBHW031054080526
44587CB00011B/677